233(bot) Acct principles & standards
194 reg. objective
7 hear better sparrow
8 IL 1980 award
31 ombudsman role

Regulating Aged Care

Dedicated to
Elemer Geza Makkai
Ida Murray
Joseph Braithwaite

Regulating Aged Care

Ritualism and the New Pyramid

John Braithwaite

Australian National University

Toni Makkai

Australian Institute of Criminology

Valerie Braithwaite

Australian National University

Edward Elgar
Cheltenham, UK • Northampton, MA, USA

Published by
Edward Elgar Publishing Limited
Glensanda House
Montpellier Parade
Cheltenham
Glos GL50 1UA
UK

Edward Elgar Publishing, Inc.
William Pratt House
9 Dewey Court
Northampton
Massachusetts 01060
USA

A catalogue record for this book
is available from the British Library

Library of Congress Cataloguing in Publication Data

Braithwaite, John.
    Regulating aged care: ritualism and the new pyramid/John Braithwaite,
Toni Makkai, Valerie Braithwaite.
        p.   cm.
    Includes bibliographical references and index.
    1. Nursing homes—Inspection—United States. 2. Nursing homes—
Inspection—Great Britain. 3. Nursing homes—Inspection—Australia.
I. Makkai, Toni. II. Braithwaite, V.A. (Valerie A.), 1951–   . III. Title.
[DNLM: 1. Homes for the Aged—legislation & jurisprudence—Australia.
2. Homes for the Aged—legislation & jurisprudence—Great Britain.
3. Homes for the Aged—legislation & jurisprudence—United States.
4. Nursing Homes—legislation & jurisprudence—Australia. 5. Nursing
Homes—legislation & jurisprudence—Great Britain. 6. Nursing Homes—
legislation & jurisprudence—United States. 7. Cross-Cultural Comparison—
Australia. 8. Cross-Cultural Comparison—Great Britain. 9. Cross-Cultural
Comparison—United States. WT 33.1 B814r 2007]
RA997.B695   2007
362.16—dc22

                                                                    2006102451

ISBN 978 1 84720 001 3

Printed and bound in Great Britain by MPG Books Ltd, Bodmin, Cornwall.

Contents

Preface

The ambitions of this study were to be a sustained and systematic comparative study of regulation and to make a fresh contribution to regulatory theory. Chapter 1 shows that the data collection was unusually comprehensive and sustained over a long period. Chapters 2–6 summarize the data for the United States (US), then England, then Australia. While the data collection was considerable in the 1980s, 1990s and 2000s for all three cases, it was most thorough for Australia in the 1980s and 1990s. Because these Australian data have been extensively written up in two dozen previous publications, this book concentrates on data that have never been published before, especially from the United States, but also from the United Kingdom (UK) and the latest unpublished data from Australia. All but three of the chapters have resisted the temptation to rehash these previous publications. Chapters 3 and 7 are exceptions that incorporate some substantial reliance on Braithwaite (1994), though most of their content is new, introducing more recent data. Chapter 8 has adapted a number of ideas from John Braithwaite (2002c). The fact that we refer to the findings of our previous published work from this study rather than rehash them means that there is an embarrassing amount of self-citation and citation of work of our colleagues.

Part II – Chapters 7–10 – develops the theoretical contribution of the project inductively from the empirical material in Part I. The theoretical contribution of Chapters 7 and 8 is to develop the idea of regulatory ritualism, to show how pervasive and multidimensional a problem it became with the rise of regulatory capitalism since the 1970s (Levi-Faur 2005, 2006). Ritualism means acceptance of institutionalized means for securing regulatory goals while losing all focus on achieving the goals or outcomes themselves (Merton 1968). Our theoretical interpretations also owe a lot to Michel Foucault because we find many of the regulatory rituals that have grown are rituals of discipline that oppress vulnerable actors. Our intellectual style is not nihilistic. In the face of a rising tide of regulatory ritualism, we document actors at many levels of the regulatory game effectively resisting and transcending ritualism. Our text abounds with stories of inspiring activism to transform aged care, advancing freedom as non-domination (Pettit 1997) and improving quality of care.

While aged care is a massive problem in its own right, we hope our data will prove of some relevance to other arenas where health-care workers such as nurses toil (for example, hospitals) and social carers (for example, child care and care of the disabled). And we hope it makes some contributions of general relevance to the study of regulation and governance.

A fundamental theoretical contribution, induced from our empirical work, was Valerie Braithwaite's idea of motivational postures. Her postures of resistance, game-playing, disengagement, capitulation and commitment have informed a new policy analysis of regulatory responsiveness, especially in the domain of tax policy in Australia and New Zealand, but in other nations and arenas too. In Chapter 9, the motivational postures are deployed to develop a response to regulatory ritualism in aged care. This book is the first of a trilogy of Regulatory Institutions Network (RegNet) contributions with Edward Elgar. In the next year another will be completed by Valerie Braithwaite that builds on the motivational postures work herein, entitled *Defiance in Taxation and Governance*. And John Braithwaite will be producing a book entitled *Regulatory Capitalism* that further develops the theme of the current book.

Finally, Chapter 10 develops the idea of 'the new pyramid' – a strengths-based pyramid that is linked to a regulatory pyramid. Judith Healy (2007) is further refining the idea in wider arenas of health regulation of complementing 'pyramids of sanctions with pyramids of supports'. We like Malcolm Sparrow's (2000) prescription of 'pick important problems and fix them'. But we conclude this is better accomplished when nursing homes also 'pick strengths and expand them'. Chapter 10 argues, relying heavily on the English data, that pyramids can work better when they network escalation. Single strands of control tend to snap, but networked webs of control can be resilient. The conclusion then seeks to rise to the challenge of integrating normative and explanatory theory to show how webs of control can be crafted to expand freedom by controlling domination. In addition, the linking of networked strength-building to networked regulatory control through the new pyramid can deliver us an empowering regulatory strategy. It does this in conditions of a least likely case of empowerment (the frail aged). We also show how the project of empowering clients is linked to the improvement of the oppressed working conditions of base-level service delivery staff whose numbers have exploded in conditions of regulatory capitalism. They are much more shockingly exploited and disciplined than the factory workers of industrial capitalism, especially in the United States. The frail aged can and do find strength in helping others, including their impoverished care workers; care workers can and sometimes do find strength through new career trajectories of excellence in helping the frail aged.

Chapter 10 also seeks to advance the epistemology of regulatory science. Nursing home regulation allows quantitative measurement of compliance with higher reliability (for example, inter-rater reliabilities from .93 to .96) and response rates (for example, response rate of 96 per cent for chief executive officer [CEO] interviews) than can be found elsewhere in the regulatory literature (Braithwaite et al. 1991). Nineteen different reliability and validity tests on our Australian data included a correlation between state-assessed and self-assessed compliance of .88 (Braithwaite et al. 1991). Chapter 7 suggests how this was possible because of the design of Australian regulation. Many multivariate analyses were run based on two waves of data collection from very different kinds of actors on different sides of the regulatory fence in Australia. Unlike our RegNet collaborations at the Australian National University (ANU) on tax compliance and restorative justice, we were unable to launch randomized controlled trials on the effects of regulatory interventions. But the health sector is more rich than any other in randomized controlled trials on a number of the regulatory questions of interest to us. We have been able to draw this rigorous work by others into our analysis.

While our epistemology values these kinds of quantitative analyses on representative samples, it also values triple-loop learning (Parker 2002) from accumulations of semi-quantitative root cause analyses on small, unrepresentative samples from highly specific contexts. Attending to this work helps us learn how to learn to do better at the governance of health and social care. Finally, we must learn how to be better clinicians who diagnose regulatory failure on an N of 1. This is important, we argue, because the world is too complex for much of it to be known or knowable by quantitative, deductive science. Our new pyramid model is also part of an epistemology of how to do a regulatory science that combines ethnographic research with high-brow and low-brow quantification to grapple with a world of complexity.

Early on David Ermann, Diane Gibson, Ann Jenkins and Debra Rickwood joined this project, made great contributions to the Australian data collection in particular, and published many extremely important works from the data during the 1990s. Readers will find numerous references to that work throughout the book. Heidi Fisse played a particularly important role in organizing the most challenging aspects of the data collection in the early 1990s. Others who made major contributions to data collection in the 1980s and 1990s were Jon Collins, Coralie Friend, Joan Hoare, Steven Jones, Miriam Landau, Malcolm Mearns, Ygtaka Shimizu and Nancy Walke. In the current decade we leaned heavily on Leah Dunn for research assistance.

The authors and their co-authors from earlier eras of the project were supported by a variety of employers across these decades. Two deserve special mention. We thank the Research School of Social Sciences at the

Australian National University and its five Directors since the time this project was conceived. John Braithwaite was at the time of writing the longest-serving member of that School, though Valerie Braithwaite has worked much longer for ANU. Toni Makkai won an Australian Research Council postdoctoral fellowship to join the project. She is now Director of the Australian Institute of Criminology. The opinions expressed in the book do not necessarily reflect the policy positions of the Institute or the Australian Government. Many colleagues in both the old and the new Coombs building, where the Regulatory Institutions Network is located, have sustained us intellectually during the long journey of this project. Single ideas in this book bear the hands of a number of different RegNet colleagues. Philip Pettit, David Levi-Faur and Peter Drahos deserve special mention, however. The American Bar Foundation was more than just one of the important funders of this research; it was a splendidly gregarious, kind and intellectually stimulating environment for us when we were undertaking our US fieldwork and introduced us to the influence of Ian Ayres. The other funders deserve our sincere thanks. They are the Australian Research Council, the Australian Department of Health, Housing and Community Services, the Australian Commission on Safety and Quality in Health Care, the Florida Department of Health and ACT Health. The greatest thanks should go to the many residents, staff, proprietors and nursing home regulatory officials whose conversations and insights drive any value this book might have.

Our special gratitude to the following colleagues who gave of their time to comment on draft chapters: Gabriele Bammer, Murray Batchelor, Mark Brandon, Kevin Bryant, Ross Bushrod, Lawrence Cram, David Crosbie, Paul Dugdale, Chris Falvey, John Finnegan, Judith Healy, Timothy Jost, Tina Magennis, Pascal Perez, Elizabeth Pringle, Carolyn Scheetz, Clifford Shearing and Kieran Walshe.

Now some notes on terminology. We try to make comparisons among cases easier by using common terms cross-nationally where we can. So we call nursing home inspectors what Americans today call 'surveyors', Australians call 'assessors' and the British call 'inspectors'. Even though we know this will aggravate Americans and Australians, 'inspectors' is the term we chose because, at some period of the history of this project, all three nations used the term 'inspector'. While all nations started out calling clients of nursing homes 'patients' at the beginning of this study, and the English today prefer 'service users', we use 'residents' because that is the term used in the other two nations today and in all three for most of the history of this project. 'Nursing homes' itself is a term falling out of official favour today in Australia and the UK, even though it remains widely used in practice. While ageing in place is eroding once clear distinctions between 'nursing homes' and 'hostels'/'care homes'/'assisted living homes', our core meaning of 'nursing homes' as residential homes for the aged that supply geriatric health-care services retains considerable meaningfulness.

John Braithwaite
Toni Makkai
Valerie Braithwaite
Canberra

PART I

Nursing Home Inspection Observed

1. History of nursing home regulation

Nursing homes can be inspiring places to visit. The love and dedication of professional staff creates an environment that is a pleasure to be in. Care staff pause to stoop to their haunches, look a resident in the eye as they hold a hand or stroke a forehead, share a bit of banter. Residents may be physically frail, but many are verbally feisty. *Joie de vivre* is in the air. Laughter and singing can be heard. A kindly Labrador wanders the corridor. The decor feels like a home. A very old woman who had been terribly sick is packing up to return home after a program of restorative nursing and physiotherapy. Another group of people, staff from care assistants up to highly qualified health professionals of many kinds, are meeting with a resident and members of his family to revise his care plan. Empowerment is in the air too.

What attracted us to the study of nursing home regulation was that it is a least likely case of empowerment. No group is harder to empower than the institutionalized aged who are more lacking than others in both the muscle and the voice to resist. 'Even prisoners can riot,' Joel Handler said to us, though we are almost pleased to report that during our fieldwork there was one riot in an Australian nursing home where furniture was overturned and fires lit! Eckstein (1975) conceives of a least likely case as one where the claims of a theory are least likely to be supported. The method is to find the least likely case; then if the theory is supported there, one can have a degree of confidence in it. So if regulatory strategies succeed by empowering clients as weak as nursing home residents, we can be more optimistic about such strategies with stronger stakeholders. Disempowered nursing home residents, closeted away in obscure corners of cities, seemed least likely stakeholders in the deliberative forms of restorative and responsive regulation we favoured as we went into this project (Ayres and Braithwaite 1992; Braithwaite 2002a). The promise of these responsive empowerment strategies is reassessed in Chapter 7.

We also became committed to the research over a long period because in the worst homes we saw horrific things. These were homes where the stench of human waste was ever present, where wailing pierced the air and no one paused to comfort the wretched soul whose plaintive voice it was. An old woman is tied at the waist into a wheelchair, both her wrists also tied to the arms of the chair, her hands in mitts, so she cannot cause trouble by pulling at tubes that feed her (unnecessarily, because with enough staff care she could be spoon-fed real food). She does not wail, she occasionally groans, hopelessly. Others are restrained by drugs, just staring. A dozen residents, all in wheelchairs, and tied in lap restraints, have been wheeled to the perimeter of the nurses' station where they can be watched. The nurses' station is a hub with spokes of corridors running out from it. From there supervisory staff can see most of what is going on, that both employees and inmates are doing what they should.

This architecture is inspired by Jeremy Bentham's Panoptic design for the prison. When we talk to the residents they tell us they feel like they are in a prison. Can we help them to get out, to get home? Toni Makkai's father recently passed away after spending his last year in an Australian nursing home. He was a refugee to Australia from Eastern Europe after World War II, and had spent time in refugee camps in Europe and Australia. By the time he entered the home he was suffering from dementia. On visits the conversation went:

> *Father:* Where am I? Am I in a refugee camp?
> *TM:* You're in a nursing home Dad.
> *Father:* Why am I here?
> *TM:* Because Mom can't look after you anymore and you need to be in a secure and safe place.
> *Father:* But I can't get out.
> *TM:* It is for your own good.
> *Father:* It's a prison.
> *TM:* No, it's a nursing home.
> *Father:* Then why can't I get out?

The intermittent clash of stainless steel, the long corridors of linoleum tell them they are in an institution. They are roused from bed, showered and fed on an institutional routine. In the worst cases this means the night shift showers them early in the morning before they hand over to the day shift. The only routine with toileting is that residents expect to wait a long time before they can be assisted with it; they learn to lie in their waste. Some have pressure sores bigger than a fist, even with maggots adding to the disgust of the wound itself. Staff claim they had them when they arrived, but admission records from the hospital reveal otherwise. In one case we learn a resident was admitted from a nursing home to a hospital with maggots in her ear.

At the extremes, we saw evidence of what we could only describe as murder, indeed serial murder, though murder convictions for nursing home abuse are rare (Long 1987). Serious sexual assault as a result of avoidable regulatory failure also deeply disturbed us:

> In Texas, thirty-three year old nurse's aide Johnny Gordon, a tall, 200 pound man with a criminal record, was allowed to care for nursing home resident Dorothy

Cooper . . . [E]vidence later revealed that several facilities within the Texas Health Enterprises chain negligently conducted required criminal checks on Gordon not once, but three times. During a required training class in his third employment stint, he was recognized by the assistant director of nurses from a previous facility who remembered his abusive behaviour. Although this assistant director reported Gordon's previous history to both the training facility's administrator and her supervisor, the facility deliberately ignored the warning . . . On July 20, 1993, Gordon brutally raped sixty-four year old Cooper not once, but twice with a showerhead during an unsupervised female patient shower. Next Gordon returned Cooper to her bed and proceeded to masturbate, discharging semen across her body. Two nurse's aides reported the suspected sexual assault to their supervisor after discovering a semen-like substance in Cooper's vaginal area. The supervisor ignored the discovery and left for lunch to shop for wallpaper. The nurse's aides then informed the charge nurse who discounted the semen-like substance as a vaginal infection. After Gordon brutally attacked Cooper, she became permanently withdrawn and refused care by staff. At night, the staff would find her terrified with her legs locked in the bed rails and often screaming.

(Phan 2002: 298)

In another home, in a large US city, a fire brigade paramedic complained against two nurses who stood around waiting for the ambulance instead of administering cardiopulmonary resuscitation (CPR) to a cardiac arrest patient. He died. When the paramedic arrived, he had to scream to get access to the patient's charts – they were locked in a room to which no one could find the key. In the paramedic's complaint he alleged: 'This is a real death-house.' On the inspection to investigate this complaint we encountered a facility with rodent droppings and actually saw a rat. Almost every feature of care had major compliance problems. The dead patient was on drugs that required regular monitoring of pulse, but this had not been done. Staff had not been trained in how to do CPR. Many residents who were supposed to get sleeping pills at 8 p.m. each evening had been receiving them at 8 a.m. for the past three weeks. No medication sheets had been filled out at all for one month. There were blank sheets signed by a doctor and a pharmacist in advance of actual entries being made on them. The previous administrator had run the place with a forged licence. The facility was depressing, apathetic, no visitors, barely alive. The home had been required to put goals into residents' care plans on a previous round of enforcement. They had put in silly goals, ritualistic goals that were easy for them to achieve. For example: 'Will not put food items in purse 3 of 7 days in week'; 'Smoke in room only 3 days a week.' Problem definition of 'upset and demanding behavior' leads to the goal of 'Will control his upset and demanding behavior 2 times a day.' Not only was the care planning ritualistic, so was the inspection. The inspectors believed it was a shocking facility that probably should be closed. But they had recently been given a torrid time by a facility lawyer on another enforcement action. The grilling left them 'washed out' and they did not want to go through it again with this facility. So the enforcement response was limp.

In an English home, residents were abused by being forced to eat faeces. In an Australian home, two nursing aides used a garden hose for an enema, puncturing the bowel. Some of the things repeated in nearby homes were eerie. We visited two homes in one US state in the same month that had both seen male residents have their penis cut off (by nursing assistants it was suspected but not proved).

On a lighter side, two nursing homes in south-east Australia housed lonely women who told us when young they had torrid affairs with Errol Flynn. (Flynn did hail from that part of the world, so perhaps they had!) Some were more than just lonely in the circumstances of the home; they were depressed looking back on their whole life. One old 'digger' told us that he had plenty of time to think about how he had done nothing of value in his life. When we bet he had helped other people to a better life, he conceded he had done one good thing in his time. In World War I he captured a German soldier. He was stopped by a young officer who reminded him about the approach they were taking to prisoners, and began to pull a pistol from its holster. The digger, lying, said he had orders to take the prisoner back to headquarters for interrogation. When the officer walked off in disgust, the German pressed his Iron Cross into the digger's hand, gratefully saying something to him in German. The old digger proudly showed us the Iron Cross. Tearfully he said he wished he knew what those German words were. We say we doubt we will ever be able to look back on anything that could give us as much pride as that. We would like to linger longer reminiscing about the old man's war, but move on to proceed with the work of this book.

Sixteen years later, with the work of the book still not completed, the digger long dead, the authors hope that the research might make some small contribution to thinking through how to make the final years of future generations less lonely, less depressed, better cared for, than that old digger endured.

THE CONCEPT OF REGULATORY RITUALISM

Robert Merton (1968) identified the five types of adaptation to a normative order – conformity, innovation, ritualism, retreatism and rebellion – where the response can be 'acceptance' (+), 'rejection' (−), or 'rejection of prevailing values and substitution of new values' (±) (see Table 1.1). In this book, we apply Merton's model, with only a little distortion, to acceptance and rejection of regulatory goals and means to achieving those goals

Table 1.1   Merton's typology of modes of individual adaptation

Modes of adaptation	Cultural goals	Institutionalized means
I. Conformity	+	+
II. Innovation	+	−
III. Ritualism	−	+
IV. Retreatism	−	−
V. Rebellion	±	±

Source: Merton (1968: 194).

institutionalized in regulatory standards. Our data finds conformity, innovation, ritualism, retreatism and rebellion all evident in responses of
nursing homes to their regulation. Conformity is found when nursing
homes endorse regulatory goals and adopt the recommended path for
achieving them. Innovation breaks with conventional means, finding new
ways of pursuing agreed regulatory objectives. Rejection of both regulatory
goals and means has already been discussed in some of the worst homes
visited in the course of this study, a condition called retreatism. When rejection of goals and means is accompanied by a switch to alternative goals and
means, nursing homes fit Merton's rebellion mode of adaptation. Rebellion
becomes most evident when regulatory agencies change their standards and
procedures. This leaves the fifth mode of adaptation – ritualism.

Ritualism is the adaptation that progressively becomes the most daunting challenge of regulatory capitalism (Levi-Faur 2005). This theme is also
evident in Michael Power's (1997) work on how, in *The Audit Society*, audit
has become a 'ritual of comfort'. Ritualism means acceptance of institutionalized means for securing regulatory goals while losing all focus on
achieving the goals or outcomes themselves. We will show in this book how
the expansive nature of nursing home regulation in the US, England and
Australia faces the significant challenge of ritualism. We will also seek an
understanding of how master practitioners and master regulators of aged
care struggle against ritualism, an unintended consequence of expansive
regulation. Our summary of what these master practitioners do is well summarized by Malcolm Sparrow's (2000) simple prescription: 'pick important
problems: fix them'. But it also involves 'pick strengths and expand them'.
This leads to the development in this book of a new strengths-building
pyramid of regulation to complement the old problem-fixing enforcement
pyramid.

In this chapter we will first have a little to say about the meaning of regulation and then explore what a nursing home means in the context of the

history of aged care in the three nations. Julia Black (2001) has explored
the different levels of generality at which the concept of regulation can be
conceived. She argues, sensibly we think, that different levels are appropriate for different analytic purposes. Regulation can be something only state
regulatory agencies do, a form of state administrative practice. Or we can
define regulation to include regulation by professions, by international
organizations, industry self-regulation and other levels of governance.
Regulation can be conceived as something that requires rules or laws that
are then enforced by a regulatory actor. Lawrence Lessig (1999: 235–9) sees
law/rules as just one of four mechanisms in his typology of regulatory
mechanisms in *Code and Other Laws of Cyberspace*. The other three are
social norms, market and architecture.

Social norms, like law, are commands, but they are enforced, according
to Lessig, by the community rather than the state, by informal social disapproval rather than by formal sanctions. Our data will show that informal
praise by inspectors is a significant factor in explaining improvement, two
years later, against quality norms among Australian nursing home managers (Makkai and Braithwaite 1993a).

Markets constrain through price. To some, it is controversial to describe
the market as a regulatory mechanism because there is no regulator who
decides on a price – the market is the antithesis of intentional social engineering (Black 2001). There is no doubt however that public and private
policy makers do make decisions to move transactions 'from hierarchy to
market' to steer the achievement of objectives such as efficiency or pollution control. The state of Illinois won a prestigious award from the
Kennedy School of Government at Harvard University when it moved in
the 1980s to increase Medicaid payments to nursing homes when quality
improved. Our data reveal, with the benefit of hindsight, that this experiment was actually a major policy disaster because rigging markets to
achieve regulatory objectives is particularly vulnerable to ritualism (see
Chapter 8).

Architecture is the environment built around an object of regulation that
physically constrains it. Disney World regulates by a Foucauldian architecture of bars, guard rails and other physical barriers (Shearing and Stenning
1985). A reinforced door to a cockpit is a way of regulating hijackers, as is
a lock. Architecture can organize natural surveillance to focus on hot spots
of vulnerability to crime – for example, kitchen windows in a housing estate
that look out onto children's playgrounds. The basic idea is the same as that
which underlies Jeremy Bentham's Panopticon prison design. We will see in
Chapter 3 that many nursing homes in the United States have adopted a
panoptic design to maximize surveillance of residents, with disastrous
implications for efforts to create homelike environments. Lessig's special

contribution to regulatory scholarship is to show the profound consequences of software code as an architectural regulator of cyberspace. Both
Bill Gates and the US-dominated regime of copyright and trademarks have
structured the architecture of the Internet to advantage certain commercial
interests and disadvantage others. Lessig argues that a lot of the power of
architectural mechanisms of regulation resides in their self-executing properties. Legal constraints, in contrast, need to be mobilized, and this may
result in delay and uncertainty. For this reason, during the cold war, the US
and USSR put in place architectural regulation to make it impossible for
one to surprise the other in a way that might cause an accidental or 'inten-
tional/accidental' nuclear war. Each agreed to make it impossible for the
other to open a missile silo and activate a warhead without an electronic
alert installed by the other side at the silo automatically triggering a
warning in the other's capital.

Nursing home care is one of many kinds of services that were once
mainly provided by the state and charities, and today are mainly supplied
by for-profit businesses. Privatization has increased public demand for regulation, partly because abuse and neglect is more prevalent with private
than public and charitable providers, as we will see in Chapter 8. We live
today in a state that does less rowing but more steering (Osborne and
Gaebler 1992), a state that is less a provider or welfare state and more a regulatory state (Day and Klein 1990). This state is not characterized by privatization and deregulation, but by privatization and regulatory growth
(Ayres and Braithwaite 1992: ch. 1). It is a society with *Freer Markets and
More Rules* (Vogel 1996). This is what Levi-Faur (2005, 2006) calls regulatory capitalism. The shift has not been simply one from the liberal nightwatchman state of the nineteenth century to the provider state that existed
from the New Deal of the 1930s to 1970, to the regulatory state. It is not
just state regulation that has expanded: so has industry self-regulation, corporate compliance systems, regulation by large corporations of smaller
suppliers and users of their products upstream and downstream, regulation
by non-governmental organizations (NGOs) and voluntary accreditation.
Regulatory capitalism seems the right name for more privatized markets
that are both more privately and more publicly regulated (Braithwaite
2005a).

We will find all of Lessig's mechanisms of regulation important in the
context of nursing home regulation. It is also the case that private accreditation is often posited as more effective than public regulation. Consequently,
a maximally broad conception of regulation will be adopted here as 'steering the flow of events' (Parker and Braithwaite 2003). Such a conception cor-
responds to the usage for a regulator in engineering as a device for regulating
the flow of, say, oxygen from a tank. This may seem to make regulation in

social science almost as broad a concept as governance and broader than government by the state. But governance is about providing and distributing as well as regulating. This book is not about how much nursing home care different levels of government ought to provide, nor how such support ought to be distributed.

RITUALISM AND THE FAILURES TO IMPROVE HEALTH AND SOCIAL CARE

Beyond nursing homes, we live in an era when recognition has dawned of serious problems in both social and health care. With social care, much of the attention in many nations has been on sexual and physical abuse scandals in care institutions, particularly for children. Decades of neglect in mental health now represents a significant challenge to governments and service providers. With health institutions, the crisis has been mainly about medical errors causing death. An Institute of Medicine study estimated that 44000–98000 US hospital patients die each year and more than a million are injured as a result of medical error (Institute of Medicine 2000). A 1995 Australian study (using the Brennan et al. 1991 Harvard methodology) estimated that 18000 Australians die each year because of medical errors, half of them preventable, and 50000 suffer permanent disability (Wilson et al. 1995). The most recent British study found hospital patient safety incidents contributed to 72000 deaths, half preventable (National Patient Safety Agency 2004). It is a death toll that positions road safety, occupational health and safety, crime and terrorism as comparatively small problems.

Sparrow's (2000) prescription 'pick important problems: fix them' seems obvious as a response. The trouble is that in a hospital, for example, paperwork like filling out forms on admission and outputs like conducting surgery are unavoidable and cause conflict if you do not do them. Identifying problems and trying to fix them, in contrast, is work that can be avoided, and it causes conflict if we do it. So people in organizations, according to Sparrow, tend to stick to the unavoidable work, and the work that will cause trouble if you do not get to it. That means problems are not fixed.

In one of the best books on this challenge, Brennan and Berwick (1996) contrast the way American health care responded to its quality problems with the way manufacturing responded to the loss of business to Japanese firms that had embraced continuous quality improvement in the 1960s and 1970s. By 1990 American business had become as serious about continuous quality improvement as Japanese business. Brennan and Berwick (1996) contend that this happened because of external pressure from competitive markets: American firms went under when they failed to pick their quality problems and fix them. But competition did not work in the health sector: health providers that failed to fix their quality problems could flourish.

In Chapter 8, we will have a lot more to say about the possibilities for health and social care competition to create the external pressure to pick problems and fix them. Like Brennan and Berwick (1996), our conclusion will be that it is difficult to make competition work anywhere near as well in nursing home care as it can in widget making. Like Brennan and Berwick (and Walshe 2003), we think regulation is needed to create that external pressure. This means, for example, regulation that can threaten to suspend a hospital's licence, or threaten the job of its CEO, if a problem that is keeping infection rates or preventable falls high is not fixed.

Unfortunately, regulatory failure can be as big a problem as market failure in not providing this external pressure to find quality and safety problems and fix them. So this book is a contribution to understanding both regulatory failure and market failure in health and social care, and how to fix them. We suspect it is possible to fix markets well enough that some of the burden can be taken off regulation, and to fix regulation well enough that some of the burden can be taken off markets. This implies, as in Lessig's (1999) analysis, that markets are conceived as another regulatory tool for creating the external pressure to fix quality problems. One reason markets fail is market ritualism. An example is using privatization as an institutionalized means to create a market, but then privatizing a public monopoly into the hands of a private monopoly. The result is that the goal of a competitive market is not achieved, as in the Russian oil industry. Equally, we will show that other forms of external regulation fail because of a variety of kinds of regulatory ritualism.

These forms of ritualism are conceived in this book as the fundamental obstacles to continuous improvement in health and social care under conditions of regulatory capitalism. Because ritualism prevents us from fixing problems, we first need to learn how to fix ritualism. Nursing home care proves a rich arena of experience for this purpose.

As a research site, nursing homes have a number of attractions. The first is that, as we will see below, nursing home regulation in the United States is about four times as well resourced as hospital regulation. So there is more regulatory activity to study. Second is as a social-care domain, there are implications for social care as well as health care, and indeed implications for rethinking health-care institutions such as hospitals in more social-care terms. Third, nursing homes are more technologically and organizationally simple organizations compared to, say, hospitals or Health Maintenance Organizations. So it is easier for the ethnographic researcher to grasp the implications of a higher frequency of observed regulatory encounters. Fourth, we will show that in Australia (though not in the United States) nursing home regulatory compliance could be measured with higher reliability than any elsewhere documented in the regulation literature. Hence superior quantitative work has been possible compared to other domains of regulation, based on survey research with the remarkable response rate of 96 per cent on the first wave of data collection from nursing homes, with inspectors then cooperating in filling out questionnaires for 406 of 410 of the sampled homes.

We are in a decade in which a revolution in health safety and quality has begun. Leape and Berwick (2005) do not yet see systematic national evidence that the National Quality Forum's '100,000 Lives Campaign' is actually saving such lives in the US. Yet they do conclude that evidence-based medicine has identified at least 12 practice changes that if they were identified across a nation to pick and fix could substantially reduce preventable death and suffering (see Table 1.2). Before moving on to the task of understanding the role of regulatory ritualism in preventing health providers from picking problems such as these and fixing them, we must return to our special context of nursing home regulation, first by describing its history in England, and then the US and Australia.

THE EVOLUTION AND DEVOLUTION OF THE NURSING HOME AND ITS REGULATION

England

The nursing home is a phenomenon of late modernity, really of the twentieth century. By the twenty-first century its evolution had begun to shift to devolution into a more complex continuum of care. For most of human history, the aged were cared for in the home of their immediate family. Yet in most families, old age as we know it today barely existed. In 1800 in England life expectancy was 36, lower in poorer nations like France, India and China. In England, it gradually rose to 69 by 1950, then much more quickly to 78 by 2000. This means that until the lifetimes of the authors, most people were productive members of their household up to what was in contemporary terms a young death. For the first time in history, during the adulthood of the authors of this book in the US, Australia and England, a typical married couple has more parents than children. And they spend more years of their lives caring for an ageing parent than for a dependent child (Tellis-Nayak 1988: 6). As the burdens of aged care have grown, so has community demand for institutional care. In the 1990s

Table 1.2   Practice changes that can substantially reduce death and suffering

Intervention	Results
Perioperative antibiotic protocol	Surgical site infections decreased by 93%
Physician computer order entry	81% reduction of medication errors
Pharmacist rounding with team	66% reduction of preventable adverse drug events 78% reduction of preventable adverse drug events
Protocol enforcement	92–95% reduction in central venous line infections
Rapid response teams	Cardiac arrests decreased by 15%
Reconciling medication practices	90% reduction in medication errors
Reconciling and standardizing medication practices	60% reduction in adverse drug events over 12 months (from 7.6 per 1000 doses to 3.1 per 1000 doses) 64% reduction in adverse drug events in 20 months (from 3.8 per 1000 doses to 1.39 per 1000 doses)
Standardized insulin dosing	Hypoglycemic episodes decreased 63% (from 2.95% of patients to 1.1%) 90% reduction in cardiac surgical wound infections (from 3.9% of patients to 0.4%)
Standardized warfarin dosing	Out-of-range international normalized ratio decreased by 60% (from 25% of tests to 10%)
Team training in labour and delivery	50% reduction in adverse outcomes in preterm deliveries
Trigger tool and automation	Adverse drug events reduced by 75% between 2001 and 2003
Ventilator bundle protocol	Ventilator-associated pneumonias decreased by 62%

Source: Leape and Berwick (2005).

nursing home care began to cost significantly more than the total cost of primary health care in England (Bowman 1997: 189).

From Elizabethan England, small numbers of elderly people whose families would not or could not care for them were housed in workhouses for the poor. These, however, were institutions for younger indigent citizens that also served as a dumping place for the elderly. Private and charitable hospitals, as they became more accessible to the ill in early modern England, became places where nursing was provided for dying elderly; by the twentieth century many hospitals came to have entire wards dedicated to this purpose. Mental hospitals became the most common places where infirm elderly were housed, especially if suffering from dementia. The asylums provided discipline more than care, and like most of the hospitals, the accommodation was barrack-like. Non-hospital care in large old Victorian homes and converted hotels began to proliferate after World War I, more rapidly after World War II. Peter Townsend's (1962) fieldwork in 173 aged care homes of various kinds in 1958 and 1959 (archived at www.esds.ac.uk) showed that while local authorities aimed to create smaller homes than the barrack-like care in former workhouses, many of the new homes were uncarpeted dormitories. Townsend's *The Last Refuge* created public concern about dehumanizing institutional care for the aged in the 1960s. The 1970s saw very rapid growth in the number of nursing homes. This continued in the 1980s and 1990s, which saw a sevenfold increase in the number of nursing home beds (Kerrison and Pollock 2001). National Health Service-funded nursing home care was no more expensive, and probably cheaper, than care in geriatric hospital wards and there is evidence that quality of care improved, and certainly that patients and relatives preferred nursing homes to geriatric wards in hospitals (Bond et al. 1989).

During the Thatcher government years, public purchasers of care were required to spend a certain proportion of their budgets on the independent sector. This produced a dramatic shift in the proportion of nursing home and residential aged care home beds that were supplied by the for-profit private sector and a proportionate decline in public sector provision. This continued under the Major and Blair governments, with two-thirds of the local authority beds that existed in 1990 having disappeared by 2004 (Office of Fair Trading 2005: 37). Churches and charities were less prominent players in the post-1970 nursing home market in England than in the US and Australia, so the big shift in the UK was from public to for-profit provision.

As nursing homes proliferated, long-stay hospital beds for the elderly were progressively closed. By the time of our 1989 fieldwork they were totally absent from many District Health Authorities (DHAs), though still in the process of disappearing in some others. The deinstitutionalization of the mentally ill resulted in many elderly mentally ill being reinstitutionalized, mostly in residential homes as opposed to nursing homes. It is hard to overstate what a profound change this was in the nature of the British health system. By the end of the 1990s, the majority of health-care beds in the UK had become non-government (for-profit or charitable) nursing home beds. 'Between 1979 and 2000, the number of National Health Service (NHS) beds in England decreased from 480,000 to 189,000, while the number of beds in the independent mainly for profit sector increased from 23,000 in 1983 to 193,000' (Kerrison and Pollock 2001: 490).

In parallel with the rise of nursing homes regulated by National Health Service DHAs, the welfare state also funded even more rapid growth in residential homes without full-time nursing care which were initially run by local councils. Over time, an increasing proportion of these homes were privately run and contracted by councils to provide residential care for the aged. In theory, the aged in residential homes were not as sick as nursing home residents. While residential homes did not have full-time nursing staff, NHS nurses visited to provide nursing care, as of course did doctors. As 'ageing in place' became more influential (allowing people to become sicker and die in the place where they are most comfortable), many residential homes came to have residents as sick as those in many nursing homes. One reason 'ageing in place' became an influential philosophy was evidence that moving a frail aged person from a familiar environment could do more harm to their health than the benefits of moving into an environment richer in nursing resources. The upshot was that the concept of the 'nursing home' was abandoned by official British discourse at the end of the twentieth century. The former residential homes became statutorily defined as care homes for older persons and the former nursing homes became care homes for older persons with nursing. They were all 'care homes' inspected by the same national inspectorate under the same standards.

Yet in the field we often heard inspectors, staff and residents refer to the facility as a 'nursing home' when there were nurses on the staff. So notwithstanding the official death of the concept of the nursing home in one of our three jurisdictions by the end of the study, we have continued to use the term 'nursing home'. Similarly, we have continued with the term 'residents', as the term still most commonly used in Australia and the US, notwithstanding the recent British preference for the term 'service users' and use of 'patients' in the early years of the study in all three countries. Finally, we use the term 'inspector' as the common term to avoid confusion, as inspector was used in all three countries at some point during the study, and is still so used in the UK, even though it has been supplanted by the term 'surveyor' in the US and 'standards monitor' followed by 'assessor' in Australia.

In England, as in the US and Australia, not only did we see at the very end of the twentieth century and the beginning of the twenty-first century a halt to the formerly steep growth in the number of aged care homes with nursing at the expense of aged care homes without nursing, we also saw rapid growth in domiciliary care – with NHS nurses visiting the aged in place in their own home, or the homes of relatives with granny flats (a partial turning back of this institutional clock). Other continuum of care developments that have expanded rapidly across the globe include aged care complexes with independent living units and a nursing home on the same site. The elderly graduate on one site from fully independent living, to independent living with visits by nurses, provision of meals and other home help, to nursing home care and care of a specialized, locked dementia unit. Even so, in 2004 there were still 410 000 elderly people in the UK in 15 700 residential care facilities.

The United States

By the end of the nineteenth century, five types of facilities were providing care for the aged – county poorhouses ('almshouses' or 'farms'), state mental hospitals, charitable homes for the aged established by Methodist, Lutheran and Jewish organizations in particular, and some early for-profit boardinghouses that evolved to provide some nursing care and nursing homes affiliated with (mostly public) hospitals. County poorhouses run by local governments were generalist custodians of the poor, orphaned children, physically disabled adults, mentally disabled, mentally ill and the aged. In 1923, more than half the 78 000 occupants of US almshouses were over 65 years of age (Vladeck 1980: 34). Progressively the generalist poorhouse was supplanted by more specialist institutions for these various categories of needy folk. Nursing homes, often originally called rest homes or convalescent homes, were part of this evolution of specialized care. By 1930, there were more people over 65 in mental hospitals than in almshouses and private nursing homes combined (Vladeck 1980: 35). It was not just deinstitutionalization of the mentally ill in the final decades of the twentieth century that was going to change this.

United States economic regulation of aged institutional care started with President Roosevelt's New Deal, specifically the Social Security Act of 1935. The New Dealers were against the use of public poorhouses to care for the poor elderly. A muckraking study by Harry Evans (1926), *The American Poor Farm and its Inmates*, was one important text that informed this first generation of advocates for the institutional reform of aged care that so influenced the New Dealers. The policy response was to make those residing in public institutions ineligible for Old Age Assistance. This spawned the growth of private nursing homes. As a consequence, during World War II, for-profit providers for the first time passed both public and charitable providers in the number of nursing home beds (Thomas 1969: 125). By 1954, 86 per cent of the 9000 nursing homes in the United States were for-profit facilities, 10 per cent charitable and 4 per cent public (Special Committee on Aging 1990a: 149). While the 1935 Social Security Act effectively shut down the poorhouses, in the 1940s mental hospitals continued to house about a quarter of the institutionalized aged (Waldman 1983: 508).

The 1947 Hill–Burton legislation provided increased health funding to states, but with mandated economic regulation of the industry that required states to issue a Certificate of Need that a particular kind of health facility was actually needed at a specific location. This rationed public support in an era when health facilities in some cities, including big ones like New York (Thomas 1969: 273), had average occupancy rates over 100 per cent. The response was a 600 per cent increase in the number of nursing home beds in the United States in the boom construction period between 1950 and 1980. This 1947 law reform introduced the first federal standards for approving physical construction and design of new facilities. The Public Health Service officials who drafted the rules had a hospital orientation. This is why to this day American nursing homes look so much more like mini-hospitals than English or Australian homes (Vladeck 1980: 43). The federal requirement for a Certificate of Need was lifted in 1982, though a few states still have a limited certificate of need process.

The era of central (federal) health planning that began in 1947 reached its high-water mark with the Comprehensive Health Planning Act of 1966 under which federal funding was provided for each state to have a State Health Planning Council. The planning era began to wane everywhere by the 1980s and in many quarters during the 1970s where the attempt to ratio-nalize the American health non-system in a holistic way through compre-hensive planning was generally pronounced a failure (Ermann 1976; O'Connor 1974). The central planning era for nursing homes coincides with what Braithwaite (2005a) has called the era of provider capitalism[1] and what others have called the Keynesian welfare state (Levi-Faur 2005, 2006). One year before the central planning high-water mark, Congress passed Public Law 89-97 to establish Medicare and Medicaid in 1965, which came to fund publicly most nursing home beds. Today 60 per cent of nursing home income is received from Medicaid, with Medicare providing a significant proportion of the remainder. It is the lever of the withdrawal of this state funding support, as in England and Australia, that gives the regulatory system most of its influence. The nursing homes that are totally dependent on Medicaid tend to be less profitable and have lower staffing levels than those with substantial revenue from wealthier private pay patients or from Medicare for short-stay (generally younger) restorative care cases in transition from hospital back to their homes.

Ermann (1976) discerned three movements in American health gover-nance: trust of professionalism, trust in comprehensive planning and trust in a mix of community empowerment and markets. The first movement that preceded the comprehensive planning attempts of provider capitalism trusted professions to run health-care organizations. Before corporatization of health gained momentum in the final third of the twentieth century,[2] even private hospitals run by doctors, and certainly charitable ones, were not seen as needing regulation. 'Why, it was asked, should we regulate organizations whose only goals are public service?' (Ermann 1976: 170). In the comprehensive planning era mid-twentieth century, professional self-regulation was no longer seen as sustainable because most of the dollars were no longer being spent on doctors; there were a lot more professional and non-professional players, such as major insurers, in the system.

Then comprehensive planning was seen as having failed for the reasons advanced by Hayek (1949). Central planners did not have enough local knowledge; their centralized schemes wrought havoc because of insensitivity to local custom and contingent variation. Ermann (1976) perceptively saw two competitors for the third wave of change. The left favoured recovering local knowledge by 'community control' of health care which was local and consumer-centred, with particular attention to the neglected needs of disadvantaged consumers. The right favoured more markets, more consumer sovereignty; the Hayekian solution of the price mechanism delivering signals from local preferences to remedy the want of local knowledge in central state planning. We will see that both developments have been very much in contest, a still unresolved contest, in the three decades since Ermann's article.

Our analysis is that this continuing contest, if you like the continuing failure of all four options in Table 1.3, leaves us reasonably positioned for crafting a more robust dispensation that involves seeing all four glasses as half full as well as half empty. It is a mistake to be utterly cynical about professional self-regulation and professional semi-autonomy. It is a mistake to give up on central planning. What we must avoid is the folly of seeing the planning of the national executive government as the only planning. What is needed for better health is a plurality of separated, semi-autonomous powers (professional, commercial, accreditation, local government, state government, federal government, consumer groups) each doing strategic planning that takes account of the strategic plans of the other separated powers (Metcalfe 1994). Because romantic schemes of top-down demand for community control of health and welfare have mostly failed, that does not mean a policy patience that waits for bottom-up community engagement, and then supports it, will fail in the same way. Because more competition in health markets mostly fails to improve health outcomes (see Chapter 8), this does not mean competition policy cannot be crafted in a way that actually does improve outcomes. Professional self-regulation,

Table 1.3   Eras of trust, eras of health sector capitalism

Era of trust	Trust professionals	Trust comprehensive planning	Trust local communities	Trust markets
Era of capitalism	Liberal nightwatchman state Nineteenth century–1935	Provider capitalism/welfare state 1935–1970s	Regulatory capitalism 1970s–	Regulatory capitalism 1970s–
Key regulatory mechanism	Professional self-regulation	Plans enforced by state command and control	Informal social control by norms	Price mechanism
Number of key partners in the regulatory dance	One (professions)	Two (state and providers)	Three (tripartite or multi-party community–provider–state)	None (deregulation)
Knowledge mechanism	Professional knowledge	Bureaucratic knowledge	Local	Invisible hand captures knowledge of sovereign consumers
Bed allocation	Professionals locate beds to suit them and their patients	Demographic analysis plans allocation through Certificate of Need to keep occupancy near 100%	Communities disperse bed entitlements through local deliberation	The invisible hand leaves poor providers with many empty beds while good providers grow

Source: Adapted from Ermann (1976).

central planning, community control and markets are all such thin reeds in health governance that they are bound to snap if we radically shift too much of the burden for improved health and social care performance on to them. We need now to tie these reeds together in new ways to weave a more robust and redundant policy fabric. At least that is the lesson we will draw from what we see as these quadruple policy failures of the twentieth century in England and Australia, albeit in different and less disastrous ways, as well as in the US. We seek to rise to this challenge in Chapter 10 where we discuss the marriage of webs of explanation and webs of governance into strategic nodes of governance.

Even in the most sophisticated market, New York State, nursing homes remained a cottage industry until the final quarter of the twentieth century. The average number of beds of for-profit nursing homes in New York increased from 14 in 1949, to 24 in 1958 and 34 in 1964 (Thomas 1969: 157). But from 1964 it took only another decade for the average number of beds in facilities nationally to double again (Vladeck 1980: 103). In Rhode Island, the average size of nursing homes increased from 32 beds in 1972 to 73 by 1978. This period saw the Rhode Island mom-and-pops (small owner-operated homes) shut down, with the number of nursing homes declining from 180 to 110. The year before this period, 1971, saw 18 homes closed for failure to meet the Life Safety Code. This process was occurring across the nation. One old-time inspector explained to us that when he joined the Michigan Department of Health in the 1970s 160 mom-and-pops were closed in one year, half on fire safety grounds: 'When I came here our objective was to close down the mom-and-pops. And we did that.'

The ratcheting up of regulatory standards, especially after 1970, meant that homes had to enjoy greater economies of scale. There were three key drivers here. First was the need for economies of scale to cover either full-time or part-time dietary consultants, pharmacy consultants, physical therapists, social workers, quality assurance committees and a wide range of other services that federal regulation ultimately came to impose. Second were fire safety standards that were more economic for purpose-built facilities on greenfield sites to meet than converted structures designed for other purposes. Third the progressively increased documentation demanded by regulators was more economically managed by being large enough to hire specialist nurses, like the now ubiquitous Minimum Data Set (MDS) managers, who manage paper more than patients. None of these drivers were as large in England, Australia and most of Europe (Meijer et al. 2000: 557), where nursing homes today average around the size they were in the US in the early 1970s.

A distinctive feature of the American industry that is not apparent in Australia or England was some involvement of organized crime in nursing home ownership (see, for example, Vladeck 1980: 106), attracted by the huge speculative profits that could be made in the industry for as long as expensive regulatory impositions could be kept at bay (Vladeck 1980: 115). As recently as the late 1980s in New York we were told of a crime boss proprietor who placed a gun on the table during an exit conference following an inspection of his home, a gesture the inspector said he noted! A considerable number of real estate speculators without a health background, some of them fraud professionals who turned their hand to health benefit fraud, were also more a feature of the US industry, though they also moved into the Australian and English industry. These proprietors were major obstacles to improving quality of care. Crime boss proprietors seem to have gone the same way as mom-and-pop proprietors, no longer being a significant part of the US nursing home industry.

In the late 1960s and early 1970s, during a stock-market boom, much of the supplanting of mom-and-pops with chains occurred. More than 50 nursing home chains issued stock in 1968 and 1969. For a short period the nursing home chain was the hottest class of stocks on the market (Vladeck 1980: 118). But chains of hundreds of nursing homes proved less than the splendid business model the investors of the period thought. They thought the stupendous rate of growth in publicly funded nursing home beds would have to continue as the population aged further, blind to the possibility that the state would respond to this fiscal blow-out by a move back to community care. Medicenters of America, which ultimately went broke, was formed by the President of Holiday Inn. But motel franchising philosophies of standardized construction plans and uniform management policies did not fit the aged care sector where management had to be more responsive to particularized needs of residents for a loving home as opposed to a holiday room. Beverly Enterprises emerged as the largest chain, with a thousand homes by the mid-1980s. During the 1980s and 1990s, quite a number of its facilities had quality of care debacles. With every new Beverly nursing home scandal, the Beverly brand became a liability that drove the company into the red. By 1999, it had downsized to 562 nursing homes. It was still the largest. The smallest of the six largest chains (Vencor) had only 291 facilities but enjoyed considerably more operating revenue than Beverly (Harrington 2001). The American chains are beginning to internationalize, though this is hardly a globalized industry. Sun Healthcare had 397 nursing homes in the US, 145 in the UK, about half that investment in the Australian industry, with significant beds in Spain (1640) and Germany (1217) as well (Harrington 2001).

Today the industry is more one of mini-chains than maxi-chains like the Beverly of the 1980s. By the 1990s a majority of nursing homes were integrated into chains (Harrington 2001). The economies of scale demanded by regulatory pressures are not easier to meet in the move from ten homes with 1000 beds across the chain to 100 with 10 000 beds. A proprietor with health industry know-how can monitor a dozen homes with sufficient early intervention to prevent a scandal that will besmirch their brand. This is much harder with a hundred facilities. Secondly, if as is typical, the chain has its facilities geographically concentrated in one region of the country, say spread across two adjacent states, then management can concentrate on maintaining close rapport with just two state regulatory administrations. It can also geographically concentrate its political influence over legislators and state-based industry associations, both of which have proved important to successful proprietors. Hybrid mini-chain business models are common, such as the proprietor who owns some facilities, manages others on a percentage of revenue basis, and contracts services to yet others – say pharmaceuticals services by a proprietor who is also vertically integrated into a pharmaceuticals supply business. This hybridized chain model also hedges reputational risks to a brand from a regulatory scandal in one part of the business. As in the UK and Australia, much of the more recent investment has gone to retirement villages that provide a continuum of care.

Nursing home regulation in the United States is an interesting case study for those interested in regulatory capitalism as a phenomenon, because it is not a case of regulation responding to the structure of the industry. Rather it is regulation that has driven the structure of the industry, the size of firms and the business models they deploy. Indeed, the very private nursing home industry was a creation of New Deal regulatory ambitions to shut down aged care in dilapidated almshouses. To understand why intimate, family-like 30-bed nursing homes can be economically viable in the UK or Australia but not in the US, this book will argue that we need to understand the nature of US regulation.

Australia

As in England, nineteenth-century residential aged care was for people who were indigent. In 1821 the government of New South Wales funded the building of a Benevolent Society Asylum, 70 per cent of whose inmates were over 60 by 1830. In 1849, the Liverpool Street Asylum was established. Probably it could be described as Australia's first nursing home, though the first Nightingale nurses did not arrive in the colony until the 1870s and Nightingale nurses only became compulsory in asylums from 1877 (Fine 1999: 12). Asylums remained the centrepiece of institutional aged care until the 1950s. The crucial impetus for change was the 1954 Aged or

Disabled Persons Homes Act which awarded government grants on a pound-for-pound basis for the capital cost of building nursing homes. This subsidy was increased over the next decade, most importantly with recurrent as well as capital support from 1963. Nursing home bed numbers doubled during the ten years from 1962 to 1972 and continued to grow faster than growth in the number of aged persons until 1983. At this time it hit a plateau with a slight and gradual increase in bed numbers that was much more gradual than the increase in the size of the aged population (Fine 1999: 14).

In 1972, the Aged or Disabled Persons Hostels Act created a distinction between nursing homes and hostels. The Act enabled a large funding investment in building new aged care hostels that did not have nurses permanently working in the facility. The aim was to get residents who did not need nursing care out of nursing homes to free up beds for waiting lists of residents who did. Hostel care would be cheaper for the government and provide a less institutional environment for residents. A considerable shift in the proportion of aged care beds from nursing homes to hostels was indeed accomplished (Gibson 1998: 56–7, 66). The Australian distinction between hostels and nursing homes was the same as the British distinction between residential homes and nursing homes and the American distinction between assisted living facilities and nursing homes. The fiscal motivation for establishing facilities with lower skill levels of the staff was the same in all three countries.[3] As demand for residential care places grew and grew, however, waiting lists often became as long for hostels as for nursing homes. The result was that extremely frail residents needing nursing care were often pleased enough to get a place in a hostel. More fundamentally, as 'ageing in place' became a more influential philosophy, hostel residents who started out not needing nursing care stayed in the hostel until they died. In response, the statutory distinction between hostels and nursing homes was abolished before the end of the twentieth century, as was the distinction between skilled and intermediate care nursing homes in the US and residential homes and nursing homes in British law.

All the residential care growth was in non-government beds, with government beds declining to become less than a sixth of the industry. As in the US, but unlike the UK, there are a substantial number of church and charitable nursing homes in Australia. Indeed, religious and charitable homes have always been more the 60 per cent of Australian homes, while for-profits have been the majority in the US since the New Deal. At the time of writing, some consolidation is occurring, with a number of charitable homes looking to sell out to private chains. Yet only seven operators in Australia have a market share greater than 1 per cent, so consolidation has a long way to go compared to other market sectors. Hence, the major long-run transition is the same in the three nations – from predominantly public/charitable toward for-profit provision in the course of the second half of the twentieth century.

In the even longer historical perspective, we had predominantly domestic care funded by families in the era of the liberal nightwatchman state; the rise of direct public provision during the era of the provider (or welfare) state from the New Deal of the 1930s to 1970; and a return to largely private provision with public subsidies during the current era of regulatory capitalism (Braithwaite 2005a; Levi-Faur 2005) from 1970. In all three nations, residential aged care has been one of the fastest growing parts of public spending. This has led from the last decade of the twentieth century to an expanding shift in public institutions from ageing in nursing homes to ageing in place with support from visiting health and welfare professionals. In 1997 a century of mostly rapid growth in the numbers of residential aged care beds ended in the UK; every year since 1997 has seen a slight decrease in the number of beds, notwithstanding growing numbers of elderly (Office of Fair Trading 2005: 39) and in the mid-2000s the number of nursing homes (though still not the numbers of residents) has begun to decline slightly in the US for the first time. This is an emerging new synthesis of the nightwatchman, provider and regulatory states; re-domestication, combined with private contracting of publicly funded services to domiciliary/community care and public regulation of that private domiciliary provision. As in the nineteenth century, over 90 per cent of the care for the aged today is provided by families and is heavily gendered (Braithwaite 1990). What is different is that a variety of publicly funded support services for both the aged and their carers are provided today to keep the aged out of institutions for as long as possible. Even so, a great many of us still spend our last days in nursing homes.

While charitable institutions are more important in the Australian market than the other two, while local government provision is more important in the British market, while the US market is both more private and more aggregated into large corporate chains, the similarities in the historical trajectory of aged care provision are more profound than the differences. In 2000 these three countries were all in the middle range of developed economies in spending on long-term care – all spending between 1.2 per cent and 1.4 per cent of gross domestic product (GDP) on it – all very different from the 2.9 per cent Sweden spends (OECD 2005: 26). Admittedly, the US is distinguished from Australia and the UK, indeed from almost all other developed economies, by the high proportion of its long-term care expenditure that is private rather than public. There are major similarities in the historical trajectory of regulation as well. Yet here we will see the cross-national differences are more profound.

HISTORY OF REGULATION OF AGED CARE

The next five chapters describe in detail the history of regulation of aged care homes in the three countries. Remembering that our chosen conception of regulation is broad, there was always some regulation. Local constables in early modern England were reluctant to intervene in the private lives of families, but intervention was known to occur when elder abuse was severe. Strong social norms in nineteenth-century parishes, villages and towns in all three societies required that elderly family members should be cared for with kindness, if not love, and gossip was a powerful form of social control against neglect when it was visible, which it mostly was not. As Michael Mann (1986) has shown, from medieval times Christendom exercised formidable ideological power to secure norms embedded in canon law. The agency of parish priests who had considerable access to the private space of families was important, but so was the Christian congregation collectively. By the twentieth century, clergy had become much less important advocates on behalf of neglected and abused elderly. Yet they still have some advocacy significance in hospitals, nursing homes and private homes. This trajectory of the residual regulatory significance of clergy is one of the common elements of the history of aged care regulation in the three nations.

The History of English Regulation

The Nursing Homes Registration Act, 1927 was the first national legislation in our three countries to mandate registration and inspection. It set a pattern for the English-speaking world that nursing homes should be subject to regulation by both pre-marketing clearance and post-marketing surveillance. Before the nursing home could be marketed to residents, its plans, facilities, fire safety, staffing and the qualifications of management had to be approved (registration), and after registration there was to be post-marketing surveillance by regular inspection. This was different from pharmaceuticals regulation in our three nations for most of the twentieth century (which was based on pre-marketing clearance only) and food and consumer product safety regulation (which was based on post-marketing surveillance only).

Both pre- and post-marketing regulation had been recommended by a Select Committee on Nursing Home Registration in 1926, before which the Royal British Nurses Association, the College of Nursing and the Society of Medical Officers of Health, but not the Ministry of Health, argued that there were serious problems of overcrowding, pressure sores, scanty food, poor sanitation, poor infection control and unsatisfactory arrangements for the removal of soiled linen. Registration and inspection under the 1927 Act was undertaken by local authorities. In 1948 homes run by local authorities themselves became subject to inspection by officers of the Ministry of Health. In 1971, the Department of Health and Social Security created an inspectorate of local authority social services that came to be called in 1985 the Social Services Inspectorate. So local authority inspectorates checked aged care homes and the Social Services Inspectorate inspected the local authority inspectors. Day and Klein (1990: 33) pointed out that its power was then, as it still is, 'chiefly hortatory', its leverage limited. They also showed considerable overlap of the responsibilities of the Social Services Inspectorate with similar work of the Audit Commission, and limited coordination between the two. This overlap was addressed from 1996 when the two agencies started to conduct joint reviews of social care agencies.

During the first two decades of regulation, from 1926, there seems to have been little distinction between nursing homes (with staff that included registered nurses) and residential homes (that provided social care without qualified nursing). But with the establishment of the NHS after World War II, nursing care facilities for the aged run by the NHS became an NHS responsibility, and in 1973 private nursing home registration and inspection also became a responsibility of Area Health Authorities in the NHS (from 1982 District Health Authorities – DHAs). Social care homes remained the responsibility of local authorities. Over time dual registration of a facility, with one part of a home registered as a nursing home by the DHA and another section registered with the local authority for residential social care, became more common. This was one reason for the ultimate collapse of the distinction between nursing homes and residential homes for the aged.

The Hospital Advisory Service was created in 1969 to inspect long-stay institutions administered by the NHS, including aged care wards in hospitals. It was ultimately abolished for England and Wales in 1997. The Hospital Advisory Service rejected a rule enforcement model in favour of a consultancy model (Day and Klein 1990: 80). Excessive use of restraints and a lack of individual care plans were the practices most commonly targeted by Hospital Advisory Service inspection reports in the 1980s.

Under the Registered Homes Act 1984, DHAs were obliged to produce written guidelines for nursing home owners, register new facilities and inspect all nursing homes in their district twice a year. This was the inspection regime we observed between 1989 and 1993. It was a regime with a national requirement for inspection but there were no national standards, the guidelines being set at the district level. We found considerable diversity in what they required (as have others, for example, Arai 1992). National Minimum Standards were introduced for the first time in the Care Standards Act, 2000.

The Thatcher government introduced a contracting-out philosophy for both nursing home and social care in 1989. National Health Service

Districts became purchasers and, mostly, private nursing homes became providers. Similarly, local authorities became purchasers of residential care beds for social care and care home operators became providers. Inspection units were to be set up at arm's length from both the purchasers and the providers. Many other government services in Britain saw this purchaser–provider split in this period. Public as well as private providers of a service similar to hospitals became competitors with other public and private hospital providers to win contracts for hospital services to a DHA (the purchaser). The model was copied in many parts of the world, including some Australian states and territories, and reversed since in some of them, as the dramatic organizational and 'value-for-money' changes the purchaser–provider split had promised did not materialize. Nevertheless, aged care was at the leading edge of the New Public Management. A more permanent shift has occurred from the provider state (or the welfare state) to regulatory capitalism (Levi-Faur 2005), wherein states do less rowing and more steering (Osborne and Gaebler 1992).

The ethos of the New Public Management of the Thatcher and Major years was decentralized value-for-money auditing rather than national standards. In those years, we will see that American and Australian nursing home regulation was becoming more centralized, with authority, particularly over standards, but also enforcement policy, shifting decisively from state to national governments. Nevertheless, the audit society (Power 1997) ethos in Britain did drive increased investment in nursing home inspection. The National Audit Office and the Audit Commission were not major players in this. These agencies did not attempt to review value for money in all aspects of health and social care provision. Rather they adopted a topic-based approach – choosing topics from cancer care to the National Blood Service – and rarely chose topics where aged care was central. Similarly, nursing homes virtually never hear from the Health Service Ombudsman: in 2001–02 they investigated only 240 complaints, mostly nothing to do with aged care (Walshe 2003: 122). This contrasts with the large presence we will see that state Long-Term Care Ombudsman programs had in US nursing homes and the effectiveness they had in improving health outcomes (Cherry 1993). Voluntary accreditation of nursing homes is also less prevalent in England than in the US and Australia. A private sector organization called the Health Quality Service does accredit, but their client base is tiny (16 nursing and residential homes accredited as of June 2005).

Even so, because of the growth of DHA inspection, the Thatcher era was not one of deregulation for nursing homes. Investment in regulation was strengthened even further with the election of the Blair government. For the first time national standards for nursing homes and residential aged care homes were introduced in 2000 and the regulatory regime moved beyond limited national inspection of local inspectorates to a national inspectorate. The Conservative Party, DHAs and the Department of Health (who were wary of public reports on the inspection of their public providers) had always been rather content with the decentralized status quo. The Labour Party and the National Consumer Council were more pro-regulation, favouring a national inspectorate under national standards; the now defunct Independent Healthcare Association, whose members tended to be large providers (nursing and residential home chains), favoured national standards from their inception at the end of the 1980s because they claimed this would deal with inconsistency in the rules required from different parts of their organizations. As large providers, they also felt they had less to fear if a Labour government drove out some of their smaller competitors with tougher standards that they would find easy to meet. Some elements of the Registered Nursing Home Association also favoured a national inspectorate.

A National Care Standards Commission (NCSC) from 2002 integrated social care inspection for services for children, adults, and the aged, including takeover of aged care home inspection from 150 local councils and 95 District Health Authorities. It was early in the implementation of this big change in 2004 when a Commission for Social Care Inspection took it (the NCSC) over and further integrated its work with other social care work of the Audit Commission and the former Social Services Inspectorate. As one industry association leader put it, nursing home and residential home inspection were merged 'with a social care perspective'. Social work rather than nursing became the dominant profession in the business of nursing home inspection. This was partly about an ideological shift, which we observed to be real at the street level, to emphasizing empowerment of residents and their social needs in inspections, and partly a pragmatic reaction to a national shortage of nurses. The Commission also inspected children's residential homes, residential special schools, nurses' agencies, adoption agencies, services for the disabled and other social care service providers. Fifty-four per cent of the 2622 total staff of the Commission, and 76 per cent of its inspection resources, at the time of our 2004 fieldwork, were working on aged care home inspection out of nine regional offices. In addition to integrating nursing home and social care regulation, the aged care regulatory coverage of the Commission for Social Care Inspection extended to domiciliary and day-care services for the aged.

Three things changed during the Blair years:

1.   There were National Minimum Standards (implemented 2002).
2.   Nursing home and aged social care homes were integrated into the one national regulatory regime.

3. The national role had changed from simply inspecting regional inspectors to directly inspecting providers.

However, the Commission took in the Social Services Inspectorate and continued to work jointly with the Audit Commission to issue star ratings of the overall social care performance of local authorities. The Secretary of State for Health for the first time in 2001 announced publicly the names of councils that had received a zero star rating. The zero star rated councils were subject to a regime of special inspections and special measures, while councils with three stars were substantially exempted from inspections for three years. At the time of writing, a policy debate is being promoted by the Commission on the possibility of extending the star ratings approach, or some kind of balanced scorecard approach, from aggregated local authority performance down to the performance of individual aged care facilities.

In the 2005 budget the government announced that by 2008 11 national inspectorates would be 'streamlined' into four (Office of the Deputy Prime Minister 2005: 31). The Adult Social Care and Health Commission would combine the current functions of the Commission for Social Care Inspection (except those for social care of children) and the inspectorates responsible for health and NHS inspections of facilities such as hospitals. This time the proposed restructure is motivated by concern over the huge increase in the cost of the regulatory state, notwithstanding government belief that 'inspection works':

> A recent MORI survey on behalf of the Local Government Association showed that over 60% of councils believe that inspection sharpens their focus and three in four, while agreeing they often dislike inspection, believe it can – when used effectively – drive improvement. However, the number of inspectorates has risen in the last five years, with nine new, two expanded, and six reconfigured. The total cost of all public service inspectorates has increased from £250 million in 1997 to over £550 million in 2002/03.
>
> (Office of the Deputy Prime Minister 2005: 30)

While we will see regulatory flux has been considerable in the US and Australia in recent decades, this does not match the constant administrative restructurings of the British state in this area, particularly under the Thatcher and Blair governments (for an overview see Walshe and Boyd 2006: 34–55). Yet one of our findings in the next chapter is that nursing home inspectorates are 'street-level bureaucracies' that in some fundamental ways are beyond the reach of meddling politicians – they are bureaucracies where the power that matters most is at the street level of the officers who interact with clients (as opposed to senior management) (Lipsky 1980). Echoing similar comments by other old hands of English nursing home inspections, an inspector who had worked through all these bureaucratic restructurings remarked about them: 'Going out and doing the job was very much the same.' Referring in 2004 to the 2002 move to new national standards, another said this was 'a whimper rather than a bang for inspectors'. We will see indeed that on the ground in England there has been more continuity than change, and that the changes since the 1980s have been modest compared to the differences between regulation in England, the US and Australia.

The History of US Regulation

The New York City Department of Hospitals started inspecting and licensing for-profit nursing homes in 1929, two years after the first English regulation (Thomas 1969: 271–2) and in 1940 the state of New York Department of Social Welfare established standards for private nursing homes. Amendments to the federal Social Security Act in 1950 required states to license nursing homes, delegating the content and enforcement of the standards to states. Federal funds flowed to states during the 1950s for state health officers to visit nursing homes, teaching techniques of restorative nursing, food services supervision, management systems and the like. This was the era when states like Virginia settled into a consultancy model of improvement through collaborative regulation. During 1988 interviews at the Virginia Department of Health, there was consensus that 'This was one of the most effective things we ever did.'

A sequence of Senate committees between 1959 and 1965 documented poor-quality care in nursing homes and impotent state government regulation. In the wake of these hearings, the advent of Medicare and Medicaid in 1965 brought with it a Department of Health Education and Welfare with authority to set federal standards for homes participating in Medicare and Medicaid and to withhold funds from facilities that did not meet them. Medicare provides health insurance for the elderly and disabled; Medicaid provides health coverage for low-income persons, including the aged. Even financially comfortable middle-class Americans run down their savings quickly during extended institutionalization in a nursing home and so become Medicaid cases. Therefore, few nursing homes survive without Medicaid certification.

Medicare and Medicaid marked the end of the era of state control of nursing home regulation. A new era had begun of federal standards, federal control of what regulatory activities would be funded and what would not, and state surveyors who administered that system. The federal government has a regional office structure and also sent out surveyors to do 'look-behind' surveys to check that state surveyors were following federal protocols properly. These federal surveyors also took their own enforcement actions on problems they discovered. Many cities and counties also have nursing home inspectors, who usually concentrate on kitchens, sanitary and life safety issues, as does the federal Veterans Administration. During our observations of state inspections, we regularly encountered other regulators in the facility. This never happened during our English fieldwork and rarely in Australia. At the operational level, the US nursing home industry during the period of this study was more heavily regulated than Braithwaite (1985) found to be the case for coal mines and pharmaceuticals (Braithwaite 1984),[4] and more so than hospitals, as we will see below. The nursing home industry is a likely candidate for the industry whose operations are most heavily regulated; its biggest competitor for that title perhaps being the nuclear industry (Rees 1994).

Between 1969 and 1973 there was another round of Senate hearings on poor quality of care and regulatory failure by the states. The Ralph Nader organization wrote reports on nursing home scandals and regulatory failure that made sense of how 32 residents could die in a fire in a new nursing home in Ohio in 1970 and how 36 could die from a salmonella (food poisoning) outbreak in a Baltimore home in the same year (Vladeck 1980: 65). In response, Congress mandated in 1972 full federal funding for state survey and certification of nursing homes. Final federal regulations to implement this law were issued in 1974. Also in 1972 the long-term care ombudsman program was introduced, which soon came to see a federally funded ombudsman program in every state. Mary Adelaide Mendelson's (1974) exposé of the nursing home industry, *Tender Loving Greed*, also had a large impact on community support for tougher regulation.

The ombudsman program has driven some of the distinctive flavour of US nursing home regulation. In many states, at many points during the past three decades, where local nursing home advocacy groups have been weak, the ombudsman's program has been a kind of stop-gap cell of reformist advocacy. This has occurred because most state ombudsmen primarily use volunteers to be their advocacy agents in nursing homes, while also using some paid staff (National Center for Long Term Care Ombudsman Resources 1989). Walshe (2003: 98) reported 927 paid ombudsman program staff nationally, compared with more than 13 000 volunteers. That said, in most states at most points in time since 1972, the state Long Term Care Ombudsman has been more quiescent than aggressively activist. But even in these contexts, people from the ombudsman's office who we repeatedly saw turn up during inspections are one significant check and balance against the capture of survey teams by the nursing home. Walshe (2003: 98) reached the same conclusion, seeing the ombudsman program as delivering the tripartism to US nursing home regulation that responsive regulatory theory conceives as a fundamental protection against capture. A secondary function of the ombudsman is that when we observed inspectors confronting situations that they felt were bad for residents, but were not covered by the standards, we would often see them call in the ombudsman to take on the matter on behalf of the resident.

The election of President Reagan in 1980 saw a number of efforts to deregulate nursing homes, including replacing federal regulation with accreditation of a kind that applied to acute care hospitals. The consumer movement organized effectively against these proposals. Public outcry was vociferous and by 1982 Health and Human Services (HHS) Secretary Richard Schweiker was promising not to 'turn back the clock' on nursing home regulation.

Yet within months of this announcement, HHS in 1983 published proposed revisions to nursing home law that would 'deem' nursing homes accredited by the Joint Commission on the Accreditation of Hospitals (now called the Joint Commission for Accreditation of Healthcare Organizations – JCAHO) to meet federal regulatory requirements (Jost 1983, 1988). Again the community backlash was great. Congress imposed a moratorium on regulatory change until the Institute of Medicine was able to produce its 1986 report, *Improving the Quality of Care in Nursing Homes*. The American Bar Association section on Legal Problems of the Elderly laid important groundwork for the regulatory reforms proposed by the Institute of Medicine. Its report represented a consensus of the stakeholders in aged care. It recommended more regulation, not less.

Only 10 per cent of nursing homes voluntarily seek JCAHO certification. The JCAHO remained the dominant health regulator for hospitals only. The deregulatory ideology of the early Reagan administration saw the number of federally funded health facility inspectors (mostly nursing home inspectors) cut from 2400 to 1800 in 1982. Yet by the end of the Reagan administration there were over 4000 inspectors (for evidence more generally on the shift from deregulation to substantial regulatory growth under Reagan, see Ayres and Braithwaite 1992: ch. 1). There was further substantial growth under the first President Bush, with a 40 per cent increase in staffing and a 70 per cent survey and certification budget increase in 1990–91 to implement the 1987 Omnibus Budget Reconciliation Act (OBRA) reforms. Ironically, the sharpest ratcheting up of nursing home regulation in US history occurred under the Republican administrations of Presidents Nixon, Reagan and the first Bush.

An interesting comparison that reveals how heavily the US came to invest in nursing home regulation is found in Walshe (2003: 102). The budget of the JCAHO, with responsibility for regulating all hospitals in the United States, but also many other kinds of health providers, has less than a quarter of the combined budget of federal and state agencies regulating nursing homes (including the ombudsman programme). The National Committee for Quality Assurance (the dominant regulator of health plans) has only one-nineteenth the budget of the nursing home regulators. As the chief nurse of one state health department put it to us, acute care providers such as hospitals are more trusted to self-regulate 'because you come out of them vertical, whereas you come out of nursing homes horizontal'. Trust in a medical profession which is more visible in hospitals is also a factor. From a synoptic perspective of health system risk, there is a misallocation of resources here. However serious the problems of US nursing homes, they do not cause 44 000–98 000 residents to die and more than a million to be injured as a result of medical error, as the Institute of Medicine (2000) estimates hospitals do. Another mismatch in regulatory resource allocation we will see is that assisted living (residential facilities for the aged that do not provide around the clock nursing) suffers from a grossly under-resourced regulatory regime compared to nursing home regulation, given the realities of ageing in place. On the latter one can detect a public mood for change as a result of the growing popularity of media exposés of atrocious quality of care in assisted living homes and concern for more regulation from organizations such as the American Association of Retired Persons. In spite of this public pressure, the federal government is reluctant to enter a huge new field of regulatory funding.

A 1990 Health Care Financing Administration (HCFA) survey found the average number of inspector-hours on site for annual nursing home inspections was 156. In 1996 this fell to 136 for annual surveys, 29 hours on average for complaint inspections and 19 for revisits. These hours increased later in the 1990s, then fell back to more like the 1990 level in 2005. This does not count off-site report-writing and enforcement processing and additional on-site hours paid for by the state to monitor add-on state standards. When there are serious problems, extra inspectors are pulled in; we found cases where as many as 15 inspectors continuously camped at a nursing home for three weeks. Nursing home inspection is as a consequence much more fine-grained and intensive than environmental, occupational health and safety, food and pharmaceuticals inspection in the US.

Electoral support for the Institute of Medicine (1986) recommendations for regulatory reform was strong. A coalition of consumers, providers, health professionals and others called the 'Campaign for Quality Care' formed to reach a consensus position on legislative implementation of the Institute of Medicine proposals. Elma Holder and Barbara Frank, who came out of the Ralph Nader organization, were leaders of the National Citizens' Coalition for Nursing Home Reform that drove the consensus-building process. The Health Care Financing Administration under the Reagan administration resisted reform. But victory fell to the National Citizens' Coalition for Nursing Home Reform with passage in 1987 of the Omnibus Budget

Reconciliation Act (Public Law 100–203). This Act completely revised the federal nursing home regulations and how they would be enforced.

The fieldwork reported in this book covers state surveys of federal requirements before and after OBRA came into effect. OBRA increased requirements for the training of nursing home staff, introduced a variety of new residents' rights, imposed quality assessment and assurance obligations on nursing homes, but most of all OBRA was intended to be about strengthening enforcement, expanding enforcement options and making enforcement more inexorable in circumstances of non-compliance of severe severity and scope.

At all points in the history of US nursing home regulation, state advocates were achieving little victories for more stringent state licensure standards over and above the federal standards on one issue or another, often in the aftermath of a scandal in that state on that issue. State innovation with higher standards, including on enforcement standards, then copied by other states and ultimately advocated federally, has been one historical dynamic ratcheting up federal standards (Bardach and Kagan 1982). Over time most states reduced costs by completely integrating state licensure and federal Medicare and Medicaid certification surveys, so they were done by the same inspectors during the same visit. This increased pressure for harmonization of state and federal standards. Today there is much less interstate variation in regulatory strategy and in the level of standards than there was during any previous decade of American history.

While state legislatures still pass some important nursing home regulatory add-ons, it is the Congress in Washington that sets the legal framework. At the start of this study the Health Care Financing Administration within the Department of Health Education and Welfare drafted the regulations and inspection protocols. Later in this study there was a name change of HCFA to the Centers for Medicare and Medicaid Services (CMS). The CMS in effect sets national nursing home standards for healthcare quality, activities, residents' rights to privacy, information, personal possessions and control of residents' financial affairs, dietary standards, pharmaceutical services, physical environment, infection control, and disaster preparedness, among other issues of vital concern to the quality of life of institutionalized people. The range of issues covered by the US regulations is much the same as in the UK and Australia, but we will see that the way they are enforced is quite different.

The History of Australian Regulation

As in both the UK and US, at all stages in the history of Australian nursing home regulation, local government had an important role in inspecting building standards, fire safety and health in the sense of sanitation and sewerage regulations. Also, as in both the UK and US, from the time of the rise of the welfare state, aged care facilities have always experienced audits and financial inspections to ensure the legitimacy and accuracy of benefits claimed. Benefit fraud has been a major problem in all three countries. One Australian nursing home proprietor returned his questionnaire for this study, apologizing for the delay because he was on the run from the Australian Federal Police in the United States! Both these areas of local government inspection and financial inspection are beyond the scope of this study, which is restricted to quality of care regulation.

All three nations saw a huge increase in investment in regulation with the rise of regulatory capitalism from 1970, the US seeing the biggest increase. While periods of rule by conservative parties saw concerted efforts to deregulate, such as those by the Reagan administration in the early 1980s and the Howard government in Australia in 1996, these were resisted or reversed, and conservative governments mostly did as much to increase regulation as social democratic parties (for example, Parker 1987: 112). All saw a centralization of regulation at the national level, with the US making this move first in the mid-twentieth century, Australia at the end of the third quarter of the twentieth century and Britain in 2000. All saw a move away from a purely health orientation to regulation and more emphasis on social care, quality of life and resident rights. We see this as part of a more general trend of regulatory capitalism towards a rights orientation. In Chapter 6, however, we argue that the rights orientation in Australian aged care has not gone as far as in the disabilities sector, for example. Australia has mandatory reporting of child abuse for professionals, but not of elder abuse. Property rights are extended in expanding markets, as illustrated most potently by the widening of intellectual property rights (Drahos with Braithwaite 2003). In aged care, public provision increasingly provides the elderly with rights effectively to buy their own provision from a plurality of residential and non-residential providers. The rights of the aged to privacy, to participation in care planning, to a homelike environment, to freedom of movement, to political participation, to lodge formal complaints, and the like, have also expanded in all three nations. Nevertheless, we will see in the next five chapters that the differences in the way regulation is organized and in the culture of enforcement are profound across these three nations.

As in the US, Australia had a major era of nursing home scandals fanned by the consumer movement in the 1970s and early 1980s. The Auditor-General (1981) reported that the federal government was failing to assure value for the money it was spending on nursing homes. Parliamentary enquiries followed (Giles Report 1985; McLeay Report 1982). These reports excoriated the quality of care in Australian nursing homes and the inadequacy of its regulation by input-oriented state government regulation. As a result there was a Commonwealth government takeover of nursing home regulation from the states in 1987, followed by a brief period when some states kept some of their quality inspection in place to duplicate federal inspection. The post-1987 standards monitoring process was more resident-centred, more outcome-oriented and more oriented to resident rights. In 1996 a conservative government with a deregulatory agenda abolished federal standards monitoring and replaced it with an accreditation regime rather like that applied to hospitals in Australia and the US. It was less outcome-oriented, more oriented to systems improvements at first and then to continuous improvement.

Deregulation engendered another wave of nursing home scandals in the late 1990s and a certain amount of re-regulation. When poor compliance was revealed by the Aged Care Standards and Accreditation Agency, government inspectors moved in more frequently in the aftermath of accreditation to impose sanctions. Both federal regulation in the late 1980s and the partial re-regulation at the end of the 1990s saw increases in the numbers of officials inspecting nursing homes, but to levels nowhere near those in the US. There continues to be media and public disquiet over the quality of care in Australian nursing homes and concern over the lack of available places. Scandals involving rape and abuse of residents culminated in a joint communiqué from the Council of Australian Ministers for Aged Care and Ageing (10 April 2006) to address the problem. Of concern had been the lack of training for staff and no protection of whistleblowers within the industry. Later in 2006 agreement was reached on the introduction of mandatory reporting of abuse in aged care homes and a uniform system of police checks for workers in the aged care industry akin to that which has long existed in the US.

METHOD

Our method is micro–macro. It takes seriously Giddens's (1976: 122) observation that:

> The proper locus for the study of social reproduction is in the immediate process of the constituting of interaction. On the other hand, just as every sentence in English expresses within itself the totality which is the 'language' as a whole, so every interaction bears the imprint of global society; that is why there is a definite point to the analysis of 'everyday life' as a phenomenon of the totality.

The totality we seek to see more richly through observing interactions in nursing homes is the phenomenon described above as regulatory capitalism.

We do so by finding Mertonian ritualism to be multidimensional and endemic to regulatory capitalism. The method is also qualitative–quantitative, particularly in our Australian study, where we were able to test regulatory theory on a quantitative study of 410 nursing homes, though it is the US that has the best quantitative resources from research conducted by others, including randomized controlled trials and substantial meta-analyses on some of the important regulatory questions.

In the course of the research we have observed routine interactions in hundreds of nursing homes (for the details, see Chapter 2 for the US, Chapter 5 for England, Chapter 6 for Australia). These include interactions among residents, staff, managers, inspectors, proprietors, family/visitors, advocates, lawyers, consultants, and doctors, and all possible dyads and triads of these actors. Most were informal interactions, but some were structured as formal meetings, such as staff meetings, resident council meetings, exit conferences between inspectors and stakeholders, care planning meetings, quality improvement committee meetings and handover meetings between one group of nursing staff and another at the end of a shift. Focus groups of staff and a face-to-face quantitative survey completed by the CEO were also a data source from 410 nursing homes. Beyond these more structured interviews, there were hundreds of interviews with key stakeholders from cabinet ministers to regulators, consumer advocates and industry leaders, and with hundreds of inspectors. This enabled the research to be qualitative–quantitative, as well as micro–macro. In addition to observing all or substantial parts of 157 inspection events,[5] we were also able to observe a number of other kinds of interactions relevant to understanding this type of regulation – meetings of advocacy groups and industry associations, consultation meetings between these groups and government, legislative hearings, formal adjudications and appeals against penalties imposed on nursing homes for breaches of regulations, complaint processing, strategy meetings of regulators at head office, voluntary accreditation processes – and we were able to join training courses and become qualified as inspectors ourselves, and in the case of the senior author fail one examination necessary to qualify!

John and Valerie Braithwaite served for a number of years on the accreditation committee of a Canberra nursing home, were actively engaged over many years in the politics of both consumer and carer advocacy around aged care, and served as consultants to the Australian government on nursing home regulation during each of the past three decades. The direct experience we as authors and you as readers have of being part of some of these interactions as visitors to family and friends in nursing homes make this an unusually communicative site for a micro–macro sociology of regulation.

Unobtrusive Observers Not

While touting these strengths of our method, we should confess the weakness that we were often not the unobtrusive observers we would have liked to be. We managed to make a spectacle of ourselves by tramping faeces through a nursing home on our shoes, be a focus of amorous attention from residents in ways that were hair-raising, get our photograph on the front page of the nursing home newsletter 'confidentially' interviewing a resident, have nurses expose the naked body and pressure sore of a resident to 'get the opinion of the visiting Australian doctor', furtively loosen the restraint of a resident who pleaded for this, and bar the door to residents seeking to disrupt a residents' council meeting! We were often asked by inspectors whether we had seen what they had seen; we are embarrassed to report our answers sometimes influenced their decision on non-compliance. In Australia, the 410 homes in our study were widely known as 'Braithwaite homes'. Memos from their bosses criticized the productivity of inspectors in not completing enough inspections per month because this was slowing the flow of 'Braithwaite homes' into our study. One director of nursing angrily complained to us that they were only getting their inspection then because they were a 'Braithwaite home'.

While we defend the practice of asking confronting questions after observing something hard to comprehend, we acknowledge more than one instance where our intrusiveness changed the flow of events in unanticipated ways. We report below an incident where our quest for understanding went too far, leaving a research imprint that was, in hindsight, bigger than we, and others, would have liked. An exit conference has just concluded in a US nursing home that seemed to John Braithwaite to be badly out of compliance on many standards:

JB: So let me clarify, no standards were out then, just a few elements?
Inspector 1: Yes, they made it; only elements were out.
JB: Why is it that elements being out is not so bad? What's so different about standards being out?
Inspector 1: What's so different? *(Points to director of nursing and her deputy.)* They'd be crying if they had standards out.
JB: Yet there were some pretty serious things here. The 9.7 per cent Med-pass error rate, for example. It seemed serious so many getting someone else's medication.
Inspector 1: Actually it was 7.8 per cent. Some of the things we had earlier counted as errors we shouldn't have. They weren't significant enough to be truly errors.
Inspector 2: But even at 7.8 per cent he's right, that is serious, that should put the standard out.
Inspector 3: Yes over 5 per cent on Med pass puts the standard out.

Inspector 1: Has he gone? [He refers to the administrator of the home who has quit the exit to photocopy their report.] It will have to be changed.

Everyone rushed upstairs in pursuit of the administrator to rewrite the report with the standard out. One inspector thanked John for drawing attention to the mistake. The others seemed less than grateful. The director of nursing was crying and being consoled as the team left. As the administrator showed John the door, he said 'Next time go to another nursing home.'

NOTES

1. Provider capitalism rather than the welfare state because there was so much expansion of state provision on non-welfare services such as air travel, telecommunication and the like.
2. Starr (1982, cited in Kane and Kane 1985) refers to the last quarter of the twentieth century as the era of corporate medicine in the United States, as do Kane and Kane (1985: 264) for Canada.
3. An important motivation in the US for legislating for the invention of the Intermediate Care Facility (as distinguished from a Skilled Nursing Facility) in 1967 was Iowa nursing home interests, later supported by their national association, persuading legislators that the ratcheting up of standards would drive out of the industry mom-and-pop providers operating in converted dwellings (Vladeck 1980: 63). History proved this to be only a holding operation for a decade or two, at the end of which the ratcheting up of standards had driven almost all of the traditional mom-and-pop homes in converted houses out of the business. By 1980 the Intermediate and Skilled distinction had become meaningless, so similar were the standards applied to the two. They then came back in under the regulatory radar again as assisted living facilities.
4. Though pharmaceuticals are more heavily regulated at the product level.
5. An inspection event is defined as any compliance visit to an aged care home by a person defined as an inspector in the Preface (surveyor, standards monitor, assessor) with a responsibility for assessing compliance with public nursing home quality of care laws. The visit can be for a full annual inspection, a follow-up to an earlier full inspection, a spot check on compliance with a specific law, or a visit to investigate a complaint.

2.   US nursing home regulation

The next three chapters are devoted to US nursing home regulation. This chapter describes the extensive empirical work which informs our description of the big picture of what makes US nursing home regulation distinctive and how the US regulatory process unfolds. The chapter ends with an extended discussion of what we find to be most distinctive of all about the US nursing home policy debate – the centrality of the enforcement question. Chapter 3 considers US nursing homes and their regulation as a set of disciplinary practices. Chapter 4 seeks to capture both the distinctiveness and the complexity of US nursing home regulatory strategies.

THE EMPIRICAL WORK

In the 1980s, much more so than today, there was a diversity of state approaches to nursing home inspection in the US. So breadth of coverage was an aim of conducting fieldwork in 26 states – the largest 20 states in numbers of nursing home beds (except Pennsylvania, which declined to participate in 1988; in 2005 it would still not grant access to the observation of inspections) and a geographically balanced selection of the six smaller states. The latter were selected purposively; for example, Rhode Island because it had the most frequent inspections, with a state law mandating at least six inspections a year. These 26 states accounted for 80 per cent of the nursing home beds in the US. Nine states were visited twice during our 14 fieldwork trips to the US between 1987 and 2006 and Chicago was visited eight times.

In addition to more breadth, there was also more depth to the US fieldwork in one locale – the city of Chicago. Of the 52 inspection events observed in the US, 22 were in Chicago, though at least one inspection was observed in 25 of the 26 states visited. Convenience and cost were reasons for selecting Chicago as the site for more intensive fieldwork – John and Valerie Braithwaite enjoyed visiting relationships with the American Bar Foundation and Northwestern University over a number of years.[1] Our colleague Diane Gibson also visited us there in 1990 and observed several inspections with us, as did David Ermann elsewhere in the US. We were able to experience the nature of change by observing separate inspections at the same Chicago nursing home in the 1980s, the 1990s and the 2000s. Of the 23 state inspectors working in the city of Chicago at the start of our fieldwork, 22 were observed doing inspections. We spent countless hours talking with them about their jobs over lunch, partying in the evening and driving to and from nursing homes. Nationally, a total of 162 state inspectors were observed doing an inspection and interviewed in the course of the inspection. In all cases inspections were observed by at least one of the authors, and for a minority two or three authors observed some or all of the same inspection. There were also five visits to both Washington, DC and Baltimore to interview national players between 1988 and 2005.

The states where surveys were observed, with the number of fieldwork trips in brackets where they were greater than one, were: Florida, California (two), Texas, Alabama, Arizona (two), Washington, Colorado, Oklahoma, Illinois (eight), Maryland (six), Missouri, Minnesota, Indiana, Wisconsin (two), Michigan, Ohio, Massachusetts, New York (two), Connecticut, New Jersey (two), Virginia (two), North Carolina, Rhode Island, Tennessee (two), Georgia, Louisiana. Beyond the 52 inspection events (each observed for a period from one to four days), 19 other US nursing homes were visited for purposive reasons, such as to observe what was reputed to be an exemplary quality assurance committee at a regular meeting. Obviously, there was a worry about selection bias with the state selecting which of the (usually multiple) surveys underway near the state capital during the week of our visit we were allowed to observe. This was one reason for the more intensive Chicago fieldwork. We were able to observe all the inspections occurring in Chicago during one three-week and three one-week periods of our choosing.

Interviews were conducted with a total of 235 state government head office officials, in addition to the 162 state inspectors. Interviews were also conducted with officers of the major state industry associations, advocacy organizations and the state ombudsman in most states visited. An annual conference of the National Citizens' Coalition for Nursing Home Reform was attended and many interviews conducted with participants at that conference. Seventeen key federal regulatory personnel were interviewed during five visits to the Health Care Financing Administration (HCFA) and the Centers for Medicare and Medicaid Services (CMS) in the 1980s, 1990s, 2004 and 2005.

Private lawyers who specialize in nursing home cases, criminal prosecutors and police abuse investigators, the leaders of national industry associations, national advocacy organizations and national professional, quality assurance and certification associations were also interviewed, in some cases on multiple occasions across the three decades. Several penalty hearings were observed, as were several accreditation visits from the Joint

Commission on the Accreditation of Healthcare Organizations, and many visits of quality assurance staff of large chains on their rounds to their nursing homes. Dozens (34 in Chicago) of care planning conferences for specific residents were observed when they took place on the day of an inspection, as were many Quality Assurance Committee meetings and dozens of meetings of nursing home residents' councils and several family council meetings. We also sat in on some senior management meetings where regulatory tactics were discussed. In sum, this was an unusually intensive, long-term fieldwork engagement, with some key informants being interviewed more than ten times in the course of the project.

THE BIG PICTURE

In Chapter 1, it has already been noted that US nursing homes are larger (mean 107 residents), more institutional, more panoptic in architectural and video surveillance, more organized into multi-facility chains, more overwhelmingly for profit and more hierarchical in their management structure than in most of the rest of the world, including Australia and England. At the bottom of that structure, nurse aides are even more poorly paid than their equivalents in the UK and Australia, considerably more so, and are more custodial in their care. In general, aides' jobs are at the very bottom of the class structure, being paid less on average per hour than work in fast-food outlets such as McDonalds. Probably a majority of aides in the nursing homes we visited were non-white. In recent decades there have been large increases in the number of Asian aides and nurses (many Philippinos in Chicago) combined with the large numbers of black and Hispanic aides who have been in this workforce since the 1960s. We observed dozens of incidents of racial tension with predominantly white residents. There was also a lot of conflict between aides of different races that adversely affected residents as well as the aides.[2] Only one or two racist incidents were observed in both our Australian and English fieldwork, where the racial composition of the hands-on care staff is more similar to that of the majority of residents. In Chapter 10 we will argue that only when part of the national mission of the aged care industry is to create higher quality job opportunities and career ladders for the nation's most disadvantaged workers will quality of care dramatically improve.

Compared to England and Australia, a higher proportion of the hands-on nursing care (over 90 per cent) is provided by nurse aides in the US with a minimal 75 hours of training. This proportion has risen in the US in response to the nursing shortage,[3] increased demand for registered nurses to move to management and documentation that drives funding (this is why aides provide over 90 per cent of the hands-on care even though they represent only 70 per cent of the nursing hours), and cost rationalization. Staff turnover in nursing homes in all three countries is high, but particularly so in the US and particularly among aides, where it is 100 per cent per annum nationally (and in Chicago) (Eaton 2000). This contributes to the greater impersonality of US nursing home care – in general, staff and residents have simply not settled in to know one another as well. The evidence is also strong that it is harder to maintain high standards of care when staff turnover is high (Burnfeind and O'Connor 1992; Castle 2001; Christensen and Beaver 1996; Harrington 1996: 466; Makkai and Braithwaite 1993c: 85; Singh et al. 1996). Registered nurses in the US spend most of their time managing risk by managing documentation and supervising staff. This reflects the fact that the US industry, because of the intensity of regulation, invests more in documentation and more in management. As one informant who had wide experience as a nursing home administrator in both Australia and Oklahoma put it in 1990, while US nursing home management is more sophisticated than Australian management, Australian hands-on care is more sophisticated and caring.

The US industry has also been more scandal-ridden than England and Australia. Nursing homes and their regulation have been a bigger political issue. This was particularly so in the 1970s and 1980s. Partly in response, nursing home inspection is much more heavily resourced than in Australia and England, and as we saw in the last chapter, much more heavily resourced than the regulation of other institutions in American health care, such as hospitals, assisted living and care in private homes. Many state health departments told us 75 per cent of their regulatory staff were devoted to nursing homes, 25 per cent to the regulation of everything else in their state health system. We observed several inspections of US nursing homes in which more than ten inspectors were involved. The modal number of inspectors was four to six, depending on the state; in Australia it was two; in England one. This comparative resource situation looks set to continue into the future, with US inspection teams overwhelmingly in the four to six range and US inspectors continuing to spend on average slightly more than twice as many days in a facility for an annual inspection (average four days including follow-up) than the English do for their annual inspection or the Australians for their triennial accreditation.

The US industry is more resigned to detailed inspection as a fact of life. They argue with inspectors much less than in Australia and England. Their attitude is 'please just tell us what hoops we must jump through and we will jump'. In Merton's (1968) terms, they are much more ritualistic – they are more focused on the hoops than on the outcomes that jumping through them will achieve. Their dominant motivational posture is more of 'capitulation' to the regulation rather than 'commitment' to it (Braithwaite 2007; see Chapter 9). United States inspection has more potent consequences. Penalties are more often imposed; they are more automatic and they are tougher. Administrators more often lose their job and lose a bonus because of a poor inspection report. The inspection process is more formal, more rule-bound and less convivial. This is even truer today than in the 1980s. Not only is the US nursing home more afflicted with paperwork, but also US inspectors are hugely more afflicted with paperwork (or rather keyboard work) than their counterparts in the UK and Australia.

Our conclusion will be that intensively ritualistic regulation of American nursing homes has had a number of positive effects. It has driven most of the crooks from the industry – the organized criminals and property fraudsters – and it has driven out financially struggling small providers ('mom-and-pops') who often provided poor quality care. The very worst homes, 'the bottom feeders' as one state regulator put it, which entered the industry during the era of provider capitalism, were driven out in the era of regulatory capitalism. As we went from state to state we were initially cynical of this claim, finding that many states had not closed any nursing homes in the past year, sometimes not in the last few years, and that three nursing homes being pushed out of the industry in one state in one year is a high number. Yet in the more aggregated view of history, Vladeck (1980: 167) concludes that of the order of a thousand nursing homes were pushed out of the industry in the US in the 1970s. This seems to have been more or less sustained in subsequent decades if we are willing to count facilities forced to sell to a better managed proprietor by regulatory pressure. Each decade, roughly a thousand facilities that cannot cope with the demands of running a nursing home are driven from the industry largely as a result of regulatory pressure. In an industry that has ranged between 10 000 and 20 000 facilities since 1970 (16 000 in 2005), this is quite significant.

There have also been identifiable specific improvements in American nursing homes since the mid-1980s. Both physical and chemical restraint declined sharply during the era of regulatory capitalism (Castle and Mor 1997; HCFA 1998: vol. 1, viii). Throughout the period of the study there have been significant declines on a range of indices – in the late 1980s 42 per cent of all residents in the US were physically restrained, down to 4 per cent by the end of the study (Centers for Medicare and Medicaid Services 2005: 104), antipsychotic nursing home prescriptions declining 52 per cent (HCFA 1998: vol. 1, viii) and hypnotics by 80 per cent (HCFA 1998: vol. 3, 440). Tube feeding of residents who could be fed by mouth with a lot of assistance has reduced since the 1980s and continues to fall (Centers for Medicare and Medicaid Services 2005: 69); and rates of urinary incontinence and catheterization have declined (Centers for Medicare and

Medicaid Services 2005: 69; Walshe and Shortell 2004). Fire safety and physical safety have generally improved (though many grandfathered buildings still did not have sprinkler systems in 2005). The science of insect control through integrated insect management reduced vermin problems. Decor and cleanliness have improved; food quality, choice and safety have improved greatly (though malnutrition remains common – HCFA 1998: vol. 1, xi). Six-bed rooms no longer exist, though the US has not seen the dramatic growth in single-bed rooms of the UK and Australia.[4] Activities programs have improved in quality, diversity and frequency; access to specialist health professionals such as consulting physicians, physical therapists, occupational therapists, dieticians, psychologists, social workers and pharmacists has increased.

At the same time, pressure ulcer rates increased 16 per cent between 1998 and 2004 (Centers for Medicaid and Medicare Services 2001: 86; 2005: 54) and are high compared to the rest of the world, and rates of bowel incontinence may have risen slightly in the 1990s (Harrington et al. 2000a). Residents get less care from qualified nurses than they used to and staff turnover has increased. With constantly changing staff, there is a problem of lack of depth of knowledge of those they are caring for. In an increasingly mobile American community, many nursing homes are becoming more cut off from their communities and residents from their relatives: a Maryland nursing home we visited that systematically recorded family contacts with residents reported only 19 in the course of a month for 107 residents, meaning the odds of having a visitor on any day were one in 169. Some residents' lives are being rendered more miserable by release into nursing homes of elderly offenders on parole who entered the prison system as a result of the more punitive policies that started with the Nixon administration and who are so institutionalized that they are incapable of living in the community. Physical and sexual assault incidents, theft, causing fires by setting other residents' beds alight, even murder and the occasional shooting of a drug dealer in a nursing home, have occurred as a result. An obverse problem is mentally ill residents and drug addicts who before deinstitutionalization from the 1970s would have lived in mental institutions, but today end up in nursing homes because they can no longer cope in the community. Today many older street people in Chicago spend winter in a nursing home and then return to the street for the summer. More residents are bed-bound today than in the early 1990s, though as in England and Australia, this may reflect a higher proportion of older and sicker residents as more of the younger, less infirm age in place.

The view that the longer list is of important specific outcomes that have improved during the period of this study is shared by old-timers of the industry who had a capacity to reflect back on what the industry was like in the 1950s, 1960s and 1970s. Physical abuse of residents is one of those areas that is hard to assess. We and these old-timers, based on our observation of the industry over a long period, believe incidence has reduced, while seeing abuse as a much bigger problem in the US than in Australia or England. This was also the view the Institute of Medicine (1986: 3) formed on the period before this study commenced: 'Although the incidence of neglect and abuse is difficult to quantify, the collective judgment of informed observers, including members of the committee and of resident advocacy organizations, is that these disturbing practices now occur less frequently.' Perhaps it had improved, yet a subsequent survey of 577 US nursing home staff found 10 per cent admitting to committing physical abuse and 36 per cent to having witnessed it (Pillemer and Moore 1989).

More generally, the Institute of Medicine (1986: 6) found that 'the consumer advocates, providers and state regulators with whom it discussed these matters believe that a larger proportion of the nursing homes today are safer and cleaner, and the quality of care, on the average, probably is better than was the case prior to 1974'. Fifteen years later the Institute of Medicine (2001) again reached the conclusion that in general quality of care had continued to improve, that regulation had been implicated in this and that further strengthening of the regulatory process was needed. At the same time as regulation removed the 'bottom feeders' from the industry, our conclusion will be that today regulation may be reducing the quality of care provided by average and high quality providers. Overall, American regulatory capitalism has eliminated the most neglectful and abusive providers (or most of them), and reduced many specific forms of neglect, but has held back good and average providers from systemic continuous improvement they would have achieved had the regulation not been in place.

The biggest improvement in the US has been that documentation has progressed in its rigour and quantity. What is questionable is whether it has improved in its integrity. We detected a great deal of systematic falsification of records, as in staff signing records of attendance at in-service training they had not attended (also reported in HCFA 1998: vol. 1, 48), and night shifts who are less busy than day shifts using their quiet time to scour documentation for the day shift to record the turning of any resident who should have been turned or to record the medication of any resident who should have been medicated, whether this had been done or not. Detection of such fraud occurred when an inspector found, for example, that a drug recorded as administered had never been supplied to the nursing home or when fictitious minutes of an infection control committee discussed the condition of a resident who had died a year before the meeting was recorded to have occurred. We were surprised at how many nursing home staff admitted falsification of records. Even the head of one state nursing home regulatory agency said: 'When I worked in the industry I tried to keep reimbursement up by keeping records of people being on services they didn't need.'

Fraud is often rationalized as necessary to 'stand by our patients' because, as the deputy director of one state department of social services put it, 'They say "The reason we can't meet the standards is that you're not giving us enough money."' Fraud and poor quality care are positively correlated because they are excused by the same technique of neutralization (Sykes and Matza 1957) – accuse the accusers (the government for not giving us enough money). One experienced criminal investigator with a state regulatory agency saw the connection between criminal neglect of residents and fraud as an iron law: 'If it's a neglect case that rises to the standard of criminality under American law that crosses that line, you will find falsified records.' Indeed it is a fact that many of the corporations that have been in deep difficulty for poor quality of care have also been in serious trouble for Medicaid fraud. The most notable example is the largest provider of nursing home care, Beverly Enterprises, who settled with the Department of Justice to pay $175 million on charges of defrauding Medicare between 1992 and 1998 by falsifying records to increase the hours of care residents appeared to receive (Harrington 2001).

When inspectors find falsified records – for example, infection control committee minutes that purport to discuss the case of long-dead residents – they write a deficiency for the failure of the infection control committee to meet quarterly, not for fraud. This makes fraudulent ritualism rational. If the fact is that your infection control committee has not met as required and you falsify minutes of the meeting, the worst thing that happens is the same thing that happens for a failure to have minutes – a citation for failing to have the meeting. In egregious cases, inspectors can also report the falsification of records to a professional registration board. But this rarely happens, unless it is falsification of the record of an individual resident in a way that endangers the health of that resident.

MANAGING COSTS, MANAGING QUALITY

For finance ministers in most developed economies, health costs are their biggest headache because they persistently grow faster than all other costs and they are such a large proportion of the budget. In turn, the aged account for the largest proportion of those health costs, and as the proportion of the population over 70 increases, this structural driver of the health cost spiral gets worse. Overservicing in the 1970s came to be seen as the biggest preventable cause of the cost spiral, as well as being a major cause of iatrogenic injury. In a system where most services were not paid for by the patient, but by a third party such as a private insurer, Medicare or Medicaid, providers were tempted to give the patient that extra service they did not really need.

Proving that individual doctors were overservicing or overprescribing drugs was difficult in an evidentiary sense. It was also costly to execute a form of enforcement that involved second-guessing a highly trained professional with an intimate knowledge of the patient's history that the would-be enforcer of overservicing lacked. Moreover, enforcement had to proceed one diagnosis at a time to solve a cost problem driven not by millions but by billions of diagnoses every year. Overprescribing drugs might cause a lot of preventable deaths and constantly drive up the proportion of the health budget consumed by pharmaceuticals, yet spending days or weeks collecting the evidence to prove one unnecessary prescription that costs $100 could never be cost-effective regulation. Finally, it was a politically costly form of regulation to be constantly challenging the integrity of a powerful medical profession that enjoyed higher levels of trust from the community than did the government itself.

Both the rate of increase in health costs and the political fear of trench warfare with the medical profession were more acute in the US than other nations. Hence, in the 1980s the US led developed economies into a more structural assault on the overservicing problem. Its biggest purchaser of health services, Medicare, replaced retrospective cost-based reimbursement for hospitals with fixed payments on the basis of the patient diagnosis. This was the diagnosis related group (DRG) system. It did stem costs while replacing a problem of poor health outcomes driven by overservicing with poor outcomes from underservicing (Jost 1988). It made sense to push a patient out of hospital when they were too sick to go home. If relapse were the consequence of such bad medicine, the hospital could start a new diagnosis on readmission and collect another payment. The encouragement of health maintenance organizations (HMOs) that are paid on a capitation rather than a fee-for-service basis was another example of this structural shift in policy. It too was effective in reducing incentives for overservicing, while increasing incentives for underservicing – a chat with a nurse on the telephone for a matter that should involve seeing a physician.

The nursing home was a different kind of structural solution to the cost blow-out problem. Frequent home visitation of doctors to the bedridden elderly was costly for Medicare. It was also something twentieth-century doctors were less willing to do than were nineteenth-century doctors who dealt with a population in which there were comparatively few people over 70 and even fewer who could afford to pay them to come out to visit their elderly relatives. What twentieth-century professional would not prefer a job where clients sat in a waiting room to see them to one where they fought city traffic to find one client after another for home consultations? The nursing home was invented in part to solve this problem. First families and then physicians and the welfare state unburdened their consciences of the need to give proper medical care to the elderly by putting them in a home run by a 'matron' who could make most of the tricky medical decisions referred to her by care staff, only calling in the doctor in extremis, and waiting to call in the doctor when there were a batch of patients with problems she could deal with in one visit.

In the long run, however, this cost-saving strategy did not work. This was because underservicing – neglect – led to scandal and regulatory reform as muckrakers, elected political opportunists, and warm-hearted consumer advocates and journalists looking for a shocking story all exposed to the public cases of neglected aged. The regulatory reform made nursing home care more costly. Nevertheless, nursing homes remained largely physician-free zones of care, something some US states are seeking to change at the time of writing. Over time the proportion of care provided by registered nurses declined. Administration of medication and treatments of wounds or of pain once done by registered nurses are today the work of Licenced Practical Nurses (LPNs) with one or two years of training. And over 90 per cent of nursing care is provided by nurse aides (minimum 75 hours' training) supervised by nurses. Finally, Medicaid-supported places in nursing homes were more aggressively rationed so that over time a form of care rendered more expensive by regulation became reserved for sicker and sicker people. This simply led to the reinvention of the virtually unregulated mid-twentieth-century nursing home as 'assisted living homes'.

Over time, more and more very sick elderly have been pushed into assisted living. Growth in the philosophy of ageing in place has supplied a kind of principled rationale for leaving once-mobile residents admitted to an assisted living home without a registered nurse after they become bedridden and afflicted with severe medical problems. All indications are that we are beginning to see a repetition of the same cycle of scandal and reform with assisted living homes, as they come to warehouse larger numbers of very sick elderly, that we saw in the 1970s and 1980s with nursing homes. Regulation will again make the cost savings from underservicing dissipate.

Nursing homes have not been hugely affected by the DRG system, though better run homes benefit from it considerably at the margin. Homes which provide good restorative nursing, physical and occupational therapy, can pick up their best profits by taking in patients whose diagnosis no longer requires hospital treatment but who cannot be cared for at home. These are attractive financial crumbs from the hospitals' table, the nursing home benefiting from the way DRGs push patients out of hospital who are not ready to go home. The negative effect is that it, along with the medically oriented Minimum Data Set, is re-medicalizing aged care after the social care reforms of the 1980s (Vladeck 2003). The incentive structure, both for hospitals and for this short-term acute care side of the nursing home business, is to 'code up' the diagnosis of patients as high as feasible upon admission and then code them down quickly to get the payout for restoring them at the lowest feasible cost of institutional care.

The bread-and-butter long-term care incentive structure for nursing homes is quite different. It is to code up the diagnoses and levels of care required as high as is feasible upon admission to the nursing home and to keep coding up as steeply and as quickly as feasible as deterioration occurs during the process of long-term care. Quality of care regulation, however, places a limit on continuous coding up to increase case-mix reimbursement. Pressure sores that get worse in severity and number can both create an entitlement of the nursing home to higher reimbursement because of more severe diagnoses in their case mix and act at the same time as a red flag for inspectors who examine whether the home should be fined or have new Medicaid admissions suspended because of poor quality care. Getting Minimum Data Set (MDS) codes right for each resident is financially the highest stake patient-level decision the nursing home makes. This is why it cannot be clerks who fill out the MDS forms. It is a job for the home's smartest registered nurse(s) below the director of nursing. It would be a cost-inefficient use of such a scarce human resource to have them actually caring for the sick. There is an optimum way of coding a bedsore as a stage 1, 2 or 3 pressure sore that is different depending on whether this is a high-risk or a low-risk resident.

A high-risk resident with a pressure sore is not a sentinel event that triggers further review under the quality indicators program. A low-risk resident with a pressure ulcer on the MDS does create such a sentinel event. That is why one sees so many nursing homes with large numbers of MDS-coded pressure ulcers for high-risk residents and zero for low-risk residents. Either the low risk must be coded up or the ulcer must be coded down and concealed. 'Fecal impaction' MDS coding is another quality indicator sentinel event. 'This is why there is always a zero return on them in the MDS, unless they have a new MDS nurse who is still learning the job' (2005 Maryland interview), as one senior state regulator explained. The return is actually 0.1 per cent nationally for fecal impaction. Minimum Data Set nurses learn to code fecal impaction down to a diagnosis of severe/repeat constipation. Dehydration (the third sentinel event under US quality indicators) also rarely gets non-zero returns on the MDS, with the national MDS-reported dehydrations coming in at 0.0 per cent in all recent years (Centers for Medicare and Medicaid 2005: 69). Obviously the national data are false; as revealed by our own eyes, nursing home residents in the US do suffer dehydration. By prioritizing something as a sentinel event, the regulatory system renders it invisible and unmeasurable.

So we have a system with widespread falsification of documentation and investment of the brightest and best in gaming the system in the midst of a nursing shortage that is partly fuelled by the fact that such very game-playing tarnishes the traditional appeal of nursing as a caring vocation. And we have the resultant pathologies of overservicing, underservicing, and documentation that provides a misleading guide to hands-on carers and to those whose job it is to hold the quality of that care accountable. All this makes the 'socialized medicine' so vilified by the American Medical Association, and in the American health-care debate generally, seem an attractive alternative. This alternative is for a public health system that is rather like public education in developed economies. This means local or regional providers of public education being given a budget by central government, allowed large discretion on how to disperse institutions and programs across their region to provide education, yet audited or peer-reviewed by central government on the comparative quality of educational outcomes achieved by different regions. While socialized, such systems are not without competition. There is competition to do well in inter-institutional and inter-regional comparisons. In higher education, this can count among the strongest competitive urges for quality – to be ranked in the top ten medical schools or even the top ten football colleges! Then there is competition from citizens who use their wealth or insurance or scholarships to opt out of the public system into a private system that seeks to innovate in ways designed to make private institutions more attractive to consumers than the default public system.

But most importantly, there is a competitive labour market for the professionals who provide the hands-on services. In American public primary education it might be argued that peer review, student ratings and other performance evaluations do not drive pay rises and promotion up a teaching career structure enough. American higher education, in contrast, might be too competitive a structure, where some public universities expend excessive transaction costs in granting annual or biennial pay rises to each professor on the basis of their publications, student ratings and other measures. In this system academics are given incentives to be constantly testing their price in the labour market by applying for faraway jobs they do not want and using their offer to get a pay rise at home. Our point is not to say that primary or tertiary public education in the US or England or Australia gets it right. Rather it is to say that it seems a possibility within a socialized education system that competition from public evaluations of outcomes, contestability from opt-out to a private-pay market and well-attuned labour market competition can have settings that deliver fine outcomes.

Socialized health and aged care seems no less promising so long as these three forms of competition within it have well-attuned settings and so long as independent regulation, legislative oversight, investigative reporting and advocacy groups are active, vigilant and sophisticated in their critiques of the quality of provision. In Chapter 8, we return to consider the socialized medicine alternative that might have more appeal in the European context[5] and Michael Porter's alternative of switching the targets of competition in private health markets, a restructuring that might have more political appeal in the US context. Whichever of those moves one finds more attractive, our submission in Chapter 8 is that American models for patient-level funding of private provision of health and aged care have failed to conquer overservicing and underservicing and documentation fraud, and have failed to deliver high quality at moderate cost. Piecemeal reform, we will conclude, cannot fix this.

THE INSPECTION PROCESS

The inspection (referred to in the US as a survey, and inspectors as surveyors) is the centrepiece of nursing home regulation. It begins with a tour of the facility and then final selection of a sample of residents who are interviewed and whose charts are audited for evidence of compliance with the standards. One of the major changes to the process during the course of this study has been a shift from selecting residents for intensive review onsite (based on detective work, interviews, the 'smell test') and selection offsite before arrival based on statistical sampling. For example, if the nursing home Minimum Data Set indicates that the number of residents with physical restraints and pressure ulcers is above the seventy-fifth percentile of all nursing homes, then residents recorded on the MDS as having physical restraints and pressure ulcers will be randomly over-sampled. Up to 2005, in many states as many as half of the residents sampled off-site would be replaced after the tour by another resident with the same risk profile. Detective work on the tour might raise deep worries about a restrained resident with a black eye; so he or she may be substituted for a sampled restrained resident. A pilot program started in 2005 to eliminate the discretion to do this substitution (an issue we will discuss at length in Chapter 7 when we discuss protocol ritualism and statistical ritualism).

On the tour we observed inspectors noting a variety of minor problems. An inspector would say to a nurse accompanying her on the tour: 'His nails need attention.' Then, 'That bed is rusting. It needs repainting.' It is rare for nursing home staff to contest such assertions or to offer any kind of excuse. Competent management will get most such problems attended to either immediately or before the team have finished the inspection. One Chicago administrator expressed a common philosophy during one tour we observed in 1989:

> I've been in the industry for ten years. I don't worry about it any more. I mean it's important. But they'll always find some things, someone who needs socks, someone who should be shaved. That's OK, we expect that. We can't be perfect. We'll fix it and try to be better next time.

Inspectors notice how quickly such problems are fixed and often commented to us that it was an indicator of how responsive the nursing home was. In the overwhelming majority of cases these little problems do not become part of a pattern that leads to writing a deficiency. Nevertheless, it is an important informal part of the process that a host of little problems get fixed on the spot. As one director of nursing said: 'They [the inspectors] have picked up some things I had not seen. Familiarity breeds contempt.' This is the 'fresh set of eyes' function of inspection that does not depend on enforcement for its effectiveness. Sometimes when problems are of a seriousness to justify writing a deficiency, the inspector will use forbearance to build goodwill toward future compliance: 'Chicago sanitarian to administrator before formal Exit begins: "I'm not going to write down that problem with the scale. Just get it fixed, okay." The administrator nods thankfully. "There are very mild deficiencies which I did not write because you are fixing them . . . [He then lists them]".' In addition, a lot of problems get fixed in the minutes between the arrival of the inspectors at the nursing home and their arrival in a particular part of the facility. Much scurrying of staff pushing brooms, wielding sponges and clean laundry begins as soon as the inspection team is seen in the car park.

Before and after every reform to the process that occurred between 1987 and 2005, most surveyor time continued to be spent checking resident charts. Sometimes this work is done sitting at the nurses' station where resident files are maintained. But mostly charts, that are normally more than the width of a brick, are carried to a room where inspectors sit for hours poring over them. First, for the resident with the restraint and the black eye, they will check that the reason for the restraint is recorded (and is a legitimate reason), that a doctor has signed off approval for the restraint, that how the black eye was obtained is recorded in the nurses' notes. The resident's care plan will be checked to see if these issues have been properly discussed and recorded in that process. Were relatives invited to the care planning meeting and did they approve use of the restraint? If the approval requires release of the restraint every two hours, is it recorded as being done every two hours of every day? If complaints have been received from relatives, the record will be checked to see if these have been followed through. If it is found that the black eye was caused by rough handling by a nurse aide, the files will be checked to ascertain if there should have been an abuse investigation and if there was one. If there was, are all its recommendations recorded as implemented? For example, was the aide dismissed and his or her conduct reported to the state abuse hotline? An issue like this will lead the inspector from scrutiny of the resident records to the staff member's file. In the US, and increasingly in Australia and the UK, the documentary focus of the regulatory process drives a philosophy of 'If it's not recorded, it didn't happen.' This is not to say that inspectors do not regularly go to the resident's room to check out a problem they see in their charts. If nurses on the inspection are worried about why a pressure sore is not improving, they often observe treatment of the ulcer. This can reveal both poor treatment technique that is spreading infection and that the pressure ulcer is recorded erroneously in terms of how serious it is.

Observation of treatments almost never happens during English and Australian inspections. The Americans reject the English view that it is an unacceptable invasion of privacy to observe something like the treatment of a bedsore on a resident's buttocks. One inspector said this was 'never' a problem if the resident is feeling sick enough: 'Residents want you to see what is happening.' This was confirmed by the observation of residents complaining that the nursing home was not treating their bedsore and asking the inspector to do so, even saying to the inspector, pointing to J. Braithwaite, 'Can you get the doctor to look at me?' So we must balance the conclusion that US inspection is more documentation driven with the qualification that nevertheless the more heavily resourced US process is more rigorous about certain forms of observational follow-up as well.[6] Obversely, we saw nurses on Australian inspection teams asked by residents to look at their pressure sore, declining to do so, and settling for checking that their care plan covered pain management for it.

Simply being out in the nursing home, as opposed to shut in a room poring over charts, creates many opportunities to observe disturbing occurrences of poor quality care. It was lunchtime in a Chicago home and a resident came out of his room shouting at a nurse aide, but in our direction: 'Tell the truth. They are from the state. Tell them the truth that I have to go and get my own tray because they are too lazy to bring it.' Later in a private interview with this resident it became clear that this outburst was intended to punish an aide who had 'threatened' him and he repeated the allegation that 'I have to get my own tray because they're too lazy to get it.' This resident had had a foot amputated as a result of gangrene and was supposed to be isolated from contact with other residents. But in this encounter we had indeed seen him dragging his bandaged leg along the floor behind a wheelchair as he headed for the kitchen.

The respect in which the US process is most systematically more observationally rigorous than that of England and Australia is observation of sufficient numbers of administrations of medications to calculate a 'medpass error rate'. On a typical survey, this occupies many inspector-hours and is nerve wracking for the staff who are observed to see if they give the right medications in the right way at the right time to all the residents on their rounds. The standard requires that the error rate not be over 5 per cent, a level that is common for homes to fail to meet. Observation of food preparation in the kitchen and of the actual feeding of residents is also more systematic in the US. This is partly record driven. The inspector records the dietary requirements of a sampled resident from their charts; then in the meal observation she checks if that resident gets the food that meets those requirements, as well as checking that it is hot, choice is adequate, assistance of disabled residents with feeding is provided, and so on.

One team member specializes in physical inspection of the building to ensure that fire safety standards are met, that the temperature in refrigerators and washing machines and the temperature of water from taps is right (they use their thermometer constantly), that the laundry is processed in a hygienic fashion, that the building is clean, that alarms on doors work, that surfaces are not slippery, that hazardous chemicals are locked away, gas cylinders secured to the wall so they cannot topple over, vermin absent, and the like. Some of this process is documentation driven too. For example, records are checked that all staff received fire safety training, that extinguishers are checked on a regular schedule, and the like.

Another important form of documentary checking is scrutiny of nursing home policies to ensure they cover all the issues required by the standards in the right way. The survey process introduced at the beginning of the 1990s to implement the 1987 OBRA reforms were touted as a move away from a documentation-driven process. The Omnibus Budget Reconciliation Act (OBRA) actually did not reduce the focus on documentation and did not change the fact that inspections were overwhelmingly documentary and much more so than English and Australian inspections. Also the numbers of worksheets inspectors were required to use tripled with OBRA. However, OBRA did make resident interviews a more significant part of the process and effectively mandated a meeting with the residents' council (the 'group interview' with residents) at which the council could articulate its concerns about the home. An early randomized controlled trial with the new process in Rhode Island showed that it did increase the number of deficiencies detected (Spector and Drugovich 1989). However, the real world of implementation proved the opposite of a randomized pilot; we will see later in this chapter that recording of deficiencies has dropped off considerably post-OBRA.

While it seems strange that it took until the 1990s for resident interviews to become an important part of the US process, in many countries during the 1980s (for example Japan, as observed by David Ermann for this project) resident interviews were not in any way part of the nursing home regulatory process. In all three countries, many inspectors accorded the testimony of residents little credibility. Many disturbing failures to take residents seriously were observed, such as the following in a 1990 Chicago inspection. The resident said to an inspector, quite articulately: 'They rough you up when turning you. They won't answer your call button or just bawl you out.' This concern did not find its way into the inspection report, was not discussed in the exit conference or shared with other members of the team and not followed up in any way. In a 1990 Oklahoma survey, a resident said in her interview that her greatest concern was that the lady who sat next to her at lunch just cried and this upset her. The resident suggested that this other resident was hungry and could not cope with the frustration of waiting a long time before food arrived. Staff could make meals more pleasant by just feeding her first. The inspector made no note of this and did nothing to follow it up. We did. We checked her at mealtime. Sure enough she was crying loudly; she said the reason was she was hungry and the meal took so long to arrive; and sure enough the meal did take a long time to arrive. When we confronted inspectors over this problem, the answers we got were typified by this New York inspector:

> If the resident tells you they get no ambulation that may or may not be good evidence. You lose credibility with the home and the court if you accept the word of an unreliable source. It takes a lot of skill then to get an aide to admit the lack of ambulation and why they don't do it.

While triangulation of evidence is important, the disturbing thing about this attitude is that while credibility in the eyes of the nursing home and external authorities is important, credibility in the eyes of residents is not so important, and this is a brute clash between the ideology of the regulatory process and its practical realities of power imbalance. A Californian inspector had a rule of thumb that was more charitable to resident empowerment: 'You might take the word of a resident against the nursing home if they are alert and the record indicates that they are alert most of the time.' This means if the nursing home says in court that this resident is not alert, is confused and should not be taken seriously, the inspector can quote the home's own records back indicating that they are mostly alert. In general, though, we saw many disturbing cases like the following in which there was a pattern of complaints from a number of residents not getting the physical therapy that the nursing home said they were. Each was discredited one by one as in the following exchange at an inspection team meeting, and there was no checking of the repeat allegations by systematic observation of the delivery of physical therapy:

> *Inspector 1:* It's the staff's word against the resident's. The records say she is getting the physical therapy, so there you are.
> *Inspector 2:* She's very confused.
> *Inspector 1:* I thought she really had her wits about her; didn't you, John?
> *J. Braithwaite:* Yes, she seemed pretty sharp to me.
> *Inspector 2 (ruling in favour of the staff):* It's so hard to tell. Sometimes they seem with it when really they're very confused. You can't judge.

In general, resident complaints in interview only lead to deficiencies if some documentary evidence consistent with the complaints can be found. This is a serious weakness in a system where fabrication of records is rampant. Interviews of staff are another important source of information, though staff interviews have a less central place than they do in the English and Australian processes.

The survey team meets at the end of each day they are at the nursing home to swap notes on what they think might be building up to become a deficiency. This is important because the team divides up responsibility for different standards to different team members. So a team member who notices something significant on another team member's standard needs to share this at the informal team meeting. The team reaches a consensus on what problems are building up to be sufficiently acute to threaten a deficiency. The administrator will normally be alerted on all of these before the team leaves the facility each day. She will also get a pre-exit just before the full exit, so she knows what she will have to handle with her staff in the exit. By the time the process reaches the exit conference, the intent is that there be 'no surprises' for management. An important reason for a 'no surprises' policy is that responsible staff will often give reasons and further information when given an informal alert that they would not give in front of their superiors at an exit. It also can give the team an early steer that they have misinterpreted some information and simply got it wrong. If a responsible staff member is shown a problem on the spot when an inspector detects it, this can reduce disputes, build feelings of procedural fairness and educate. For example, an Arizona inspector in 2003 sees a dignity issue. A large female resident (425 lbs) has her buttock and upper thigh exposed:

> *Inspector to charge nurse:* You tell me what you see.
> *Nurse:* I can't see anything.
> *Inspector:* Look again, you'll find it.

The final team meeting before the exit conference reaches a final consensus on which deficiencies will be written up in their report.

At the conclusion of the survey, an exit conference is held which is normally attended by all members of the inspection team, the administrator, director of nursing, heads of other departments such as dietary, often a quality assurance (QA) advisor from the headquarters of a chain, and often a staff representative and a representative of the residents' council. It is normally a gathering of 10–20 people around a table. If a serious deficiency has been detected in the survey, the supervisor of the team will have been advised of this by telephone, will have expressed views on how the serious matter should be handled and will often be present for the exit. The results of the survey are reported orally in a way that focuses almost totally on explaining deficiencies, though there was often some discussion of what kind of plan of correction was required. The HCFA video training John Braithwaite did in 1990 had a test question: 'Which is *not* a reason for conducting an exit conference?' The correct answer was: 'Allowing provider an opportunity to present their plan of correction.' If no standards are reported to be out of compliance at the exit, there will normally be a little restrained celebration in the exit by the nursing home staff, followed often by quite a joyous, backslapping ritual of celebration after the team leaves (which we observed many times, verifying how important these processes are in the life of a nursing home professional).

The decision on whether the plan of correction is satisfactory to rectify the deficiencies reported is not made by the team but by their supervisors at the regional office. There is normally no checking that what is promised in the plan of correction is actually delivered within the time lines promised and no follow-up to see if last year's plan of correction has been completed at the time of the next year's survey. Except where stated above, these features of the survey process have remained remarkably constant through the 1980s, 1990s and 2000s.

The HCFA regional office used to select 5 per cent of inspections to conduct a validation or 'look-behind' survey soon after the state inspection to double-check that the inspectors had successfully detected and reported non-compliance. Since 1995 the feds instead go on-site with state inspectors to watch them do interviews, record reviews and observe team meetings and other facets of the survey for compliance with federal procedures. Federal audits of documentation packages prepared by state agencies after annual inspections and complaint investigations are also conducted. When non-compliance is found, the state survey agency must prepare a plan of correction. Some of these plans of correction have elements, such as an in-service training for inspectors, rather like elements found in facility plans of correction. When state inspection agencies have a poor compliance record with the feds, there have been many occasions in the history of the Medicaid program when states have had severe financial penalties imposed on them. The inter-governmental regime is therefore disciplinary, punitive and ritualistic. Referring to CMS audits of state survey agency records, one state official said: 'They're not outcome-oriented at all. We manage to get better nursing homes than Illinois, but because Illinois gets its paperwork done with all the ticks in all the right boxes, while we left some of our ticks out, we get cut some of our money and they don't.'

Complaint inspections in most states are a separate process from the annual inspection. Only small states handle fewer than a thousand complaints a year and have a separate ombudsman's program that also handles fewer than a thousand. Large states like New York have 8000–10 000 complaints each year. Inspectors often go out when a few have accumulated in the same facility and normally spend a day in the facility, often with more than one inspector, checking compliance with the standards that are the subject of the complaint. The volume of complaints received and formally processed in the US is much greater than in Australia and hugely greater than in England.

ENFORCEMENT

Enforcement is the central issue in debates about US nursing home regulatory strategy. The most influential government reports on the topic are overwhelmingly about how to activate enforcement. This is absolutely not the case in the English and Australian policy debates. Apart from its much superior resources, the most distinctive feature of US nursing home regulation compared to the UK and Australia is the frequency of its resort to penalties. That said, we do not want to create the false impression that this is a regime where inspectors seize on every little breach of the rules they detect to impose a fine. At least 90 per cent of failures to live up to the standards that were detected during our fieldwork were not written up in any way. Then the overwhelming majority that are written are recorded with a scope and severity that requires no more than a plan of correction to be prepared. Of the minority of deficiencies that do lead to a proposed penalty, more than 90 per cent of the time no penalty is imposed because the facility has come into substantial compliance by the time of revisit (HCFA 1998: vol. 1, 274).[7] During all periods of this study, fixing a deficiency almost immediately in most states virtually guaranteed there would be no penalty. As Keith Hawkins (1984, 2002) found with British environmental and occupational health and safety inspectors, intentional as opposed to negligent violation, or breaches that seemed inexcusable,

Severity	Scope		
	Isolated	Pattern	Widespread
Immediate jeopardy to resident health and safety			
Actual harm, no immediate jeopardy			
No actual harm, potential for more than minimal harm			
No actual harm, potential for minimal harm			

Figure 2.1　　Post-1995 scope and severity grid

resulted in more heavy-handed enforcement, even if intentionality and exculpation were irrelevant in law. For example, an Indiana inspector: 'There's no excuse for them not following this. They have no excuse so I think I should write it.' A Massachusetts inspector: 'If it's a repeat offence and there was an intent to fix it, they tried to correct the deficiency, then you wouldn't punish them.'

A change came to make inspectors less 'street-level bureaucrats' (Lipsky 1980) with the post-OBRA scope and severity grid introduced in 1995. The size of fines also increased from 1995 – up to $10 000 per day per serious deficiency. The grid has different levels of severity on one axis, different levels of scope on the other – isolated, pattern, widespread (see Figure 2.1). When deficiencies fall in certain boxes of higher scope and severity on that grid certain kinds of sanctions became non-discretionary. Note how this model is contrary to the prescriptions of responsive regulation; instead of enforcement that is flexibly responsive to corporate transformation into the future, enforcement is boxed in by the scope and severity of past wrongs.

However, this automaticity drove inspectors to write even fewer deficiencies to save facilities from automatic penalties and themselves from being tied up in appeals against them. The average number of deficiencies written per facility decreased by 44 per cent from 8.8 in 1995 to 4.9 in 1997; in the same period, the number found to have no deficiencies increased by 100 per cent (Walshe 2001). However, in response to a new wave of NGO, US Senate and General Accounting Office critique for enforcement weakness in 1998, the average number of deficiencies per facility gradually began to recover, increasing each year between 1998 and 2004 until in 2004, for the first time, it returned to the level before 1995 when the supposedly tougher OBRA enforcement reforms were introduced (Centers for Medicare and Medicaid Services 2001: 144; Harrington et al. 2005: 78).

Even then, in the nine years to 2004 the proportions of higher scope and severity deficiencies fell. These are the deficiencies that drive automatically punitive enforcement responses (Center for Medicare and Medicaid Services 2001: 150; 2005: 110–16; Harrington et al. 2005: 80). The proportion of deficiencies at the actual harm level or higher and the percentage of inspections resulting in substandard quality of care declarations (that drive revisits) have both progressively decreased each year since the OBRA enforcement reforms of 1995. Since 1995 there have been many years when five or more states averted mandated federal enforcement by citing no facilities for any substandard care deficiencies. Basically, the response to criticism of the regulators for implementing OBRA in a way that reduced the citation of deficiencies has been to increase citations of deficiencies that require only a ritualistic plan of correction.

Between 1990 and 1992, when the first tranche of OBRA measures to tighten enforcement were implemented into the survey process, there was also a drop in the amount of enforcement that actually occurred (compare the data in Gardiner and Malec [1989] for the late 1980s with 1990–92 data in Department of Health and Human Services [1996: 22, table 400]). Each year between these two watersheds of OBRA implementation of 'tougher' enforcement – 1993, 1994 and 1995 – there was also a small further drop in the number of deficiencies cited and a considerable further increase in the percentage of facilities where no deficiencies were found (Harrington and Carrillo 1999).

Street-level bureaucrats have a tendency to drag discretion back from Washington to the level of the street. Squeeze at one place on the toothpaste tube of discretion and street-level discretion can move to another place.[8] One of the changes after 1995 was that if a facility is deficient on three consecutive surveys on a particular standard, or if it fails to correct deficiencies in 90 days, an immediate ban is placed on payments for new Medicare or Medicaid admissions. What we observed inspectors doing after 1995 to protect nursing homes from this consequence when they thought it was not justified was to write the new deficiency under a different standard number than it had been written under the last time it was detected.

One common scenario here is as follows. Standard X is reported as non-compliant in an inspection. A plan of correction is then received that is accepted as fixing the problem. Then the state regulator receives a complaint, say, 88 days after the original inspection. The new complaint inspection reveals that the information provided in the complaint is correct and the nursing home is again non-compliant on standard X. The violation might not be especially serious and may be substantively rather different from the matter that caused non-compliance 88 days earlier, but because the facility cannot possibly fix it in two days, they are hit with substantial automatic penalties and reputational costs. Advocates have been known to time their complaint lodgement at the end of a 90-day cycle purposely to hurt nursing homes in this way. In these circumstances the street-level bureaucrat may be reluctant to make a finding of non-compliance, or may write out the non-compliance under another standard that will not cause automatic defunding of new residents.

Consider the inspector who finds a resident whose care plan says they should be turned every two hours. Two hours elapse without a turning recorded or observed. The inspector will almost never write this in the report unless that omission is part of a wider pattern of omission detected around that standard. As in England and Australia, one slip does not lead to a deficiency unless it is a slip with catastrophic consequences.

In general, more deficiencies mean more work – more writing, more explaining and defending, more conflict with the home, returning to the home on a six-month instead of a 12-month cycle,[9] more quizzing by supervisors and the possibility of a hearing. In recent years in particular we noted that inspectors were pressured by their peers to be circumspect about 'having a concern'. We saw one inspector with a reputation for toughness exposed to two rather similar encounters with inspectors at different times and places during 2004:

> *Inspector 1 to 2 in Inspector Jane's presence (superciliously):* Jane has 7 concerns.
> *Inspector 3 to Inspector 4 in Jane's presence (superciliously):* How many does Jane have today?

A widely used expression is that an inspector is 'too picky'. More routinely, inspectors play devil's advocate with one another's intention to write deficiencies; they try to make it easy for one another to back down by revealing fanciful and real things that could go wrong in an enforcement hearing (particularly when reliance is being placed on the testimony of residents as opposed to documentary evidence). Another incentive problem is that some states have put their public relations people onto announcing reductions in the number of serious deficiencies being written as evidence that the state has improved quality of care. Today in states like New York this means averting deficiencies of high scope and severity is a performance criterion of sorts.

While industry often alleges a 'gotcha' mentality, we observed little of that, for example, few communications between inspectors to the effect of 'Here's our chance to get them.' But we constantly observed exchanges of 'Oh no. Oh God. We're going to have to write them out on this.' This would happen, for example, during the med-pass observation of drug administration when inspectors would be observed uttering their hopes and prayers that there would not be another error that would put the facility above the 5 per cent error rate that makes for a serious deficiency.

The high-water mark of nursing home enforcement nationally in the US clearly was 1989. It was the campaign for OBRA that drove enforcement up; with implementation of the law itself, enforcement slipped back. In 1989 almost all states actually imposed administrative penalties on fewer than a hundred occasions, though California and Texas were punitive states with 1800 and 1700 administrative penalties respectively (Gardiner and Malec 1989: 8–9). This was a big increase compared to 1983, when only 900 civil or administrative fines were imposed nationally (Institute of Medicine 1986: 342). Many states did not make use at all of the next most popular sanction in 1989, suspending new admissions or suspending funding for new Medicare/Medicaid admissions, though most did (Gardiner and Malec 1989: 8–9). By 2003, this sanction was imposed in all but four states, but it was imposed much less frequently than in 1989, especially at the level of the suspension of all new admissions (whether Medicaid or not).[10]

Suspending new admissions is a sanction more damaging to nursing homes than a slap-on-the-wrist civil monetary penalty (imposed 1979 times across the US in 2003). In addition to the great financial cost of reduced income from 'slowly tightening the vice' as more residents are turned away, there is the adverse publicity of having to advise residents that they cannot be admitted to empty beds in the facility because of an enforcement action. Some states require notices to be posted at the door of the home when new admissions have been suspended. Evidence of how profoundly these reputation costs are felt is that we found some facilities deciding to take new admissions for free from hospitals that supply them rather than be forced to explain that they had had their funding suspended for new admissions. These are reasons why a moratorium on admissions is much less frequently contested than a large fine; the nursing home wants to concentrate on fixing the problem to lift the freeze as soon as possible.

During our interviews with enforcement specialists in state after state we were told that while the fact of a deficiency was rarely contested, its level and the level of fine associated with it were regularly contested in hearings; suspension of new admissions was almost never contested, however. Because residents are most costly to care for at the time of admission, freezing new admissions actually cuts the income flow of the nursing home while freeing up resources in the short term to concentrate on compliance for the residents who are already there. A problem that emerged with the greater imposition of fines in the 1980s is that in many states the amounts collected were less than half the amounts imposed, and the process of trying to collect them was costly. A freeze on new admissions was easier to enforce at every level. There was real enforcement genius in this enforcement innovation of the late twentieth century. Again Texas, a state that had had some unusually horrific nursing home scandals earlier in the 1980s, was the most frequent user of this sanction in 1989 (218 cases) followed by New Jersey (130) (Gardiner and Malec 1989: 8–9).

More interventionist sanctions still at the end of the 1980s were the capacity most states had to appoint a receiver to run a non-compliant nursing home or designate a monitor appointed by the state and paid for by the nursing home to report back to the regulators on progress. Few states that used these remedies did so more than once or twice a year, with the exception of the comparatively frequent use of monitors in Illinois and Indiana.

The ultimate sanction against a nursing home in all states is licence revocation. In most states in most years it was never used for fear of what would become of the residents after a home was closed. Only 13 states used this sanction in 1989, with three states also suspending licences rather than revoking them (Gardiner and Malec 1989: 11–12). Georgia revoked ten licences, with Kansas, New Jersey and Illinois each revoking eight. For most nursing homes, federal Medicaid decertification is as clearly a corporate death sentence as state licence revocation, given that more than two-thirds of beds nationally were and are Medicaid funded. There were 25 Medicaid decertifications in Massachusetts in 1989, 37 in Texas and 14 in Oregon. Overall 53 nursing homes had their licences revoked in the US in 1989, while 130 were decertified for the receipt of Medicaid benefits (Gardiner and Malec 1989: 15). In most years in the US during the period of this study, more than a hundred nursing homes were effectively closed because of their poor compliance. It was more common for them to voluntarily close because of enforcement pressure, but most states also compulsorily closed homes most years, both by state revocation of licence and federal decertification as a Medicaid provider.

Table 2.1 shows that the big story of enforcement is that since the 1989 high-water mark, sanctions have become less frequently proposed following inspections across most of the country, and once proposed are much less likely to be actually imposed. The biggest effect of OBRA has been a shift from state-level sanctions that were imposed 90 per cent of the time once proposed, to federal sanctions not imposed 90 per cent of the time once proposed by inspectors and their supervisors. Other federal sanctions

Table 2.1   *Comparison of 1989 state enforcement data[1] aggregated for the US with 2003 federal enforcement data[2]*

	1989		%	2003		%
	Proposed	Imposed		Proposed	Imposed	
Civil monetary penalty	5054	4969	98.3	1979	209	10.6
Denial of payment for new admissions	486	455	93.6	698	16	2.3
Directed in-service training	Not used	Not used	Not used	362	10	2.8
State monitoring	74	47	63.5	124	5	4.0
Directed plan of correction	Not used	Not used	Not used	83	26	31.3

Notes:
1.   Data are actually either fiscal 1989 or calendar 1988 from Gardiner and Malec (1989).
2.   Supplied to the authors by CMS.

were available but never used in 2003 and most other recent years – transfer of residents, facility closure, and denial of payment for all residents. Termination and CMS-approved alternative state remedies were each used once.

Some qualifications are in order here. While many states have totally or substantially deferred enforcement to the federal survey process after 1995, many have not. So there is a lot of state enforcement action not captured in the 2003 figures in Table 2.1. In states such as Wisconsin and Washington, most of the enforcement action remains at the state level and fixing a problem immediately does not guarantee dropping of the action if the breach were serious. One data source that combines state and federal sanctions of 720 nursing home administrators in 1997 found that 18 per cent of them (122) had an enforcement action proposed as a result of their most recent inspection, and only 19 per cent of these (22) had a sanction or remedy (such as directed plan of correction or directed in-service) imposed (HCFA 1998: vol. 3, 462). While we can be confident that 1989 has been the US enforcement high-water mark for most of the country, state nursing home regulation see-saws so much as administrations change and local scandals erupt that we cannot be sure just how much of the US we mean when we say 'most of the country'. Another big qualification is that assisted living homes that have become de facto nursing homes are being subjected to increasing state enforcement in many jurisdictions. So if we count them as nursing homes, as we should, and as assisted living enforcement increases, as it will, it is not even clear whether or not the US is beginning a process that will surpass that 1989 high-water mark in the late years of the current decade.

Throughout the study period it has been extremely rare for criminal penalties to be imposed on nursing home organizations for breaches of quality-of-care standards or for bribing regulators (Connolly 2002). In most states organizational criminal penalties have never been used. Celebrated corporate homicide prosecutions for neglect of residents in nursing homes have failed in the courts, though there were successful prosecutions of individual executives for homicide in the 1980s (Long 1987; Pray 1986; Schudson et al. 1984). All states refer charges against individuals who abuse residents for criminal investigations by state prosecutors. There have been hundreds of criminal penalties for patient abuse imposed in most years in the United States since the early 1980s (Institute of Medicine 1986: 342), compared to only a handful of criminal abuse convictions each year in England and Australia combined, and some years when there were none. Abuse enforcement across the United States shifted to a criminal law model in the 1980s and criminal enforcement has become more intensive since.[11] In the 1980s in Illinois, abuse was mostly responded to civilly; today police are seconded to the Illinois Department of Public Health to secure a criminal law model for abuse cases detected by frontline inspectors.

Some states initiate large numbers of enforcement actions that they never formally implement because they reach settlement agreements with the nursing homes. States that did this routinely, such as Massachusetts at the time of the late 1980s high-water mark of enforcement, appeared to have a worse enforcement record than they had. Consent agreements sometimes contained onerous provisions, such as California's 1986 agreement that Beverly Enterprises pay a fine of $800 000 and set up a substantial quality assurance program that seemed to be viewed as state of the art for the time by many independent commentators. Quality assurance programs that later became a universal regulatory requirement were first imposed in innovative consent agreements. The head of one state enforcement agency said that her strategy in serious cases was often to:

> go for revocation of their licence and then negotiate a settlement. You don't want to make it totally obvious that you are willing to settle for less than revocation. Nor do you want to overplay the problem so that you get the public so stirred up that you can't manage the situation and patients get upset and worried.

To assist such negotiation, Tennessee inspectors in the 1980s were trained to increase bargaining power in cases that might be heard in open court by writing into inspection reports statements like the following, which the nursing home would not want the media to get their hands on: 'On each of three days of the survey, the director of nursing on arrival was reading a romance novel concealed behind patient charts.'

An extensive critical literature built up in the 1970s and 1980s attacking the weakness of American nursing home enforcement in both the mass media and the scholarly literature (Blum and Wadleigh 1983; Brown 1975; Butler 1979; General Accounting Office 1987; Institute of Medicine 1986; Johnson 1985; Long 1987). Yet the US has tougher nursing home enforcement than any country we know. The literature attacking regulators for enforcement weakness may be one of the factors that caused American regulation to get tougher throughout the 1980s. Yet armchair scholarly commentators read these critical popular and scholarly literatures as evidence that enforcement is weak and regulation is weak. The truth is that it is precisely in regulatory domains that lack such critical literatures (for example, nursing home regulation in the United States during the 25 years after World War II or in Japan in the 1970s and 1980s or hospitals regulation in the US until very recently) that we are most likely to find weak enforcement. Armchair commentators on an industry, who seek truth in the weight of popular critiques, rather than through systematic empirical comparison, may obscure the truth. Yet at the same time they may play a role in social constructions of an industry and its regulator that lead to change. The social construction 'American nursing home regulation is weak' is shown to have a rather limited truth claim when one asks 'Weaker than what?' It turns out that it is tougher and better resourced than at earlier points of American history (prior to the mid-1980s), tougher and better resourced than in any other nation we know of, and tougher and better resourced than other domains of American business regulation we know of. Yet scholarly acceptance of the social construction reinforces it, even legitimates it to the point where opinion leaders in the community, some regulators themselves, and many legislators come to accept it as fact. When this happens, the widespread perception of regulatory weakness can cause a response that is likely to deliver tougher, less discretionary regulation. In the worst case, scholars read the popular critiques of enforcement failure as the raw data for their own construction of the world after those critiques have already done their work in changing the world (see Figure 2.2).

Today there is a less critical literature on the enforcement question and, as we have seen, less enforcement than when enforcement activity hit its peak immediately before OBRA implementation in October 1990. Edelman (1998: 1) correctly detected a return to the situation of the early 1980s where: 'The failure to correct deficiencies, rather than the existence of deficiencies, is the basis of enforcement. Deficiencies in the new statutory areas of residents' rights and quality of life are virtually ignored by the enforcement system.' Even so, compared with England and Australia, US

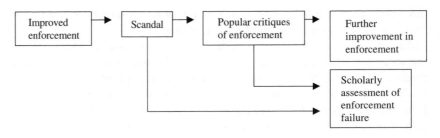

Figure 2.2   Lagged scholarly assessment of enforcement failure as a result of enforcement improving

nursing home regulation fits Robert Kagan's (1991) model of 'adversarial legalism'. Part of this is a low level of trust, as illustrated by the following exchange in 1989 in a Chicago nursing home. (There is no documentation signed by the physician or in the nursing notes indicating awareness of an allergy the resident suffers. The inspectors are concerned that the doctor has prescribed medications without knowing of the allergy.)

> *Pharmacist:* I'm saying the doctor was told. I wouldn't lie.
> *Inspector 1:* We don't know that.
> *Pharmacist:* Yes you do because I'm a professional and I wouldn't do that of course.
> *Inspector 2:* Professionals lie to us all the time.
> *(Later to J. Braithwaite, after pharmacist had left) Inspector 1:* I think he is lying.

The upshot of these encounters where professionals are treated as untrustworthy is that they feel less trusted. Systematic Australian research from 410 nursing homes shows that when directors of nursing feel more trusted during government inspections, compliance improves in the two years after the inspection (Braithwaite and Makkai 1994). While dragging inspectors to court is rare, it is routine in many states for any serious penalties or enforcement actions to be challenged through alternative dispute resolution or a formal administrative law hearing (often a private legal practitioner sitting as a hearing officer). Many states had in-house counsel who could take cases right through to court; other inspection agencies were represented in court by the state Attorney-General's office. A survey by Jost (1985: 165) found that the minority of state agencies who were represented by in-house counsel were more satisfied with their legal representation.

Allegations concerning some major cases against chains were extraordinary at times, and had no counterparts in the course of the Australian and English fieldwork. They included bribery of a District Attorney, the deputy head of a state regulatory agency, offer of bribes to inspectors, large campaign contributions to state legislators in return for political pressure to have a particular inspector removed from a particular case, campaign contributions to judges who hear nursing home cases in states where judges are elected, seeking to destroy the career of enforcement officials by, for example, litigation against them for alleged impropriety or disclosure in open court of any adverse matter involving them in their personnel file or from other sources, and setting up a whistle-blower with criminal proceedings for resident abuse. Political interference to thwart enforcement action has become less common in the last three decades because 'politicians have been burned for defending nursing homes with real problems' and regulators learnt that they could expose political interference by leaking to advocacy groups. It remains a large problem in many states, but not a major issue in many others.

We found appeals that state nursing home regulators lose often produce great reform at the facility level. This happened because while the case was winding its way up to the hearing officer or court, proprietors would fix things in the home, mount in-service training and fire incompetent managers in order to win their case, especially when the looming consequences were large, such as closure. This phenomenon of regulators losing the battle but winning the war was first demonstrated in Waldman's (1978) study where defendant companies won antitrust cases by reforming their anticompetitive practices.

Tort litigation did not loom large as an issue in the 1980s and early 1990s, but over the past decade lawyers specializing in suing nursing homes on behalf of residents have begun to advertise aggressively, especially in states with large nursing home populations, such as Florida, and seem to be winning bigger payouts (as high as $83 million in a Texas case and $94 million in a California case – Brady 2001) than they were in previous eras (Harrington 2001). During the current decade in Florida and Texas, which between them accounted for the majority of nursing home tort litigation in the US, tort became a major factor in the web of nursing home controls (Stevenson and Studdert 2003). Tort payouts in fact increased progressively throughout the period of this study and at the time of writing there is a tort reform debate in the US Congress about capping such payouts.

TRIPARTISM

Walshe (2001: 140–41) has criticized US nursing home enforcement for being insufficiently tripartite (Ayres and Braithwaite 1992: ch. 3). While Walshe is right that US nursing home regulation is not as tripartite as occupational health and safety regulation in many nations, it is more so than most

American regulatory domains. A number of senior state health department officials contrasted the absence of external pressure to enforce the law in hospitals and other areas of health regulation with nursing home regulation where 'consumer groups are there to keep you on your toes'. When we visited Oklahoma at the end of the 1980s, citizen observers from statewide advocacy organizations accompanied inspectors when they were investigating complaints. Iowa had a 'nursing home watch' program in which community representatives were formally charged with monitoring quality of care in facilities. Each Iowa nursing home was required to establish a 'Care Review Committee' of members of the community in which it was located. The Care Review Committee conducted complaint investigations, quarterly inspections and liaison with the annual state inspections.

One of the OBRA reforms implemented in 1990 was effectively a meeting with the residents' council (the 'group interview') as a standard part of the inspection process. In many states it is standard practice for either volunteers or employed staff from the state ombudsman to attend this residents' council meeting and the initial tour of the facility with the inspector. In California and some other states the Long-Term Care Ombudsman's representative has long attended citation review conferences where facilities contest enforcement actions by the regulator. Complainants, affected residents or their representatives also have long had legal rights to attend citation or civil penalty review hearings in these jurisdictions. In some states tripartism worked with the bite that matched the ideal in Ayres and Braithwaite (1992: ch. 3). In New York at the end of the 1980s, some well-placed informants had the strong view that no fewer than 'every receivership has been forced by the ombudsperson or consumer groups'.

Ombudsmen also sometimes attend exit conferences in all states. This is an especially tripartite phenomenon in a state like Michigan where the Long-Term Care Ombudsman program is administered by the leading community advocacy organization for nursing home reform in the state – the Citizens for Better Care – or in New York where the state ombudsman program was run by the New York State Office for the Aging, but where its area agencies contracted out to local voluntary organizations to run the program through 400 volunteers in their areas. The CEO of Michigan Citizens for Better Care had a vision of their role grounded in tripartism: 'We don't mind playing left field to keep them in centre field. So long as they act in good faith.' In Michigan, Citizens for Better Care received copies of all complaint reports, facilitating their involvement as a third party when this was important or strategic. Tripartism was also fostered in Michigan by providing for complainants to receive a proportion of civil penalties imposed as a result of a complaint. Nationally, there has been in the current decade a large escalation in the number of private False Claims Act qui tam actions against nursing homes, in which the private litigant obtains up to 35 per cent of the penalty imposed on the home (Kapp 2002).

A September 1991 survey of 520 facilities in 40 states found representatives of the ombudsman to be present at a quarter of exit conferences; residents from the facility were present in half, while attorneys were present in only 2.5 per cent (American Association of Homes for the Aging 1991). A 1990 interview with a leader of the statewide Washington State Nursing Home Residents' Councils expressed the rationale for a tripartite philosophy of resident participation in exit conferences and other parts of the inspection process in the following way: 'A lot of things you have to live it in order to see it.' Some ombudsmen report that when they are able to get copies of their nursing home's deficiencies in a timely manner following an inspection, they check that deficiencies are corrected during their regular visits (HCFA 1998: vol. 3, 481).

Most state ombudsmen have been active since the 1990s in promoting family councils in nursing homes; they also sometimes send representatives to exits. Forty-one per cent of nursing homes had them in 2004, down from 46 per cent in 1998 (Harrington et al. 2005: 28), and 95 per cent have residents' councils (up from 92 per cent in 1998). On the debit side, the breadth of participation in exit conferences in some states has been a casualty of federal standardization of the survey process. The Illinois Citizens for Better Care were still banned from attending exit conferences during our 2004–05 fieldwork for fear that some of their members were 'aggressive individuals who would go to the press'. In some states in the 1980s we observed wider participation of staff from different levels and departments of the nursing home than we observe today. Sometimes a representative of the union in the nursing home was also present. Representatives of the residents' council were also routinely present at the exit in these states and often representatives of a family council as well. We also observed the old state Medicare–Medicaid Inspection of Care process, absorbed into inspections post-OBRA, to have rather tripartite exit conferences in many states.

An interesting perspective on multipartite participation in exit conferences came in 1989 from the executive director of one state private nursing home association. When one of his members lobbied a politician to pressure the regulator about demands from a specific inspection team, he confided this was not always good for him and his organization. It created limited opportunities and considerable risks to his good relationships with the regulator, the politician and the member nursing home. He adopted the practice of encouraging the politician to attend the exit conference. In the days of the late 1980s when exit conferences were highly dialogic (before participation became ritualized – see Chapter 7) this gave a useful outlet for the skills of a politician. The nursing home association executive director's experience of this was that the politician would tend to play a useful role in brokering a peace and building commitment to a workable plan of correction. The politician's presence at the behest of the facility would certainly prevent the regulator from indulging in overkill and unreasonableness. But mostly 'they tended to join with the department in saying they need to fix it'. This deliberative response seemed so much better for all the parties than the usual response that the politician's office calls the inspector's boss saying that a complaint about their regulatory unreasonableness has been received and they are concerned. A policy of invitation to the exit discourages this kind of unconsidered, pro forma political interference and the ill will it can create in provider–regulator and regulator–legislator relationships.

CONCLUSION

American nursing home regulation is a story of American exceptionalism and adversarial legalism (Kagan 1991; Kagan and Axelrad 2000). The amount of inspection resources and enforcement is extraordinary compared to nursing home regulation in any other nation we know and compared to most other domains of American business regulation. This made it a site of considerable enforcement innovation and innovation in regulatory tripartism. The innovation and energy on enforcement and tripartism is, however, less today than it was at the end of the 1980s thanks to federal disciplining of state innovation, one of the topics of the next chapter. For all that central discipline, state nursing home inspectorates remain street-level bureaucracies. Inspectors have managed to take back discretion in a way that has thwarted political intent to increase the frequency and stringency of enforcement. While nothing could be more the antithesis of responsive regulation than the enforcement automaticity of the scope and severity grid, street-level enforcement has proved more resiliently responsive in practice. This is a theme we return to in Chapter 4.

NOTES

1. Chicago nursing homes were a focus of national attention in the early 1970s as scandal after scandal of deplorable care occurred. This prompted the Illinois Department of Public Health to put in place some of the most rigorous inspection policies of the time. By the late 1970s many commentators believed that Illinois homes had moved from being among the worst in the nation to somewhat above average (Tellis-Nyack 1988: 38). By the time our fieldwork started in 1987, Chicago was not generally perceived as unusually bad or unusually outstanding either in terms of the quality of care or the quality of regulation. After seeing both in action in 25 other states, at the end of our fieldwork we suspect this is pretty much so.

2. Black aides in one nursing home alleged that white aides, some with Ku Klux Klan affiliations, got relatives to complain against black aides. White aides, it was alleged, would pour water on sheets after a black aide just finished changing a bed and then complain about the job done. The president of the residents' council in another nursing home said: 'There's a lot of discrimination here. The black staff do not like the Philippino staff and the Philippino staff do not like the white staff. Each group does not work with the other. There is no liason, no coordination, between different departments for this reason.' In Chicago, we observed a deal of anti-Semitism of residents toward Jewish owners (sometimes connected to resentment over having to eat kosher food) and of non-Jewish toward Jewish proprietors (causing division within the Chicago industry lobby and petty resentments over issues like kosher food at industry dinners). We also observed tacit racism of inspectors, as with the following statement of a Chicago inspector: 'The staff they get at the southside facilities, I shouldn't say this but they're retarded or apathetic or something. They don't care. On the south, the conditions are just terrible. The contrast with the northside homes is great.' Another Chicago inspector commented: 'The Jewish owners they do anything for the extra dollar. If they can save money and the patients suffer for it, they'll save the money.'

3. While the US spends far more on health per capita than any Organisation for Economic Co-operation and Development (OECD) nation, its citizens get comparatively little care from qualified nurses. While Australia and the UK also have a nursing shortage, the US has fewer nurses per capita than the UK, Australia and the OECD average, and in the decade 1992–2002 the number of US nurses grew at half the rate of OECD median growth (Anderson et al. 2005: 907).

4. Assisted living homes have seen more growth in single room accommodation than nursing homes.

5. Denmark, for example, does not have for-profit nursing home beds: 72 per cent of beds are public and 28 per cent private non-profit (Meijer et al. 2000: 557).

6. The HCFA (1998: vol. 1, iii) also reports that contemporary US surveys also give more priority to direct observation of residents than Joint Commission certifications of nursing homes and other health-care providers.

7. While revisit is not normally triggered by simply writing a deficiency, it is normally triggered by the proposed imposition of a penalty.

8. We were impressed that some of our inspector informants were able to predict in the late 1980s and early 1990s that this would be the effect of OBRA implementation: 'If enforcement is automatic, upshot would be less citation. For me I would prefer to plead with staff to fix it before we go' (Maryland inspector). Criminologists have known this phenomenon for many decades; for example, that the effect of a mandatory death penalty for rape is fewer police charges and fewer rape convictions.

9. Michigan inspector (1990): 'We don't like to put conditions out because no sooner have we got our report through the system and we've got to come out and start working on another one.'

10. Data supplied by Centers for Medicare and Medicaid Services, Baltimore and from Gardiner and Malec (1989).

11. Notwithstanding the increase in police enforcement, there is some evidence from the 1990s of a reduced willingness of inspectors to write abuse deficiencies (HCFA 1998: vol. 3, 572).

3. The disciplinary society and its enemies

We have seen that regulation has been fundamentally responsible for driving the mom-and-pops out of business and making American nursing homes much larger than those of England and Australia. Being less intimate, they are also prone to be more institutional. In this chapter we will see that regulation was also directly involved in making them more institutional. They are mostly disciplinary institutions in many of the senses Michel Foucault (1977) evocatively described prisons to be. Prisoners in maximum security prisons are not tied into chairs and beds, and most have freedom to roam larger indoor and outdoor spaces than residents in locked dementia wings of nursing homes. Even in a country with as high an imprisonment rate as the US, a much larger proportion of citizens spend an important part of their lives in a nursing home than in a prison. American nursing homes not only discipline the bodies of residents to comply with institutional regimes, the majority of staff are also impoverished and disciplined people; even the administrator is much more lacking freedom than other professionals thanks to a regulatory process that makes their very tenure in the position of authority quite fragile. Nursing home chain management often tapes exit conferences to monitor the performance of their administrators in these crucial encounters with state authority. Nursing home regulation, we find, is hardly a domain of neoliberal governmentality, as in the work of the late Foucault (1991). This is more a domain of discipline and punishment (Foucault 1977).

Seeing this clearly is part of our wider project (that is not about Foucault) of questioning how accurate it is to believe we live in an era of neoliberalism as opposed to regulatory capitalism (Braithwaite 2005a; Levi-Faur 2005, 2006). Neoliberalism is conceived in this project as a program of privatization and deregulation, of a diminished public sphere and an enhanced role for markets. The regulatory capitalism argument is that what we see today in developed economies is not privatization and deregulation, but privatization and regulatory growth, an enhanced role for markets but also for regulation. This book documents the fact that health and aged care reform since 1980 fit the regulatory capitalism analysis in the sense that while states might be doing less rowing (less direct provision of aged care beds in public hospitals), they are doing more steering of a predominately private industry.

A second strand of this argument we explore is that contemporary societies are not very 'liberal', as is evidenced by a massive growth in what Foucault called the disciplines. It is not the case that with the passing of the industrial revolution neoliberal governmentalities have replaced discipline. Rather we live in a world in which there is both more governing through markets and more discipline, more people in prison, more people in nursing homes and assisted living facilities, more people under surveillance by agents of state security. Nursing homes are no less quintessentially part of the new service economy than serving fast food or information technology. We argue that nursing homes became more not less disciplinary than the Fordist factories and hospitals that so fascinated Foucault.

A reason that markets and discipline grow hand in hand is that discipline is marketed. Criminologists have documented how privatized prisons create an entrepreneurial class who tout the virtues of prisons as solutions to problems, just as two centuries ago certain shipping interests touted the virtues of transportation of convicts to remote places like Australia (Christie 1993; Feeley 2002). Today organizations like the American Nursing Homes Association lobby in Washington for more public dollars to subsidize the highly institutionalized models of care of the aged in which their members are expert. The Posey Corporation of California, the largest vendor of physical restraints, (unsuccessfully) lobbied industry and regulators against an overreaction to the Untie the Elderly Campaign. Security technology companies lobby for more state surveillance; the Halliburton Corporation lobbies for an invasion of Iraq buttressed by privatized security.

The final section of the chapter argues that this disciplinary society has its enemies. There are providers of community care for the aged who argue for shifting Medicaid dollars away from disciplinary institutional care. We will document the important role of restraint-free nursing homes who play on community fears of excessive discipline to market an alternative. We will document the important role of advocacy groups, particularly the National Citizens' Coalition for Nursing Home Reform, in linking arms with providers exploiting an anti-discipline market niche. Finally, we document the role of professional model-mongers of more emancipatory models of care, such as the Eden alternative. All these enemies of the disciplinary society have been fighting back across the period of this study, and they have had some important successes.

THE MARKET FOR DISCIPLINE

While it is true that there are fewer citizens disciplined in institutions such as factories, mental hospitals and orphanages than in the heyday of industrial capitalism and the welfare state, the numbers disciplined in prisons have more than doubled since Foucault wrote *Discipline and Punish* (1977), and so has the number in aged care institutions (at least if we add assisted living institutions to the rather stable numbers for nursing homes proper) in the US, Australia and England; indeed in most Western economies. In Asian societies, the growth of even more disciplinary[1] institutions for the aged has been more recent and rapid: there were only 27 nursing homes in Japan in 1965, over a thousand by 1980 (Shimuzu et al. 1985). Since the 1980s nursing homes in the US started to employ more workers than the auto and steel industries combined (Eaton 2000). In addition, we have whole new layers of disciplinary control under the banner of homeland security and regulation of refugees. Even more so when we leave the homeland, we are disciplined to our socks – policed, frisked, fingerprint-identified, surveyed by covert cameras – through the anti-terror state. Schools remain fundamentally disciplinary institutions, and citizens spend more years in them than they did during industrial capitalism, and universities have become more disciplinary than they used to be – more like schools, less the courageously free and wonderfully unruly places where your authors had their tertiary education.

This is not to say that the trends are without complexity. In schools, as we will document for nursing homes, there are forces of resistance to the disciplines. Moreover, we will see that in nursing homes there is coexistence and interaction between the disciplines (which for Foucault is a politics of the human body) and 'regulatory controls' (which for Foucault is a politics of populations, managing populations actuarially without necessarily focusing upon the individual).[2] Foucault accommodated this in his account of the growth of regulatory controls (Foucault 1984: 139, 149; O'Malley 1992). We see actuarialism in the use of the Minimum Data Set to select for review actuarially low-risk residents with pressure sores, then disciplinary control to turn the bodies of those residents two-hourly, or to discipline them to get up from their bed, and to discipline the treatments staff are observed to give the pressure sore. All this is informed by an architecture for bodies: so for a group of residents requiring two-hourly turning, staff can be disciplined to turn their bodies toward the window on odd turns, toward the door on the next turn. Then any resident pointing to the door when all others point to the window raises a question for aides and supervisors of a need to check if the last turn has been overlooked. In 2003 we observed an Arizona nursing home in which all residents with a weight loss problem had a napkin of a particular colour to cue aides to check that they ate. Our point is simply that this book is a contribution to questioning sweeping claims that this is an era of neoliberalism where governance through markets has swept past discipline, and to strengthening claims that post-1980 is an era of regulatory capitalism.

We have been helped to see how Foucaultian our understanding of nursing homes is by Shearing and Stenning's (1985) classic on Disney World. Shearing and Stenning reject the interpretation of Foucault that discipline requires soul-training, moral reform. To identify discipline with soul-training fails to distinguish between Foucault's generic concept of discipline and his more historically specific analysis of carceral punishment as one form of discipline. What is distinctive about discipline is that it is a type of power 'comprising a whole set of instruments, techniques, procedures, levels of application, targets; it is a "physics" or anatomy of power, technology' (Foucault 1977: 215). Unlike state power to execute or torture, it is not 'located outside and above the social relations to be controlled but is integrated into them. As it is part of the social fabric it is everywhere, and yet it is nowhere, because it does not have an identifiable locus' (Shearing and Stenning 1985: 337). Without in any way seeking to train our souls, these disciplines (the barriers and bars; compare nursing bedrails) keep our bodies safe as they are hurled around at speed in devices designed to give us fun. Private security is also shown in Shearing and Stenning as devoid of moral reform as a basis of control. They allude to Oscar Newman's work on 'defensible space' to design buildings for providing routine crime prevention through natural surveillance of children's playgrounds, for example, from kitchen windows.

What is interesting about the nursing home case is that some of the technologies of carceral discipline, such as panoptic architecture, are present in a fabric of discipline that is 'non-carceral' in the sense that much of the time there is no soul-training, only body-constraint. Far from training souls, nursing home discipline often infantilizes, as when residents, often with affection, can be referred to as 'our babies'. What is interesting about discipline is the way it is hybridized in contingent mixes of body and soul regulation, individualized and actuarial regulation. Stenning and Shearing have done a service to the social sciences in making us see expanding discipline in as obscure a site as Disney World. Ours is a more banal extrapolation of disciplinary understanding from the context of the prison, the hospital or the factory to the American nursing home chain of the late twentieth century as an aged care factory that markets its own distinctive mix of disciplines. Stenning and Shearing helped us see architectural discipline not as the discipline of the past. We can now more clearly see it as a discipline of the future, as we are disciplined by Microsoft architecture in producing this very text (Lessig 1999). Equally, we can see the centrality in a networked knowledge economy of open software Internet architectures that contest and move around would-be monopoly architectures for disciplining our knowledge-production (Nicol and Hope 2007).

At the top of the regulatory chain today, disciplining by software is particularly important. The feds regulate state regulators not only by a state procedures manual and by look-behind federal inspections to check inspectors are doing things right, but also by software that in effect makes it impossible to enter the wrong kind of information, or incomplete information, in the same way that websites refuse to let us purchase or register for something unless we provide a zip code with the right number of characters. It is less possible these days to never get around to resolving a complaint; the central complaint tracking system may hold up reimbursement from the federal to the state government if an unresolved complaint prods the software to raise a red flag. These information systems also strip discretion from inspectors to decide which residents to look at during an inspection; the information systems select a targeted set of residents centrally. In Chapter 7, we consider how regulation by computer architecture is now reaching right down to the regulation of nurse aides by nurses.

PANOPTIC DESIGN

United States nursing homes (like the limited number of Canadian[3] and Japanese ones that David Ermann and the authors observed for this project, though less so English and Australian homes) are disciplinary societies. Many homes built in the great American construction boom from the 1960s to the 1980s have to this day explicitly panoptic designs – nurses' stations are hubs from which radiate wings of rooms. Residents whom it is thought unwise to leave unsupervised in their room are wheeled, typically in the 1980s tied, into a position adjacent to the nurses' station.[4] Often a dozen or more silent, sullen, slumped subjects are congregated around the nurses' station. The corridors of each wing and the front rooms of each – often public areas such as activities rooms, television and dining rooms – can be subjected to surveillance from the nurses' stations (see Figure 3.1). Duffy et al. (1986) showed that US nursing home administrators had a clear preference for more over less panoptic nursing home architecture. Residents were less supportive of designs that fostered interaction between residents and had a stronger preference for designs that secured privacy than did either administrators or architects. This difference of preference was particularly strong with the design of lounge areas, where almost all administrators preferred configurations of chairs so people were facing one another, while 70 per cent of residents preferred configurations where they were not.

We are not saying panoptic design characterizes the majority of American nursing homes. We do contend it is distinctively much more present in the US than in England or Australia, where 'privacy and dignity' and 'homelike environment' standards would never allow some of the panoptic practices we observed in the US. In England or Australia we have

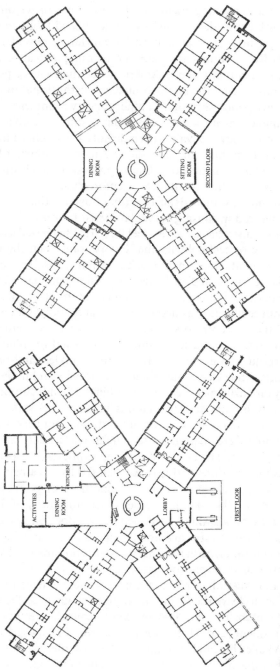

DINING ROOM

SITTING ROOM

SECOND FLOOR

ACTIVITIES

DINING ROOM

KITCHEN

LOBBY

FIRST FLOOR

Figure 3.1   Panoptic design of two floors of an American nursing home

79

never seen the seating arrangement in a Beverly Enterprises dining room where all the problem feeders sat at horseshoe-shaped tables with an aide standing inside the horseshoe, enjoying a frontal view of how all his charges were eating. Al Reiss, commenting on one of our publications from the 1990s that made this point about American distinctiveness, pointed out that: 'this is a more general American medical institutional model: many hospitals also have panoptic designs: in the recovery room with all its monitors the surveillance institution reaches its highest form, with almost total abandonment of privacy as a value' (Braithwaite 1994: 42). In more subtle ways than panoptic architecture, almost all American nursing homes are designed as surveillance institutions. Our hypothesis is much stronger than that this manifests a failure of the US to enforce the privacy, dignity and homelike environment standards of other nations; it is that US regulation was centrally involved in causing surveillance institutions.

In England and Australia, as well as the US, during the past decade we have seen increasing use of technologies that compensate when the number of short spokes that radiate from a panoptic hub is limited. Sometimes this technology is simple yet surprisingly effective in extending human gaze. A nurse at a corner where two very long corridors intersect can get a remarkable view to the end of both corridors in a curved mirror that occupies the corner where the ceilings of the two corridors meet opposite a nurses' station. Closed-circuit television screens are also a more common sight to enhance surveillance in modern nursing homes, as are electronic anklets and bracelets on targeted residents, while electronic monitoring of exits and doors to locked units (generally for Alzheimer's residents) within the facility are virtually universal. Nursing home building regulations in many US states have long required a view of all corridors from a nurses' station. For very old buildings constructed before this regulation, closed-circuit television (CCTV) surveillance can be required to achieve the outcome. A difference between the US and England is that because of this rule, when CCTV became affordable it effectively became mandated in the US in conditions of poor surveillance, whereas in the 1980s in the UK when some homes introduced CCTV, District Health Authorities initially threatened their licences for doing so on grounds that no one would want to stay in a hotel with CCTV monitoring their daily movements. The current British national standards prohibit CCTV except for external security reasons in entrance areas.

In English and Australian nursing homes, residents have much greater effective freedom to leave the facility to go to a favourite coffee shop, hairdresser, pub or club. In one 2004 residents' council meeting held with inspectors, a resident said: 'I'm happy here. But I'm locked in and not allowed out. What crime did I commit?' We had last observed an inspection of this nursing home in 1991; freedom of movement was greater then. Since

1991 the neighbourhood had gentrified; the more respectable neighbours who had moved in began to complain when unkempt residents wandered out into the neighbourhood, especially into their prim gardens.

THE MIXED IMPACTS OF THE ENEMIES OF DISCIPLINE

To summarize our hypotheses in this chapter so far: the disciplinary nature of American nursing homes is driven by their comparatively large size, distant management and institutional structure. This is a product of regulation; the disciplinary nature of American nursing homes is connected to the disciplinary nature of their regulation; the disciplinary nature of both American nursing homes and American nursing home regulation makes ritualism an inevitable pathology; and therefore, a key point of intervention to deal with the dual problems of ritualism and disciplinary oppression is radical transformation of the regulatory framework. The disciplinary character of US nursing homes explains why there has been a more vibrant social movement for nursing home regulatory reform in the US than in Australia or England. Sadly though, an unintended consequence of their activism has been to make homes even more disciplinary. The same can be said of US tort lawyers who specialize in nursing home abuse and neglect cases for a contingency fee.

The disciplinary nature of nursing homes explains why the US also has a vibrant social movement not to reform nursing homes, but to abolish them in favour of community care, and why Australia and England do not have such social movement politics. Another reason an NGO such as ADAPT (American Disabled for Attendant Programs Today) (Figure 3.2) became in the 1990s such an aggressive force for total liberation of residents from nursing homes, with a medium-term objective of shifting 25 per cent of the Medicaid budget into community care, is that ADAPT drew on energetic support of people and corporations who were home health-care providers. We found these home health-care providers associated with ADAPT to be sincere in their commitment to a 'wiser, more humane way' than nursing homes. It may be that some of them became home health-care providers because of their activist commitment to that more humane way, as opposed to becoming activists because they had an interest as providers. We simply remark that the synergy of liberationist activism and American interest group politics gave resources and energy to a vibrant abolitionist politics that was absent in Australia and England.

Finally we will suggest that the key to change lies within the dynamics of this social movement politics. Good regulatory scholarship can help with showing advocacy groups paths from ritualism to innovation. Moreover, it can persuade some regulators and progressive providers to promote

**Washington State
Nursing Home
Resident Councils...**

**THE VOICE
OF THE
NURSING HOME
CONSUMER**

*Figure 3.2   On the left, ADAPT's logo in the iconography of abolitionism;
on the right, the mainstream advocacy group iconography of
empowerment within institutions*

alternative strategies, thereby creating the possibility of a plural coalition of
advocates, providers, regulators and researchers who share that vision of a
shift from ritualism to innovation that improves quality of life for the aged.

UNTYING THE ELDERLY

The most important instance where such a plural coalition happened on a
specific issue in the US was the Untie the Elderly Campaign led by the

National Citizens' Coalition for Nursing Home Reform, supported by progressive regulators and providers who sought a competitive advantage by promoting 'restraint-free' homes and gerontologists who produced evidence that challenged industry claims that regulation to require major reductions of restraint would cost 'a billion dollars a year'. Phillips et al. (1993) showed in a staff time study of care for 11 932 residents that, after controlling for differences in impairment and control needs, physically restrained residents required more nursing care than other residents (for further evidence of this see HCFA 1998: vol. 2, 344). Tinetti et al. (1990) found that continuously restrained residents were three times as likely to suffer serious injuries as those who were never restrained. Restraint is also a cause of pressure sores. Even a decade and a half ago the National Pressure Ulcer Advisory Panel estimated healing a pressure sore was then costing between $5000 and $25 000 (HCFA 1998: vol. 2, 341). These kinds of numbers give some insight into how the comparatively competitive, privatized, yet highly disciplinary American health system costs so much compared to many other nations, yet delivers worse health outcomes. Other researchers showed that tort risks caused by restraints were far greater than tort risks prevented by them and that insurers were more concerned about risks of overuse than of failure to use (Special Committee on Aging 1990b: 22–56). Researchers matter in reform coalitions that strike blows like this against ritualism by showing political leaders that there are cost-effective regulatory alternatives, by showing progressive providers that they can secure a brand advantage by being early movers to adopt them (Porter 1990) or by showing an entire industry that they are wrong to think that they will be worse off as a result of the change.

The disciplinary nature of American nursing homes is most apparent in the visual surveillance described above, which, as oppressive of privacy and dignity as are its effects, is nevertheless motivated by a well-meaning desire to protect residents from harm and to protect the home from negligence litigation. Similarly, with the other most visible sign of the disciplinary order of the American nursing home – the shocking level of physical restraint.[5] Unlike the discourse of discipline in a prison, the brutal reality of restraint in a nursing home is encased in a vocabulary of caring. Physical restraint is often characterized as 'postural support'. The dominant supplier of restraints, the Posey company of California (Poseys were also widely used in Australia) has such a cosy name, warm like a tea cosy,[6] for forms of vests with straps for tying residents that they reported to us felt more like straitjackets. It was not just our conversations with restrained residents that made us think that; it was our observation of them wailing, for example: 'Nurse please don't tie me up.'

Consider this deficiency citation for a Beverly Enterprises home: 'Resident #13 was found . . . with her right hand restrained to the bedrail with mitt in place. The hand and lower arm were swollen and cyanotic. Indentation marks from the strings were noted where tied . . . The resident has no mitt restraint order.'

When we questioned staff in the 1980s and early 1990s they said (usually both mistakenly and sincerely) that restraint was necessary to protect the residents by preventing falls and to protect the nursing home from lawsuits and regulatory sanctions.[7] Less commonly, they conceded it represents a policy of the corporation to save staff time on the management of difficult residents. Because restraint causes psychiatric and physical morbidity that includes loss of dignity, urinary incontinence, pressure sores, skin abrasions, nerve damage and muscle atrophy (Evans and Strumpf 1989, 1990; Meyers 2002; Miles and Irvine 1992; Tinetti et al. 1991, 1992; Werner et al. 1989) US regulation requires that restrained residents be released, exercised and repositioned every two hours to avert these deleterious consequences.

The fact that restraint can be a tool of discipline is demonstrated by a study of what were the predictors of failure to comply with these rules for the release of restraints. The three main predictors of residents remaining continuously restrained were staff perceptions of residents' verbal aggressiveness, their physical aggressiveness and their unpleasantness (Schnelle et al. 1992). In the 1980s we even saw it recorded in nursing notes that a resident was being tied up to be punished. Evans and Strumpf (1990: 126) quote one resident who indicates how punishing it can be: 'I felt like I was a dog and cried all night. It hurt me to have to be tied up. I felt like I was a nobody, that I was dirt. It makes me cry to talk about it (tears). The hospital is worse than a jail.' An 84-year-old woman experienced restraint like this:

> I don't remember misbehaving, but I may have been deranged from all the pills they gave me. Normally, I am spirited, but I am also good and obedient. Nevertheless, the nurse tied me down like Jesus on the cross, by bandaging both wrists and ankles . . . It felt awful, I hurt and I worried, 'What if I get leg cramps; what will I do when I can't move?' . . . Because I am a cooperative person, I felt so resentful. Callers, including men friends, saw me like that and I lost something; I lost a little personal prestige. I was embarrassed, like a child placed in a corner for being bad. I have been important . . . and to be tied down in bed took a big toll . . . I haven't forgotten the pain and indignity of being tied.
>
> (Evans and Strumpf 1990: 126)

More fundamentally than being a form of punitive discipline, throughout and presumably prior to the 1980s, restraint was routinized discipline. In our 1988 fieldwork we discovered the following remarkable quality assurance program (see Table 3.1) being implemented in several Chicago nursing homes by the quality assurance manager of a chain. It was a program that from 1990, after the Untie the Elderly Campaign, might have cost a nursing home its licence. But in 1988, we saw it implemented without any critical

Table 3.1   Resident risk assessment program

Mild or no risk	Moderate risk	High risk
0–4	5–7	8–11
Two rails up	Two rails up	Two rails up
May need instructions for safety	Vest when warranted. Patient must be assisted in all activity	Close to nursing station if possible. Vest at all times. Hand restraints, when necessary. Check patient frequently

comment and indeed with an implied commendation that at least the head office of the chain was investing in a QA manager to do this.

When we questioned whether it was appropriate to automatically restrain high-risk residents, the QA manager simply told us better safe than sorry, better to do too much than too little. Then when we queried whether some low-risk residents determined to be mobile would be put at greater risk by bedrails when they climbed over them, it was conceded that some would be safer with the bedrails down. There could be discretion here. But best to train the aides with a simple standard rule to keep the bedrails up.

Given how entrenched the problem was, the reduction in the level of restraint seemed remarkable when in the early 1990s we observed it being halved. The improvement then progressively continued. At the time of writing the US has a recorded level of physical restraint of 4 per cent compared to 42 per cent in the late 1980s. At first, cynics argued that chemical restraint was being used as a substitute for physical restraint. But it is now clear this was not right. While antidepressant use is up (a good thing in the view of most experts because depression in nursing homes is under-diagnosed and under-treated) (Harrington et al. 2005: 40), antipsychotic prescriptions have halved in US nursing homes since the social movement against physical and chemical restraint was launched (Garrard et al. 1995; HCFA 1998: vol. 3, 417–49).

The data do not support any causal association between increased enforcement actions concerning restraint and this reduction. On the contrary, restraint citations have fallen considerably since the 1980s, as one would expect with so much less restraint happening.[8] That said, we observed the Untie the Elderly Campaign to change the way inspectors responded to restraint. In the 1980s we observed a great deal of what Patterson (1982) has shown to be the ineffective social control technique of 'nattering' on the restraint issue. Here is a typical 1989 encounter with nattering:

Inspector: She doesn't need to be restrained.
Nurse: Well the doctor thinks so, that she is at risk of a fall.

While the inspector is not convinced and does not look convinced, she does not press a confrontation on the issue. She just walks on and the resident continues to be tied up. After 1990 we noticed that nattering disapproval in these cases was replaced by confrontational disapproval: 'I don't care how many doctors orders you have, you have not documented a convincing case that this resident should be restrained' (1993 inspection). The inspector post-1990 would keep on the nurses' backs until they called the doctor while the inspection was still underway to say the inspectors were challenging the necessity to restrain this resident (see Chapter 4 for their strategies to accomplish this). By the pre-exit conference, the administrator was in a position to advise inspectors that the restraint order had been revoked or that the care plan was being changed to implement a gradual reduction of restraint. No restraint deficiency would be written. The street-level regulatory accomplishment was not achieved by formal sanctions, but by a shift from nattering disapproval to confrontational disapproval with follow-through.

Educative appeals by inspectors were also important. Inspectors would talk about what other facilities who were respected industry leaders had done to reduce their level of restraint. Inspectors were the street-level communicators for disseminating the change of elite professional opinion accomplished by the Untie the Elderly Campaign. They would explain that restraint was more a cause than a solution to tort risk; they would argue that in the long run reduced restraint would reduce rather than increase demands on staff time. But all of this was enabled by the campaigning genius of Elma Holder and the National Citizens' Coalition's ability to network with progressive industry leaders who were already restraint-free. The coalition made these industry leaders national heroes at their annual conferences and on Capitol Hill in Congressional hearings associated with the Untie the Elderly Campaign. It was what we will call in Chapters 4 and 10 a strengths-based campaign, where informal praise rather than formal fines was the key regulatory tool.

At the state level, the coalition also gave favourable publicity to states who were early movers in achieving dramatic reductions in levels of restraint, such as Vermont, New Hampshire and Florida. In Chapter 4, we discuss how Florida educated its providers toward the vision of becoming a restraint-free state, leading other states in this regard. Only later did the strategy involve state advocacy organizations attacking state regulators who were national laggards in reducing levels of restraint. In 1991, California, which went along with industry submissions that reforms such as the restraint provisions would make OBRA too expensive, and so resisted implementation, began to come in for public criticism. During this period, the Little Hoover Commission and the National Senior Citizens Law Center vilified California for leaving over 68 per cent of its nursing home residents restrained while most other states were achieving dramatic reductions in restraint (Spiegel 1991: A1). The campaign worked mainly through pride, but there was naming and shaming of states and facilities as well. By 2001 the median level of physical restraint in Californian nursing homes was 2 per cent according to CMS records.

At different points during the 1990s and 2000s states that fell slightly behind other states in restraint reduction experienced campaigns to remedy this situation. For example, between 1994 and 1997 Connecticut saw a Breaking the Bonds Coalition of nursing home personnel, researchers, state officials and professional and industry associations bring its level of restraint down through educational conferences and other means of consciousness raising (HCFA 1998: vol. 2, 355, 374). Wisconsin halved its level of restraint in the early years of the current decade after its normal position as a national leader was put in question by levels of restraint that were above the national average. Georgia did the same in 1996 when the Georgia Nursing Home Association led a consciousness-raising campaign. During the mid-1990s the association sent a letter annually to each home comparing its use of restraints to that of other facilities. Facilities reducing restraints below 10 per cent were awarded certificates by their industry association (HCFA 1998: vol. 2, 356, 374).

The big accomplishments were from what we will call in Chapter 10 moving up a strengths-based pyramid (a politics of professional pride). Then the mopping-up improvements were accomplished by moving up an enforcement pyramid (a politics of professional shame directed at both laggard nursing homes/chains and laggard state regulators and state industry associations). Finally, it must be seen as an accomplishment of networked governance, of a reform coalition nodally led by Elma Holder, that tied together researchers, tort lawyers, progressive providers, leaders of health professions, legislators, insurers, regulatory leaders and street-level inspectors. The National Citizens' Coalition for Nursing Home Reform (NCCNHR) was a node of governance that tied together a web of actors employing a web of regulatory tools – evidence on risks, education, role-modelling excellence, praise and pride, shaming and shame, consultation on alternative solutions and a shift from nattering to inspectorial confrontation with follow-through. Because the old enforcement of the 1980s was ritualistic – ensuring doctors' orders were up to date, ensuring restraints were loosened every two hours instead of removing them altogether – little was lost from the reduction in the actual level of formal enforcement that occurred.

LESS VISIBLE DISCIPLINES

The most visible manifestations of the disciplinary society (restraint and visual surveillance) are complemented by an infinity of smaller less visible disciplines. These include institutional timetabling of visiting, eating, exercising, bathing and moving discretionary control over savings from residents to relatives. In the most disciplinary nursing homes, even when punishment is replaced by attempts to individualize reward and praise, it is done in a way that can be read as discipline, regimenting dignity. For example, in one Chicago nursing home we encountered on corridor walls two certificates headed 'Award for Special Achievement. To John Smith for Six Months Sobriety.'

The regulatory order creates opportunities for relatives to discipline residents even when the facility opts for freedom. In 2004 we attended a heartbreaking informal dispute resolution over an abuse and 'immediate jeopardy' citation of a rural county nursing home in the Midwest. The son of a 92-year-old female resident complained that an 89-year-old male resident was sexually abusing her. All the evidence at the hearing was that there was a sexual relationship, but that it was consensual. The citation had been issued because the son claimed to be his mother's guardian, and his view was that she was incapable of making a decision about a sexual relationship. The evidence was that while she had some cognitive deficits, they did not render her incapable of consenting to a sexual relationship. While only minor formal sanctions were imposed on the nursing home for allowing the relationship to continue, this was a case where *The Process is the Punishment* (Feeley 1979). The male resident was terrified that he might be put in jail. The female resident was mortified at the invasion of privacy of an interview in which she was asked intimate details of her sexual encounters with the man. The staff member who was required to conduct the interview was distraught and ashamed at having done so. All staff of the nursing home, the Ombudsman and everyone at the hearing were struck by the tragedy of a beautiful relationship between two old people ended by fear and repression. The root cause of the tragedy was regulation, rather regulators believing that the 'play safe' position in a matter as sensitive as a sexual abuse complaint was 'if the guardian says no, best to interpret consent as absent. Therefore this is sexual abuse. Therefore the nursing home should be sanctioned for putting the resident in immediate jeopardy.'

In many parts of the United States, nursing home residents do not have what we might call a right to be fat. Mrs Smith, who has enjoyed eating to excess and put up with being fat for 80 long years, is forced to diet when she enters a nursing home. Why? Because the dietician is concerned at what might happen when the inspectors see in Mrs Smith's chart that she is overweight and that the home has failed to protect her health by putting her on a diet. This might get the dietary department a deficiency (and therefore cost the dietician a bonus for a deficiency-free inspection). Even if, in fact, the nursing home is likely to get enlightened inspectors who would not count Mrs Smith's not being on a diet as a strike against the home, the disciplinary order of nursing home employment counsels the dietician to play it safe ('Who ever got a deficiency for putting a fat person on a diet?'). There is in general a contest over the right to do risky things that are utterly uncontested for adults outside the institution: 'Best nursing care may not be possible by allowing them the right to smoke' (nurse nearing retirement in 1987 reflecting on how resident rights had gone too far).

A good illustration of protective discipline being applied arose during an inspection on the East Coast of the US in a nursing home specializing in the needs of Asian residents. The inspectors observed many of the residents, as would be customary in their own homes, to remain all day in housecoats like bathrobes. Following a cultural pattern, they did not wear underwear. Old people being as they are, this resulted in incidents of exposure of private parts observed by the inspectors. The inspectors said they did not want to discourage the residents from customary modes of dress, but they wanted staff to be more sensitive to the privacy and dignity issues involved, and in any case they could not ignore the standard. So they wrote the following citation: 'Privacy and dignity was not always maintained: i.e., four patients were observed with their personal parts exposed and they lacked underwear.' The following plan of correction came back from the nursing home: 'Staff to be in-serviced further on patient dignity and the need to maintain the privacy of all patients. Underwear to be purchased for patients who lack them; underwear to be worn.'

The disciplining of bodies in American nursing homes is not just about their medical regimentation. Grooming was a big issue in many Chicago care planning conferences we observed. For example, a resident whose hair was diagnosed as too greasy would have the care planning objective set for her (without her participation): 'hair to be washed three times a week'. In a New York nursing home we saw documents headed 'Personal hygiene audit sheet'. These included boxes to be ticked beside words like 'neat'; it covered the appearance of clothing, shoes, hair, wheelchairs, and so on.

INSTITUTIONAL SCALE, ROUTINE AND NORMALIZATION

These illustrations of less visible disciplines remind us of Foucault's (1977: 222) aphorism that 'the "Enlightenment" which discovered the liberties, also invented the disciplines'. Indeed, one is tempted to extend it to the present by saying that the post-war United States, which claims some credit for spreading the liberties behind the iron curtain, imposed the disciplines on its own elderly and then sought to export the disciplines through the international expansion of its nursing home chains. There is a global gerontological epistemic community that is American dominated. Even in countries like Australia, which has experienced only modest market penetration by American nursing home chains, there is still some percolation of the American model, mediated through textbooks, gerontology journals, marketing men with new surveillance technologies, industry associations that see more of a future in corporatized caring than in a cottage industry, and visiting gurus. There was even a group that managed 13 Australian nursing homes in the 1990s called Conforme Management! A South Australian director of nursing captured well the concern some feel about the direction of change: 'It's no longer a cottage industry. They are individual people with needs to us. In the new factory industry, they are units. That's why we now need complaints systems and the rest.'

This is an interesting quote, because by making the connection with the 'factory', this director of nursing, doubtless without having read Foucault, is tapping into Foucault's key idea of the carceral archipelago: 'Is it surprising that prisons resemble factories, schools, barracks, hospitals, which all resemble prisons?' (Foucault 1977: 228). The large American nursing home chains cannot help but spread the disciplines. They operate in an industry that poses large regulatory risks, as the near bankruptcy of Beverly Enterprises in the late 1980s illustrates. There is no choice for them, therefore, but to follow the logic of regulatory risk management. That means highly disciplined institutions in which risks (read people) are monitored, recorded and subjected to preventive controls (or at least the appearance of preventive control, so that the organization can be seen not to have neglected the risks embodied in hundreds of standards).

We have already seen how the large American chains owe their very existence to the imperatives of largeness and institutionalization that were products of regulatory choices made in the United States in the 1970s and 1980s, different regulatory choices from those made in other countries. The risk with large institutions is that people and problems can fall between the cracks. Size therefore motivates surveillance, record-keeping and control. Hence, for example, larger facilities are more routine and excessive users of antipsychotic drugs to control people (Hughes et al. 2000; Schmidt et al. 1998). This is the essence of Foucault's notion of power as discipline. Disciplinary power does not grow out of the barrel of a gun, not from the edicts of a monarch or a judge, not from the control of capital, as do other forms of power. Disciplinary power works through the construction of routine; it can be seen in its most developed form when a total institutional environment is designed as a technostructure of control. Bauman summarizes well the change Foucault sees in the way power is exercised with the growth in discipline:

> Power moved from the distant horizon into the very center of daily life. Its object, previously the goods possessed or produced by the subject, was now the subject himself, his daily rhythm, his time, his bodily actions, his mode of life. . . . It wanted to impose one ubiquitous pattern of normality and eliminate everything and everybody which the pattern could not fit. Unlike the sovereign power which required only a ceremonial reminder of the timeless limits to autonomy, the emergent power could be maintained only by a dense web of interlocking authorities in constant communication with the subject and in a physical proximity to the subject which permitted a perpetual surveillance of, possibly, the totality of his life process.
>
> (Bauman 1982: 40)

The crucial theoretical limitation of the Foucaultian perspective for the present problem is that it assumes that disciplinary power is used for 'normalization', by which Foucault means bringing under control, back to normal, the slightest irregularity of conduct. Foucault sees the clinical sciences as instruments of normalization. Yet the clinical sciences and regulation can be instruments of individualization rather than normalization. Chapter 10 is about how Bauman's webs of interlocking regulation can empower residents and personal care workers. Ironically, there is a literature on 'normalization' in gerontology. The author of the term, Wolfensberger (1972, 1985), a gerontologist, means exactly the opposite to the meaning Foucault gives the term.[9] For Wolfensberger and the many health-care professionals influenced by the idea, normalization means shifting power back from institutional routine to individual residents – allowing them to live in a nursing home as free, choosing individuals, just as they do in the 'normal' outside community. Put another way, these health-care professionals have the agenda of normalizing the institution instead of normalizing the subject of the institution. The normalization movement of the 1970s and 1980s laid the foundations for the contemporary regenerative care movement discussed in Chapters 9 and 10 and later in this chapter.

Garland (1990: 174) made the point in his critique of Foucault that there is no inevitability that regulation destroys freedom; regulation, equally, can constitute freedom. Cases in point are standards that require nursing homes to guarantee 'privacy and dignity', a variety of specific 'freedoms', including the wonderful Australian legal mischief of the 'right to take risks' (Commonwealth/State Working Party on Nursing Homes Standards 1987: 49). A useful way of comprehending what is happening within the nursing home industry in the modern world is as a battle between the two normal-izations. Health-care professionals are warriors on both sides of this battle; regulation is a weapon used on both sides of the barricades, though the modalities of regulation favoured by the two sides are very different.[10]

Furthermore, we must not forget that it is specific regulatory choices that created the conditions for a factory industry. Smallness dissolves many of the disciplinary imperatives of the chains of large institutions. For example, the less disciplined staff in smaller organizations tend to have lower turnover (Cotton and Tuttle 1986). Tiny English nursing homes can be justifiably criticized for sloppy record-keeping and abysmal care planning. Yet, in their defence, they do not need such discipline as do American insti-tutions managed by a remote corporate headquarters on the other side of the country. When there are only 18 residents in the home and low staff turnover, the director of nursing knows the problems of all of them per-sonally and intimately. She does not need a systematic information system to ensure that problems do not fall through the cracks. She does not have to worry so much about shuffling staff from A wing, where they know the residents, to F wing, where they do not, because there is only one wing. She does not need a pervasive surveillance system to cover the nursing home because she herself, like all staff, gets into every part of the nursing home many times every day. The more intimate knowledge of every resident's needs that can be accomplished when all staff get to know all the residents means that particularized solutions can be found to problems that more bureaucratized institutions feel they can only handle with a form of disci-pline such as restraint. This is why there is a long history of research in the US and UK showing that smaller homes achieve higher resident satisfac-tion, higher activity levels and lower isolation (Curry and Ratliff 1973; Greenwald and Linn 1971; Townsend 1962). Another factor here is that because convenience of location drives the frequency of visiting (Minichiello 1989), a diaspora of small homes closer to family residences will be more integrated into the community than a smaller number of cen-tralized institutions.

LAYERS OF DISCIPLINE AS DRIVERS OF RITUALISM

The structural imperatives of scale and bureaucratization therefore combine with a disciplinary regulatory system (that is forgiving so long as the appear-ance of remedial inputs is documented) to create disciplinary institutions for the elderly. A little more should be said on how the disciplinary regulatory system is created. What we are describing is a disciplinary regress. Mrs Smith is disciplined by the dietician onto a diet. The dietician has been in turn disciplined to do this by the existence of a state inspector, who is unlikely to understand the details of Mrs Smith's preferences as well as the dietician and who therefore may react to the appearance of poor health care when overweight residents overeat. The state inspector, in turn, is disciplined by the existence of supervisors, a state procedures manual and federal look-behind inspectors, who are even less likely to get close to a nuanced understanding of Mrs Smith's case, but who can readily pick up a failure of an inspector to notice an unclosed loop in records the inspector should have checked. A regulatory system has been created where everyone is regulated by someone else in a culture of distrust in which all are ground through the disciplinary mincer. Demands for regulatory accountability are met with ever more layers of regulation, usually heavily documented to vindicate the new discipline.

Structurally, this situation conduces to ritualism. Getting the documentation right is the way to protect yourself. The way to persuade the disciplinary actor above you is to show her that you are a credible agent for her discipline, passing it on to those below in a way that can be documented to those above. It is the documents and the disciplinary practices that are your defence, not any imaginative or dedicated things you might have done to improve the quality of life of residents. That is, ritualism is your defence – devoting your energies to institutionalized means rather than to a goal like reducing pain. The contrast is palpable at every layer of the regulatory apparatus, in the United States and England or Australia, in the proportion of the time people spend working on documentary defence rather than hands-on problem-solving. Nurses in the United States spend little of their time giving care to residents; that must be left to nurse aides because practically all of the registered nurse's time must be dedicated to the more important task of keeping documents in order. This, in turn, exacerbates the disciplinary quality of nursing homes because there is evidence that registered nurses are less 'custodial' in their attitudes to residents than are licensed practical nurses and that licensed practical nurses are less custodial than nurse aides (Bagshaw and Adams 1986: 242). And many researchers have associated a custodial orientation to poor quality care (Fawcett et al. 1980; Lieberman and Tobin 1983; Moos 1981; Wolk and Telleen 1976). Nurses, with their more caring, patient-centred professional socialization, are sorely needed on the front line as role models of non-custodial care. At the level of the nurse aide, a custodial quality is often engendered in their work by the sheer scope of the difficulties they must oversee, as the following extract from our notes of a Chicago inspection illustrates:

A resident gets up from her seat to move her tray of food [in the dining room] elsewhere.

Aide: 'You can't just get up and move somewhere else.'
   Then the aide finds another spot in the dining room, points to it, says 'you sit there', then walks out. The resident wanders about until I help her, for which she is very grateful. When the aide returns, the surveyor asks her why a resident, who can use only one hand and needs a straw, is not getting help with eating.
Surveyor (to aide): 'What's your name?'
Aide (aggressively): 'Why do you want to know my name?'
   I notice, but the aide has not noticed, that one of the residents has had orange peel in his mouth chewing on it for 5 minutes, during which time two other residents have been laughing at this.
   There is a general pandemonium in the dining room. One resident has wandered around with a spoon full of food and forgotten where his plate is. He is eating another resident's stew with that resident's spoon. Even though it has been brought to the attention of the administrator yesterday that it is against the regulations for residents to be smoking in the dining room especially while others are eating, this is happening again today.

This is the noisy, messy drama of the dining room. The fundamental reason why this is such a punitive encounter, like one sees between a young black man and a police officer on the streets of Chicago, is that a dining room of 25 residents, many of whom need assistance with eating, is supervised by one aide. This aide has three days' experience on the job and has not even learnt that even when a surveyor acts like a cop, you do not respond to them as if they were a cop by declining to give your name! Observing the bedlam, even as an observer one craves the peace of Foucault's 'capillary form' of power which 'reaches into the very grain of individuals', a power where, yes, that resident would sit where the aide told him in his usual seat, where the aide would see the orange peel and remove it from the mouth, where more food found its way into residents' mouths instead of slopped across the table and onto the floor. Such a capillary form of power is what this inspector believes good nursing homes provide. It is missing here, so the nursing home is going to be disciplined at the exit. (They were.) The nursing home in turn will discipline the aide. Indeed, they suggest in their plan of correction that they will take 'appropriate disciplinary action' against the aide, and they will assure that a second aide who is sometimes in this dining room at mealtime (but not today) will always be present (or always be present when inspectors arrive perhaps!) so that the residents will be better disciplined. What will not happen is that enough caring, well-trained staff support will be provided to empower residents to make choices to consume the food they want in an eating experience that is serene. 'That is a possibility in the nursing homes out at Evanston with their considerable numbers of private pay residents.' Here in the city where none are private pay, can that ever happen? Here it is the surveyors enforcing factory care in preference to bedlam.

Nurses' aides have low unionization (12 per cent, concentrated in public and not-for-profit homes), low pay (lower than McDonalds), are more likely to be injured than workers in coal mines or manufacturing plants, and have high annual turnover rates (100 per cent for aides, 56 per cent for registered nurses, 27 per cent for administrators) (Eaton 2000). Most aides work in what Eaton (2000) calls 'Low Quality Nursing Homes' (70 per cent of the homes in Eaton's study) like the Chicago home just described.

Inspectors in the United States spend most of their time alone in a room poring over resident charts. The theory of the OBRA reforms fully implemented from 1995 was that the inspection process would become more resident centred and less document centred. But our research team's observation is of no significant change because the new element of resident interviews has been balanced by extra documents for inspectors to check and extra pieces of paper for them to fill out. Enormous resources are dedicated to documentary accountability checks to ensure that inspectors have completed all their records in the right way; few resources are dedicated to evaluating whether they have done anything to improve quality of care or even to talking with them about how better to accomplish this.

At every level in this hierarchy of mistrust, actors have a more jaundiced view than they should of the competence and capacity for responsibility of those they wish to discipline. The social scientists who advise US governments on the design of nursing home surveys, for example, widely have the view of nursing home inspectors as incompetents who are incapable of dialogic problem-solving, who must be disciplined against deviating from 'objective' survey protocols. These are registered nurses whom they view as incapable of the responsible exercise of discretion, some of whom have run much larger organizations than the departments in which the academics work. The social scientists typically have acquired this stereotype of the untrustworthy, incompetent inspector without ever seriously interacting with inspectors on the job about their reflections on how they achieve progress. Instead, they sit at their computers designing protocols for inspectors-as-dopes, thereby increasing the prospects that inspectors will become dopes. Our truth is that it is the dopes at each level who create dopes at the next rung down on the disciplinary ladder. Good managers empower their staff: in the best nursing homes, one sees nurse aides actively involved in decision-making and rising to the challenge of exercising their discretion to better serve the residents who are their responsibility (Tellis-Nayak 1988). In the worst homes, care managers manifest the jaundiced view of the competence and trustworthiness of aides of this Australian director of nursing: 'A checklist was my way of getting it done. We have to accept that we are dealing with girls who are rote learners. So it's the way I get them to learn. It's not checked off so they say, "Oh, I haven't done it."'

Breaking out of the hierarchical culture of mistrust and ritualism requires advocacy of a new regulatory maturity, a radical break with the documentation-driven obsessions of the past. American social scientists and health scholars who work in this field hold out limited hope because they are central communicators of the culture of mistrust. They tend to view the industry as rapacious and untrustworthy, regulatory managers as captured and feckless, and inspectors as incompetent. Managers in the industry are the actors least capable of effecting a profound change in regulatory culture, notwithstanding the conventional incantations about the power of capital. This is because they are the most mistrusted in a culture of mistrust, because they have most to gain by being untrustworthy. The federal regulators are in a better position to lead than the industry, though they still suffer from considerable mistrust as 'captured regulators' and they have a poor record of policy entrepreneurship, probably because of their structurally weak position within a spending agency driven by the imperative to keep costs down.

NEW ENEMIES FROM WITHIN THE DISCIPLINARY SOCIETY

At an NCCNHR Annual Meeting four visionary providers who had not known each other were placed on the same panel. This meeting was a catalyst for providers with emancipatory visions of aged care to work together to form in 1997 the Pioneer Network. The Pioneer principles are:

- Respond to spirit, as well as mind and body.
- Put person before task.
- All elders are entitled to self-determination.
- Community is the antidote to institutionalization.
- Do unto others as you would have them do unto you.
- Practise self-examination, searching for new creativity and opportunities for doing better.

The Pioneer providers place a lot of emphasis on abolishing institutional dining. Residents are enabled to dine whenever they are hungry with a kitchen that operates like a restaurant. Meals are made to order. A family council as well as the residents' council are seen as important instruments of supporting residents to take control over life choices from the professionals. Residents and staff are grouped into small communities within a larger facility and residents have specific staff assigned to their care within that community of care. The architecture is changed. Central nurses'

Table 3.2   The Pioneer Network culture change

Change from	Change to
Staff write care plan based on what they think is best for your diagnosis	Resident, family, staff develop care plan that reflects what resident desires for him/herself
Care plan attempts to fit resident into facility routine	Care plan identifies resident's lifelong routine and how to continue it in nursing home

stations go. A non-institutional environment is created by an emphasis on animals, plants, gardens and kitchenettes, and homelike decor. Animals and children are also central to revitalized activities that emphasize inter-generational exchange and opportunities for residents to give care. Some of the juxtapositions the Pioneer Network advocates to change the culture of care planning include those in Table 3.2.

An example of a Pioneer Network approach to resident-directed care planning with a diet case is shown in Table 3.3.

Another particularly influential model for transforming institutional care from within that emerged in the 1990s is the Eden Alternative, which has captured the imagination of 300 nursing homes across the US and now is spreading in Canada, Europe, Japan and Australia. There is much shared vision between the Eden Alternative and the Pioneer Network. Eden also emphasizes eliminating the nurses' station as the panoptic hub of an insti-tution. It also emphasizes contact with and responsibility for children, plants and animals. Loving companionship is seen as vital to community-building; loneliness, helplessness and boredom are seen as constant dangers in an aged care institution. Giving care, as in the Pioneer Network, is seen as important for residents. Trust and valorizing the wisdom of elders are also central principles. As in the Pioneer Network, democratizing staff and resident decision-making are important strategies of emancipation as are replacing institutional routines of bathing, eating, sleeping, and so on with resident choice over when all these formerly routinized activities occur.

These principles are even redefining the thinking of the largest, histori-cally most institutional provider of nursing home services in the world, Beverly Enterprises. Beverly is experimenting with the market implications of renovating and breaking up 39 of its institutional homes into 'neigh-bourhoods' of 24 residents with dedicated staff for each sub-community. Pioneer and Eden are simply the most influential variants of emancipatory epistemic community-building in gerontology. In less dramatic ways, one can observe elements of emancipatory models of transcending the

Table 3.3   Illustrating the Pioneer Network shift in care planning

TRADITIONAL CARE PLAN		
Problem	Goal	Interventions
Non-compliant with 1800 cal. ADA diet	Resident will eat only foods approved in ordered diet	Educate resident regarding diabetes, her diet and impact to her health if non-compliant Notify nurse of food hidden in room Monitor for s/s hypo and hyper glycemia Check blood sugar 6 a.m. and 8 p.m. Administer insulin as ordered
RESIDENT-DIRECTED CARE PLAN		
Needs	Goal	Approach
I have diabetes and I take insulin I am aware of recommended dietary restrictions and I choose to exercise my right to eat what I enjoy	I will enjoy moderate foods of my choice	Please provide me a regular diet with no concentrated sweets. Ask me prior to each meal what I would like Honour my requests Daily arguments about food will anger me Check my blood sugar daily at 6 a.m. and 8 p.m. If it is too low or too high, I will discuss with the nurse what I ate that day, and will take responsibility to make better choices Administer my insulin as ordered

disciplined institution being insinuated into institutions by emancipatory professionals. These professionals are the enemy within. They might have been emboldened by NCCNHR and visionary state advocacy groups and ombudsmen, but on the floor, institution by institution, they are the innovators working with residents' and family councils to transform the disciplinary society.

WEBS OF HOPE

The greatest hope for policy leadership toward a radical shift in the culture of US nursing home regulation thence continues to reside with the constituency who have been the policy entrepreneurs in recent decades – the consumer advocates. The National Citizens' Coalition for Nursing Home Reform was particularly effective in shaping the agenda in the 1980s and continues to be important, as does the American Association of Retired Persons. They enjoy a surprising degree of grudging respect from their adversaries in industry and the state. They are in touch with the grassroots of their constituency – the nursing home residents. This gives them a grasp of the failures of regulation from a resident-centred perspective. It is this grasp that led them to campaign so vigorously and effectively for reform in the use of restraints – reform, as we have seen, that has challenged the ritualism of regulation that accepted a pile of physicians' orders as sufficient justification for restraint. The NCCNHR is a coalition of some 200 advocacy organizations and 1000 individual members. A senior Missouri state official said in 1990: 'The most powerful person in the US nursing home industry is not the Beverly CEO (he is weak), not the head of HCFA, nor ANHA, it is Elma Holder.' Elma Holder was the NCCNHR founder and CEO who started out with the support of Ralph Nader, then the Long-Term Care Action Project of the Gray Panthers and then the financial support of the American Association of Retired Persons for NCCNHR.

At the same time, advocacy of a radical renegotiation of the ground rules of US nursing home regulation poses risks and threats to an organization such as the NCCNHR. First, there is the risk that major accomplishments of their social movement would be lost in a radically redesigned regulatory order. One of these, for example, is that the United States is perhaps the only country in the world with a demonstrated capacity to frequently take tough formal enforcement action against nursing homes with deplorable standards. Second, there is the threat involved in conceding that the consumer movement shares with the industry, the lawyers, the regulators and the social scientists a significant part of the blame for the disciplinary, ritualistic quality of American nursing home regulation. The consumer movement does share in this blame because it has been at the forefront of demanding new layers of discipline, the filling out of more pieces of paper to ensure residents are protected. The consumer movement position has not been without paradox in this regard. While it has been an advocate of more and more specific new regulations that require new pieces of paper, in the main it has been an advocate of a more resident-centred process that is less oriented to checking documentation. The policy it has advocated as a matter of broad regulatory strategy has been at cross-purposes with the aggregation of its piecemeal advocacy of an extra bit of discipline here and there. In this, the consumer movement is no less guilty than the industry associations that call for regulatory simplification as a matter of broad regulatory strategy and scream for tighter specification (ergo, multiplication) of regulations as soon as their members complain of inconsistent application of a broader rule.

As politically difficult as it would be for them, it is perhaps only the NCCNHR who have the political respect to initiate a cooperative process with the other industry players to fundamentally rethink the culture of American nursing home regulation. This is what they did on the way to OBRA in 1987 when they brought together many key industry associations, professional associations and other consumer groups such as the Gray Panthers and the American Association of Retired Persons to sign on to consensus positions on how all aspects of nursing home reform should proceed (National Citizens' Coalition for Nursing Home Reform 1987). Ulsperger's (2002: 397) data show that US media coverage of NCCNHR increased every year between 1987 and 1990, and then plummeted in the four years after the major reforms were implemented. It took off again between 1995 and 1999 as the second wave of OBRA reforms were implemented and resisted by the industry in many states.

The success of the Untie the Elderly Campaign is a taste for them of what can be accomplished down this path for the people they represent. Moreover, they already have succeeded with some path-breaking reforms in the direction of an alternative accountability model instead of more and more layers of discipline. These involve increased empowerment of advocacy groups outside nursing homes and of residents' councils within them. Examples are the OBRA reforms empowering representatives of residents' councils and advocates to participate in exit conferences at the conclusion of inspections and earlier reforms to give discussions with residents' councils an important role during the inspection process and to give residents more effective access to inspection reports.

One of the arguments of this book is that dialogic, local accountability based on broad outcome-oriented standards and well-resourced local advocacy is a more hopeful strategy than national accountability based on demands for detailed documentation and a myriad of inputs (see Handler 1986). The American consumer movement has successfully lobbied for a new accountability model based on dialogue with consumers and advocates, though this has been allowed to grow alongside the oppressive old accountability model based on ritualized inputs and paper warfare. So there are grounds for both hope and despair about the future. A next step might be to open up a dialogue about a coherent program to affect the demise of this old accountability model. While it is hard to break out of cycles of mistrust, it should be possible to persuade consumers, workers, owners and bureaucrats that a less disciplining industry culture would allow them all more rewarding lives.

NOTES

1. Asian nursing home development is historically much more recent than in the West and considerably influenced by American models of corporatized care. Our impressions are of a highly disciplined form of institutional care often in large facilities. A recent study reported a prevalence of physical restraint in Taiwanese nursing homes similar to the appalling levels that existed in the United States in the late 1970s (Yeh et al. 2003: 215).
2. We prefer to think of Foucault's discipline of individuals and his actuarial regulation of populations both as forms of regulation, especially in light of our findings on how they work together to steer the flow of events in nursing homes. But this is not a quibble we need to settle to use these concepts in advancing our understanding of what is actually happening at these sites.
3. Consistent with our limited observation that Canada may have been more like the US than England, Cape (1983) found restraint use was greater in Canada than in England by a ratio of 8:1.
4. A reason for watching restrained residents is that physical restraints are an important cause of death in nursing homes (Miles and Irvine 1982). Forty-two per cent of dead restraint victims were found suspended from chairs and 58 per cent from beds. One study estimated that every year one or two residents per thousand die from strangulation by a restraint; in 1992, even after restraint levels had begun to plummet, it was estimated that over 200 Americans were being killed by restraints (Meyers 2002). Higher levels of restraint in the US historically have therefore been a reason for higher levels of surveillance.
5. Chemical restraint may be even more pernicious, though it is less visible. Some surveys have found as many as 50 per cent of nursing home residents on antipsychotic or sedative/hypnotic drugs when only 10 per cent of the sample had a clearly documented mental illness (Sherman 1988). National Nursing Home Survey data analysed by the National Institute of Mental Health found 62 per cent of residents to be on psychiatric drugs, though only 5 per cent of them had psychiatric diagnoses (Special Committee on Aging 1990b: 40). As one state inspector who was a qualified pharmacist put it, in many nursing homes 'drugs can be causing more confusion than psychosis'.
6. Poseys were named after the original owner of the company, Mr Posey, so the warm connotations of the brand name was a coincidental marketing plus.
7. In truth, there have been more successful lawsuits in the United States about residents strangling on restraints than about residents who fell for want of a restraint. Indeed, it is likely that there have been very few successful lawsuits of the latter type (see Special Committee on Aging 1990b: 33 and elsewhere; see also Evans and Strumpf 1989).
8. Immediately pre- and post- the 1995 introduction of the OBRA enforcement guidelines, physical restraints increased slightly as a percentage of citations from 2.5 per cent to 2.9 per cent, but as the absolute number of citations fell sharply in this period, restraint citations also fell in absolute terms (even in this period) from tiny in number to tinier (HCFA 1998: vol. 3, 546).
9. See Wolfensberger (1972). In the 1980s, Wolfensberger reformulated his normalization concept somewhat as 'social role valorization' (Wolfensberger 1985): 'The most explicit and highest goal of normalisation must be the creation, support and defence of valued social roles for people who are at risk of social devaluation' (Wolfensberger 1983: 235). In his Japanese fieldwork for this project, David Ermann found the term 'normalization' to be used in Japanese nursing homes, just as we found it to have been widely imported into Australia.

10. The battle is joined on one side by the majority in the corporatized caring sector who want to be 'given the rules of the game so we can play by them' and the rulebook regulators. On the other side are the bulk of the consumer movement and the outcome-oriented regulators who are interested in a regulatory process that includes dialogue about resident rights and freedoms. We see this contest in an Australian director of nursing who complained about inspectors insisting on individualized care plans: 'Individual care plans are impractical. Nursing homes do not have enough nurses to cope with everyone's choice. There need to be rules.' The same director of nursing also said: 'Restraints are necessary. It is criminal to allow residents to fall when this could be prevented.' The contest over discipline and freedom are not peculiar to the US, only more central in the history of its regulation.

4. American regulatory strategies

While this book finds the US to be an exceptional case of more adversarial aged care regulation than the rest of the world (Kagan 1991), the bigger story of this chapter is that there is on the ground, nevertheless, great diversity of regulatory strategy. While the big American contest has been between deterrence and consultancy visions of regulation, strengths-based approaches, praise, education, persuasion, incapacitation, leadership to push up through a ceiling in a way that pulls laggards above a floor, 'just wearing them down' and a great variety of other approaches are part of the regulatory mosaic.

Day and Klein (1987b) conducted an exploratory study of nursing home regulation in New York, Virginia and England. They concluded that in terms of Reiss's (1984) dichotomy, New York was a case of deterrence regulation, England and Virginia of compliance regulation. Our own fieldwork in the late 1980s and early 1990s in these three jurisdictions broadly confirmed their conclusion, based on interviews and observation of a completely different set of actors in the field than Day and Klein's informants. We found, however, that the concepts our informants used were not quite deterrence versus compliance, but deterrence or enforcement versus consultancy. Not only is using consultancy more faithful to our informants' conceptualization, it is also a more analytically concise concept, as we hope will be revealed in the discussion below. While Virginia fell between the extremes of New York and England, when we first visited in 1988 it was more like England. We were told that in the past 40 years the state had only taken a nursing home to court once. They had had only half a dozen formal hearing processes with nursing homes in the previous four years. By follow-up fieldwork in all three jurisdictions in 2004, Virginia was more like New York and less like England. Consultancy as a regulatory strategy had substantially withered. The regulatory process had become more formal, though hardly more demanding. New York also converged toward Virginia in that 1990 was the high-water mark of deterrence in New York nursing home regulation (Harrington et al. 2004; Rudder and Phillips 1995).

We found Virginia in 2004 to have moved further away from the consultancy model of inspectors advising homes on what they might do to improve compliance. Both we and Day and Klein (1987b: 333) found New York populated by state program administrators strongly animated by a desire to prevent field staff from playing a consultancy role: 'We have to continuously remind them that they shouldn't be consultants.' In fact, today all US states exercise a lot of discipline over inspectors against consultancy through their middle managers who are accountable to CMS (the federal regulator).

At the same time, in 2004–05 we found the phenomenon of heads of state health departments who felt they were finally making some real progress with a consultancy approach to eliciting continuous improvement in their hospitals and had become critics of the highly prescriptive, deterrence approach that CMS in Baltimore forced them to adopt in the nursing home side of their regulation. The head of the health department in one large state said this was a 'sore point' with Baltimore, but he was quite defiant about changing his people – 'we try to be creative' in doing more education and consultation. Outside the annual survey (inspection) process there remain to this day significant consultancy aspects to American regulatory strategy. When a nursing home opens a new wing, for example, state agencies will often do a 'consultation' on how to meet the standards in the circumstances of the new layout. Of course, when the state puts in a receiver to run a home that has persistently failed to meet standards, this in a sense is a draconian form of consultation! Other evidence comes from the Medicaid Inspection of Care (IOC) to assess whether individual residents were getting the care mandated by their level of Medicaid funding (and that this was appropriate to their level of disability). The OBRA reform implementation of 1991 abolished the IOC in most states. Until 1991 some states had twice as many IOC nurses visiting nursing homes annually as surveyors. The IOC nurse inspectors who we often encountered and observed in nursing homes before 1991 were much more consultative than the surveyors.

The City of Chicago nursing home inspectors who we also saw regularly at work were also even more consultative than the state surveyors. They were much less thorough than state inspectors, but had more of a relationship with home management because they were dropping in four times a year (in the mid-1980s it was monthly). Veterans' Administration inspectors who came to check on the care veterans received were also consultative. And so were fire marshals and accreditors of the Joint Commission on Accreditation of Healthcare Organizations when they came in. Nursing home beauty shop inspections by state boards of cosmetology, Blue Cross inspections, city and county building inspections, city and county sanitation or health inspections also were often consultative. Most importantly of all, every state in the US has an ombudsman program, many with volunteers of limited experience, but also a core of professionals with a great deal of experience, who have always done considerable consultancy. As the New York Ombudsperson put it, 'We are problem solvers, not policemen.'

Hence, viewed as a whole, there was a great deal of consultancy regulation going on in US nursing homes, and there still is, though not as much as there was, and not as much as in England and Australia.

The inspection philosophy is that if inspectors advise a nursing home on what they should put in their plan of correction for a failure to meet a mandated outcome and then it turns out this solution does not work, the state might be compromised in its capacity to take enforcement action against the home for subsequently persistently failing to meet the standard. If nursing homes need consultancy advice, they should buy it in, not use state inspectors in a way that confuses their role as law enforcers. We were told the story of an inspector who noticed that the 'roof is leaking' and told the administrator to 'fix the roof', something that cost $300 000. Unfortunately, it subsequently became clear that the stains on the ceiling were condensation from a pipe.

Consumer groups have consistently advocated an anti-consultancy line and CMS has long agreed that it must not fund state inspectors to do any consultancy and must discipline them if they slip into it. This started in the 1970s campaigns to toughen enforcement. It is a classic case study of US adversarial legalism (Kagan 1991). Many health lawyers promoted this analysis in alliance with consumer groups; indeed, many of the consumer group leaders were legally trained. Chapter 4 of the Ohio Nursing Home Commission report (1978), *A Program in Crisis*, was entitled 'The failure of the consultancy model.' This report in turn cites a like report of the Texas Attorney-General: 'The role of consultant demands that agency personnel view violations of regulations as problems to be overcome through better consultancy and not as conduct to be punished' (Ohio Nursing Home Commission 1978: 56). The report notes the commitment of the Ohio Department of Health to consultancy and links this causally to various cases of nursing homes providing egregiously poor care without being closed by the department. The possibility that a regulator might simultaneously have a commitment to consultancy at the base of a regulatory pyramid escalating up to closing of nursing homes when consultancy persistently fails was not considered. This would have been the responsive regulation analysis of the data in the Ohio Commission report of 1978 – that the problem was not the presence of consultancy but the absence of the backbone to take tough enforcement against substandard homes.

The leadership of most state survey agencies in the late 1980s were resisters to the crushing of the consultancy model, though there were important exceptions such as California, whose leadership had an absolute commitment to the displacement of consultancy with enforcement. By the late 1990s most of those resisting state regulatory leaders had gone; capitulation to the demise of consultancy was near universal. In many states, however, we saw different leaderships come and go that would in effect see-saw back and forth between more emphasis on deterrence and more on consultancy, and these were the terms in which they articulated the contest of regulatory models. The current decade has actually seen a rediscovery of the value of consultancy, top-down from CMS. This has arisen because of a new safety and quality movement in hospitals being rolled out by CMS through federal funding for state Quality Improvement Organizations with a general remit to cover quality improvement in all health services, including nursing homes. In the nursing home domain, however, this state-supported consultancy is kept totally separate from state enforcement agencies.

In this new mood of tolerance of the feds for the very idea of publicly funded consultancy, however, state survey agencies such as Maryland, New Jersey, California and Wisconsin have established small separate state-funded nursing home consultants. This was a big shift for California where in this decade, in contrast to the 1980s, we were told by inspectors that both the state and CMS have less of a 'gotcha' attitude. The largest and perhaps most sophisticated of the new generation of consultancy programs is in Washington, where the state survey agency has 30 registered nurses who visit unannounced and do quality assurance assessments. It is notable, given the fear that state consultancy will corrupt state enforcement, that Washington, which has the best resources for consultancy, had the highest rank of all states for enforcement in Harrington et al.'s (2004: 66) study.

Of course, such consultants raise in reverse the problem of role confusion. What does the state consultant do when she sees unusually serious non-compliance that is putting residents at risk? In Maryland in 2005 we were told that if their state Technical Assistance Unit sees something serious, the nursing home will be called in for a meeting with top management of the Department of Health to mark the seriousness of the non-compliance. There is a stern talk and they are told that they will be given a break; there will be no enforcement action because this problem was detected by the Technical Assistance team, so long as the problem is fixed immediately to make residents safe. Because it was only necessary to do this six times between 2000 and 2005, Maryland nursing homes are now more trusting that it will not get them into trouble to be open with the unit. A good way of describing the QA visits conducted by the unit is that they are rather like the English nursing home inspections we will describe in the next chapter.

At all periods during this empirical research, we found quite a bit of wilful, furtive defiance of the injunction against consultancy. Consultancy would generally not occur in set-piece collective encounters such as exit conferences, but sometimes it did. Mostly consultancy would occur one on one. Inspections where some non-compliance was detected, but none of it of sufficient severity or scope to cite, were particularly popular contexts for inspectors to offer advice on what could be done to ensure that this non-compliance was prevented from becoming a pattern. Inspectors see this as about building goodwill, being helpful. Sure the home can hire consultants, 'but since I am here with yet another set of fresh eyes on what's wrong, why not be helpful and give them my point of view?' In one 1990 exit conference that started with an announcement that there were 'no findings or deficiencies but a few things to talk about' one inspector asked if staff could work harder at their care plans. Some issues on a particular resident were instanced in a directive way: 'Can you increase roughage in the diet? Can you address diet in her care plan?' Then the administrator was asked if he could remind the pharmacist to tighten up on his documentation in various ways. In a further spirit of building goodwill for future compliance, the team then ran down a list of positive things they had found (again something the HCFA did not want them to do, lest this be quoted back at the agency by a lawyer should some future enforcement action be taken in this area). Finally, the exit ended with the inspection team leader saying: 'Keep up the good work.' The administrator replied: 'Thank you for your recommendations.' Mission accomplished, goodwill secured, from the perspective of this inspection team defying federal and state policies on how the survey should be conducted. This at a time when the procedural guidelines for the survey process stated:

It is HCFA's policy that facility operators who are in business to provide a certain type of health care, should be qualified to independently manage and operate their institutions in accordance with good business practice. If a facility needs the services of a professional consultant to advise them on business or health related matters, then they should undertake to hire one. Surveyors should not provide such consultation since budget allocations to the States for surveyor staffing resources do not include funding for consultative services. [It did until the mid-1980s.] Also, the surveyor's role as inspector and enforcer may be compromised if the surveyor approves plans of correction that accommodate only the surveyor's suggested remedial action and do not necessarily address the real problem . . . surveyors should never function as consultants and should not delve into the facility's policies and procedures to determine the root cause of a deficiency.

(Health Care Financing Administration 1988: 2)

At the same time, protocols in the 1980s required inspectors to report not only 'deficiencies' which required a plan of correction to be written by the facility, but also 'findings' which did not have sufficient scope (pattern) or severity to warrant a plan of correction or a citation and penalty. This allowed inspectors in semi-formal ways to give the nursing home a break, but implicitly on condition that they work on this problem, because if they did not they might be hit hard next time: 'I'm going to put the standard back in but I'm going to write a statement about grooming. If you don't attend to it, there will be more problems. Miss Francis may want to include that in your next in-service program.'

Today's protocols do not make this distinction between findings and deficiencies, thus institutionalizing fewer opportunities in the process to 'give them a break' while 'giving them a warning'. On the other hand, street-level bureaucrats find their own ways of doing the same thing – for example, a 2004 California inspector's warning to nursing home administrator: 'I'm not going to write it, but I'm just pointing it out so it does not slip further.' In the same year, in one day of observing a Michigan inspection we counted a dozen little consultations akin to the following that included a diagnosis of a root cause (in this case poor communication between dietary and nursing staff): 'I'll hand it to the dietician; she recognized the problem but nursing did not carry it through. So you have to work together.' In another the sanitarian noticed a resident trip on a beige-coloured fan on a beige carpet: 'Put some bright red tape on them or something.' Many administrators said to us in the US, as in England and Australia, that they look upon the inspectors as a resource, even when they belong to a chain with quality assurance consultants who they view as smarter and more experienced than the inspectors. They still view inspectors as adding a value over and above their sophisticated corporate consultants because in recent times they have been to nursing homes all over the state. Preventing carbon copy accidents is one area where consultancy is frequently used and valued. For example, a Texas sanitarian notices oil leaking from the hydraulic mechanism in a lifting chair. He tells the nurse: 'Have a medical repair mechanic check this.' Then he tells a cautionary tale of a bad accident in another facility where a chair crashed after oil had been leaking from the hydraulic mechanism for weeks before.

The most common piece of highly valued advice inspectors give is 'X home upstate had the same problem as you. If you give Mary Smith a call at X and mention my name if you wish, I am sure she will give you the benefit of their experience.' Note also that this does not run the risk of the nursing home implementing a solution that does not work and then pleading in mitigation that they were just doing what the inspector told them to do. In this common scenario, the consultancy of the inspector goes no further than the suggestion that Mary Smith could be a helpful person to chat with in deciding how you craft your own plan of correction. The head of one state survey agency said:

What we've done in the US is cut off communication with the industry and it's led to a downgrading of care. Who has more information about how things are done in the health care industry than surveyors? So long as they say when they are passing on experience from other facilities: 'It worked for them. It might not work for you.'

Helping is what comes naturally to a nurse socialized as a caring professional; a role focused ruthlessly on law enforcement does not. 'By helping the facility, we are helping the residents' (Chicago nurse inspector). Our interviews also confirmed that nursing home administrators appreciated this kind of encounter: 'We do things automatically. We need someone to come in from outside and make us look at things differently. See ourselves from a different perspective. That's good . . . They don't consult but when they do you open up more – say this is my problem, what do you think?' (Chicago administrator 1990).

While some inspectors in the late 1980s agreed with the federal policy of banning consultancy, a lot of agreement among both the inspectors and the inspected was expressed that this was a policy that would reduce openness and trust. Here their thinking was in line with that of Zartman and Berman (1982: 33) in *The Practical Negotiator*: 'Trust is enhanced if a negotiator can demonstrate a genuine interest in trying to help the other side reach its objective while retaining his own objective and making the two appear compatible.' Another suburban Chicago administrator described a 1988 meeting 'with the feds' in which the HCFA officials said: ' "Why should we give you a cookbook? You have been in the game for long enough." We administrators were furious. I see this as the feds fostering an adversarial atmosphere.' In another 1990 Chicago inspection, a director of nursing said:

> We don't want them in as policemen. They get more respect from us if they come and help us out. It does not help if they act like they have a whip to hit us with. If you are not trying, Gestapo tactics might be OK. When you are doing your best, they should be more gentle. When you are coming here you are coming into our home. Just like anyone's home, you're going to see some irregularities. But you shouldn't go by the book. You should find out why. Take into account individuality. The book is not a human being. They need a little more feeling and understanding.

Today this is not such a lively debate. The industry has capitulated to the policy of in general eschewing consultation in favour of enforcement. Nevertheless in 2004 and 2005 we observed a lot of consulting on the side that was appreciated by homes, often little things like a dietician inspector helping the kitchen to make up a recipe for a powdered protein for a resident who needed it. All health professionals have histories that mean for some of the multifarious problems that come up they are the only person in the room who has experience about best practice in that particular situation. In one Chicago home two nurses were pondering, but did not know what to do, when an aide told them he could not understand how this resident's pan came to have a small amount of urine with sediment in it. The inspector arrived on the scene and asked the aide: 'Has he just done this or has it been sitting for a long time?' Aide: 'Don't know.' Inspector: 'Get him to do another and if it looks like that, test it.' Experienced inspectors know that this kind of advice only takes 20 seconds, builds goodwill because it is so appreciated, helps the home and a patient, and is very unlikely to return to bite the inspector.

There is routinely a deep tension between consultation effectiveness and enforcement effectiveness which most of the time in the US even today is tacitly decided in favour of consultancy effectiveness. The Chicago nurse inspector observes a poor infection control practice in the treatment of a wound. She turns to John Braithwaite and explains that her choice now is to observe a lot more wound treatments over the next three days to establish a pattern of poor practice on such a serious matter that will result in the home getting a heavy fine. Or she can correct the nurse immediately and explain to her why her care runs a grave risk of spreading infection from the wound. As soon as she puts the home on notice that something this significant has happened during the inspection, she can be sure that all nurses who treat wounds will be told they need to be especially careful not to make this mistake again during the next few days.

Dietician inspectors explained that enforcement action is much more likely to be successful for nursing homes failing to comply with special diets if residents are observed actually eating what they should never be allowed to eat. But of course the instinct of a caring health professional is to intervene as soon as he sees a resident about to ingest something they should not. With the administration of medications, the tension between gathering evidence for enforcement versus problem-fixing is particularly acute. In the case of the med-pass observation, inspectors generally do not stop the LPN from issuing the wrong drug or the wrong dosage because the whole point of the process is to validly compute a med-pass (drug administration) error rate. However, if they detect in time something life threatening as a result of Mrs Smith getting Mrs Smythes's pills, they do intervene to prevent the harm and compromise the calculation of the error rate.

STRENGTHS-BASED INSPECTION

It is unusual for consulting and praise for improvement to occur in the actual exit. A more common recourse is to conduct the exit by the book, and then, as the team packs up to leave, throw out comments like: 'Communication at mealtime is what impresses me about this place. The staff working together. "This one needs some help. You do this and I'll do that." They're really talking to each other.' As the head of one state agency said: 'If you say only negative things you leave there and it looks like everyone has been whipped to death.'[1] We did indeed observe that scene many times in the US. Though the survey process is designed entirely around correcting weaknesses, it was common in the US, though less so than in England and Australia, for inspectors to have a strengths-based philosophy. This philosophy is that the best way to improve is to build out from your strengths and ultimately these strengths will grow to conquer weaknesses or to compensate for them.

Another part of the strengths-based philosophy is the belief that human organization is collective. So with an old person, concentrate on regenerating strengths – they can lean on their friends, family and carers for their weaknesses. Similarly, with nursing home staff, if we build out from everyone's strengths, the chances that the weaknesses of one individual in a work group will be covered by the strengths of another will be much improved. Similarly with a team inspection – cultivate the strengths of individuals and compose teams to complement one inspector's weaknesses with another's strengths. A virtue seen in this philosophy by regulators who subscribe to it is that everyone in aged care is part of a community of care, each helping one another to build their strengths. Whether one is a resident, a provider or a regulator, one can share in the integrity, the holism of a strengths-based philosophy.

Contemporary nursing and aged care professionalism around ideals such as regenerative care and restorative nursing are hospitable to a strengths-based approach, as are various strands of contemporary regulatory thinking around restorative justice and continuous improvement. So it is perhaps not surprising that this philosophy has been so tenacious in the United States against the pressure of three decades of deterrence-oriented regulatory reform and bureaucratic discipline utterly hostile to strengths-based inspection.

Partly this is also a strategic philosophy of inspection. In any organization there will be friends and enemies of compliance. On this philosophy, it is more important to know your friends than to know your enemies. What you try to do is 'strengthen the hand of those who are going in the right direction internally'. It has been a recurrent observation in the occupational health and safety literature, for example, that inspectors will often find the safety manager as their ally in a coal mine or a factory whose management are committed to cutting corners on safety. Once a good relationship has been established with that safety manager, they will often lead the inspector to a problem they have been unable to persuade management to fix (Braithwaite 1985; Hawkins 1984, 2002). The inspector and the safety officer in effect conspire to get that problem written up in the inspector's report, so the safety manager can say to senior management that now they must fix this or they will be exposed to future penalties or future civil litigation for failing to solve a problem identified by the state. We saw a lot of this in nursing homes, the inspector who winks at a department head as he walks out of the exit conference and whispers 'Did I do a good enough job for you?' Inspections can strengthen the quality-conscious administrator's hand in dealing with resistant staff as well. For example, a North Carolina administrator: 'An advantage of the regulations is that you can avoid arguments with staff who don't want to do things. It takes the personalization away from a lot of the things that need to be done. It's not me asking for it, it's the law.'

Many problems of neglect are subtle, nuanced, matters of degree and therefore matters of difficult judgment. I might observe a dining-room scene and pick out a resident who I believe is neglected because they are not receiving enough assistance from the aides with eating. You might disagree upon observing the same scene. You might think that resident is not eating because you, like the aides, have noticed a cue from the resident that suggests they have already had enough to eat. While going hungry is a matter of profound importance, it is just plain difficult to judge who is right in this situation. The standard contemporary American inspection approach to this dilemma is to follow a certain kind of rule of optimism (Dingwall et al. 1983): if there is doubt about your capacity to prove neglect, ignore it. If the team leader perceives a lack of consensus within the team on whether a deficiency should be written, they will normally veto it in accord with this rule of optimism. The strengths-based inspector reframes this problem by a focus on excellence rather than neglect. She spends a lot of time in the dining room. When she sees attentiveness to residents who need assistance with eating, she praises that. Then she might gather all the aides together in the dining room at the end of the meal, summarize all the good things she has seen, and ask them how they could improve further. 'Are there any other residents who you think might need the extra assistance that I saw you give Mrs Jones?' Perhaps they will mention Mr Smith, who the inspector is concerned about. If not, she can say, 'What about Mr Smith? He is the only one who I wondered if he needed more help.' Perhaps then the inspectors will learn that they are wrong about Mr Smith and perhaps the aides will learn that they need to build on their strengths to make Mr Smith a beneficiary of them. Whichever of the foregoing is true, the philosophy of the strengths-based inspector is that uncertainty about an important concern is not a reason for doing nothing. The rule of optimism of the enforcement-oriented inspector is the path to neglect.

A key skill of the strengths-based inspector is being a good listener. You cannot build strengths without empowering those with the strength. A mistake we observed many neophyte inspectors in Australia to make when they had a strengths-based philosophy, but executed it badly, was to jump in quickly with communicating expectations on what kind of improvement is desired. More sophisticated practitioners of this philosophy were more patient, encouraging nursing home staff to tell their own story of how they were building on their strengths, what their plans were for future improvement. Kay Pranis (2000) argues you can tell how powerful a person is by how many listen to their stories. When the President visits a town, many come to listen; when a beggar arrives in a town, most try not to listen to what he utters. It follows that we can empower people by the simple act of listening to their stories, making their stories the point of reference for the stories we contribute to our conversation with them. Therefore, good strengths-based inspectors are accomplished listeners. Through their listening they help convince staff that yes they do have the power in their own hands to improve further. American inspectors are mostly very good listeners to nursing homes' interpretations of whether they, the inspectors, have got their facts right in finding a deficiency. They are good at speaking first with their story on why they think the home is not meeting the standard and then listening to why they might be wrong. This is because they are socialized to a conservative approach to writing deficiencies – better for your career if the home tells you that you are wrong before the matter is written than for your boss or a judge to do so. They listen to check their stories because they follow a rule of optimism (Dingwall et al. 1983) about nursing home compliance – if in doubt, assume compliance. But this is not listening that builds strengths in quality of care; it is listening that builds competence in game-playing with excuses, mostly documentary excuses, that make it possible for the inspector to follow the trouble-free course of the rule of optimism. It is not strengths-based listening because the starting point is not the home's story of what they are doing to build quality.

In Chapters 6 and 9, we will see that Australia is the jurisdiction that has the strongest strengths-based practice of nursing home inspection. In this section, however, we have seen that there are more than glimpses of it in the US, just as there are in England. Strengths-based inspection is part of the complex tapestry of how inspectors, in all nations we have been able to observe, manage to get things done.

CATALYSING CURE OF ROOT CAUSES

A common compromise for inspectors who wanted to help solve problems without disempowering the home was to consult in a non-directive way – what Bardach and Kagan (1982) would call diagnostic inspection and we

would call catalytic inspection: 'We need more creative juices on care planning' (silence, waiting for creative juices to come back!). Often catalytic
inspection would take the form of enforced self-regulation. Instead of
telling the nursing home how to solve a problem, the inspector would tell
them they expected to see a written plan to solve that problem and evidence
that the plan was being implemented and working. This could range from
big issues like requiring an infection control plan to noticing a single minor
incident of a resident with jagged nails and suggesting a nail care program
that makes it impossible for any resident's nails to be forgotten. Or the
freshness of the bread:

> *Inspector:* I'm not writing it, but maybe you need to look if your system for rotat-
> ing the bread is working.
> *Administrator:* We will. I think there is an issue with the Kosher bread.

The following inspector had a more generic approach to catalysing self-
regulation:

> *Inspector:* Self-inspection is the key to deficiency-free surveys.
> *Administrator:* We'll be doing that every three months on each department soon.

One of the mysteries of US official nursing home regulatory policy is how
regulators can judge whether a plan of correction is satisfactory without
having a view on what are the root causes it should address. This is the
essence of the ritualism of the US plan of correction process. In previous decades the inspector who visited the home would approve the plan
of correction. Today a supervisor in a regional or head office does that.
They approve plans of correction not so much on the basis of a judgement of whether they will work to solve the problem, but on the basis of
whether they will pass the muster of audit by a federal officer. In 2004 a
Virginia supervisor said: 'Do we guide them? We probably do. It's a
phone tag kind of game.' But the phone tag is not consultancy on how
to solve the problem so much as consultancy on how to fit in with the
requirements of the information architecture of federal regulation of
state regulation.

The diagnostic/catalytic inspector, in contrast, is implicitly looking for
root causes and demanding systemic solutions that work. One inspector
explained how she defied federal policy of not diagnosing root causes by
asking questions such as, 'Why do you think these systems aren't working?'
A New York state survey regional office manager said: 'The more the
system is closely defined for us the more we lose our ability to see the big
picture.' In other words, only street-level bureaucrats have the holistic local
knowledge to see root causes clearly. This approach fails, however, when

management of the nursing home lacks the managerial competence either to craft a systemic solution or to implement it effectively. Just as consultation after consultation will not work in these cases, so plan of correction after plan of correction will not work, and so punitive penalty after punitive penalty will not work. In contexts of 'yo-yo compliance', regulators must do the root cause analysis and find the root cause of the recurrent problems when management is not up to the complex task of assuring quality of care. Deterrence regulation then must be replaced with an incapacitative remedy such as forcing the proprietor to put in a new management team, imposing a state-appointed administrator, forcing the proprietor to sell or, if there is no hope along these paths, closing the facility and moving residents to a safer place.

PRAISE

The most important communication tactic for building out from strengths is of course praise. Both we and Day and Klein (1987b) found US nursing home regulation to be more formal and less familiar than English inspection. On an initial tour of the facility during the English and Australian inspections, there was much more emphasis on the administrator or director of nursing accompanying the team and introducing the team to all and sundry staff. English and Australian inspectors were more likely than American inspectors to offer praise to a staff member both during the tour and throughout the inspection, for example for a problem in their area that had been fixed or improved since the last inspection, or for some innovative quality improvement initiative they were working on. Following Australian inspections, 68 per cent of directors of nursing reported that the inspectors used either 'a great deal' or 'a fair amount' of praise. Many US inspectors who told us they were surveying for negatives, not for positives, nevertheless were observed to use praise informally. Some of these inspectors would even tacitly use praise in the maximally formal setting of the exit conference. For example, a Californian inspector who was very big on saying to us that it was not his job to praise the nursing home for positives went to a deal of trouble to present non-negatives in a way that implied praise! So in the pre-exit meeting of the inspection team he said: 'We'll cover [med-pass] first, where they had no errors, so we can stroke them a bit first.'

Actually we did not see a US inspection where at some point some informal praise was not expressed. Often it was a little statement that seemed to have a big impact. For example, an inspector was talking to the administrator in her office. The person responsible for pest control came in.

> *Inspector:* I'm really impressed with the progress on roaches. It's miraculous really
> the way we've seen that problem under control compared to a few months ago.
> *Administrator:* You've made his day.
> *Pest man:* You've made my week.

We saw evidence in the US of virtuous circles of praise, as in an administrator writing a letter of appreciation to the state headquarters of the
survey agency about the professionalism of a particular inspector. We had
observed this encounter between that inspector and the director of nursing
at an exit in front of her peers:

> *Inspector:* Documentation in the doctor's progress notes is so much better than
> other nursing homes. They are the same doctors, so I don't know why.
> *Director of nursing:* I'm so proud you brought that up because we worked hard
> at that.

The head of nursing home licensure in Florida in 1990 said she liked each
exit to have a 'bouquets' section and a 'watch for the future' section. The
former builds strength and confidence to do the latter well. Care staff get
many of their rewards from the job from evidence that they have done
something that has made things better for a person who is suffering. But
this intrinsic feedback occurs less frequently in care of the frail aged than
in acute care in, say, hospital nursing. With the sickest residents needing
the most intensive care, communication is too minimal to permit this
encouraging feedback. This is the context of praise from inspectors being
important. Massachusetts director of nursing: 'The rewards of nursing
are thanks from your patients. With nursing home patients, they aren't
very responsive. Sometimes facilities are not there or not encouraging. So
it's important for the surveyor to give praise.' In our qualitative research
we would see Mrs Jones glow after an inspector said to her: 'Mrs Jones,
you're a wonderful nurse.' After an exit with a lot of praise, we observed
90 minutes later another manager stopping the director of nursing in the
corridor, putting his arm around her, almost cuddling her: 'Good job.'
Director of nursing: 'The whole staff did this.' So we observed self-
conscious communication work to fuse multiple individual prides into
corporate pride. Praise by these US inspectors triggered processes of
intra-corporate praise that engendered the collective pride that is the
stuff of high workplace morale and high performance (Cotton and Hart
2003).

Systematic quantitative evidence from 410 Australian nursing homes is
consistent with our ethnographic work in this regard. Inspection teams who
used praise a lot as a regulatory strategy improved compliance in the two
years following an inspection significantly more than inspection teams that

did not (Makkai and Braithwaite 1993a). This remained true after efforts to control for how deserving of the praise homes were. The study concluded that when collectivities are praised, all involved individuals want to share in the credit and when individual members of a collective are praised, the collective claims a share of the individual praise. In contrast, when collectivities are blamed or punished, each involved individual tends to believe it is someone other than them who is responsible; when individuals are blamed, the collectivity tends to disown or distance itself from the individual. This is why the collective dynamics of informal praise make it a more powerful form of social control of collectivities than blaming.

In the 1980s, a number of US states presented 'Superior Facility' awards or five- and six-star rating certificates that would be seen hanging conspicuously in the entrance lobby. This fell out of favour in the 1990s. In Illinois, there were also Governor's awards for 'Excellence in the Field of Long Term Care' and one would see in the 1980s framed in the entrance lobby letters of congratulation sent by local members of Congress to facilities that had performed outstandingly during inspections. The state of New York Department of Health put out press releases each quarter listing the nursing homes found to have no deficiencies. Outside New York City, it was not uncommon for local newspapers to pick up these press releases to run a story about a nursing home providing exemplary care.

While not an officially encouraged part of US inspection strategy today, we have seen that street-level bureaucrats in the US actually use praise a lot. However, one reason they do not use it as much as English and Australian inspectors is that central policies animated by adversarial legalism (Kagan 1991) have real effects in discouraging it, as the following story illustrates. We observed a Californian inspection of a home that had some serious problems. At the pre-exit discussion among the inspection team the consensus was clearly expressed that while there were still some significant deficiencies, there had been substantial improvement since the last inspection. At the exit itself, the deficiencies were soberly read out, one after the other. After undertaking to get moving on fixing these problems, the administrator said: 'Would you have any comment on whether we have improved since last year?' Team leader (uncomfortably): 'No we couldn't comment on this at this stage.' When we questioned the team leader about this later, pointing out the inspectors had agreed at the pre-exit discussion that there had been substantial improvement on many fronts, she said: 'I don't know. We're not allowed to.' Her supervisor, who had joined us for this debriefing, then chimed in: 'We're here in an enforcement role. If Mary says you've done a great job, the administrator will say to another evaluator that Mary says we are great. It makes our job harder. We're here in an enforcement role, not to massage their ego.'

EDUCATION AND PERSUASION

One of the classics of regulatory scholarship is Robert Kagan and John Scholz's (1984) 'The "criminology of the corporation" and regulatory enforcement strategies.' It argues that for those types of corporations that are *amoral calculators*, who will cut corners to increase profit, tough prompt deterrence is the best strategy. Businesses that are *political citizens* generally feel an obligation to comply with law, but are prepared to disobey in domains where the law seems unprincipled, or its implementation capricious or unreasonable. For the political citizens, Kagan and Scholz commend the regulatory strategy of persuasion. A third category of corporation is *organizationally incompetent*. They fail to comply with environmental laws, for example, because they lack managerial competence in environmental management systems or technical competence in say environmental engineering. Education and consultancy are the strategies Kagan and Scholz commend for them. Fairman and Yapp's (2005) study of British local government food inspectorates found that more educative regulators achieved much better compliance outcomes for a sample of 81 small and medium-sized enterprises (SMEs), which most nursing home groups are. They concluded that regulatory education both helps SMEs 'make sense' of requirements (assisting the non-compliant political citizen) and helps remove blockages to compliance and coping with the complexity of compliance (assisting the organizationally incompetent).

Education and persuasion becomes the dominant strategy when new standards and procedures are being introduced in the US, as in England and Australia. As OBRA was being introduced, a large proportion of inspector time was devoted to explaining what they were doing, why they were doing it, why the new process would improve quality of care and convincing management that they would be able to cope with it. One nurse asked of some of the OBRA changes, especially on restraint: 'But is this just a fad that they will change two years from now?'

> *Inspector 1:* No, it's here to stay.
> *Inspector 2:* That's right.
> *Nursing home doctor (with a mixture of irony and sincerity):* Resident rights. We're not for that, are we? We want them to do as they're told, don't we?

The inspector responded non-verbally with a smile and a frown at the same time and gently waved her finger at him. This home had a 'making OBRA fun' program whereby, for example, each staff member simply spent five minutes talking to a resident, getting to know them better. As long as two years after the introduction of OBRA, we observed inspectors refer to the newness of OBRA in saying, 'There are some things I won't cite this year that I would next year.' We found some states to have an unwritten rule that no deficiencies would be found in the first survey for a new facility; it would be an educative survey.

One of the strands of the web of controls that secured the remarkable accomplishment of the post-OBRA reductions in levels of restraint was education and persuasion. The head of the Florida survey agency announced that she wanted Florida to become no less than a restraint-free state. Many educational seminars in cooperation with the industry were convened on how to solve problems without restraining people. Improved statewide performance was announced with recurrent fanfare. 'We have reduced physical restraint from 44 per cent to 37 per cent.' 'Physical restraint is now 22.5 per cent in Florida.' Training and feedback on how the state and the facility were going without any particular incentives, 'the vision thing', was the strategy in Florida. But Florida was also keen to be competitive and successful in comparison to other states in accomplishing the vision. Many states put a lot of effort into persuading physicians who worked in nursing homes to show leadership in support of OBRA, not only on the restraints issue. Missouri, for example, set up a Physician Advisory Committee to consult and build commitment on OBRA implementation.

While enforcement-oriented and consultancy-oriented inspectors tend to disagree on the virtues of praise, they tend to agree that an important part of regulatory strategy is to educate providers on what the standards require and persuade them that the standards are desirable. Consultants think they are in a better position to do this because of the goodwill they cultivate and because they make themselves available to the provider as a resource. Some enforcement-oriented inspectors think this is neither here nor there as it is better to separate education and persuasion from enforcement. Regulators ought on this view to deal with education and persuasion through training courses on the standards, and not rely on the inspection process to sell the standards.

However, when compliance is demanded and withheld during an inspection because the provider thinks the demand is not in the interests of residents, it can be more cost-effective to try to turn around that resistance than in effect say 'well we'll have to see you in court then'. We saw many both enforcement- and consultation-oriented inspectors with formidable skills in the simple art of being 'gentle but firm', as a Connecticut inspector put it. We observed a nurse argue with a Korean-born Chicago inspector in a way that betrayed a misunderstanding of the fault that had to be corrected. She touched the nurse on the hand to stop the retort, and gently but firmly explained why this was not good enough. In fact she insisted on the expected standard twice in this way; a gentle touch, a smile, caring eye contact, then kindly, insistent speech.

David Ermann found education and persuasion to be much more central in Japanese than in US nursing home regulation. He found that inspectors were to 'encourage smooth management' of nursing homes 'through law, advice and leadership'. The sanctions available were few and essentially not used. The function of law was not to underwrite enforcement, but to confer legitimacy and to facilitate coordination between inspector and provider expectations around a focal outcome (McAdams and Nadler 2005). The coordination role of law is not that the law makes it more legitimate to drive on the right than the left side of the road, but that law provides a salient outcome that can prevent cars bumping into other cars, or inspectors bumping into proprietors. Here are some of Ermann's notes from a conversation with a Tokyo nursing home administrator during one of the inspections he observed:

> Asked to characterize inspectors, first adjective was 'gentle'. They exercise their power by suggesting, 'Maybe you can improve things this way.' If there is disagreement, then there is discussion. I asked what happened if the disagreement was unresolved. 'More discussion.' And I asked if the discussion did not convince ever. After again being reminded that inspectors had knowledge from other nursing homes they inspected, I was told such an impasse had never been reached in the 15 years of the administrator's experience. All of this discussion about basic disagreement was pained, strained, highly hypothetical. I asked if they found this discussion too hypothetical and they quickly and strongly agreed despite this being a criticism of my questions. In general, once again I was struck by how willingly nursing home people suspend judgment when faced with the authority of the government. My interpreter, who had spent two years in the US, shared this view of Japanese/Western differences. There seems to be no view here of inherent antagonism between inspectors and nursing homes. Instead it is cooperative with the inspectors having the weight of authority. Eventually we did get a case where the administrator said he had not gotten the required four signatures on a contract, and was told by the inspectors that 'you should improve'. What if you didn't improve? 'They would send a letter.' Still no improvement? The head of the nursing home, and probably the person making the errors, would be fired, though this rarely happens. The nursing home head would be fired because he is perceived (accurately, I think) as having the authority to make things happen.

While these notes reveal much Japanese distinctiveness, it would be wrong to read them as Japanese exceptionalism. It is the contemporary US that is most internationally exceptional. England is more like Japan than the contemporary US. Indeed, Virginia in 1988 was more like Japan than the contemporary US. In explaining why they had only been in court with a nursing home once since 1947, the following exchange occurred between John Braithwaite and a senior Virginian state official:

JB: Do nursing homes ever dig their heels in and say they're not going to institute a plan of correction? Anyone who said 'take us to court and make us'?
Official: Not had anybody tell me we're not going to do it. Not had anybody put
something on a plan of correction and not follow through eventually. Have had
some problem crop up again later, however, having fixed it last time.
JB: What about cases that went to a hearing?
Official: All cases where they said they were going to do it. Cases where we
weren't satisfied that they did it well enough and they think they have done it well
enough.

As in Japan, the providers we met in Virginia in the 1980s viewed the state
as all powerful. In Virginia, as we will see for England in Chapter 5, this
was not grounded in regular imposition of penalties, but in the belief that
ultimately they had the power to close the business, that they were a benign
big gun (Ayres and Braithwaite 1992: ch. 2). The state was also respected,
viewed as responsive and authoritative. A proprietor explains at the end of
one Virginia inspection that he thinks the state might have got its facts
wrong and they need to check this before writing their plan of correction:
'Our experience is that they have not usually got their facts wrong. Its more
often us who have got it wrong.' A longstanding Virginia administrator
made the surprising statement in 1988 that, 'We have never had an unreasonable deficiency. That is, they persuaded us or we persuaded them.'[2] The
contrast is with this genre of plan of correction from a 2004 Wisconsin
inspection that we saw quite frequently around the US, especially in the
latter years of this study:

> Preparation and execution of the Plan of Correction does not constitute admis-
> sion or agreement by this provider of the truth of the facts alleged or conclu-
> sions set forth in the statement of deficiencies. The Plan of Correction is
> prepared and executed solely because the provisions of Federal and State law
> require it. This provider maintains that the alleged deficiencies do not individu-
> ally or collectively jeopardize the health and safety of the residents nor are they
> of such a character as to limit the provider's capacity to render adequate care.

Virginia industry old hands would refer to earlier periods in the twentieth
century where the industry resisted regulation, but by the 1980s it was
accepted as something they learnt from, that improved care for their residents, that was mostly fair. In the 1980s Beverly Enterprises had deep
conflicts in many jurisdictions such as California, but in many others,
including Virginia, Beverly was working productively with the state regulator and seemed to have strong quality assurance systems compared to those
of other providers of that era. This suggests the hypothesis, that we return
to with our English and Australian data, that the culture of regional regulatory communities of regulators, providers, advocates and professions

(Meidinger 1987) may be more important to explaining outcomes for residents than the corporate cultures of chains. As one Virginia inspector said in 1988: 'It may be that what you expect of them is what you get.' Making a rather 'regulatory community' analytic point to explain why some chains that were regarded as problems elsewhere were not in Virginia, she went on: 'It doesn't hurt that you've got an alumni working in private enterprise. Some of their QA staff in homes.' The ombudsman program and the good relationship it has with the regulator was also seen in Virginia as a great network of micro-influence to build a regulatory community for quality care.

The head of the Virginia state regulatory agency said 'We do put homes on termination track. We'd be reluctant to go to court, but we make it clear that we're willing to . . .' [in a rather Japanese way, he said they don't end up in court because 'we wear them down long before then']. Ermann's Japanese notes capture rather well this notion of achieving results through education and persuasion just wearing down resistance and disengagement.

In 1988, while there were states such as California that were more punitive, less into education and persuasion, and more determinedly against consultancy than New York, there were many states that were as reluctant to litigate and as committed to the education and persuasion and consultancy models as Virginia. The head of the Virginia agency in 1988 said to us that Virginia was 'probably around the middle to lower level of all states in punitiveness'. In fact, it has always been in the bottom quartile of punitiveness of all states (see, for example, Harrington et al. 2004).

If 'smooth management', albeit with a great deal of ritualism, is the result of education and persuasion being the central regulatory strategy in Japan, the less central place of education and persuasion in the US compared with all the jurisdictions we have visited has the result that 'cat and mouse' characterizes behaviour at one level of the regulatory game in response to other levels that discipline it:

> *State inspector:* It's a game. Always trying to stay one step ahead of who's regulating you. We are trying to beat the federal government. The facilities are trying to get around us.

One might add the aides are trying to get around management and the residents are often trying to get around the discipline of the aides to make them diet, get out of bed when it suits the aides, refrain from expressing their sexuality, and so on (as discussed in Chapter 3). American culture is deeply suspicious of all levels of the nursing home game because regulatory discipline far too quickly supplants regulatory conversation that might craft communal commitment to a good way of living for the sick aged.

WATCHING THE OLD HANDS

United States inspectors rely on the clout of their own organization much more than British inspectors (see Chapter 5), who compensate most creatively for their punitive weakness by weaving together webs of external influences. Nevertheless, good US inspectors often prefer to keep their own threats in the background by foregrounding their desire to protect the facility from other threats such as tort liability:

> *The inspector testing the temperature of water from a bathroom tap:* It's awfully hot. Some of these people are going to be burned bad. Do you keep records [on temperature checks]?
> *Administrator:* No.
> *Inspector:* Hard to be too careful in this day and age. There's a lawsuit going at the moment as a result of a resident being badly burned by hot water.

We observed that new inspectors were less skilled at such tactics of insistence without making threats than old hands. We also noted that when new regimes were being bedded down, such as the OBRA reforms in the US in 1990–91, and the introduction of the standards monitoring process in Australia in 1988, both sides tend to struggle more with the uncertainties of the new situation by greater recourse to threat. But in normal times, managers such as this one from Missouri represent the conventional wisdom when they say: 'A surveyor who says you do this or I'll pull your licence is out of line. We have fired such people in the past.' We know from the psychological experiments on how people behave in prisoner's dilemma games that irrational competition is reduced by more and higher quality communication between players (Kahn 1984: 298). Weimann's (1982) experiment on the citizen side of dealing with a government bureaucracy found that the least effective strategy in negotiating to get what they want is reciprocal-negative: 'If you don't help me, I will have to turn to your superiors. I will complain.' When the bureaucracy is a government regulator, the most effective appeals are altruistic: 'Please help me. It is a personal problem and you can help me. I really need it.' Almost as effective an appeal in dealing with most types of bureaucracies is reciprocal-positive: 'I appreciate your help. I will thank you personally. You will see that it pays.' Of intermediate effectiveness between these extremes are normative appeals to bureaucrats: 'I deserve this service. Your organization is meant to provide this service.' We therefore interpret the evolution of cooperation (Axelrod 1984) between new inspectors and new nursing home managers, and as new regimes bed down, as experiential learning of how to get improved outcomes for residents with less pain for the negotiators of those outcomes.

Our observations are that deterrence theorists are right to see part of this conversational evolution as capture of the inspectors by nursing homes that actually are well connected politically and can cause inspectors pain by complaining to their superiors. Equally, however, we observe it to involve capture of the nursing home by the inspectors. Mutually empathic, yet assertive, adjustment is a kind of mutual capture of each by the interests of the other. This is not a new insight in the regulation literature. Stenning et al. once likened financial regulation to elephant training, in which elephants and trainers pose very different but real kinds of threats to the other:

> As any experienced elephant trainer will attest, this animal, while potentially very dangerous to work with, can also be a remarkably compliant beast. Even when it is in a docile mood, however, the sheer size and power of an elephant poses a special problem for anyone seeking its cooperation. Indeed, in order to reduce the risk to him and to others to an acceptable minimum, the trainer of an elephant in captivity must develop a sympathetic understanding of the animal. A degree of mutual trust must be established between animal and trainer, such that the trainer's behaviour is as predictable to the elephant as the elephant's is to the trainer. A high degree of skill, tact and sensitivity is required, and the training of an elephant involves not so much the imposition of discipline by the trainer on the animal, as a cooperative acceptance by them both of the need for disciplined behaviour and mutual respect. Since such a relationship does not come naturally to either, it is usually best achieved through a judicious blend of techniques which include persuasion, rewards and sanctions.
>
> (Stenning et al. 1990: 89)

Rickwood and Braithwaite (1994) analysed our data from two rounds of Australian inspections to show that from the nursing home's side, open communication with inspectors pays. First, it pays in improving the quality of care because outcomes improve more in inspections where nursing homes are open with inspectors, after controlling for other influences on improvement. Second, it pays because inspectors know there is a correlation between cover-up and incompetence and dishonesty. So when nursing homes decide not to be open, they run up a red flag. These Australian data therefore support the received wisdom we heard, from both sides of the fence at the street level of US inspection, that openness pays and openness works.

GRADUALLY RAISING THE BAR

Many old hands among both inspectors and the industry had a gradualist vision of the possibilities for accumulated historical change that only becomes major in the long run. While this vision is not completely correct, in that there are periods when rapid reform occurs, as with the sudden reductions in levels of restraint from 1990, we see some validity to it in the way hard things like crowding and choice of food and soft things like decor and activities have gradually but significantly improved.

These old hands have an intuitive grasp of the law and economics insight that there is a turning point beyond which the stringency of change demanded by a regulator actually reverses change in the opposite direction to that desired by the regulator. There is a point where the expected cost of extra staff time to meet regulatory demands becomes greater than the expected punishment cost of attempting to get away with non-compliance. This means it is not true that the more stringent the demands for improvement, the more improvement there will be. Rather there is an optimal level of stringency to entice the economically rational actor to maximize improvement.[3] But, of course, in an iterated regulatory game over the years, once certain kinds of investments have been sunk in past decisions to comply, it can be rational to comply this year when expectations are edged up a bit further rather than face new punishment costs. If expected punishment costs are $10 000 this year, it is rational to spend $8000 to comply, even if one sunk another $8000 last year to avoid last year's punishment threat.

The 'gradual improvement of standards' theorist also says he or she is seeking to achieve 'attitude change' over time. This might be attitude change that this kind of improvement is the right thing to do, or that it is necessary to remain competitive in the struggle to keep the facility full, or some other motivational appeal. On all these fronts, it follows that what will be too high a demand for some providers will be sub-optimally low for others who have already been led further down the path to improvement. The head of the survey agency in one middle-sized state had a sign on his desk:

> See everything,
> overlook a lot,
> correct a little.
> *Pope John-Paul II*

As a former head of nursing home inspection in Australia who subscribed to this philosophy put it:

> You want to encourage the best homes to leapfrog ahead to become front-runners and take pride in the fact that you hold them up as an example of excellence. Then try to get the poor performers to catch up as much as they will voluntarily. Then years later get tough to bed down a new minimum that has been pulled up by the process of front-running and catching up by the average provider.

The idea is that a smart, incremental regulatory strategy uses those who push up through the ceiling to ultimately pull up the floor. Part of this philosophy is that the homes that push up through a ceiling on one issue might be the laggards on another. One 'gradual improvement philosophy' inspector explained to us that you will look to a 30-bed home to be exemplars of excellence on how to create a loving community environment that is like a family home; you will not look to a 200-bed facility for that, but you might look to them to lead up the laggards on excellence in management systems.

When inspectors are pushing excellent facilities to leapfrog further ahead of the pack, collective pride rather than shame or punitive threat tends to be the lever of choice. A collegial model of how staff can help one another improve through in-service training, conversation at staff meetings, care planning meetings and quality assurance committee meetings, or just encouraging conversations on the run in the corridor or at the handover between shifts, are the stuff of improvement. Indeed, the inspector is looking to ensure regulation does not excessively distract the leapfrogging nursing home from nurturing a wider family of influences for improvement. Hence, the following encounter observed in 1990 at an Australian nursing home makes such an inspector glow:

> *Inspector:* Do you feel comfortable talking to staff?
> *Daughter-in-law of resident:* Yes, I'm part of the family.

When the possibilities for a family model of informal social control prevail (Braithwaite 1989: 54–68), this kind of inspector within certain limits of appropriateness will encourage the relative with a grievance to sort out even a serious grievance in direct conversation with staff of the home in preference to tying a caring, responsive nursing home up in a formal complaint process. In the 1980s we met many American inspectors with this kind of philosophy of nurturing a collegial family model of improvement by their best providers, especially in rural and small-town America. We encountered many inspectors in England and Australia during the current decade who fit this model, but not in the United States.

THE DIFFICULTY OF CONSISTENT PUNISHMENT

Inspectors have theories of how far they can push nursing homes before staff will give up and adopt the motivational postures of resistant defiance or disengagement: 'If you point too many things out on the first day they can get defensive. So save some for the second day. You don't want to get their backs up.' Day and Klein (1987b), like us, found all of these agencies to be street-level bureaucracies (Lipsky 1980) where the real work is done by inspectors out in nursing homes remote from their supervisors. In the inspections we observed over 90 per cent of detected violations were minor and were dealt with by means other than formal enforcement action. It is simply not an option to launch enforcement actions for a majority of detected violations. Nor is it an option to write up all the little breaches that are observed. Hence, even in the well resourced New York of the late 1980s, many minor breaches were dealt with by pointing them out and allowing them to be fixed on the spot or while the team was still in the home. If necessary a bit of advice on how to fix it there and then would be offered so that the team could leave with a clear conscience that this unrecorded breach was at least no longer in existence. So when New York is described as a deterrence regulator, something with comparative force is said, but this is still a regulatory agency that always got most of its compliance by means other than deterrence. Even when voluntary compliance broke down and the state of New York proceeded with a formal enforcement action, most of these were resolved at a settlement conference before the proposed penalty went to an administrative hearing, let alone the courts. While New York was a comparatively litigious jurisdiction in the 1980s at least, going to court was always a rare event. A number of our informants also argued that there is a big difference between New York City and upstate: 'Its not for the most part a problem in getting compliance upstate, even without regulations to cover it. They will take notice if we suggest something. But it's a different story in New York City' (upstate supervisor, 1988).

A former head of nursing home inspection in Georgia explained that:

> Some will comply in spite of the regulations. Some will try to go as close to the line as they can at every turn. They'll try to get away with what they can [these are the homes he went on to explain need a deterrence approach]. Most are in the middle and we can always influence them to do better.

We also found New York inspectors in 1988 to see cooperative compliance strategies as a good way of working the cross-cutting allegiances within regulated organizations to get staff to volunteer information that might later be used in a formal enforcement action. A New York inspector commented: 'How do you get staff to give you incriminating evidence? You don't get it by going in as a poker-faced regulator.' Australian inspectors proffer the same advice: 'I try to call them [the staff] by name always to encourage familiarity. Then by the second day it's all "Hello Mary", and they are at ease with me and will start to tell me things about the place.' A coordinator of inspector training in Illinois said her hidden curriculum is that 'you catch more flies with honey than with vinegar'. Paradoxically then, cultivating cooperative compliance was seen as a path to securing the occasional big enforcement hit. Without exception, in the 49 jurisdictions in the five nations where inspections were observed for this research the most common industry response to a detected formal violation was to accept it and agree on a plan of correction without any threat being issued. And the most common regulatory response to that voluntary compliance was to accept the plan of correction and decline to impose any sanction. This was not just mostly true; it was overwhelmingly the pattern – everywhere. The big reason for this is the impossibility of getting the job done by consistently enforcing rules. In addition, Day and Klein report a phenomenon of convergence in professional nursing culture:

> Indeed the inspector interviewed, whether in New York, Virginia, or England, showed a remarkable consistency in the way they described their actual methods of inspection, irrespective of the official model of regulation. Often they used the same words to describe a process of quickly summing up the general atmosphere and smell of a nursing home before getting down to the specific regulatory requirements demanded of them by federal, state or DHA codes and guidelines. And the reason they did so was because most of them were nurses, and spoke as nurses trained to observe the same things. If political cultures pull regulatory models in different directions, professional culture pulls regulatory practice together again.
>
> (Day and Klein 1987b: 335)

Making threats about enforcement action in the US is almost as rare as enforcement action itself. Making threats was hardly necessary in jurisdictions such as New York that had a demonstrated capacity to take tough enforcement action. The record speaks for itself: if the nursing home 'plays the game' (an expression that recurred cross-nationally during our fieldwork) and agrees to fix the problem, the regulator is most unlikely to take enforcement action, even if the initial problem is quite serious; if the nursing home refuses to play the voluntary compliance game, it will not shake the regulator off its back so easily, and if it persists with resistance on a matter of some seriousness, enforcement action becomes likely. Even in 2004, with the salience that physical abuse of residents had by then as an enforcement issue, we observed US residents report problems of abuse to inspectors in a residents' council meeting. When the inspectors were told that the responsible nurse aide had already been dismissed for this, nothing was written on the incidents of abuse in their inspection report. Centers for Medicare and Medicaid Services policy is that serious problems should be written as deficiencies even if they are fixed on the spot. But resistance to this is strong not only from street-level bureaucrats, but from many heads of state regulatory agencies such as the one who said in 2004 that 'I wanted to get rid of the gotcha mentality'; he wanted to encourage facilities to phone in, voluntarily disclose and discuss compliance problems they were confronting. He explained that when inspectors detected past non-compliance that was no longer evident at the time of the inspection, it would have to be very serious to produce a deficiency. If the facility's quality assurance system had got involved with the problem and fixed it, it was viewed as important not to write a deficiency so vigilant quality assurance would be rewarded.

In jurisdictions that, unlike New York, have always lacked a credible will to enforcement (for example, Louisiana, most English health authorities in 1990) the process is nevertheless very similar in this fundamental way: most of the action is voluntary compliance without threat. Whereas in New York resistance triggered a regulatory attention cycle that may well lead to enforcement, in Louisiana or England resistance triggered a regulatory attention cycle that gave the appearance that it may well lead to enforcement, without the fact of enforcement. Hawkins (1984) called the latter process 'bargain and bluff'. But note that bargain and bluff is not the standard approach of toothless nursing home regulators; the standard approach is to eschew all suggestion of threat; bargain and bluff only comes into play in the unusual cases where there is resistance.

Yet in a way it is wrong to say that 90 per cent of the time compliance is achieved without invocation of deterrent threats; in these cases deterrence is either implicit and real (New York) or implicit and imaginary – based on bluff (England) or, as we explain in Chapter 5, based on networked informal deterrence. This is not to say that, at the moment of voluntary compliance, it is fear of implied sanctions that mostly motivates compliance. The empirical evidence of nursing home deterrence suggests this is not the main story (Braithwaite and Makkai 1991; Makkai and Braithwaite 1994a). The capacity for deterrence is part of what lends authority to the state when it requests compliance with the law (or the doing of things that will make life better for nursing home residents even if that is not precisely required by the law). Perhaps Durkheim (1961: 10) was closer to the truth on this question: 'Punishment does not give discipline its authority, but it prevents discipline from losing its authority.'

Nursing home compliance arises more from a desire to go along with authoritative requests to comply with the law or authoritative suggestions to act in a professionally responsible way than from any rational weighing of the costs and benefits of compliance. This is why bargain and bluff, while it sometimes fails, works better than would be predicted by a rational actor model. Voluntary compliance is underwritten by deterrence, but not in a way that often leads the nursing home operator to calculate about the actual levels and probabilities of deterrent threats. Because of this, even when these actual levels and probabilities are zero, orchestration of an appearance that they are non-zero will often be enough to do the job: 'This is the government talking. And ultimately they have the authority to make their demands stick when you are acting outside the law.' Needless to say, however, such state authority is a fragile accomplishment and therefore a shaky basis for sound regulatory policy. In this respect, it is New York that had the more robust and principled policy settings in the late 1980s. The following statement by a New York inspector could never be made by a typical English inspector:

> You can maintain the same demeanour when confronted with tension and stress, when the facility gets aggressive and unpleasant. You can be friendly if they don't correct. You just pass it on. You never have to be anything but assured and friendly. The enforcement system will take on the battle . . . the team leader just tells them what the repercussions are if you don't correct. You just let the system take over. That's all you have to do. A good team leader is confident, friendly, and explains consequences.

This assurance and composure in New York is underwritten by the capacity to 'pass the case on' to the agency lawyers. It enables accomplished New York inspectors to project a demeanour of inevitability about compliance, an inexorability about enforcement escalation when confronted with resistance, a capacity to communicate the (slightly misleading) implication that 'if you want to go off and fight with the lawyers about this, that's fine and that's your right. It won't be my problem; it will be your problem and the lawyers' problem.' When inspectors have productivity targets to meet and another inspection to start tomorrow, handing over a recalcitrant non-complier to the enforcement system can be attractive so long as they will not also be later caught up in a hearing.

RITUALISM AND OTHER MERTONIAN MODES OF ADAPTATION

The foregoing discussion might be read as suggesting that the major problem with nursing home regulation is the resister to regulatory commands. This is not so: determined resistance to regulatory commands by nursing homes is quite rare, even in comparatively adversarial and litigious New York.[4] Statements like the following by an Indiana director of nursing were not unusual: 'Probably 98 per cent of citations we agree with.' The politics of rebellion against regulatory commands is much more common at the level of industry association resistance than at the individual nursing home level. At the nursing home level, what Merton (1968: 194) calls ritualism is the greater problem than what he calls rebellion. Ritualism is a more effective means of holding regulation at bay than rebellion because it is less confrontational and more subtle. Rather than resist the objective of reducing chemical restraint that management does not really accept, the services of a captive physician can be retained to complete medication orders required by the law whenever management requests them. This section is an extended development of how American ritualism works, followed by a more brief treatment of Merton's other adaptations of rebellion, retreatism, innovation and conformity (see Table 1.1 in Chapter 1).

It is generally regarded as imprudent in the nursing home industry to force a confrontation with the state by openly refusing to comply. Typically the legal costs of such a confrontation will exceed the expected penalties the proprietor seeks to avoid and the costs of compliance, which are usually not high in any specific case (Braithwaite et al. 1990: 94). Moreover, nursing home regulatory agencies in most of the jurisdictions we have studied, even in New York, have a good track record at winning their infrequent legal battles. As a result, rebellion is often motivated by reasons such as professional pride rather than rational economic calculation, as in the anger of a nursing home client reported by one American defence attorney: 'I didn't do this. I want to fight it whatever it takes.' The 'check's always in the mail' strategy, as some regulators refer to it, is the more effective one for those who wish to cut corners on compliance. First, all regulatory agencies have less than perfect mechanisms for confirming that checks are actually paid or that plans of correction are implemented. Second, it is often possible to write a plan of correction that follows institutionalized means for securing regulatory goals but that in practice can be implemented in a perfunctory fashion, as the following exchange illustrates:

> *Administrator for chain:* You can win the battle and lose the war. There's the fear of retaliation next time round. When we disagree, sometimes the best policy is to lie down and play dead. Just put in a plan of correction that will make them happy.
> *JB:* And then what? Do you mean you have only perfunctory compliance with the plan of correction, enough to get them off your backs?
> *Administrator:* Yes.

The nursing home might agree to write a new policy – a piece of paper that changes little in terms of how things are actually done – or it can agree to run an in-service program to train staff in how to avoid non-compliance in future. Such plans of correction can be hard to reject as unsatisfactory and can readily be shown to have been implemented. But organizations that opt for such ritualism are likely to become what the regulators call roller-coaster nursing homes – they make a few changes to come into compliance only to be found out of compliance again at the next survey because of their fundamental lack of commitment to regulatory goals. Some large American nursing home chains are like this. They respond to a finding of non-compliance in one nursing home with a plan of correction to put extra staff onto the problem. The extra staff are simply shifted from another home in the chain. Once the first home has been certified as back in compliance the extra staff may drift back to the second home, which meantime has been out of compliance in some other area because of the staff shortage. If this violation is detected by another survey team, staff may be temporarily shifted from a third facility to plug this gap. In this way a ritualistic corporation can have roller-coaster compliance in all its facilities. Chains that claim to be 'playing the game' can actually be taking the regulators for a ride! This is the idea of gaming as a resistant rather than a compliant motivational posture, discussed in Chapter 9.

The game is easy to play because the regulatory system does not fund follow-up to check that a standard plan of correction works in solving the problem. The philosophy is that compliance on that standard will be checked anew without particular attention to the plan of correction at the next annual inspection. In the worst case, this makes it possible for the plan of correction to be just a piece of paper, or perhaps a piece of paper that is only brought to life in the weeks just before the next survey is completed. Plans of correction are in some states not even read by the inspection team who visit the nursing home. We heard two inspectors explain to a director of nursing that the plan of correction does not go to them: 'Our supervisor will read it and will talk to us if there is any problem.' When we drove with one inspection team to lunch, one of them explained to the general accord of others: 'Anything that's the least bit acceptable will be approved because we have so few days to turn these around. Unless it's right out in left field, we'll accept it.' Here is another example from 1991 Chicago fieldwork notes of ritualistic compliance to get the inspector off the administrator's back in the short term:

> The sanitarian explained that the door to the kitchen had to be closed at all times because it is a fire door. The administrator says to me [JB] after the sanitarian has left: '15 years they've been coming and that door is always open. No one has ever mentioned it before. I suppose she's right. She seems to know the regulations. But isn't it incredible that they never mentioned it before? [She props the door open.] You see how hot it is in this kitchen. You think we will keep this door closed after they leave?' [Interpretive note: This probably means propping this door open will be on the list of things staff must rush around and fix whenever an inspector arrives – during the minutes when the administrator delays the team with initial pleasantries, offers of coffee, when inspectors arrive.]

Industry informants in both Australia and the United States were often quite open about their commitment to ritualism: 'I wrote it [the plan of correction] to pacify them [the regulators].' Our favourite example of ritualism is of an

Australian director of nursing who did not want to oppose an inspection team who 'made a big heap out of ethnic diet' under an Australian standard that requires sensitivity to cultural preferences for different types of food: 'So we bought ethnic diet books – a ragout, goulash is a stew – give it a foreign name and they'll be happy.' In Christine Parker's (2006) terms these are facilities where undertakings are made to the regulator without the moral message in the law being communicated and accepted as a result of the regulatory interaction. In many American states the virtues of ritualism are a deeply ingrained part of the received wisdom of the industry: it is repeatedly pointed out to you that the facilities with the highest levels of compliance are not the best facilities: 'They are the best facilities at keeping the paperwork on the particular things required', said one Chicago nursing home administrator. Ritualism can also be a source of profound injustice. With more serious matters, the administrator will sometimes fire the director of nursing in a plan of correction as a ritualistic sacrifice because, said a Midwestern inspector: 'It's his [the administrator's] butt or hers [the director of nursing] when actually it's him who is the problem and she's doing a reasonable job.'

That ritualism, rather than rebellion, is the main problem with nursing home regulation takes us back to the claim that inspectors cannot rely on deterrence to deliver compliance most of the time. Unless they can coax and caress nursing home management into a commitment to regulatory goals, they will confront endemic roller-coaster compliance from organizations that correct some inputs or processes (institutionalized means in Merton's terms) without tackling the underlying causes of chronic non-compliance. Effectiveness, therefore, crucially depends on embracing both 'compliance' and 'deterrence' strategies. Compliance without deterrence regulation puts inspectors at risk of having their bluff called; deterrence without compliance regulation puts them at risk of accepting ritualism rather than commitment to regulatory goals. American street-level bureaucrats who articulate the truth of the latter claim (actually, quite a large proportion of them) defy federal and state policies that forbid the evil practices of 'consultancy' and 'education' during inspections. They usually do not recommend institutionalized means that the home must follow to secure compliance. The strategy is more often to be a catalyst, to get the administrator to analyse and remedy the root causes of failure to attain regulatory goals, as explained by one experienced New York inspector:

The feds say: 'Do not survey for root causes.' New York State has always surveyed for underlying causes [a statement that would horrify those in head office in Albany who espouse the official line]. We talk with the administrator prior to the exit: 'Gee, there's a lot of problems here in this area – X,Y, and Z. What do you think about the competence of the department head?' Or, 'Why do you think these systems aren't working?'

Sophisticated street-level bureaucrats first seek to persuade management that regulatory goals really are desirable if evidence of this management commitment is lacking. Then they will help the nursing home do their own diagnosis of the problems of their organization that must be solved if compliance is to be sustained (see Bardach and Kagan 1982: 148–9; Braithwaite 1985: 101–3). Unfortunately, however, the regulatory process in most American states does not readily accommodate the coaxing of compliance at these two levels. Consider the following example of a citation of a Southern nursing home:

> Each resident did not receive care necessary to prevent skin breakdown as evidenced by three decubiti that developed in the facility.
> *Plan of Correction Written by Nursing Home:* The medical director examined the residents in which the alleged decubiti were found. He did not feel that two of the three residents had evidence of decubiti. However, all three residents were placed on treatment schedule to prevent further skin breakdown.

Legally, it is hard to reject such a plan of correction as unsatisfactory. Yet its acceptance succumbed to two regulatory failures. First, there was a failure to persuade the nursing home that they had a serious problem (or if not that failure, a failure of the inspection team to admit they were wrong and that there was no problem). Dialogue is needed to persuade the home that skin breakdowns representing even the early stages of pressure ulcers on three separate residents is a problem of a seriousness that should not be tolerated by responsible management. Second, there was a regulatory failure to persuade the nursing home to rethink their whole prevention program with regard to skin breakdowns instead of just offering to patch up the three detected cases. Dialogue is needed to diagnose the deficiencies in prevention programs and to catalyse the serious redesign of policies and procedures required. What happened instead was the triumph of ritualism with the acceptance of the proffered plan of correction.

The deadlines that deliver the impressively reliable annual inspection cycle in the United States, combined with the official policies against 'consultation', make this dialogue difficult. Yet we have seen some rays of hope, of change. One reason for the oppressively high levels of restraint in American nursing homes in the 1980s was a failure to engage in regulatory dialogue with homes. While we discussed the restraint issue in the last chapter, we return to it at length in this chapter and several subsequent ones. More than any other issue, restraint allows us to illuminate the big questions of regulatory strategy – in this section, the challenge of ritualism and how to respond to it through dialogue and a multidimensional web of controls. What we observed in the 1980s was inspectors nattering about restraints followed by ritualistic responses to the natter about their levels of restraint. Repeatedly between 1987 and 1990 we observed regulatory inertia in the face of nursing homes that inspectors knew, or should have known, had unacceptable levels of restraint. As soon as management could produce signed physicians' orders for all residents who were restrained, that was the end of the story. The right piece of paper would keep them out of trouble even if it were signed by a medical automaton who rarely saw the residents, who was a captive of nursing home management (for a suitable fee) and who signed everything that the nurses put in front of them. 'Ninety-five per cent of psychotropic orders and restraint orders are initiated by nurses' (New Jersey inspector, 1990). Consistently studies in the US in the 1970s and 1980s showed that while only about 10 per cent of nursing home residents had documented mental illness, around 50 per cent were prescribed antipsychotic or sedative/hypnotic drugs (Sherman 1988).

In 1990, in the aftermath of the brilliant Untie the Elderly Campaign (see Chapter 3), nursing home professionals and progressive state regulators were required to put their stamp on the interpretation of nursing home reform laws implemented that year, and we observed regulatory practices becoming more dialogic on the restraint issue. Even where the nursing home could produce physicians' orders for all restraints, inspectors persisted with questioning.

> But why is the restraint needed? Don't you think you need a more detailed assessment than this? What about an assessment by a psychiatrist? What are your procedures for reviewing restraints? Aren't you worried about litigation for the improper use of restraints? Have you thought about why you have so many more restrained residents than other facilities in our region? Did you know that X [an industry opinion leader] has halved the number of physically restrained residents in her facility in the past six months, and she says that it's the best thing she's ever done for the residents and for the staff?

These industry role models of improvement, especially those who proclaimed that they managed to achieve a 'restraint-free home', were critical to what was accomplished.

The aides rose to the challenge across the country. Storytelling was important about why there was no situation for which there was not some creative alternative to restraint. Our favourite is of Georgie who would bump, bump, and bump all day on a wall. Georgie was also a resident who believed he heard voices from God. One day the administrator turned on the public address system and boomed 'Georgie, Georgie, Georgie. Stop that bumping.' Georgie said this was a voice from God and never did it again. In the section on education and persuasion in this chapter we saw that another important strand of the web of controls that prevented restraint being imposed on residents were educative, particularly stories about how other states, other facilities are achieving remarkable reductions in restraint by being variously creative in the professional alternatives they craft. It became a matter of professional pride to manifest this creativity and professional shame to have large numbers of restrained residents. The right stories are what help professionals change a practice from being a knee-jerk response to an absolute last resort (Shearing and Ericson 1991).

The sight that so shocked us when we saw it regularly in the 1980s – inspectors accepting situations where residents had both hands tied to the arms of a chair with mittens on both hands – was to become a sight we would not see a decade later. And we would certainly not encounter a 1989 incident when a resident had nets enmeshing her entire bed just a couple of feet from her face. One inspector explained the change in attitude in such cases: 'I don't care if you have ten doctors' orders. You're not using those nets.' In the course of 1990 we saw one of our Chicago homes reduce the number of restraints from 147 to 17. In the 1980s there was a great difference between the number of US nursing home residents we would observe manifesting signs of long-term psychotropic drug use – repeated mouth movements, repeated blinking, other repeated movements, the 'Mellaril shuffle'[5] – and the number that we would observe in English and Australian nursing homes. Today, there may be differences, but they are no longer so great as to be something that is striking and obvious to observers spending a lot of time in nursing homes in the three nations.

It is the combination of the processes of regulatory dialogue described above driven by the community-wide clamour for reform (see Chapter 3) of the Untie the Elderly Campaign and the OBRA 1987 campaign that delivered dramatic change.

Like the reduction of physical restraint, the accomplishment of reduced chemical restraint and more prudent use of drugs in nursing homes generally was not primarily enforcement driven. Indeed, the direct actions of inspectors were not very central and certainly less central than with physical restraint. It was driven by regulation that made consultant pharmacists rather than inspectors the crucial drivers of challenges to the ritualistic defence that 'this is what the doctor prescribed'. The more serious adverse drug events in nursing homes seem to be the most preventable; Gurwitz et al. (2000) estimate that there are around 20 000 life-threatening adverse events in US nursing homes every year, 80 per cent of them preventable. From 1974, pharmacists were required to do a drug regimen review. This was an important and effective regulatory step. It was taken a step further in 1982 when HCFA introduced a set of indicators to be checked in effective drug regimen reviews. These included things like: 'Use of antipsychotic or antidepressant medication for less than 3 days; Use of multiple antipsychotic medications on the same patient.' The HCFA (1998: 418–21) reports that 23 studies were undertaken up to 1985 on the impact of pharmacist conducted drug regimen reviews, showing effects such as reductions in unnecessary medications, hospitalizations, adverse drug interactions and costs of care. While few of the studies were methodologically strong, such effects seemed robust across many studies and large. The OBRA 1987 reforms further increased the sophistication of and investment in drug regimen reviews and saw an increase in the sophistication of their evaluation. One of these studies (Ray et al. 1993) showed how education of nursing home staff in practical 'down to earth' ways of dealing with the ten most common behavioural symptoms encountered in nursing homes could reduce use of psychotropic drugs by 59 per cent and physical restraint use by 31 per cent as an unexpected by-product. Ray et al. (1993) argue that this is an accomplishment of a synergy between education and regulation. There is a more than credible evidence base that enforced self-regulation has dramatically reduced chemical restraint and generally improved prescribing of drugs in nursing homes (HCFA 1998: 418–48).

Starting in the beginning of the nineteenth century, before there existed a nursing home industry, there was an earlier professional and public campaign against restraints in mental hospitals (Special Committee on Aging 1990b: 39–40). This was rather effective in the nineteenth century in making hospitals in England, Scotland, the Netherlands, Sweden, Denmark, and probably North-Eastern Europe generally, mostly restraint-free. This was not accomplished in the US, even though this campaign perhaps had some limited US effects, so when the nursing home industry grew in America, it grew out of the ethos of a heavily restrained elderly population in hospitals. America also became the home of dominant restraint manufacturers like Posey, who marketed a non-evidence-based philosophy of risk management through restraint. Indeed, Posey circumvented the generation of an evidence base by filing no death reports with the US Food and Drug Administration, in violation of federal rules (Rigert and Lerner 1990: 1). A critical OBRA micro-reform was the requirement that all nursing homes select a quality problem each year where the performance of the home was unacceptable and have their quality assurance committee come up with a plan to reduce that problem, implement it and monitor whether improvement occurred. In the regulatory climate of 1990–91, it was almost impossible to have a level of physical restraint over 50 per cent and not target that through the quality assurance committee as something that just had to be reduced.

So often scholars of regulation lose sight of the possibility that the year-by-year regulatory failures they see during long periods of regulatory inertia ought to be qualified by noticing that there are periods of history when dramatic regulatory accomplishments are secured in a relatively short space of time. Sometimes these are later reversed. But often they are not. We predict that the regulatory progress on nursing home restraint will never be reversed, but will be cumulative, in the same way that the United States will never return to the unsafe conditions of rail travel of the late nineteenth century when it was standard for hundreds to be killed in rail accidents in just one state in one year, or return to the shocking death rates of US coal mines of a century ago (Braithwaite 1985). Twenty-first century Americans will look on late twentieth century practices of tying up the infirm elderly as incomprehensible barbarism to which it would be unthinkable to return.

While regulatory dialogue over the restraint issue manifests some mellowing of the official US doctrine that inspectors are law enforcers whose job is simply to rate the nursing home for compliance with the standards, not consultants, the dialogue remains limited. Moreover, US inspectors receive training, consistent with the official policy, which is unsuitable for preparing them for a dialogic role. Federal training of state inspectors has emphasized the need for inspectors to be in control during exit conferences, not to be distracted by questions raised by nursing home staff, to stick to the facts of the deficiencies that require a written plan of correction. Occasionally we saw surveyors take this training depressingly seriously, as by refusing to answer questions from nursing home management as to whether, in spite of their deficiencies, they had improved since the last survey. As Albert J. Reiss Jr pointed out in commenting on one of our earlier manuscripts on this issue, it is the inspectors who are being ritualistic by shying away from positive feedback that might help sustain regulatory goals. Fortunately, such an extremist interpretation of law enforcement ritualism is not typical among the street-level bureaucrats who make the regulation work. Unfortunately, nevertheless, exit conferences in the US have become less deliberative in recent years. Often they are perfunctory; one 2004 exit meeting was observed to last four minutes.

In terms of Merton's typology, we have so far discussed conformity, rebellion, and ritualism. Retreatism, where there is a disengagement of commitment to both regulatory goals and institutionalized means of attaining them, does occur from time to time, particularly when the chief executive of the organization is 'burnt out' by the pressures of running a health-care institution (see Braithwaite et al. 1992: app. E). Indeed, it is when burnout happens that some of the more draconian regulatory interventions occur, such as putting in a government-appointed administrator to run the facility. Some of the disengaged nursing home managers we have seen have been alcoholics, one of Merton's classic types of retreatists. While it is a less common occurrence in the United States than ritualism, when retreatism does occur, the consequences for everyone concerned can be disastrous.

Innovation – achieving regulatory goals but by other than the institutionally approved means – has been substantially destroyed by decades of input-oriented regulation. As the head of one large state industry association put it, 'You manage facilities according to the standards written rather than according to what's best for patient care. You quickly learn how to play the game, to give them what's required to meet the standards.' This displacement of innovation with game-playing is today widely recognized – by scholarly commentators, governments, industry, and professional and consumer groups – to have been a bad thing. American nursing home regulatory policy claims from time to time that it is undoing this regulatory stultification of innovation by shifting strategy from input- to outcome-oriented regulation. The theory is that the law should specify quality of life and quality of care outcomes for nursing home residents, allowing facilities to achieve them through whatever means they see fit. In our view, the shifts in US policy toward more outcome-oriented nursing home regulation have been very marginal. Australian government policy from 1988 did match the rhetoric with more genuinely outcome-oriented regulatory practices than one sees in the United States, as we will see in Chapter 6, even though input regulation still has an important place on the Australian scene.

Australian regulatory policy, as we will see in Chapter 6, has also had a more explicit commitment to innovation in a variety of ways. In 1997 the HCFA launched a 'Sharing Innovations in Quality' initiative, a 'collaborative project designed to develop a repository of the innovative ideas and best practices in long term care that have improved outcomes for nursing home residents'. Limited numbers of innovations were put up on the website, partly, according to informants, for fear of losing any competitive edge the innovations deliver, but mostly, in the non-innovative culture of the US industry, because people could not be bothered to put their ideas and accomplishments up on the site.

In summary, then, American nursing home regulation achieves a surprising degree of voluntary conformity, a great deal of ritualism, and occasional retreatism and rebellion, and it tends to result in the systematic destruction of innovation. While American nursing home regulation uses deterrence much more than in other countries, it still relies heavily on compliance strategies, though not heavily enough to grapple with widespread ritualism.

SELF-REGULATION

Our fieldwork was attentive to self-regulation as well as government regulation. We interviewed people at industry associations who claimed to run self-regulation schemes; we visited the Joint Commission on Accreditation of Healthcare Organizations and interviewed both surveyors and nursing homes that had been through, or were preparing for, their accreditation process in different parts of the country; we attended a meeting of the Accreditation Committee of the American College of Health Care Administrators; we sat in on 39 care planning conferences in nursing homes and 12 meetings of facility quality assurance committees in the US.

In its short history, the US nursing home industry has moved quickly from being totally unregulated to heavy government regulation. There has never been an era when self-regulation was the primary control strategy. The Reagan administration tried unsuccessfully to change this situation in 1981. There has long been the Joint Commission on Accreditation of Hospitals (JCAH), which changed its name to the Joint Commission on the Accreditation of Healthcare Organizations (JCAHO) in the 1980s, with an eye to the nursing home business in particular. In Texas, JCAHO accreditation was deemed to satisfy state licensure, but not federal certification, which requires a government inspection. The penetration of the Commission's voluntary accreditation has always been weak, as the vice president for quality assurance with one nursing home chain explained: 'The Joint Commission accredits only 3 per cent of the nursing homes in the country and it's decreasing [actually it has been fairly stable at 8–9 per cent]. Forget it, we're up to here [signifies her neck] in inspection.' Most of the industry is not remotely interested in applying for accreditation and is totally unaffected by this self-regulation process. The entrance to the accreditation market of the Long-term care Evaluation and Accreditation Program (LEAP) in the 1990s did not significantly change that.

The 1981 proposal to waive federally mandated inspection for nursing homes accredited by the JCAHO was resisted on a number of grounds (Jost 1983, 1988). First, the JCAHO had no enforcement powers. Second, its reports were treated as confidential quality assurance feedback to management that was not available to consumers (they are more publicly accessible today). Third, its standard accreditation cycle was three years instead of the one-year minimum government cycle (two months in Rhode Island). Fourth, it was rightly criticized for an extremely input-oriented (ritualistic) approach to self-regulation. The JCAHO has been as bad as government regulation in the United States in stultifying innovation to deliver better health-care outcomes. Accepting some truth in the latter criticism, the JCAHO sought to move to a somewhat more outcome-oriented approach in the 1990s, but as with US government regulation, outcome orientation at the JCAHO remains more a matter of rhetoric than reality.

Over the years, some state industry associations have developed self-regulatory schemes to ensure that their members have satisfactory quality assurance programs as a condition of membership. Some state associations (for example, Virginia) run low-key voluntary peer review programs for administrators. The American Health Care Association has a Quality First initiative, which we found to be only a tiny presence in the field compared to state regulation. Industry associations are of as limited importance as vehicles of self-regulation as we found them to be in England and Australia (Chapters 5 and 6). Professional associations continue to play important roles in accrediting health-care professionals. Of particular interest in the nursing home industry is the American College of Health Care Administrators, which accredits administrators. Some of the professional development plans developed with nursing home administrators during their accreditation process amount to quality assurance programs for the facilities they run (American College of Health Care Administrators 1987). Doctors have been subject to peer review organizations (Jost 1988). This may have been important in hospitals where doctors exercise great power, but in nursing homes where doctors are generally part-timers with minimal involvement in organizational decision-making, this form of self-regulation has had a small impact.[6] In any case, in the entire American health care sector up to September 1987, only 54 health-care providers had been excluded from Medicare, with another 25 being subjected to monetary penalties, as a result of peer-review organization deliberations (Jost 1988: 591).

The self-regulatory action that counts most is at the level of particular nursing home organizations themselves rather than at the level of national or state associations. For years, many nursing home chains have had quality assurance programs, often headed by a vice president for quality assurance. Some of these have impressive manuals. Our observation is, however, that most corporate quality assurance programs demand no more than is required by government regulation. This contrasts with quality assurance programs in the pharmaceutical industry that often demand much higher standards than those imposed by the law (Braithwaite 1984). The function of the vice president for quality assurance in a nursing home chain tends to be to get his or her facilities up to speed when a government inspection is due. The objective, in other words, is not so much to improve quality as to minimize deficiencies detected by the regulators, a form of legal risk management. This reality is reflected in the incentive systems of the chains, which pay bonuses to administrators who obtain low numbers of deficiencies in government inspections rather than to administrators who are rated by corporate quality assurance systems as delivering good quality outcomes. At worst, corporate quality assurance personnel train staff in the art of ritualism. But this is not always the case. For example, the national quality assurance program mandated by a 1986 Californian consent agreement with

Beverly Enterprises – a past master of ritualism and roller-coaster compliance – according to several knowledgeable informants and our own limited observation of the Beverly quality assurance program in operation, was seriously oriented to improving the quality of care and probably did so for a number of years.

The Beverly consent agreement was a pioneering example of government-mandated self-regulation in this industry. This was taken a big step further with the implementation of OBRA's requirement from 1990 that each home have a quality assurance program coordinated by a quality assurance committee. The home is allowed a lot of discretion in choosing whatever quality assurance objectives seem most needed in each area of its operation. This seems a paradigm shift away from command-and-control regulation and toward fostering self-regulation, and in important ways it is. However, the culture of an industry inured to government command and control, indeed, to government discipline, pervades the quality assurance process. Ritualism is endemic. The question that holds centre stage during quality assurance meetings is not, 'What is the best way to design this program to deliver maximum improvement in quality of care?' but, 'What is it that they [the regulators] want of us here? What is the minimum we have to do to satisfy the requirement of having a quality assurance program?' We could illustrate this with some shameless instances of ritualism during quality assurance meetings. The following 1990 interaction is a more subtle case that is closer to the modal reality of quality assurance ritualism:

> *Director of nursing:* Are you looking for 100 per cent [with your outcome evaluation]? What are you going to do about it if it's 95 per cent?
> *Dietician:* An in-service.
> *Quality assurance coordinator:* Shoot for 100 per cent and put 90 per cent [on the written evaluation plan]. Don't hesitate to change the design to make it more realistic. They [the state] don't mind that. You don't get penalized for not meeting your quality assurance objectives. You'll get penalized for failing to take action on the problems you find. Do we all agree? Ninety per cent.

Here the parameters of the quality assurance program are being set so as to avert the need for any follow-up action to improve quality. In the most blatant cases of ritualism, the very selection of quality assurance evaluation is driven by a search for non-problems that will guarantee a near 100 per cent result. Ritualism cannot therefore be simply fixed by changing the structure of the law away from command and control. Ritualism is a deeper problem of regulatory culture. It is also a problem of infinite regress. This was illustrated in one quality assurance committee meeting when linking quality assurance data to employee evaluations was discussed: 'In my area, if we specify clearly their employee evaluation criteria, they won't do anything else.' Ritualism is such a deeply embedded, multilayered problem in the American nursing home industry that nothing short of a cultural revolution in the industry and its regulation may be needed to conquer it. Perhaps we are seeing the beginnings of this with the innovative breaking away from ritualism that was illustrated in Chapter 3 with the Pioneer Network and Eden Alternative.

Within a few years of the introduction of OBRA, inspectors followed a guideline of routinely not actually reading and discussing quality assurance committee reports. This policy shift occurred in response to the reasonable point that industry might not frankly report and uncover problems in quality assurance reports if inspectors came in to check them and used the nursing home's own self-assessment to punish it. But in the ritualistic culture of this regulatory system, it meant when inspectors walked into the home they simply checked that the required kinds of people were members of the quality assurance committee and that it met regularly. Whether they did anything of strategic value when they did meet became of no concern. This is not quite fair because when inspectors discover a problem of wide scope and severity, they are expected to ask if a problem of this salience has been addressed by the quality assurance committee and to see the minutes where it has been tackled. Obviously there is not a problem of using the home's self-detection against it when the inspectors have independently discovered a pattern of non-compliance.

CONCLUSION

We have seen that self-regulation, enforced self-regulation (as in mandated quality assurance processes), and state regulation have all been vulnerable to ritualism. For all that, as we saw in Chapter 2, these different levels of regulation have all played roles in a substantial list of specific historic improvements in the quality of care. The most dramatic of these, notably in the use of restraint, are not in this analysis found to be accomplishments of consistent deterrence mandated by national or state legislators. Rather they are accomplishments of networked governance of quality by advocacy groups, professions, business innovators and street-level bureaucrats.

Deterrent threats, delivering on them and bluffing about them, are certainly among the tools street-level bureaucrats have used to achieve the successes of restraining residents less and giving them more choice of a variety of kinds. While deterrence is deployed much more frequently in the US than in England and Australia, our conclusion is that street-level bureaucrats have more in common in the three nations than one might be led to expect by the large differences in the formal architecture of regulation in the three countries. To understand how safer, better care has been accomplished in America, we need to understand the whole complex of street-level strategies described in this chapter, not just the enforcement policies that are the stuff of Congressional debates. At the same time, we need to see that many strands of the American web of regulatory controls have been frayed by obsession with enforcement. In the next chapter, England supplies a counterfactual case. While America has allowed its preoccupation with enforcement to partially crush consultancy, education, persuasion and innovation, endemic English enforcement enfeeblement historically resulted in clever street-work by inspectors to braid such alternative strands into a more variegated and resilient fabric of control, at least in the locales where inspectors were most vigilant.

Our conclusion will be that we need to understand American regulation as a story of both accomplishment and counterproductivity. We need to be puzzled why, if regulation works in important respects, as this book shows it does, America's vastly superior funding of nursing home regulation does not give it nursing homes that are better places to live in than English homes. Responsive regulation was developed out of our experience with nursing home and coal mine regulation. So it should not be a surprise that we see responsive regulation as clarifying this puzzle. Enforcement can do much to improve the quality of outcomes. But enforcement can be applied either in ways that unravel other strands in webs of control or tie them into a tighter fabric. America, on our analysis, has received benefits from its superior enforcement capability compared to other nations. England has benefited from the ingenuity of its street-level bureaucrats in compensating for its enforcement deficits. So why is it not possible to have the best of both worlds? Responsive regulatory theory suggests it is possible to have tougher American-style enforcement without boxing in street-level discretion with a scope and severity grid (Figure 2.1 in Chapter 2). It is possible to have formalism that empowers and enables informal social control to work flexibly, in all its rich, innovative, contextual possibilities for variety. It is possible to clean out the 'bottom feeders' of an industry, while liberating the elite and the mainstream of the industry to innovate in quality improvement. In the campaign for OBRA (as opposed to its implementation), in Pioneer and Eden, America is not without glimpses of this possibility. American aged care and health safety and quality suffers from seeds of self-destruction, while also being ripe with seeds of self-transformation. Our data reveal American regulation as many sided and not a stable thing. In seeking to understand its past successes and their limitations, and its future possibilities, the worst thing we could do is oversimplify the street-level reality of American regulatory inspection.

NOTES

1. On the other hand, one New York inspector explained that over time in an almost totally negative regulatory system, players adjust in how they frame the meaning of feedback: 'If they understand it's a negative process, not a positive process, they think it's fair and don't get upset at what we say. They know we only have to find the negative things. And they know that if they are not getting many negatives they must be doing something right.'
2. That was Virginia, 1988. One Virginia 2004 comment from a chain CEO was 'That's the dumbest thing I've ever seen. But I'm going to do it because they like it.'
3. Makkai and Braithwaite (1993b) found that Australian nursing home CEOs do not behave quite like this economic analysis of law suggests. Compliance did reduce as expected costs of compliance increased. However, this relationship was not monotonic because of CEOs with a motivational posture of 'disengagement' (see Chapter 9) who had poor compliance in the face of low expected compliance costs.
4. The following statement of an inspector from a southern state is typical: 'In most cases – 95 per cent – the plan of correction is acceptable. We write back to the 5 per cent saying it's not an acceptable plan of correction. Mostly it's unacceptable dates – beyond 90 days. Then the vast majority come back with an acceptable plan. Much of it is sorted out on the telephone.'
5. To be technically correct, these symptoms we were observing, before we understood what they were, were tardive dyskinesia and acute extrapyramidal side effects.
6. Contemporary state and federal regulation began in the middle of the current decade to force nursing home medical directors to play a more active oversight role with the quality of care.

5. English nursing home regulation

This is a study of English rather than British regulation because all fieldwork conducted by the three authors was in England. While the fieldwork was much less than in the US and Australia, it was still substantial with a total of 37 inspections of homes being observed in seven fieldwork trips in 1989, 1991, 1993, 1998, 2000, 2004 and 2006. Forty-three different inspectors were observed doing inspections. An additional 17 nursing homes were visited with inspectors for reasons other than inspections. Only four of the inspections were of what were called residential care homes for the aged, the rest being nursing home inspections. The most intensive wave of fieldwork was between 1989 and 1993 when inspections were observed in 14 District Health Authorities (DHAs): Brighton, Canterbury and Thanet, Exeter, Torbay, South Birmingham and Central Birmingham (which were amalgamating at the time), South-West Hertfordshire, North Hertfordshire, Haringey, Liverpool, Blackpool, East Suffolk, West Suffolk and Norwich. No inspections were observed at the fifteenth DHA, Bury, but interviews were conducted there and six nursing homes visited. These were selected to represent a spread across all regions of England, concentrating in 1989 on the DHAs with most beds, and in 1991 on the DHAs we were told were most distinctively different from those we had already visited. The DHA approached in one selected region declined to cooperate with the research. This was the only refusal to cooperate. There was a purposive bias toward DHAs with a lot of nursing homes, though some DHAs with small numbers of homes were included.

Sixty-two staff from the 15 DHAs were interviewed between 1989 and 1993. Many of these staff had worked in other DHAs and told us a great deal about differences between their current and former authorities. This spread was necessary because in this era there were no national standards and DHAs adopted disparate approaches to inspection and registration. Only four inspections, involving only seven inspectors, could be observed in 2004 after the establishment of the Commission for Social Care Inspection (CSCI), two in the London area and two in Leeds-Bradford. Inspections in both periods in England tended to last just one day, more often two to three hours. There were opportunities during the day and while travelling to and from the facility to interview the inspectors, and also to get the perspective of various levels of nursing home staff on what was happening in the inspection and of residents and relatives who were visiting on the day. In the average day in the field observing inspections, there would be significant conversations with a dozen or more people (inspectors, residents, staff or proprietors). This means that while the English fieldwork was much more modest than in the US or Australia, it encompassed conversations with around a thousand stakeholders in the regulatory process about that process.

Vertical depth as well as horizontal breadth was accomplished in the data collection. The Chair of the Commission for Social Care Inspection and the National Care Standards Commission, the Chief Inspector, and most of their top management group with responsibilities related to aged care inspection were interviewed. Also interviewed were senior management of the District Health Authorities, the local council authorities, the nursing home directors of nursing and their staff, and management of nursing home groups that we visited. Other interviews were with NGO leaders, Community Health Council chairs, the Association of Community Health Councils, a number of care home industry association executives at the regional and national level, including the chief executives of the Registered Nursing Home Association and the Independent Healthcare Association from different eras, lawyers who represented nursing homes, consultant geriatricians, the National Association of Health Authorities and Trusts, the National Patient Safety Agency, the Social Services Inspectorate of the 1980s and 1990s, senior civil servants of health and social security and influential members of parliament from different times across the three decades, prominent consultants and authors of government reports.

In the US, we found the middle period of our study, the 1990s, the most instructive. In the next chapter we will find the most recent period in the history of Australian regulation the most instructive. In this chapter, we find the early period of our research in England the most illuminating. This is because 1980s and early 1990s English nursing home regulation shows how street-level inspectors can be formidable local change agents even when they cannot rely on national enforcement capabilities. By the 2000s, English inspectors were backed up by more national enforcement capacity, though still a puny form of it compared to the US.[1] We try in this chapter to give some sense of how English inspectors protect the elderly by mobilizing a local club governance even today. In England national institutions seem to come and go (a lot) while local inspectors go on forever, largely oblivious to what is happening in the political stratosphere of London.

THE BIG PICTURE

While there was much more diversity of nursing home regulatory standards and practices across different regions of England during the 1980s and 1990s than was true of the United States and Australia, the big picture is that variation across both space and time within England is much less than the difference between the English approach and that of the US and Australia. Some of the differences are doubtless driven by the nature of the industry. In the 1988–93 period when most fieldwork was conducted, the average number of beds in UK nursing homes was 29; in Australia, it was 38; in the US, it was approaching 100. Although the average size of English nursing homes has increased, it remains much smaller than US homes; in 2005 the average was 46 (Commission for Social Care Inspection 2005b: 78). Residential homes were even smaller, on average at 33 places in 2005 (Commission for Social Care Inspection 2005b: 78).

One reason English nursing homes are smaller is that a majority of the DHAs visited between 1989 and 1993 were either reluctant to register homes with more than 40, or even 30, residents or simply refused to do so. They had no legal authority to do this, but many authorities did it, based on a commitment to keeping facilities intimate and non-institutional. Sometimes this was accomplished by lobbying local government planning authorities to withhold planning approval for larger institutions.[2] There was an ethos of regulatory resistance to large chains with large facilities taking over the industry as had happened in the US. In most ways that mattered the English homes were less institutional than Australian homes and massively less institutional than in the US.[3] Most US nursing homes we visited did not have gardens; almost all of the 54 English institutions visited had gardens (all the homes in the Bennett [1986: 88] study had a garden). This puts some perspective on the importance of gardens in the Pioneer Network and Eden Alternative discussed in Chapter 3.

While today quite a large proportion of US and Australian homes have many areas carpeted in an effort to recapture a homelike environment, rather than covered in institutional linoleum, two decades ago most English nursing homes were mostly carpeted. In every way their decor was more warm and inviting. This was partly driven by the nature of the English real estate market, which meant that most English nursing homes were, and still are, in stately old (often Victorian) residences or converted little hotels[4] (particularly in the seaside clustering of nursing homes at places like Brighton and Blackpool). In the eyes of these foreign authors, such buildings tend to be architecturally interesting and inviting with their fireplaces and sitting rooms under high ceilings, while the American chain institutions built on greenfield sites appear sterile and soulless. The latter, however, are designed for superior fire safety, and make infection control, movement, management and surveillance easier.

Love can no more be quantified than architectural charm, but staff seemed to us more loving toward the elderly in English homes. They certainly knew their residents more intimately than in the US and Australia, easier to accomplish of course in a smaller facility. Managers also tended to know all their staff well and to have much larger numbers of relatives visiting than in the US. The overwhelming majority of nursing homes in England today have a keyworker system, where each resident has a staff member assigned to regularly monitor all their needs and to ensure their care plan reflects those needs and to ensure that the resident is integrated into the social life of the home as much as possible. Some nursing homes had a sign near each resident's bed stating 'My Nurse is . . . My Keyworker is . . . .' English regulation does not mandate the keyworker system, though the pre-inspection questionnaire all homes must fill out before their annual announced inspection invites them to list the name of the keyworker beside the name of each resident. Inspectors were also routinely observed to enquire: 'Who is Mrs Jones's keyworker?'

In the English homes, residents might have had less convenient access to a toilet, but they had more personal space and they used it in more personalized ways. More than half of them for the entire period of this research had a private bedroom[5] that in many cases had an individualized decor such that when the door was shut, it was not so easy to tell that this was a room in an institution as opposed to the bedroom of a sick elderly person in their own home. As in Australia, there was continuous improvement throughout the period of this study in the proportion of beds in single-occupancy rooms. In reporting on key performance indicators for 2004–05 the Commission for Social Care Inspection found that on average 94 per cent of single adults and older people going into permanent residential and nursing care were allocated a single room (Commission for Social Care Inspection 2005c: 154). More money has been spent on things like curtains in England than in the US and Australia. In Bennett's (1986: 90) study, 50 per cent of residents in the mid-1980s had been out of the nursing home in the previous six months for some kind of visit.

The nursing of English residents is not only more caring, it is more professional. English residents get more of their hands-on care from staff who are registered or enrolled nurses than do Americans. Most English nurses are not 'too posh to wash'; most nurses in US homes are. Darton (1987) found qualified nurses provided 25 per cent of staff time in nursing homes and 5 per cent in residential homes during a 1987 survey of 86 homes, bigger numbers than in the same types of American institutions.

On the other hand, managerial professionalism, including director of nursing managerial professionalism, is more impressive in the US than in both England and Australia. Managerial control of the quality of everything from laundry to food to medications is superior in the US. This does not mean American residents get superior quality care on such dimensions. On the contrary, inferior managerial control of superior staff usually delivers better care than superior control of inferior staff. For example, we found it to be rare for English homes to have any residents with pressure sores; we found it rare for American homes not to have them[6] and quite common for them to have a dozen or more. The biggest difference in the 1980s was on restraint. In none of the 54 English homes we visited did we see any resident restrained with a tied form of restraint. Today this big difference has disappeared: physical restraint is down in the US to 4 per cent of residents at the time of writing, a similar level to that which has continuously existed in England throughout this period.

Food is a clear exception to the pattern we are describing here. English nursing home food is by any standard inferior in quality and degree of choice to US and Australian nursing home food. Some of the cost-cutting on food that is highly visible in English nursing homes was appalling to foreign eyes. Observations like the following in our 1990 fieldwork notes were more common in England:

> I saw 3 evening meals being served between 4 and 5 pm. One was meat sandwiches. Another was 3–4 little link sausages, toast and tomato sauce. The third was a slice of horrible meat (was it spam?) emulsion with a blob of chutney and bread. The vegetarian alternative was unappetizing cheese sandwiches with marmite. No adverse comment was made on any of these meals by the inspector. The inspector excused sandwiches to me because 'hospitals do it'.

In the US and Australia, firm enforcement action against this nursing home over the quality of the food and the lack of choice would have occurred.

Like Australian nursing homes, most English homes are run by a registered manager who is usually also the director of nursing, traditionally referred to as the matron. Few English homes beyond major chains have an administrator, in the American tradition, above the director of nursing in the management structure. In the American tradition, the director of nursing is at the same formal level in the management structure as the head of housekeeping, or dietary, though effectively the top nurse is usually number two. In English and Australian nursing homes, managers responsible for non-nursing functions are below all registered nurses in the hierarchy of facilities which are nursocracies. While professional nursing care is more hands-on in English facilities, US facilities are more likely to have other professionals on staff such as physiotherapists (physical therapists), social workers, occupational therapists, dieticians and activities officers, though regular effective access to a doctor of the resident's choice is more available in both England and Australia than the US.[7] United States facilities are serviced by physicians retained by the nursing home, rather than by the residents; these US physicians are rarely to be seen in residents' rooms. In Bennett's (1986: 92) study, 72 per cent of Brighton nursing home residents continued to have care from a general practitioner (GP) who served them before entering the nursing home. We were told that this number is much lower today, though we have not seen systematic data. Doctors in Australia are more likely to be advocates of residents against the home than in the US, where they are more captured by the home, and the UK, where they are more captured by the National Health Service.

The superior professionalism of US activities officers drives vastly superior activities programs in US nursing homes than in English ones. While bingo is ubiquitous in the three countries, diversity of choice in activities is markedly limited in England. That said, there is evidence of improvement under more recent regulatory arrangements, with considerably more activities in homes we observed in 2004 compared to 1989. The dearth of stimulating activities in English nursing homes is a clear case of regulatory failure, and of some limited regulatory success in the US and Australia. English inspectors do not get on the backs of nursing homes, do not take enforcement action for poor quality, availability and diversity of activities programs. If they did, we might see the growth of activities professionalism we have seen in the US.

CARE PLANNING AND EMPOWERMENT

Not all aspects of nursing care are superior in England. Care planning is more rigorous in Australia and vastly more so in the US. This was true across the period of this study. English care plans were brief, often two sheets of information incorporated in a Kardex system and often titled 'Nursing Care Plan', and tended to utterly neglect non-nursing forms of care. The English regulatory system prior to 2000 discouraged multidisciplinary, holistic care. Only doctors from the health authority could read doctors' notes.

Consequently, it was necessary to include doctors on inspection teams from time to time. This was a particularly ridiculous limitation on pharmacists auditing prescriptions written by doctors to check on contraindications, adverse drug interactions, overprescribing and chemical restraint. Pharmacy inspections were required in aged care homes that employed a pharmacist, not in those that did not, creating a perverse regulatory incentive not to invest in pharmacy professionalism.

United States care plans are much larger, more thorough, multidisciplinary documents. They are also more living documents. There is more checking that the requirements of care plans are being met – both by nursing home staff and by inspectors. Probably the latter is a cause of the former. In the US, care plans are also updated on a more regular cycle and the revision process is more participatory. Relatives of the resident are written to, advising the date of the care planning meeting. More residents and relatives, in addition to a wider disciplinary range of care staff, attend US care planning meetings than English and Australian meetings. English regulation has failed both to effectively mandate such care planning meetings and to mandate the invitation of residents and relatives to them, in the way US regulation has. While more attention was being devoted to improving care planning in homes observed during 2004, and more attention was devoted to this than to any other issue, the attention was rather documentation oriented, as opposed to an orientation to making the care plan a living, participatory accomplishment. The Commission for Social Care Inspection (2005b: 25) itself notes that there is still little involvement of people who use services in developing care plans: 'An Older person: "The care plan meant nothing to anyone except to the person who wrote it" ' (cited in the Commission for Social Care Inspection 2005b: 180). American inspectors would mostly move from interviews or observation of problems with patients to checking how these issues were made real in the care plan. English inspectors moved in the opposite direction, or more often just noted documentation omissions in the care plans without even subsequently following the issue through to an interview of that resident or observation of care of the resident.

More generally, the greatest weakness of English regulation is on the empowerment of residents. Only a few of the homes we visited had residents' committees; some of the DHAs said none of their nursing homes had them. From the 49 homes we saw between 1989 and 1993 it seems safe to assume during this period that fewer than 10 per cent of English nursing homes had residents' committees, whereas over 90 per cent of US and Australian nursing homes had them. It is regulation that has driven virtually all nursing homes in comparable countries such as the US, Australia and Germany to have such committees. Moreover, a meeting with the residents' council is in effect a formal part of the US inspection process, as is the checking of the minutes of the council for problems that should be addressed.

Complaints systems are much less organized and accessible in the UK (Kerrison and Pollock 2001) than in the US and Australia. Both posters with complaints hotlines and posters about advocacy organizations or ombudsmen are much less to be seen in English nursing homes and these services are much less used. Most of the DHAs visited between 1989 and 1993 were processing fewer than ten complaints a year! Even the DHAs with the largest and best organized complaints processes were averaging fewer than two complaints per nursing home per year in the early 1990s. All large American states were dealing with a lot more nursing home complaints than all of England, a situation that still seems true today (Commission for Social Care Inspection 2005a: 25).

Exit conferences at the conclusion of inspections were much more participatory in the US and Australia across the three decades – in terms of residents, relatives and different kinds of staff – than in England. At the conclusion of an inspection, inspectors tend to meet only with the registered manager and perhaps their deputy and/or the owner. Community Health Councils did not have a right to enter homes under the post-1984 regulatory framework. Non-governmental organizations were generally weak players in the regulatory regime compared to the situation in Australia and the US. On the other hand, residents, as in the US and Australia, have over the period of this research been granted more effective access to inspection reports. They are today available on the Internet and mostly accessible physically in the nursing home and on admission.

RIGHTS OF RESIDENTS IN THE REGULATORY PROCESS

Generally the emphasis on resident rights has been less marked in England than in the US and Australia, though in 2005 the Chairman of the Commission for Social Care Inspection signalled a shift to a more 'rights based approach'. Moreover, the devolved nature of regulatory authority in England has always allowed some interesting rights-sensitive innovation. When a Hindu proprietor felt he was being subject to racist harassment by inspectors, one DHA put the President of the Hindu Association on the inspection team. English nursing home care is more paternalistic in its spirit than in the other two countries. The right to vote and be politically engaged, which is given considerable importance in the Australian process, never arose in any of the English inspections observed.

Privacy rights are a much less sensitive issue. The research team observed more instances of English inspectors entering a resident's room without knocking than instances where all the much larger numbers of US and Australian inspectors combined were observed to do this. Means of screening that would be unacceptable in the US and Australia (such as portable partitions as opposed to ceiling to floor tracked curtains in dual occupancy rooms) were seen to be accepted as sufficiently private in English inspections. On the other hand, for the whole period of this study, from the 1980s to the current decade, English inspectors eschewed observation of treatments (for example, treating pressure sores) on the grounds that this was an invasion of the private relationship between resident and nurse. In the US observation of treatments was an important part of inspecting for quality.[8]

Paternalistic communication that failed to respect residents' dignity was much more tolerated by English inspectors. For example, we saw inspectors as they observed nurses saying: 'These are our babies as we call them.' This would not attract any adverse comment from the inspector, nor would it be mentioned as a dignity issue in their report.

At every stage since 1988 the English regulatory process has been less resident-centred than the process in the US and Australia, though some radical proposals are currently under consideration, including service users becoming part of inspection teams (Commission for Social Care Inspection 2005b). While resident interviews are a more important source of information today than they were in the 1990s, and while a more prominent place in the inspection process is devoted to resident interviews, this is still a less prominent place than in the other two countries. Interviews with staff below the registered manager and with visitors were also much less frequent in English than in Australian and US inspections between 1988 and 1993, though by 2004 the English process had been reformed to place much greater emphasis on evidence-gathering from a plurality of stakeholders. Even so, the proportion of the inspection spent in the director of nursing's office, asking him or her questions and asking to see documentation, was consistently much higher in England than in the other two countries.

During some inspections, both the registered manager and his or her deputy were observed to sit with the inspector answering questions and offering interpretations during the entire time that the inspectors were checking care plans. Many inspections comprised more than an hour chatting with the registered manager mainly about documentation, and less than half an hour looking around the home and talking to someone other than the boss. One inspection observed in 2004 began with five hours sitting in the same room with the registered manager, chatting and checking various items of documentation with her. Perhaps for these reasons, the average English inspection identified fewer problems that require attention than the average Australian and US inspection until the mid-1990s. While this difference was great, it was not so after 2000, when English inspections were recording more breaches and US and Australian inspections fewer.

REGULATORY RESOURCES

Good training is one of the most important resources for regulatory inspectorates because it helps inspectors make more strategic use of their limited time. There was no national training (and in most DHAs in the 1990s no district training for nursing home inspectors) right up to 2005, though from 1990 the Department of Health (1990) did distribute a training workbook and audio tape. Inspectorate staffing levels were considerably lower in England than Australia, and hugely lower than in the US between 1989 and 1993. The resources devoted to inspection by the 15 DHAs visited were really rather similar – around, often under, one full-time equivalent inspector for each 20 nursing homes.[9] These human resources were responsible not only for inspection but also registration and complaints handling. By 2005 staffing levels were more similar to those in Australia, but the government had announced an intention to cut the number of inspectors. One of the advantages of DHA location of inspectors in the 1980s and 1990s was that they could call on a variety of health profession specializations. Medical practitioners frequently joined inspections, as did social workers, occasionally physiotherapists, fire officers and architectural experts. Pharmacists from the DHA regularly visited nursing homes.

On the other hand, the absence of paperwork burden in the job during the 1990s, and even today in comparison to the US, means that inspectors can get around nursing homes quicker to check the things that matter. While the average English nursing home inspection was taking about four inspector-hours in 1989–93, in this period the average US inspection was taking more than ten inspector-days. But the English inspectors were visiting nursing homes much more often. Most, but not all, of the DHAs were able to meet their statutory obligation of two inspections a year.[10] Nursing homes with serious problems could receive visits weekly or even more frequently. The majority of these inspections between 1989 and 1993 were by a single inspector, though many authorities had one inspection a year with two or three inspectors covering a range of disciplines beyond nursing.[11] Compared to the regular inspection process for homes already registered, the initial registration process tended to be more multidisciplinary – with the involvement of nurses, doctors, pharmacists, planning officers, engineers, environmental health officers, fire safety officers and architects (see, for example, Davis 1987: 11). During the 1980s and 1990s inspections were short where no serious problem was evident. It was and still is a regime of more frequent, shorter, less enforcement-oriented inspections, with smaller inspection teams than in the US and Australia. Aspects of the regulatory inspection literature are consistent with the notion that frequent tap-on-the-shoulder inspections, which never impose penalties with a probability or severity large enough to make it economically rational to comply, can actually be useful in motivating compliance (for example, Gunningham and Grabosky 1998; Scholz and Gray 1990). This might be because inspection works more by reminding business people of obligations they accept but lose sight of, more than because of fear of punishment.

Many health authorities in the 1980s and 1990s were doing one announced and one unannounced inspection a year, though some were doing them all unannounced. The former became the national standard a decade later. It is still not necessary for inspectors to cover all key standards in each inspection – so long as this is accomplished across all inspections during the year. This enables frequent but short drop-ins on problem facilities where perhaps only a few standards are covered.

STREET-LEVEL BUREAUCRATS

At every point in the history of English nursing home regulation, inspectors more decisively fit Michael Lipsky's (1980) depiction of street-level bureaucrats than Australian inspectors, and much more so than American inspectors. Lipsky conceived street-level bureaucrats as public servants who have a lot of face-to-face interaction with the public and are granted considerable discretion in how to conduct that interaction.

American inspectors are quite regimented by the detailed nature of the national regulatory regime they must comply with, by federal inspectors who follow their inspections to check that they are doing things by the book, by a tyranny of documentation they must fill out on the inspection process and by rigorous supervisory arrangements within state government bureaucracies. English inspectors at all periods of this study were observed at times to ignore blatant breaches of standards when they personally felt the standards were not very important (for example, thinking it is not particularly important that the home meet requirements to make inspection reports readily available to residents) or where they thought compliance with the standard was not especially important in a particular context. American inspectors do not dare make any big decisions to do something without calling their supervisor first, though they do make big decisions to ignore problems without doing so. It was only in a few English DHAs we visited in the early 1990s that supervisors at head office exerted any significant checking of what inspectors were requiring. Often a head office bureaucrat signed the formal letter that was sent to the home after the inspection, but this was typically perfunctory, done without reading the file or talking to the inspector, and in any case most of what was negotiated during the inspection was never recorded in the letter. Today inspection reports are much more detailed and more informative to consumers than the letters of often only one page in the 1989–93 period, and are read by supervisors, though to nothing like the degree of checking in the US. But it remains the case today that power is concentrated at street level rather than in an office in London or the regions.

Between 1989 and 1993, in most DHAs the inspector also had effective control over registration of new facilities and new beds. This secured their power on the street during a period when the industry was expanding, most homes were full to capacity and desperately wanting approval of new beds. Well into the 1990s many homes had a grandfathered registration that did not meet the requirements of the 1984 Act. Such homes wanted to get 1984 Act registration because this was an asset when they came to sell to a new proprietor who might not be able to call upon the protection of grand-fathering. So we observed interactions like the following: 'Unless you put that sluice in, I will not put you up to the health authority [for a certificate under the 1984 Act]' (inspector in 1990). While there had been a small number of deregistrations and a larger but still modest number of prose-cutions of residential homes in the districts where our research was con-ducted in this period, none of the DHAs we visited had prosecuted or deregistered a nursing home. Over a two-year period in the mid-1980s Day and Klein (1987a: 1022) found only six nursing homes across the entire country that had actually been deregistered, though they found 31 other cases where steps had been taken down the path toward deregistration. Across the nation during this period at least ten times as many deregistra-tions of residential homes seemed to occur as of nursing homes. This was a common grievance of the inspectors against their DHA superiors: 'I get fed up with being told to "go and sort it out with them Mary". The problem is no one wants confrontation.' Today nursing home and residential home deregistration statistics are combined. Their level, however, does not seem greatly different from the level that has prevailed over the previous two decades. In 2002–03 26 care homes for older people were deregistered in England (Dalley et al. 2004: 42) and from March 2004 to December 2005 there were 11 urgent closures as a result of enforcement action by the CSCI (Commission for Social Care Inspection 2005b: 247).

ENFORCEMENT POWERS AND STREET-LEVEL CAPABILITIES

The power of inspectors came not from such formal enforcement power, but from influence over approval of new beds, new homes and buildings. Inspectors also exercised reputational influence. They could and did spread word among those who decided nursing home placements that a certain facility was badly managed. This could hurt the nursing home, leaving it with substantial numbers of empty beds. Bear in mind that nursing homes got about a third of their referrals from hospitals funded by the same DHA that employed the inspector. On the carrots as opposed to sticks side of the equation, we were surprised at the degree to which English inspectors were a kind of business consultant to many less sophisticated providers in a market of small providers where most were not very sophisticated in a business sense. We observed them giving advice on the level at which they should set their fees, on numbers of beds that were too small to be economic, that 'you must sell yourselves' to get private paying patients, and in one case even assisting with writing a prospectus for home owners who were selling up. 'The local sole proprietor needs you. You hold their hand', a DHA inspector explained. Another said: 'I have made money for them by taking my advice, on staffing rotas etc.'

We did not see American inspectors ever play a significant role of this sort and we saw it quite rarely among Australian inspectors. Influence certainly comes from playing this role, as became clear when we learnt that inspectors 'frequently' took calls for advice on 'should I buy this nursing home?' One inspector said she would sometimes say 'Yes this is the kind of nursing home that would suit your style' or vice versa. She would divulge problems that might show the home to be overvalued. So at the end of the day, when owners sell up, the inspector can affect their capital gain or loss, perhaps markedly, at least with the way district regulation worked before there was a national inspectorate.

It is easy for English inspectors to turn a blind eye to failures to comply, even considerably easier than for American inspectors. Gifts of forbearance are widely used to entice a posture of cooperation: 'They know I'm a dangerous person to cross. I can come down like a ton of bricks. I can also turn a blind eye as long as patients are OK.' In another DHA we got this kind of story from the proprietor's side in 1991:

> I was wanting to keep the registration people at a distance at first when I got going. But I learnt that was a mistake. I have nothing to fear from them. In fact [local inspector] helped me with showing how to market this place when we were struggling to get going. We had our backs to the wall and they were flexible on staffing and other things during that tough time. If they wanted to nail me, they would have nailed me then, so I have no reason to fear them now.

District Health Authority inspectors between 1989 and 1993 often had the ability to write and revise district guidelines for quality care more or less at will. And the guidelines mattered in that world where there were no national standards and where local compliance was secured by sometimes weak, sometimes potent, informal levers, and where the legitimacy of all of this was extremely unlikely ever to be tested in a court. Street-level bureaucrats used this discretion to bring into existence a diverse plurality of guidelines throughout the nation. This diversity became a resource for national standard setting in the late 1990s and subsequently. An example of how

DHA guidelines empowered street-level bureaucrats was the Torbay 'Notes for guidance for the registration of nursing homes, 1990': '3.1 . . . Conditions may be varied by the Registering Authority in the light of circumstances specific to individual establishments. Any such conditions specified would be notified by the Registering Authority to the person registered.'

Postures of resistant defiance and disengagement, on the other hand, were responded to with harassment. One inspector's opening line with a new registered manager observed in 1990 was: 'Be honest with me. If there is something wrong, tell me and we'll sort it out. If you try to hide things, then . . . I can make life difficult for you.' The inspector explained later that this meant unannounced visits at very awkward times. This inspector described himself as 'a benevolent dictator – pleasant, happy, but ignore my advice and I'll give you hell'. While inspectors could not credibly threaten them with prosecution, they did credibly threaten with weekly, even daily, inspections until something was fixed, and an accumulation of formal letters that proprietors could worry might build a record to threaten present and future registrations of beds. One inspector explained this as 'The dripping tap technique works.' Part of a harassment strategy was often to mobilize other inspectorates to get on their case – local authority public health inspectors and environmental health inspectors, occupational health service (OHS) inspectors, the benefit fraud inspectorate, gas installation engineers, police fraud and sexual abuse investigators, approved electrical contractor certifications, consultants who provide written assessments for control of substances hazardous to health, disposal of soiled waste and SHARPS contractors, pharmacy suppliers or consultants who sign off pharmacy compliance, fire officers and others.

The nursing homes that have the biggest quality of care problems are often struggling financially. For them, the most powerful actor in their environment is a bank who they are counting on to lend them more money. These banks have become an increasingly important network partner for inspectors securing improved compliance as inspection reports have become available on the Internet and publicly displayed in facilities. Best banking practice when lending to care homes today is to check their inspection reports. So when street-level bureaucrats tacitly threaten an excoriating inspection report, they can in these circumstances be threatening the proprietor with bankruptcy.

Receivership is a complex process of different players sounding out one another's risks and how they might be managed. Usually the bank initiates the conversation with the inspectorate rather than the reverse. That is, the bank starts paying attention to a proprietor who is getting deeper into debt; then when they check the inspection report and find they have some serious issues with the regulator, they decide to talk to the frontline inspector about how intractable these problems are. In these conversations the question is raised whether in all the circumstances receivership would be wise. Both banks and inspectors have networked relationships with business people and care home chains that specialize in taking over ailing homes which have either gone into receivership or are on the verge of it. These receivership specialists have a track record of building up a home struggling with regulatory compliance and a level of quality that can fill its beds. After building it up they sell it on for a healthy capital gain. Struggling proprietors know that recurrent failure to meet standards is one of the major causes of bankruptcy, that the inspectorate has often in the past pushed homes into bankruptcy to solve a quality of care problem. They know that banks and inspectors can tacitly conspire against them to hand their business over to the 'vultures' that profit from reviving homes that have lost the confidence of the inspectorate. They know this, for example, from presentations that banks and finance houses give at industry seminars on what they require by way of meeting minimum standards for finance in their sector. More homes close or change ownership because proprietors see this coming down the track than are closed through formal processes of deregistration. Incapacitation of neglectful or abusive organizations occurs not through formally legal means, but by signalling and feinting at catastrophic inspection reports that motivate the proprietor to sell up before the value of his or her investment plummets.

In saying that formal enforcement almost never happens in the UK, this should be qualified by the fact that a few DHAs in the 1990s had on more than one occasion suspended funding for new admissions to a nursing home until something was fixed. In one DHA there had been three freezes on new admissions in the three years to 1991. Both prosecutions and deregistration of residential homes by local authorities in the 1980s and 1990s were more common, we were told, because local authorities had in-house lawyers with experience of prosecution in other regulatory domains (and DHAs did not), and because residential homes more often than nursing homes blew up on local authorities as political scandals in the media. But in the care home sector generally both then and today prosecution for failure to meet legal standards of quality of care is rare.[12] Until 2000 the legislative framework did not provide for it; with the Care Standards Act 2000 there is the option of prosecution (CSCI 2005b: 95). When prosecution does happen it is for some aspect of the home's financial management, though the prosecution case can be prioritized if residents are being abused or neglected. The dearth of both scandal and tough enforcement in England during the 1980s and 1990s is part of a more placid political picture of nursing home regulation in comparison to the tumult occurring in the US and Australia.

A senior Department of Health official said in 1991 that he 'took comfort from four things': (1) consumer groups were not expressing concern about nursing home care; (2) serious tribunal hearing problems were rare; (3) complaints were few; (4) scandals were few. He continued: 'We tend to be reactive rather than proactive and there is nothing to react to!' No senior aged care bureaucrat in the US or Australia in the 1980s and 1990s would say any one of these things about the political scene they managed (except for some US and Australian jurisdictions where it would have been said that hearings were rare). Yet, this British bureaucrat said that the reverse of most of these four things was true on residential homes for the aged. When we asked the senior Department of Health official responsible for nursing homes in the 1990s whether he saw non-compliance with agreed action plans following nursing home inspections as a problem, given that there was no system for checking that plans of action were actually implemented (there is today), he said he was 'not getting many problems'. Then he later conceded that he was perhaps not in a position to know. This was an honest concession that in the Thatcher–Major era there was a 'see no evil, hear no evil' approach to nursing home quality. The central bureaucrats in both London and even the DHAs thus relinquished the field to the street-level bureaucrats in the 1980s and 1990s. Since 2000 the constant bureaucratic restructurings of the Blair government created so much top-down unproductive work for the central bureaucrats that the still untrained street-level inspectors by default continued mostly to be able to keep things under their local street-level control in more or less the way they always had been. The thinking that surrounded the top-down grand restructurings of inspectorates seemed to take little account of the fact that what was being restructured was a street-level bureaucracy. There seemed limited interest in understanding the good and bad things inspectors were currently accomplishing, and then steering that accomplishment.

Enforcement capability probably stepped up with the creation of the Commission for Social Care Inspection. Client surveys conducted by the Commission in 2004 indicated that service users wanted a much tougher approach to enforcement, including more unannounced inspections. The Chief Inspector and Chairman both told us that enforcement actions against care homes had more than doubled by 2004, but when we asked for statistics on enforcement actions at various levels of the Commission, no one could provide any. Information on enforcement was highly decentralized and non-systematic. In 2005 the CSCI published an impressive document on the state of social care in England, which included enforcement data. Unfortunately the data were aggregated across all social care services. So it is not possible to attach evidentiary credibility to claims that enforcement more than doubled in the middle of the present decade. And it remains a safe inference that at all points during the past three decades English nursing home inspection had less enforcement grunt than Australian and American inspection.

Another thing that 2005 speeches by the Chair and Chief Inspector of the Commission indicated was about to change was the remarkable total absence of investment in national training for inspectors. But again, at the time of writing we have not seen the evidence of this happening.

JOB SATISFACTION OF THE STREET-LEVEL BUREAUCRAT

Many English inspectors said they enjoyed the freedom and professional challenge of being a self-trained street-level bureaucrat, just as many American inspectors said they hated being a low-level functionary of a more top-down bureaucracy. The dedication of English inspectors in some cases was extraordinary. Without being paid overtime, they would do inspections at 5 a.m. on a Saturday morning to catch staff asleep on the job because they felt the obligations of their office, felt only they stood between corner-cutting proprietors and the exploitation of the elderly. A dozen of them spontaneously said to us that they enjoyed their work and felt they were achieving things. We suspect that to varying degrees, even in the cases where they thought that half the time their advice was not followed (some said it was followed 90 per cent of the time or more), the tenor of general opinion was of inspector job satisfaction. Between 1989 and 1993, English inspectors were consultants. They had no qualms about offering advice to nursing homes on exactly what they should do to fix a problem. At this time, the philosophy in both Australia and the US, in contrast, was that the job of inspectors was to detect and report failures to meet standards. It was the job of the nursing home to come up with the strategies to get themselves back in compliance. In the present decade, English policy has aligned with the US and Australia in this respect, though English inspectors still have more discretionary latitude to offer advice on precisely what they want the nursing home to do when they feel moved to do this. And they still do it frequently, but much less than in the 1990s and 1980s.

English inspectors who dictate what homes should do deploy some interesting tactics for keeping power at the street level. In one DHA the inspector in the 1980s had complete discretion over the content of letters directing homes as to what was required following an inspection. She told us that sometimes proprietors try to go over her head to her boss at the DHA. 'When this happens, I say no negotiation. We'll do it all by the book now.'

OTHER STREET-LEVEL COMPLIANCE LEVERS

Nursing staff feared the capacity of inspectors to initiate action against their professional registration by the United Kingdom Central Council for Nursing – the statutory body responsible for registration of nurses. 'Companies think they own someone body and soul. But if they employ professionals, they have professional duties that can override loyalty to their employer' (DHA inspector, 1990). More importantly, inspectors could get nurses and other health professionals blacklisted in their health authority; indeed even in distant health authorities blacklisted matrons could suffer. This was variously described as the DHA's 'naughty nurses list' or its 'Don't touch with a bargepole list.' We were surprised that inspectors actually sent circulars to all their nursing homes advising that 'If X applies, please contact us.' Then they would be given the contact details of a previous employer who had dismissed them. We wondered how much procedural justice there was in getting on and off these lists when a nurse was unjustly accused of something. What was clear was that this was quite important in underwriting the inspector's limited formal power. Some DHA inspectors described the most important part of their job as to 'get the right person to be in charge'. This is a big difference from the thinking of American inspectors. Our fieldwork does indeed suggest that the quality of the CEO of a nursing home does drive the quality of care very considerably. But in more extreme cases, the attitude seemed to be if the person in charge was competent and trustworthy, everything else would fall into place without much need to worry about regulatory oversight. The most interesting thing about this approach was that DHA inspectors felt they had sufficient influence to wear down an incompetent or untrustworthy manager until the owner felt the only sensible option was to replace them, or at least that this could be accomplished much of the time.

Similarly to what Hawkins (1984, 2002) has found with both British environmental and OHS inspectors, there is much more bargain and bluff in British than in US nursing home regulation. We have seen that it was possible to bluff providers into planning for nursing homes with inferior economies of scale, when Registered Homes Tribunal decisions, in cases where this bluff was called, were quite clear in saying that there was no legal authority to do this.

A handful of nursing homes had been harassed out of business when, as one inspector put it, '[I] made myself such a pest that they decided to get out.' Another put it this way: 'I just hung around being unpleasant. I asked them to do expensive things to keep their registration and I kept at them and at them. Sometimes I was there day after day every day. Until they decided life would be easier just to sell up.' One of the expensive things that could be done was issuing a notice under Section 25(3) of the 1984 Registered Nursing Homes Act to specify the numbers and qualifications of nursing staff the home must have. On the other hand, the English process includes a lot of 'nattering' about things that might be done better, without confronting them in the ritual seriousness of an exit conference that was characteristic of most US and Australian jurisdictions in most time periods. For many inspectors, as one explained, the main levers are praise and disapproval: 'If you give them a pat on the back when things are going well, but point out to the same people things that are wrong, they know you are serious.'

One DHA described a clear hierarchy of interventions when a serious problem existed and was not fixed: step 1 was a revisit; then a stern letter if the problem was still there after the revisit; then a meeting with senior management of the health authority (this had happened only three times in 1990), the proprietor being called before a semi-formal meeting of the health authority itself to discuss why the registration of the home should not be withdrawn;[13] and finally a tribunal hearing to formally seek withdrawal of registration (see Figure 5.1). In the midst of escalation up this pyramid, if the nursing home was a member of the Registered Nursing Home Association, their inspector would be called in to provide a second opinion on the problem and offer advice to the home on how it might be addressed. The escalation to a Registered Homes Tribunal hearing part of the pyramid was mostly bluff during the 1980s and 1990s. Rosalind Brooke Ross's (1987: 2) systematic research on appeals of nursing homes to the tribunal showed that nursing home owners were more likely to win than health authorities: 'Registration and Inspection Officers have found tribunals fraught – cross examinations have been unpleasant, often undermining their credibility . . . There is a tendency for tribunal members to see the owners as victims and to disregard the plight of residents . . . Relatives and friends who could be useful witnesses are frightened and put off by the process.' The Registered Nursing Home Association (RNHA) claimed in a 1990 interview that they had led 40 Registered Homes Tribunal cases on behalf of members in the previous four years and had not lost one. Inspectors pointed out that in many of these cases, however, compromise settlements were actually reached during the tribunal process. And during this period it seems that health authorities were winning a majority of cases that were not backed by the Registered Nursing Home Association.

Another DHA in the early 1990s also had a clear sense of an enforcement pyramid. At the base was an informal caution, then a letter from the inspector, then a letter of intent from the inspector's manager with a schedule of things that must be fixed and dates by which this must be accomplished, then a formal meeting at the health authority, then the service of a

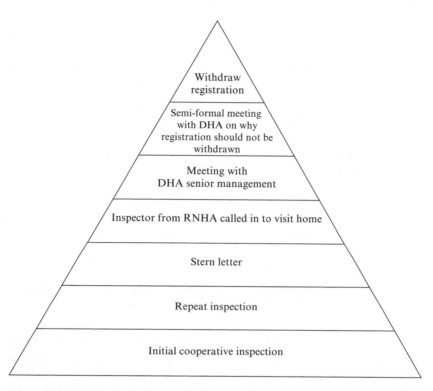

Figure 5.1   One English District Health Authority's nursing home enforcement pyramid in the 1980s

formal notice, then another formal notice, then prosecution and then deregistration. The lead inspector in this DHA said: 'They are left in no doubt
that if necessary we will use the powers we have even though you are reluctant to use them. But you must make them understand that reluctance is
not a sign of weakness.' She also confided that sole proprietor nursing
homes 'think we have more powers than we do and we don't disabuse them
of that'. But bluff does not work with the chains, who know exactly what
powers the inspectorate has.

NETWORKED GOVERNANCE COORDINATED BY INSPECTORS

In the above sections we have shown that while British inspectors have
always had weak enforcement capabilities compared to their colleagues in

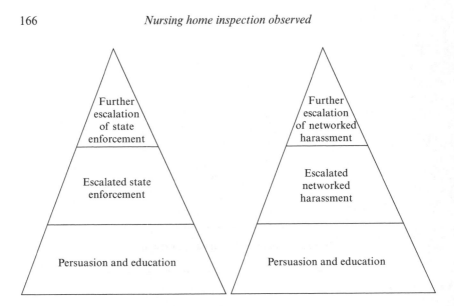

*Figure 5.2   Responsive regulatory pyramid of escalated state intervention
                (left) and escalated networked governance (right)*

other nations, they have adapted to this situation by networking regulatory
clout, networking with those who make final decisions over registering new
beds, networking in other inspectorates to campaigns of harassment, networking in social workers who control the flow of placements into the
nursing home, networking in the influence of banks who lend to nursing
homes and even networking in business opportunities through putting in a
good word for them and offering strategic advice that actually is useful. If
street-level bureaucrats are free enough from top-down control and care
enough about achieving regulatory objectives, and English inspectors are
very free and mostly do care a lot, they can be remarkably creative in networking informal enforcement capability. This fits a large literature (for
example, Hawkins 1984, 2002) on inspectors as creative in adapting informal capability in the absence of formal powers. It also fits the idea that
formally weak regulators, such as poorly resourced and legally unsophisti-
cated regulators in developing countries, can still mobilize a sophisticated
responsive regulatory pyramid by escalating up through more and more
networking of pressure on a recalcitrant firm, as opposed to escalating up
through progressively more intensive state enforcement (Figure 5.2 represents this idea – adapted from Drahos 2004).

  Indeed, if we believe that partnership achieves more than power assertion, if we believe that we have entered an era of networked governance
where hierarchical command and control does not work as well as it did in

the decades of the wave of regulatory state growth following the New Deal (Braithwaite 2005a; Castells 1996; Shearing and Wood 2003), there is the possibility of paradox here. This possibility is that the crazy British history of constant restructuring of inspectorates left inspectors a lot of space to be creative in their networking and therefore reasonably effective in their work. Responsive regulatory theorists like the authors of this book would never create inspectorates with such weak powers, such poor training, so buffeted by bureaucratic restructurings. Yet we were able to observe these inspectors regularly having an impact in improving quality in variegated idiosyncratic ways. Our observations fitted their own reports of success in securing voluntary compliance more often than not when poor practice was detected. Ritualistic compliance was also a problem, but not as much as in the US. English inspectors were interested in improved outcomes, even when their standards were input oriented. Their mentality was not that of the US inspector who felt that they had done their job if all their documentation for the survey met federal standards, who felt that whether the plan of correction would actually improve things was not their concern. When English inspectors thought something was really important, they would move beyond nattering to relentless following up until the problem was fixed. We can stand back and say that as we ourselves move closer to retirement, we would rather end up in the English nursing homes we visited (especially now that their food is improving!) than the Australian homes, and even more so most of the US homes we saw. While the data are poor, like us the English commentators who have the greatest observational experience cross-nationally and across time also conclude that English care has improved and that regulation has probably driven some of this (Day et al. 1996; Walshe 2003: 50–51).

So it is tempting to conclude that it can be quite a good thing to just leave it to untrained street-level bureaucrats with limited tools to be creative in the networked governance of quality. We do not quite reach this conclusion, though we do conclude that such poorly trained inspectors with limited formal responsive regulatory capability achieve a huge amount compared to what would happen in their absence. One cannot be completely sanguine about the English outcomes because we also saw so much that could have been better – elders having to put up with terrible food of limited choice, inspectors who did not check out pressure sores that might have been crawling with maggots for all they knew, inspectors who in other respects showed scant concern for the privacy of residents as evidenced by not knocking as they entered their room, street-level bureaucrats who sometimes got things done by methods that were unjust, unaccountable and even tyrannical. So we see it as possible to learn from the accomplishments of the adaptive flare of English street-level bureaucrats, to put checks and balances in place against occasional procedural unfairness, to give them formal powers to use when partnership and networked escalation fails, as we observed (and they said) it often does.

LEARNING

While the English inspectors were coming up with many more creative networked governance ideas for achieving results, when good things happened in Australia and the US, there were much better avenues for disseminating the learnings. Training was one way of doing it. But more importantly, Australian and American street-level bureaucrats were observed to learn much more from their inspection teammates during the inspection process, in the car on the way to and from inspections, over conversations during the lunch break, than English inspectors. English inspectors were much more often on their own when they went into the field and were much more fundamentally self-taught.[14] There was less of what Christine Parker (2002) has called triple-loop learning in the English nursing home industry (see Figure 5.3).

Triple-loop learning can mean that, in response to a regulatory conversation (Black 1997) with an inspector, a quality innovation is put in place to fix the problem in one facility or one wing of one facility. The second loop is that the innovation is diffused to all wings of the facility, all facilities in a nursing home chain or all provision across one trust. The third loop is that the

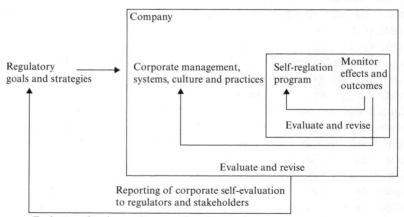

Source: Parker (2002: 278).

Figure 5.3   Triple-loop learning

regulatory system diffuses the innovation to all nursing homes across the nation. National training is one way this can happen. Another is the dissemination of innovations through the kinds of publications associated with the Australian Better Practice in Aged Care Awards discussed in the next chapter. The adaptability of English inspectors in interaction with the excellence of English nursing professionalism produced across the past three decades a record of single-loop learning in the interaction between inspectors and nursing home staff that we found inspiring. But the English record of double- and triple-loop learning is comparatively poor. One of the things the triple-loop learning in Figure 5.3 accomplishes is continual renewal of the content and process of regulation itself. It is not just that health providers learn how to learn; the entire regulatory system learns how to learn.

CLUB GOVERNANCE

There is an interesting literature on financial regulation in the City of London and other domains of British regulation fitting in some ways a model of club governance in comparison to the adversarial regulatory governance characteristic of the US (for example, Moran 2003). The image of British business regulation as the work of a gentlemen's club is contested in that literature; many researchers believe that even if this once was an adequate characterization of British regulation, it dissipated with the arrival of Rupert Murdoch and Texas tycoons who seemed more like cowboys than gentlemen to English public school networks.

Equally though, there is a consensus that English regulation at the very least retains a more club-like residue than American regulation. Nursing home regulation in Britain is more a ladies' than a gentlemen's club. The ladies do not come from elite public schools, not even from the elite of the nursing profession because geriatric nursing is low status in the English professions, as in Australia and the US. But nursing is a small world, a regional market where nurses want jobs where their partners also work and where their children go to school, a world where reputations drive promotion and where opportunities for promotion are quite plentiful. So inspectors, Registered General Nurses (RGNs), nursing home proprietors and regional industry association executives do belong to a little club. Doubtless like all forms of club governance in the UK, it is under threat today as nursing home regulation becomes more effectively national. It is also under threat from the gradual growth of chains, whose employees are promoted in national rather than regional reputational networks.[15] Chains are also not vulnerable to the bluff, the informal sticks and carrots discussed above that can work rather well with less legally sophisticated proprietors.

The reach of an inspector as a uniquely influential regional club member was illustrated in 1990 at one DHA where an inspector told us of the recent demise of the president of the regional branch of the Registered Nursing Home Association. This president was adversarial, assertive on 'the rights of nursing homes' and lambasted the 'Gestapo tactics of regulators'. The senior inspector in this health authority told us that he had approached another local *éminence grise* of the industry at church with: 'You need to get rid of him if you want to get anywhere. He's a real Arthur Scargill [the leader of the coal miners' strike crushed by Margaret Thatcher].' They did.

The club does not assemble in one place much at all. It is a networked club. Regional training events, sometimes convened by the regulators, sometimes by the industry, are one venue where large numbers of club members do get together. The English investment in such quality assurance training has been somewhat greater than in the US, somewhat less than in Australia. A rule of the club was to solve problems cooperatively, without confrontation whenever possible. When we referred to the remarkable record of the Registered Nursing Home Association in never losing tribunal cases in the years before the interview, the response was interesting:

> *JB:* With a 40 out of 40 record, you have a strong bargaining position. Why don't you play hardball as the Americans would say?
> *Industry association executive:* As a policy matter we would prefer our members to give way on all reasonable demands.

One reason for this is that the tribunal game is not seen as the main game; the main game is played on the turf of street-level bureaucrats:

> *Another industry association executive:* Confrontation is the last thing we want.
> *JB:* But you have the whip-hand. With your successful record on appeal, surely you could dig your heels in successfully?
> *Industry association executive:* We could win a lot of minor battles. But we would generate a lot of antagonism. She [the local inspector] can make life difficult for a nursing home.
> *JB:* How do you get this culture of cooperation? Is it because the association turns away members who ask the association to back them in confrontation or do members not even ask the association to back them?
> *Industry association executive:* I rather think members don't ask. They have to feel really aggrieved to ask for the association to be involved.

This in spite of the fact that a national industry association that backs them is likely to prevail on their behalf. One national association leader said that if he wrote to a DHA general manager, '90 per cent of cases they will back down. They will find a formula to resolve the problem.' A regional industry association secretary said the marching orders they had from association head office was to 'establish cooperative working relationships with your health authorities. And if in conflict, try to work it out reasonably yourselves, with logic rather than confrontation.' In both Australia and the US confrontation loomed as more important in such relationships. In the ultimate vindication of the existence of a kind of club, this local industry official also said: 'I suppose we [the industry and the health authority] are a mutual admiration society.' In one of the DHAs we visited in the early 1990s there was bad blood between the health authority and the association. Perhaps for this reason fewer than 20 per cent of the nursing homes in this district were members of the association. At the head offices of the national industry associations we were told that they did not receive many complaints from members on poor treatment by nursing home inspectors. This was a very different reality than that of Australia and the US. On the other hand, in common with the US and Australia, the industry associations reported that there was a general concern from their members about inconsistent interpretation of standards. The Chair and Chief Inspector of the Commission for Social Care Inspection in response both listed in various speeches in 2004 and 2005 improved consistency as one of their reform objectives.

As the foregoing paragraphs also illustrate, these clubs are local and one of their norms is to resolve things locally. In one late 1980s conflict where the Registered Nursing Home Association decided to take it to the tribunal, bearing in mind that a national precedent could be set – for good or ill – the District Health Authority just backed off. The inspector explained: 'I took on this job to play village cricket, not to open the batting for England.' When proprietors seek to break out of the rules of the club, one tactic of inspectors is to offer the proprietor an even bigger opportunity to break ranks with other members of the club, a prospect the proprietor finds terrifying:

A proprietor sometimes says other homes are getting away with this. I then say, 'I don't think so. But let's do a joint visit to the nursing homes where you think this is the case and we'll see together if it is true. You come with me.' Then he backs off. 'It could be a misunderstanding.'

This prospect is terrifying because the club is a community of shared fate (Rees 1994). Rees found the US nuclear industry to be a community of fate after the Three Mile Island near meltdown of a nuclear reactor. The industry believed that the result of another of their competitors going down like this could be that they would all go down because nuclear power would be so discredited. We see the same phenomenon in a document of the Registered Nursing Home Association entitled 'Factors for consideration when planning a nursing home':

> The most important ingredient in a nursing home is without doubt a good qualified nurse in charge . . . It is not sufficient to say that you can offer an attractive salary and position and so entice a nurse from another unit. This is totally irresponsible and liable to lead to deterioration in the standard of care offered in the homes in any particular area. Recent publicity shows us all too clearly that all homes can be tarred with the same brush when one is in trouble and so your responsibility in opening a home is not just to your own operation but to the quality of care offered generally in the area.

The club character of the regulatory community is also manifest in the less ruthless competition between industry associations for the same members than we see in the US and Australia. The Registered Nursing Home Association and the Independent Healthcare Association in the 1990s met together on the Joint Care Committee and made joint press statements at times on matters of industry policy. Eventually the Independent Healthcare Association went out of business, ending its limited competition with the Registered Nursing Home Association. At the same time, since 2000 with national standards and a national inspectorate, there has been some movement from local club governance to the more hierarchical regulatory state noted by Moran (2003). In spite of this, the English inspector continues to exercise more street-level control than his or her Australian and American counterparts, and he or she manages that less by mobilizing national enforcement powers, and more by mobilizing local networks of aged care elites.

CONCLUSION

We conclude that English nursing home regulation has at all times during the past three decades been a non-punitive form of regional club governance. It has also been an instance of networked governance (Rhodes 1997), where a dearth of formal enforcement capability is compensated for by escalated networking of pressure and harassment on recalcitrant nursing homes by actors as different as banks, other inspectorates and the nursing homes' own industry association. Consumer and advocacy groups are remarkably quiescent in regulatory politics/enforcement in comparison to the history of US and Australian regulation, more active in Scotland than in England (Office of Fair Trading 2005: 133–4). Age Concern may be a respected advocate for the aged, but is hardly an aggressive setter of policy agendas. This is likely the explanation for a regulatory politics less driven by media scandals of abuse and neglect than in the other two nations. It also explains why resident empowerment and resident rights are less central foci of English than of American and Australian regulation.

Inspectors are both key local figures in the regional club governance of the industry and key nodal actors in pulling together networks of governance. Inspectors have a much less political and less strategic role in the governance of nursing homes in the United States. They do not praise nursing homes when they are seen to have improved to the extent we observed English inspectors to do.

The US inspector's role is much more one of 'objectively' reporting the facts, leaving it to the 'higher-ups' in hierarchical state bureaucracies what to make of those facts and whether to initiate this or that kind of enforcement action. Those regional office decisions in the US are not made according to responsive regulatory principles. They are made by supervisors, who did not participate in the inspection, on the basis of a scope and severity grid that makes for a mandated response rather than one that is responsive to the commitment of the facility to compliance and improvement. English enforcement practice we have found to be more responsive, and creatively so, run from below by street-level bureaucrats who enrol more senior bureaucrats to their projects of quality improvement as needed. One suggestion of the critical literature on responsive regulation is that it can only work when regulation is heavily resourced. Yet comparative nursing home regulation reveals a richly resourced American modality of regulation that is non-responsive and much more poorly resourced English regulation that is responsive. Yet this does not totally refute the critique because nursing home regulation in England is still well resourced compared to other domains of English regulation.

These are major cross-national differences. However, while we are yet to consider Australian regulation in detail, this is a good point to list a number of bigger and smaller ways where we observed nursing home regulation in the three nations to be similar:

- While the investment varies, all nations have invested substantial resources into inspecting nursing homes, and expanding resources, compared to other regulatory domains and earlier periods of history. The English investment is less than in the US, but still around 2000 regulatory personnel.
- Regulation has become more nationally centralized, with Britain being the last to make this shift.
- While the three nations vary in the specificity of the standards, the standards cover the same basic range of issues in the three nations. In all three nations the list of standards has lengthened over the decades.
- There has been a shift away from standards that are concerned only with health issues to standards that emphasize social care, fulfilment, activities, resident empowerment and especially resident rights.

- Resident interviews have become a more central part of the process in all three countries. However, more time is spent poring over documentation than in talking to residents about the services they receive.
- Complaint procedures have become more formalized and better resourced over time, with England lagging behind the other two countries in this movement.
- While the reality of accomplishment of a homelike environment varies greatly among the three nations (with the English accomplishment the most impressive), all three nations have seen an increasing emphasis on the importance of a homelike environment in the standards themselves.
- Inspections mostly begin with a tour of the facility[16] and end with some kind of meeting with management of the nursing home where they get an indication of the problems that have been found. Each day of a multi-day inspection also tends to end with an exit meeting with management.
- Proprietors get a subsequent written report and this is made public on the Internet and within the facility.
- At least some of the inspections are unannounced.
- There has been some shift across the three decades from direct state regulation of standards to meta-regulation – regulated self-regulation where, for example, the nursing home is required by regulation to put quality assurance processes in place that set quality priorities and monitor their achievement.

NOTES

1. The Commission for Social Care Inspection (2005b: 95) has indicated that as part of a review of regulations the Commission will be seeking an expansion of the current range of enforcement options.
2. Even the official Department of Health (1990: 6–7) training manual implied the legitimacy of such informal restriction: 'However, the numbers of people engaged in an operation will have a crucial influence on the character of the setting, and it should not surprise us to find that while there is no legal requirement concerning size, regulating authorities often stipulate the maximum or ideal numbers of people to be accommodated . . . *Nursing homes* may also accommodate as few as 8 or 9 people though in the main they are larger with 25–30 patients being usual.'
3. Townsend's (1962) fieldwork notes from 1958–59 reveal that local nursing home regulators in the UK back then were keen to promote small homes that move away from the workhouse dormitory model.
4. Darton (1987: 9) found 54 per cent of nursing homes and residential homes to be former hotels in Canterbury and Thanet.
5. For example, Bennett (1986: 86) found in 1984–85 that 67 per cent of nursing home rooms were single occupancy (26 per cent double occupancy), this percentage being 78 per cent for residential care homes for the aged in the same district. But in a 1987 survey

of both residential and nursing homes in Canterbury and Thanet, across 86 homes, 48 per cent of the beds were in single rooms.

6. In 2003, 16.2 per cent of all residents in US nursing homes had pressure sores (National Healthcare Quality Report 2004).

7. Day et al. (1988: 32) reported that as far back as the mid-1980s, Hospital Advisory Service inspections of DHA services for the elderly made recommendations in a majority of their reports for extra physiotherapists and occupational therapists, and in a third of reports recommended more chiropodists, speech therapists and dieticians.

8. Day (1988: 51) has an alternative interpretation of this difference, which has some validity: '[T]here is more emphasis [in the US] on process or the way in which patients in nursing homes are treated. Here the stress is on providing active treatment using the medical model rather than, as in Britain, on a homely environment. Secondly, the American system, in sharp contrast to Britain's, focuses on individual patients.'

9. Day and Klein's (1987a: 1021) survey of 144 DHAs in 1984 found that for 97 of them most of the work fell on two part-time inspectors, mainly nurses, with occasional help from other district staff, including doctors. Half of our 15 health authorities were like this, the other half having nurse inspectors who were virtually full-time. Here we must bear in mind our bias toward districts where nursing homes were concentrated.

10. Under the 1984 Act residential care homes were required to have only one inspection a year.

11. Bennett (1987: 33) reported that in nine of 15 DHAs surveyed, doctors worked as a regular part of the registration/inspection team, and in five others a named doctor was available if needed.

12. From March 2004 to December 2005 the CSCI reported that there had been eight prosecutions for offences (Commission for Social Care Inspection 2005b: 247).

13. As an inspector from another DHA said of this option: 'Sounds like a lot of jaw jaw, but in the end it does bite.'

14. Or, as one inspector put it, consistent with a club governance interpretation: 'The people who have taught me my job are the very people I am inspecting.'

15. Perhaps American chains entering to compete with their members were the subtextual cowboys when the Registered Nursing Home Association put out a press release in 1990 that said: 'There are always a few bad apples in every barrel and the arrival of the "cowboy" riding at speed onto the health care ranch is a phenomenon of expansion – and one which is giving the quality care industry cause of considerable alarm.'

16. The tour is normally preceded by a brief courtesy call to the person in charge, though in England the initial meeting with the registered manager can take more than an hour and is a matter of greater inspectorial discretion.

6.   Australian nursing home regulation

The Australian case provides a study of two rather different regimes – the standards monitoring process implemented after the federal government took over nursing home regulation from the states in 1987, and the accreditation regime that replaced it after 1997. These regimes are not only different from each other; both are quite different from those we have been discussing for the US and England. Actually, our data also gives us some glimpses at the pre-1987 state government regimes in Australia that had quite a bit in common with the pre-2000 English regimes. Just as our conclusion has been that there have been some significant accomplishments of both the US and English regimes in improving quality of care, our conclusion will be that both Australian regimes have some significant accomplishments, as different as they all are. Equally, we will conclude that both Australian regimes, like the current regimes in the US and England, have some major limitations. The post-1997 Australian regime is more captured by the industry than the English and US regimes. Things have to be bad for non-compliance to be recorded or strong criticisms to be made in an accreditation report. Over 99 per cent of occasions when compliance with an expected outcome is assessed, compliance is the finding. In the very few cases where non-compliance is found, sanctions are rare.

For all that, just as there is much Australia can learn from the accomplishments of American and English inspection, there is much that other countries can learn from Australian approaches. The big accomplishment of the contemporary Australian regime is that it has given more salience to institutionalizing systems that pursue continuous improvement. We came to the current Australian system as critics of its enfeeblement of enforcement, and still are critical of that. However, we are impressed by what we have observed of how a captured regulatory regime can in a variety of ways still achieve a lot of good by building out from strengths. An argument of this book is that all of these regimes have productive and counterproductive features. All could do much better by eliminating the counterproductive qualities we identify empirically and by learning from strengths of the other regimes, adapting them to their conditions. The possibility of such adaptation is reinforced by our observations of subversive practices of street-level bureaucrats already adapting just those features that are policies of another system but not their own.

THE DATA

As in the US and English cases, interviews were conducted with key national figures from industry and professional associations, advocacy groups, heads of committees of enquiry into the industry, the law and government. The difference is that we were able to do more interviews in Australia, with some major national figures being interviewed more than ten times. In Australia, we also had the resources for a quantitative survey of the attitudes and practices of 191 inspectors and program managers (completed in 1992 with a 93 per cent response rate). In the 1980s and 1990s, but not in the current decade, we were able to interview all the key figures in all state and territory jurisdictions across the nation and observe inspections in all jurisdictions except the Northern Territory. Australian industry, professional, government and advocacy stakeholders in 1987–88 were also involved in the design of the entire study. We were able to attend many more conferences in Australia, to complete training courses for inspectors, to participate as members of industry liaison committees and advisory committees on specific issues, to sit on committees to make awards to the industry for excellence in quality of care, to be volunteers on the accreditation committee of a local facility near our home in Canberra, to observe meetings of inspectors with their supervisors on enforcement decisions, and to act in the 1980s, 1990s and the current decade as minor players of the policy game as consultants to the government, and in our policy research collaboration with the Australian Commission on Health Safety and Quality. In Australia, we were able to observe more of the day-to-day quality assurance, such as the entire process for admitting residents, in-services and consultancy visits.

Our requests to observe inspections (site visits) in 1999–2000 were denied, though we were granted interviews with the key players of the accreditation agency and the government at that time. The current CEO of the accreditation agency and his senior staff have been much more open, granting us access to observing 11 accreditation inspections in 2005 and 2006. This brings the total inspection events where the authors (with some observed by our 1990 co-authors David Ermann and Diane Gibson) have been able to observe all or a substantial part of the visit to 69 homes. John Braithwaite participated in the observation of 85 per cent of these inspections, often together with a co-author or two.

The data collection also involved quantitative data from 410 randomly sampled Australian nursing homes[1] (response rate 96 per cent) at which one of our research staff conducted interviews with the director of nursing (who was the CEO of the facility), a follow-up survey two years later after they had had a second inspection, qualitative interviews with proprietors of these nursing homes and a discussion group meeting with a number of staff of each nursing home. A reliability study was conducted at another 50 homes in which nurses on our research staff visited the home at the same time as the government team to rate compliance with the standards independently of the government ratings. A unique kind of qualitative data arose from the meetings between our nurses and the government inspectors at which each attempted to persuade the other why they were wrong and should change their compliance rating in one direction or another.

All in all, we were able to collect qualitative data from 507 Australian nursing homes and quantitative data on almost 460, for most of them at two or more points in time. As in Chicago, there was the opportunity to see the same nursing home inspected under different systems in the 1980s, 1990s and 2000s.

THE REGULATORY PROCESS

In common with the American and English process, both Australian standards monitoring and Australian accreditation inspections started with a team of at least two, normally two or three (at least one a registered nurse), having an initial meeting with the facility CEO, then a tour, and ended with an exit conference. At the exit conference, the inspectors (called assessors today, standards monitors under the old regime and inspectors under the even older state regimes) advise the nursing home of their interim conclusions about compliance in advance of actually writing their report. This was called a negotiation meeting originally with standards monitoring; it involved more detailed discussion around possible plans of action than under all the other regimes, in one case lasting five hours! If there is significant non-compliance in Australia, it is more common than in the US for sparks to fly. There is more resistant defiance in Australia than in the US and England, not the kind of capitulation we observed from American administrators when deficiencies are found with which nurses do not agree. After this meeting, a report is now made publicly available on the Internet as in England and the US. A number of informants mentioned a tendency not to put in the formal report information that was highly critical of the home.

Under standards monitoring, the home was then required either to dispute the ratings or prepare an action plan equivalent to an American plan of correction that must then be approved by supervisors as satisfactory. If instances of non-compliance were significant, the Australian process (like the English process) has always been more intensive than the US process in following up to ensure that the action plan is satisfactorily implemented and that it works in fixing the problem. About half these homes got a second standards monitoring revisit (meaning a third visit).

Under accreditation, if non-compliance is found, the agency puts in place a timetable for improvement. During the defined period within which corrective action must occur, the agency schedules a series of 'support contacts' to assess progress. If progress falls behind expectations during the defined periods, the intensity and frequency of support contacts is stepped up. If lifting support does not work, the 'sledgehammer' of a review audit (another full inspection covering all standards) will be applied. Accreditation might then be revoked, which is viewed as a serious action by providers. If at the end of the defined period there is still non-compliance, or there is evidence of 'a serious risk to the health, safety or well-being of a person receiving care', the provider is referred to the Federal Department of Health and Ageing for consideration of sanctions. These sanctions are mostly one or both of two kinds. The first is a notice to revoke the home's status as an approved provider for federally funded residents (most residents), revocation that is deferred if an approved adviser (mostly an outstanding director of nursing) is appointed jointly by the home and the department to work with the home to sort out its compliance problems. The second common sanction is suspension of government funding support on new admissions (normally for six months, though often lifted during this period). Most homes are totally dependent on government-funded places.

The rationale for these sanctions in the discourse of the department is in no way a deterrent rationale; decisions are conceived totally in a discourse of removing risks to residents and removing residents from risk. When we referred to the department teams that recommend sanctions as enforcement teams, we were corrected. Enforcement is not a word the department uses to describe what they do; they are 'compliance teams'. Only three homes have been closed by the federal government in the course of the past decade by revoking the home's status as an approved provider for federally funded residents.[2] In 'perhaps three or four other cases' homes closed of their own accord as a result of being unable to cope with what was being demanded under the shadow of a threat of revocation. This means formal and de facto closure of the home is something considerably less likely to happen to Australian than to English and American nursing homes. It also means it is less likely in the Australia of the 2000s than of the 1980s and 1990s,[3] when, in addition to occasional federal government revocation, there was more frequent state government licence revocation (something that no longer happens since states have almost totally ceded responsibility for aged care to the federal government).

The Department of Health and Ageing sends out a 'compliance team' to visit the home and make recommendations to the department's legal team in Canberra to put the home on a sanctions pathway; there are multiple opportunities to rectify before sanctions are actually imposed unless the non-compliance that leads to sanctions is an 'immediate and severe risk' (which in 80 per cent of sanctions cases it is). If the risk is not immediate and severe, the department normally calls the proprietor into their state headquarters for a firm warning that they are heading toward a sanctions path unless quick action is taken to secure compliance. Often representatives of peak industry bodies attend these meetings; in practice their role is less one of representing their member home against the department, more one of emphasizing to their member that the department is very serious and they need to mobilize professional commitment to improved compliance immediately. The association explains that they would hate to see their business wrecked in the way they have seen happen in other sanctions cases. The Department of Health and Ageing uses the industry association for the kind of networked escalation we describe in Figure 10.3 (Chapter 10). Before sanctions can be lifted the home has to show the 'sustainability of the system' they have put in place to ensure non-compliance will not recur. This is a nice feature of the current Australian regulatory framework in terms of preventing the kind of ritualistic plan of correction that we found to be so common in the US. In an 'immediate and severe risk' case, the accreditation agency is required to visit the home every day to monitor the well-being of residents until such a sustainable system is securely in place. In addition department inspectors visit weekly to check that the home is removing the risk.

A difference between the two Australian regimes is that under accreditation the nursing home completes a self-assessment on what it has done to improve and how it assesses its own performance against the standards prior to the arrival of the inspectors at the home. Inspectors arrive having read this and ready with a variety of questions about the improvements or problems reported.

Between the initial meeting with the director of nursing and exit after a second or third day at the facility a similar range of things occurred under both standards monitoring and accreditation. Interviews with a number of residents and relatives would be conducted. They would not be sampled quasi-scientifically as in the United States. Under standards monitoring, they were selected based on judgements of interviewability and in order to follow up, detective-style, concerns observed during the tour. Under accreditation, the director of nursing normally supplies names of residents who are highly communicative (a worrying bias, as inspectors often tend to concentrate on these residents) and are required to supply the names of residents who wish to speak with inspectors. The American practice of a group interview with a meeting of the residents' council (called residents' committee in Australia), that ensures there is an open opportunity for the most outspoken critics to speak up regardless of whether they are selected for interview or care plan review, is not part of the Australian process.

Problems detected on the tour or from the interviews with residents and staff, or from the self-assessment, are normally followed through to an audit of the resident's care plan, nurses' notes and other records. This is the reverse of the predominant English tradition of following problems from record review to interview with residents, relatives and staff.

Australian regulation has seen a shift from an emphasis on facility inputs such as staffing levels and the linen in the cupboards under pre-1987 state inspection, to outcomes measured in a resident-centred way under standards monitoring, to quality systems under accreditation. A criticism of the standards monitoring program often heard today is that it naively sought to measure outcomes without sufficiently evaluating holistic systems that deliver outcomes. Accreditation involved a return to emphasizing selected inputs assessed as relevant to evaluating critical quality systems, including management systems and staffing; but retained the essence of the shift to an outcome orientation, including the shift to social and resident rights outcomes, that characterized standards monitoring. While standards monitoring was more interested in the absolute level of outcomes, accreditation gives more emphasis to continuous improvement in outcomes and continuous improvement in systems. A large proportion of Australian nursing homes hire consultants to measure whether targeted outcomes are improving for their nursing home, comparing those outcomes to data from other homes. A key difference between standards monitoring and English and US inspection, on the one hand, and contemporary Australian accreditation, on the other, is that the latter sees inspectors spend a lot of time poring over such continuous improvement data.

While Australian accreditation puts much more emphasis on measuring and evaluating continuous improvement than Joint Commission accreditation in the US, the Australian accreditation model has been considerably influenced by the American tradition of health accreditation. As in American accreditation, the main decision in Australian accreditation is whether the facility will be accredited for three years. Ninety-two per cent of nursing homes get three-year accreditation (as of 2005). This compares to Australian Council on Heathcare Standards accreditation of hospitals, where the proportion of applicants getting full (four-year) accreditation fell from 80 per cent in 2002 to one-third in 2003 and 2004 (Healy 2007: ch. 5). Even though the prospects of failing accreditation are very low in Australian aged care, the Department of Health and Ageing pointed out in commenting on a draft of this book that it does seem to discriminate:

Almost all ongoing aged care homes were awarded three years' accreditation in the first round (93%) that took place between September 1999 and December 2000. By contrast, the majority of aged care homes (74%) that discontinued operating between Rounds 1 and 2 were awarded accreditation for periods of up to two years only. Therefore, there would appear to be a direct link between the Aged Care Standards and Accreditation Agency's action in relation to non-compliance, and a decision to leave the industry.[4]

When nursing home standards monitoring was introduced in 1987, the intention was a one-year inspection cycle. The inadequate resources for the program meant it struggled to achieve a two-year cycle for standard cases and achieved that with considerable inconsistency. Accreditation was in part a surrender of the government to its unwillingness in the mid-1990s to fund inspection on a cycle that was consistently one or even two years. The theory was that the systems orientation of accreditation would mean self-audit of quality would continue during the years when outside inspectors were not arriving at the facility. Ironically though, after new waves of nursing home scandals at the end of the 1990s and in 2006, and the media critiques of the enforcement weakness of accreditation during those periods, resources for accreditation were increased to the point where most homes that get three-year accreditation now receive at least one 'support contact' during which compliance is assessed each year that they are not assessed for their three-year accreditation. In 2005, homes received an average of 1.5 accreditation visits each, expected to increase to 1.75 in 2006–2007. This will include at least one unannounced visit a year.

One respect in which the difference between Australian accreditation and US inspection approximates the difference between US Joint Commission accreditation and US inspection is on the proportion of time devoted to different information sources. More accreditation time in both nations is spent on the review of documents, particularly those relevant to demonstrating the implementation of policies and quality assurance systems. There is also a somewhat greater emphasis with accreditation in checking resident records and interviews with management about systems, proportionately somewhat less emphasis with accreditation on interviews individually and collectively with residents and relatives (see, for example, the US data in HCFA 1998: vol. 1, 211), and less emphasis on observation of resident care (for example, minimal or no observation of treatment of pressure sores, no systematic med-pass observation to count drug administration errors).

One form of observation that was given more priority in the old standards monitoring than in any of the other regimes we observed was observation of the staff handover at the end of shifts. As one standards monitor explained, she liked to observe the handover because you see a lot about individuation of residents, or lack thereof, and you see how well staff use

documentation. We agree this was a strength of the old standards monitoring process, so much so that during our own fieldwork we frequently
asked if we could observe handovers. Both standards monitoring and
Australian accreditation gave a similar proportionate emphasis to non-
management staff interviews as the US process and a lesser emphasis on
this than English inspection.

With both standards monitoring and accreditation, the facility received
notice of the normal inspection. With both regimes, however, inspections
without notice and inspections outside daylight hours would occur when
facilities were identified as problem homes. Following criticism of the
accreditation agency for the rarity of unannounced spot checks, these have
increased. By 2006 28 per cent of support contacts were unannounced spot
checks.[5] This compares with all American and just under half of English
inspections continuing to be unannounced in 2004–05 (Commission for
Social Care Inspection 2005a: 23).

THE POLITICS OF REGULATORY GROWTH

The dynamics of how nursing home regulation became a political issue from
the late 1970s involved similar players to the US. Consumer groups from the
late 1970s and throughout the 1980s targeted the issue as a concern and generated information for the media by, for example, conducting abuse and
neglect phone-ins for nursing home residents and relatives (Social Welfare
Action Group 1982), by conducting reader surveys of residential aged care
in the consumer movement's flagship magazine, *Choice*, and more (Gibson
1998: 114). Horror stories of abuse and neglect became a common fare for
tabloids in most states, which started to do their own investigative work. The
Auditor-General (1981) (mirroring the comparable role of the General
Accounting Office in the US) reported that the federal government was
failing to assure value for the money it was spending on nursing homes.
Parliamentary enquiries followed (Giles Report 1985; McLeay Report
1982). These reports were extremely critical of the quality of care in
Australia's nursing homes. The Giles Report shocked the nation with
horrific colour photographs of pressure sores on the bodies of residents and
recommended a federal takeover of regulation from the states.

QUALITY OF CARE IMPROVES

In the mid-1980s idealistic and visionary public servants implemented the
new federal inspection regime with a strong rights ideology and considerable

empowerment of residents. There was a rise in the estimated percentage of nursing homes with residents' committees ranging from the largest increase in Queensland (from 3 per cent in 1986 to 90 per cent in 1991) to the smallest but still substantial increase in South Australia (from 34 per cent in 1986 to 81 per cent in 1991) (Braithwaite et al. 1992: 60). There was evidence from our research that nursing home managers in this period became more oriented to residents' rights more generally (Gibson 1998: 166–83), less task oriented and more oriented to resident outcomes, more willing to allow residents to take risks, began to put more emphasis on documenting care plans (while remaining way behind the US in the rigour and documentary detail of care planning) and increased in-service training of staff.

By the second wave of our data collection in 1991, directors of nursing were reporting more commitment to making their facility homelike, using outside consultants more to help them improve, involving residents more in decision-making, involving staff in decision-making, involving relatives and other carers, and emphasizing activities programs. On the other hand, their commitment to 'restraining residents who pose a danger to themselves' had fallen (Braithwaite et al. 1992: 25).

At the time, our systematic data from a large stratified random sample of homes indicated that directors of nursing, ordinary staff and proprietors themselves believed that standards monitoring had improved quality of care. Seventy per cent of 405 directors of nursing reported that their first inspection encouraged their motivation to improve the quality of resident care, 3 per cent that it discouraged them and 28 per cent said it made no difference to their motivation (Braithwaite et al. 1992: 23). The results were similar for the second inspection, though the percentage discouraged increased to 5 per cent in the second round. Results for ordinary staff were similar. Seventy-four per cent of directors of nursing felt the inspection had stimulated them to 'rethink many of our management practices' and 72 per cent reported being stimulated to 'rethink many of our working patterns' (Braithwaite et al. 1992: 25). This was mainly driven by the process motivating them to do their own diagnosis of their facility, perhaps in collaboration with consultants they retained. Only 43 per cent of them said they got any good ideas directly from the inspectors on how to improve the care of residents and only 32 per cent said they got any good ideas directly from the inspectors on how to improve management systems (Braithwaite et al. 1992: 24). Overall only 16 per cent of directors of nursing went along with the negative assessment that 'The standards monitoring program has not made nursing home residents any better off' (Braithwaite et al. 1992: 29).

Overwhelmingly our data suggested that rank-and-file members of the industry agreed with the new standards, understood them, believed they had been fairly consulted about their introduction and believed that they were implemented in a procedurally fair manner by the inspection team that visited their nursing home. Our data also revealed surprisingly high consistency in ratings, at least within the same state, but not necessarily between states (Braithwaite et al. 1992: chs 9 and 12).

Braithwaite et al. (1992: 28–9) argued that the improvements they observed being made in the late 1980s and early 1990s as a result of Australian agreed action plans following inspections were more major than were observed as a result of more perfunctory English action plans during that period and ritualistic American plans of correction. In the first few years, on these and a number of other criteria, our research suggested that the standards monitoring program was a growth in regulation that was significantly improving the quality of care in Australian nursing homes, even though it was badly under-resourced, shied away from unannounced inspections and was weak in its enforcement record. And it was bringing the line managers and staff of the industry, as well as the consumer groups, along with it in accepting that what was being accomplished was right and fair.

The federal government increased its investment not only in nursing home inspection but also in a complaints resolution scheme, a community visitor's scheme and funding for aged care advocacy groups in each state and territory. These continue to exist in 2006. The Aged Care Complaints Resolution Scheme covers all Australian government-funded aged care services, not just nursing homes, and deals with only a thousand complaints a year – a fraction of the number of complaints large US states deal with for nursing homes each year. While American complaints routinely trigger inspections of 19 inspector-hours' average duration and frequently lead to fines, Australian complaints mostly do not trigger visits to nursing homes and are universally steered to dispute resolution strategies, excluding enforcement and sanctions. A 2005 Senate inquiry concluded the complaints process was user-unfriendly and unresponsive, with the Aged Care Lobby Group, for example, arguing that family members have given up on complaining because 'their complaints are trivialised' (Parliament of Australia 2005: 60–65). The high-profile case of a GP who believed poor care of her mother had caused shocking bruising and ultimately death, and who had to pay $94 000 in legal fees and suffer a Federal Court case before getting access to the report of the investigation team on her complaint, became a book that excoriated both the complaints and accreditation systems (Meyer 2006). This book also documented the ritualism of Australian administrative law, making a case that the Commonwealth Ombudsman's office had 'more interest in creating the illusion of justice than in serving justice itself' (Meyer 2006: 42). The Australian Capital Territory Disability, Aged and Carer Advocacy Service argued before the

Senate enquiry that complaints were chilled by provider retribution against complainants, reporting 55 instances of actual retribution in aged care facilities in the Australian Capital Territory between 2001 and 2004.

Notwithstanding forceful systemic advocacy such as this from the ACT, both the advocacy organizations and community visitors mostly act for individual residents; they are today largely apolitical and tend not to be publicly visible critics of the regulatory arrangements. They themselves fear retribution of withdrawal of government funding, as befell the most activist advocates of the 1980s and early 1990s. We were told if they criticize the government, it has a 'long memory'. Their funding contracts with the government have clauses that explicitly fetter their capacity to criticize government policy without notice or even to criticize named providers who they believe should be closed. Government by contrast attempts to ensure this is advocacy with a small 'a'. The community visitor's scheme is a substantial program, with a high level of presence and acceptance by the industry, coordinating 6588 volunteer visitors. From its inception, however, the community visitor's scheme lost the empowerment edge advanced in its conception in the 1989 Ronalds report (Gibson 1998: 117). The government's response to vigorous opposition from private industry associations to what they dubbed the 'community busybodies scheme' was to insist that community visitors leave matters of compliance with standards to standards monitoring and stay away from legal conflicts with nursing homes to assert rights.

For more than a decade the government has been attempting to steer the community visitors and advocacy programs from the rights perspective that gave them birth to a 'partnership' perspective with the industry to improve quality. While many advocates cling to a rights perspective, and while resident rights are taken much more seriously than they were at the time of the Ronalds report, aged care is a long way behind the disability sector in terms of rights, and other sectors as well. One state advocacy organization told us they believed sexual assaults by staff against residents to have occurred at 22 per cent of the nursing homes in their jurisdiction. Advocates believe that the reason these almost never result in criminal prosecutions is that the norm is for nursing home management to conspire to cover them up. This, of course, was the norm in many sectors in the past. Yet advocates point out that while it would be extremely foolish today for a school principal to cover up a sexual assault by a teacher against a student, or for a child-care centre or a Catholic parish to engage in such cover-up today in the way that was common in the past, the rights of nursing home residents are still not taken as seriously as those of other categories of vulnerable people. This, combined with the political neutering of advocates, makes whistle-blower protection for nursing home staff one imperative reform (see Faunce and Bolsin 2004). A spate of allegations of rape of residents by staff in three different Australian jurisdictions in 2006 has finally prompted announcement of a uniform system of police checks for aged care workers, mandatory reporting of sexual and serious physical assault in aged care homes, some protection for whistle-blowers and a more vigorous complaints investigation regime. This has taken six years since a 2000 case when the ACT Chief Magistrate, in sentencing a nursing home staff member for sexual offences against an 85-year-old resident, expressed alarm about the employment of a man in the industry with a known history of sexual offences. There is also a debate underway at the time of writing on mandatory reporting of abuse allegations, something being vigorously resisted by the industry.

THE POLITICS OF CAPTURE

Long before Labor lost power in 1996, standards monitoring had lost the momentum and consensual support that our data from the late 1980s and early 1990s indicated it enjoyed. First, many of the advocacy groups became disillusioned at the continuing failure to achieve even a two-year inspection cycle, let alone move to the promised one-year cycle, as a belt-tightening government recovered from the 1991 recession. Advocates turned their attention to other issues in aged care and consumer protection where they thought they could make more strategic progress; to the extent they stuck with nursing homes as an issue, the focus was on the terms of contracts with residents to guarantee their rights – reforms that did not involve government dollars.

The leadership of the nursing home industry associations had had a torrid time in the 1980s. They knew that the worst providers in the industry were putting residents at risk and they could not defend the indefensible. During this period they cooperated constructively with the ambitions of a reformist government, seeking to ameliorate regulatory excess that might disadvantage their members in unreasonable ways. They could take some heart as the advocacy groups disengaged from nursing home enforcement as an issue and the pace of reform stalled. Indeed, this disengagement allowed them to quickly take the upper hand in policy debates. Key recommendations of the Ronalds et al. (1989) and Braithwaite et al. (1992) reports for unannounced inspections and a stepping up of enforcement at the peak of a responsive regulatory pyramid were not implemented by the government. After the first generation of visionary leaders of the standards monitoring program moved on, their successors found themselves in a political environment where the Labor government looked weak and unlikely to win the next election. In this environment regulatory bureau-crats became wary of being viewed as anti-business.

The biggest casualty was the vision of the founders of the program that over time the standards would be gradually interpreted more stringently. As the standards of the industry continued to improve from 1987, the Department of Health and Ageing[6] would 'raise the bar' on the standards. The industry lobby was unsympathetic to this vision. With the advocacy groups not watching the situation, the department decisively rejected the 'raise the bar' vision. By 1994 the standards were being interpreted as 'minimum standards' and pride was being taken as the percentages of nursing homes complying with the standards increased year by year. With advocacy groups no longer as aggressively engaged as they were, the media were doing few nursing home scandal stories as Australia moved into the 1990s. External audiences in the media and the parliament seemed com-fortable that this was a problem the government had taken by the horns; the annual reports showing increasing compliance with the standards were interpreted as evidence of the progress being made.

What they were evidence of was a regulatory regime that had moved remarkably quickly through Marver Bernstein's (1955) life cycle of public interests progressively subordinated to those of the regulated industry.[7] The visionary founders' commitment to raising the bar on the standards had been supplanted by what we are describing in this book as a more ritualis-tic form of regulation. On the ground, the morale of inspectors was sapped by the failure to back their reports with the credible enforcement they deserved, by the failure to introduce the unannounced inspections most of them firmly believed were needed,[8] but most of all by the failure to provide the program with the resources it needed to achieve its announced objec-tives. The job of Australian inspectors was always politically tougher than that of American and English inspectors in that nursing home proprietors were more willing to defy their authority, to complain to their superiors about their alleged unreasonableness and to lambast their performance in speeches in front of their Minister and in industry newsletters. This was a result of the interesting private industry association politics of the 1980s and 1990s.

During the 1980s when the Australian Nursing Homes Association (which became the Aged Care Association Australia) was so embattled by advocacy groups, in the media and the parliament, and was cooperating so constructively with the government, it came under attack from an antireg-ulation segment of the industry led by the largest nursing home chain, the Moran group. Essentially its patriarch, Doug Moran, formed a competing industry association in 1988, the National Association of Nursing Homes and Private Hospitals. This forced the Australian Nursing Homes

Association (ANHA) to become combative with the standards monitoring program in order to keep its most defiant members from defecting to Moran's new grouping. There was competition to outmuscle each other in their resistance to standards monitors. The ANHA asked members to fill out 'monitor the monitors' questionnaires and maintained dossiers on inspectors.

The Moran-backed industry association was not granted much legitimacy by the Labor government. But the ANHA, like the senior bureaucrats they were dealing with in the Department of Health and Ageing, believed the Labor government would not last long after the 1991 recession. Doug Moran was a power broker in, and major financial contributor to, Australia's major conservative party (the Liberal Party). The ANHA could not allow themselves to become as politically irrelevant under a conservative government as the Moran group was under Labor. Nursing home inspectors were left politically stranded, even more demoralized, as their bureaucratic bosses became captured by these political dynamics.

When the government did finally change, much later than most commentators expected, in 1996, it quickly announced that government inspection of nursing homes would be abolished. Standards monitoring and state enforcement would be replaced by an 'independent' accreditation body with minimal public funding that would be funded largely by industry accreditation fees (of approximately US$7000 for a larger home of 60 beds, less for smaller facilities). A unique feature of the new inspection regime was that one member of the inspection team (of normally two or three) could be nominated by the facility. Interestingly, while this was what the industry lobbyists wanted, over time it became rare for homes to request a peer from the industry who had been trained as an assessor.[9] By 2005 only 20 per cent of homes bothered to make a nomination and 90 per cent of those nominated a full-time employee of the agency. The Aged Care Standards and Accreditation Agency was to become a company limited by guarantee wholly owned by the Australian government. Essentially this was a move to deregulate nursing home inspection to an accreditation model similar to that which applies to hospitals in Australia and the United States – less enforcement, more advance notice of inspections, though with standards set by the state rather than by providers themselves.

In the first three years of accreditation, government funding was withdrawn from just one home (there are and were 3000 nationally) for failing to meet the standards. At the same time it was announced that elderly citizens entering nursing homes would have to pay large up-front charges in order to expand the funding base for the industry. More quietly, the advocacy organizations that had been the biggest thorns in the side of the industry had their government funding terminated. In the approval of new beds, there was a huge increase in the proportion allocated to private as opposed to charitable providers (which still account for 61 per cent of aged care beds); in 2000 one provider, the Moran Health Care Group, was allocated 12 per cent of the new beds as the financial press heralded, 'Moran the big winner as aged care goes private' in coverage that drew attention to Moran's generous funding of Liberal Party candidates (Tingle 2001: 2).

This was what the for-profit industry lobbyists wanted, indeed their dream package. But it was a political mistake. Suddenly nursing homes were an issue for the media again. By the end of the 1990s the press was exposing new scandals of horrific nursing home care. The Australian Nursing Federation was back in the media complaining that surveys of its members showed they were leaving aged care because of inadequate staffing; the Australian Consumers' Association was back in the fray complaining that consumers were getting poor quality regulation and poor quality access to and transparency of accreditation reports. Nancy's Aged Care Site, which the Minister at the time denounced as a 'rogue site', appeared on the Internet, listing Australia's worst nursing homes and the government's worst regulatory failures.

The media scandals were linked to failures of the accreditation regime to trigger any enforcement action against the nursing home in the face of overwhelming evidence of reckless neglect. The issue became a major minus for the Howard government in its early years and helped end the formidable ministerial careers of its first three Ministers for Aged Care – Judi Moylan (a talented minister who briefly served subsequently as Minister for Women's Affairs before being dumped), Warwick Smith (once the Liberal Party's youngest Member of Parliament and rising star, who lost his seat in 1998, and is now an Executive Director of Macquarie Bank) and Bronwyn Bishop (in the early 1990s the front-running contender to challenge the Howard leadership). Indeed, the issue in combination with fear of a new Good and Services Tax almost lost the government the 1998 election. Poll support for the government among over-fifties slumped from 58 per cent in the 1996 election to 46 per cent throughout 1998 (the year after the introduction of accreditation and the Aged Care Act 1997).

An increase in the proportion of unannounced inspections[10] was one feature of the reforms the federal government put in place at the end of the decade, along with a substantial increase in the budget for the accreditation agency. Departmental processes for imposing sanctions were beefed up, so the industry was faced with a two-level regulatory regime where, if accreditation discovered really serious problems, the department would send in its own inspection team to investigate sanctions against the home. With the 2006 announcement of an Aged Care Commissioner to investigate and take action on complaints, including complaints of failures of departmental enforcement, to some degree there may be a third-level regulatory game. The level of enforcement has risen in the current decade to more or less the level that had prevailed in the latter years of the previous Labor government (Gibson 1998: 105), but hardly to US levels. In the 2005 financial year seven facilities had a ban on funding for new admissions combined with the appointment of an adviser, three the appointment of an adviser only, one a ban on funding for all admissions only and one a ban on government funding for high level of care residents. For one of these, the ban on government-funded admissions was never lifted because the home chose to close. These were the only sanctions imposed; 208 received formal notices of non-compliance that implicitly threatened sanctions if problems were not fixed.

There are on average only 20 appeals a year to the accreditation agency over its accreditation decisions. It is extremely rare for appeals to go to a more formal legal adjudication. As of 2002, a grand total of only six appeals had been to the Administrative Appeals Tribunal (of which four were withdrawn/dismissed and one settled) (Australian National Audit Office 2003: 77). In the 1990s the Victoria police homicide squad estab-lished a task force on the deaths of 21 residents in one nursing home. This was 22 per cent of the residents in the home who all died in the course of one month. In the end, no prosecution proceeded. As in England, criminal prosecutions for neglectful care never occur in Australia.

The accreditation agency clung to the ideology that it was a child born of industry deregulation. Yes, there was re-regulation in the current decade, but this was something the department, not the agency, was choosing to do in response to political imperatives. The chief executive of the agency said: 'We are not a regulator. The department is a regulator. We're an accreditor. We're about promoting quality of care.' Figure 6.1 shows the way the mixed system of regulation and accreditation works at the time of writing. There has not been the deregulation of the market for new beds that we have seen in the US (96.2 per cent occupancy in 2003) and the government still essen-tially funds and certifies buildings before accreditation begins.

Most interestingly of all, raising the bar was back in vogue, albeit in new non-adversarial, non-punitive garb, as continuous improvement. During 2002–05, the political attention cycle again tired of nursing home regula-tion. When Julie Bishop was promoted out of the Age Care portfolio into cabinet at the end of this period, the ABC's *7.30 Report* opined that her pro-motion was because she had 'done the job of killing it [nursing homes] off as an issue' in a way her three unfortunate predecessors, and in 2006 her successor, failed to do. The accreditation agency found 89 per cent of nursing homes to be free of non-compliance on any standard in the latest accreditation round (up from 67 per cent in the first round). Of nursing

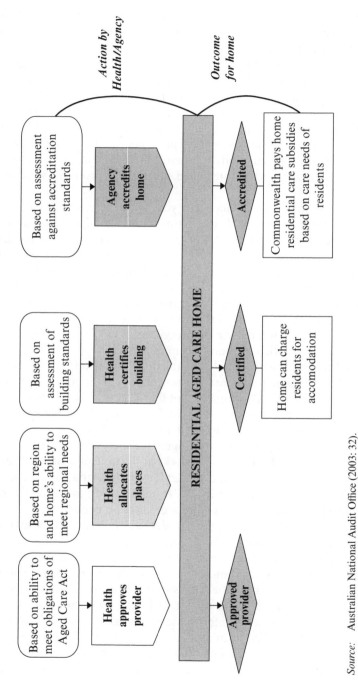

Source: Australian National Audit Office (2003: 32).

Figure 6.1 Certifying and accrediting nursing homes

homes which were rated as having some non-compliance, half were non-compliant on one standard only and all 3000 homes were rated as compliant on 34 or more of the 44 standards. The agency has as a key performance indicator in its corporate plan '94% in compliance at any point in time' (Aged Care Standards and Accredition Agency 2004–05: 23). In the agency's 2004–05 Annual Report the compliance performance indicator is defined as 'Percentage of services with 44 compliant expected outcomes.' The reported result of 98.7 per cent compliance is reached by counting as 'compliant' homes found non-compliant in the annual inspection, but which at some subsequent time were found to return to compliance on the problem standards. Indeed, if non-compliance is observed during an inspection and fixed in the course of the inspection, in general it will never be written as non-compliant in the first place.

Of course given what we know about roller-coaster compliance, this methodology is certain to give a false estimate of the actual level of compliance, as most homes in the course of three years will at some point drop out of compliance on a number of standards. The Department of Health and Ageing also gives an account in its annual report of percentage compliance as a performance indicator that must be seen to improve each year, driving compliance to ridiculously, artificially high levels over the years. Senior officers of the department argued to us quite unselfconsciously that '98 per cent of homes are fully compliant, up from 92 per cent in 2004'. Another argued that notwithstanding the media hype about the problems of the industry in 2006, 'far more homes are compliant than there were previously'.

This performance pressure helped make sense of our observation of indefensible ratings of compliance during our fieldwork. In one case, many problems of non-compliance were observed from multiple sources during an inspection, and all three assessors agreed at the pre-exit that they were worried about the poor standard of care in the home and the feeble evidence of continuous improvement. Yet at the exit no negative findings of any kind were reported even verbally, no non-compliance was written, but praise was provided of some of the positives observed. In other cases, inspectors expressed concern to us that recommendations of finding non-compliance would be changed by their supervisors without the reason being explained, without even a discussion with the inspectors who visited the facility. They assumed that their recommendations were not followed by the agency because of submissions from providers that providers have a right to make, but they did not know if this was the reason. Hence, no learning occurred about the reasons why it was felt inspectors got it wrong. Hence, cynicism was nurtured about the wisdom of forthrightly writing non-compliance. When non-compliance is so rare in the culture of inspection, the consequences of even the slightest non-compliance begin to loom large. So one nurse explained to us why she was so worried even about a non-compliance rating that could be fixed with no risk of sanctions: 'If you've got even one non-compliance the department may not approve you for new beds.'

The agency almost universally today manages to deal with problems of poor quality care while keeping them out of the media. The government mostly quietly threatens poor providers with withdrawal of government funding, mostly keeping abuse and neglect entirely out of the courts or any other public arena. It may be that the political message in Australia is not so different from the message Bruce Vladeck, who headed HCFA in the 1990s, says is the implicit set of instructions from American politicians:

> Maintain the highest possible standards of nursing home care without requiring more than incremental increases in Medicaid expenditures and don't stir up a political fuss. Avoid visible disasters like nursing home fires at all costs, but keep the industry off our backs. Don't appear officious, arbitrary, or capricious. The people in nursing homes must be protected, but remember that nursing home operators are constituents too.
>
> (Vladeck 1980: 173)

One head of a US state regulatory agency more succinctly put his objective when appointed 'to remove the Division of Ageing from the political realm'. Vladeck (1980: 173) thinks that politics is the art of displeasing the smallest number of potential voters 'by attempting to do a little something for everybody', even if those somethings become contradictory. Politically, responsive regulation can be conceived as a strategy for doing a little something for everybody – a little help to industry with continuous improvement strategies here, a little tough enforcement to placate advocates and the media there – but in a way that is not contradictory, that has integrity and coherence. The Australian accreditation agency used the 2002–05 period of peace to move up a notch from inspections that ensure sound quality assurance systems are in place, to requiring evidence that these systems are actually delivering continuous improvement. There is an implicit message to the government that this approach of building out from strengths will reduce political risks of future scandals by actually improving quality of care. The next section discusses how they are executing this strategy. We find that the contemporary Australian regulatory regime is, at the end of this tumultuous history, captured and quiescent in terms of enforcement, yet that the continuous improvement strategy is delivering some positive results, and that there is some validity to the claims of its leadership that the agency is not discredited and ritualistic in the way the mature standards monitoring process of the mid-1990s was.

A 2005 Senate report, *Quality and Equity in Aged Care* (Parliament of Australia 2005), lists the same criticisms from the industry that were at the top of the list with the old standards monitoring program and the same as in the US and England. These were proprietor and management advocates arguing before the Senate that regulation distracted staff from providing hands-on care by demanding increased documentation, and that compliance was rated inconsistently. Union and staff advocates argued that the regulation failed to mandate adequate levels of qualified staff. Some elderly advocates argued this as well as criticizing weak enforcement and insufficient inspections that were genuinely unannounced. These seem invariably the main criticisms of these constituencies, reflecting as they do their dominant concerns, whatever the regime and whatever the country. One reason is that there is invariably some validity in the assertion that care could improve if each of these issues were to be managed better. Notwithstanding the fact that these old criticisms have not disappeared, most stakeholders in Australia, and not only producer interests, believe accreditation has improved standards.

MICRO-DYNAMICS OF CAPTURE

At the level of the specific case, there was none of the open articulation of capture that we sometimes encountered in our American fieldwork: 'If a provider is a major donor to the Governor's campaign, we sure won't be closing them down. But we may be able to get them to fix the place up' (Ohio nursing home regulator; in Ohio at this time, as in many other states, the nursing home industry, because it was heavily regulated, was the third or second biggest industry in state political campaign donations); 'Unfortunately, sometimes we have to recognize the Golden Rule: he who has the gold rules' (Texas nursing home regulator; see Long [1987] for more specific documentation of Texas political interference to compromise enforcement).

Nor did we encounter any allegations of corrupt payments to regulators or inspectors associated with either standards monitoring or accreditation, while we did encounter five such allegations during our US fieldwork, at least two of which were unquestionably accurate. Nor did we encounter in Australia any political interference as vivid as the story of a Georgia legislator who prevented inspectors from entering a nursing home to take enforcement action by literally barring the door! Our favourite Chicago fieldwork story is of inspector humour in the face of politicians arriving on the scene:

We had nine nurses in at the same time. You see there really were a lot of problems, but he complained it was Gestapo tactics, harassing him. He tried to intimidate us by dropping the names of all the politicians he knew. Next day the state representative came in. And we just told him it was the law that we be there. Then the day after that he brought the state senator in. Sam (one inspector) said to him: 'Hey let us know if the President is coming tomorrow so we can wear our best clothes.'

We were told several stories of senior US state officials who lost their jobs for failing to respond to political interference on enforcement matters; there were no such stories during our Australian nursing home fieldwork.

Australian business regulation has always been characterized by a formidable revolving door between business and its regulators. Grabosky and Braithwaite (1986) found that in 31 of the 96 major business regulatory agencies in the 1980s, a majority of inspectors, investigators or complaints officers were recruited from industry. The empirical evidence is quite mixed on whether recruitment from the industry fosters pro-industry decisions (Cohen 1986; Gormley 1979; Quirk 1981). Makkai and Braithwaite's (1992) data from 173 Australian nursing home standards monitors and their inspections of 410 nursing homes found absolutely no effect on how tough they were from whether they had worked in the industry and whether they had worked as a CEO or number two in a nursing home. Makkai and Braithwaite concluded that regulators had much to lose and little to gain by being wary of appointments from the regulated industry. Not only did they find that the revolving door in did not explain capture; but nor did the revolving door out have much explanatory power. Inspectors reporting that they had plans to move in future to the nursing home industry also had no effect on how tough they were in rating non-compliance with standards. The effects of moving in and out of the revolving door on what might be called captured (pro-industry) attitudes were small and inconsistent.

During our qualitative research in the 1980s and early 1990s we also observed little that made us suspicious that inspectors were tempering their enforcement with an eye to getting good job offers in the industry. We did have that suspicion at times during our observations in the 2000s of regulatory encounters. Some accreditation staff did not seem to accept the message frequently communicated in the training of American inspectors: 'if you do this job properly, you will lose more friends than you make'.[11]

We have also increasingly suspected tempering of enforcement with an eye to a job in the industry during the 2000s in other domains of Australian regulation with which we have long experience. We do wonder today whether our findings of 1992 would be true today if that work were replicated. A decade and a half on, jobs for corporate compliance officers and work for compliance consultants have become infinitely more plentiful as a result of the growth of enforced self-regulation or meta-regulation as a favoured strategy in Australia. This is certainly true in the nursing home industry where corporate quality assurance jobs with chains were still rare a decade ago. Perhaps as a consequence, corporate compliance jobs are also hugely more lucrative for talented people than jobs with regulators. This differential was nowhere near as great in decades past. Accreditation agency staff tend not to last long in the job. From talking to them, most are positioning themselves for jobs with better pay and conditions than the agency offers. Many go to line management positions such as director of nursing in an aged care home.

In other agencies we know, like the Australian Competition and Consumer Commission, we also see the phenomenon of many of the best people positioning themselves for more highly paid jobs in the compliance industry or to set up their own compliance consultancy business. The sad thing for the quality and effectiveness of such regulatory work is that it is so often the brightest, most creative regulators who are tempted by this move. More committed regulators are prone to disillusionment when ministers, senior bureaucrats and regional office bureaucrats sacrifice the regulatory mission for a comfortable relationship with the industry, as suggested by Makkai and Braithwaite's (1992: 72) finding that it was the tougher nursing home inspectors who were more likely to quit. We interviewed a number of standards monitors during the 1990s after they decided to leave. One who was an extraordinarily competent, demanding and effective nurse grieved that there was a 'big emphasis on natural justice for nursing homes', but not much 'natural justice for residents'. The 'process takes so long that the person is often dead' by the time non-compliance was addressed. This happened in the view of many of these very capable inspectors because there was 'no resolve' on the part of more senior officials above them, up to the Minister, who wanted to appease the 'industry lobby'. The larger worry is that the temptation to capture is so much bigger today. There is more inducement to capture and indeed a phenomenon of bright young professionals getting experience with regulators for no reason other than to position themselves for a better private sector job, a phenomenon we have long seen in domains like tax enforcement, where experience with the Australian Tax Office is used to position oneself for a lucrative job in a major accounting or law firm.

Christine Parker (2002) argues that a distinctive role of the corporate compliance officer is to render the corporation more permeable to public regulatory values, the compliance officer as normative bridge between the world of the regulator and the world of business. As such, they might communicate public values in the language of the business case and business values in a public-regarding discourse. In that two-way permeability, we fear from our observation of Australian business regulation over four decades that today business values are capturing regulatory values more than the reverse. When those regulatory values are about protecting the most vulnerable members of our society from abuse and neglect, the community should be concerned.

STRENGTHS-BASED STRATEGIES

The leadership of the accreditation agency rejects a 'detection mentality, a "we caught them" mentality. How can we help people get compliance? That's what we want.' In common with the standards monitoring philosophy, the accreditation philosophy is not to be consultants, but to motivate homes to draw on consultants, while being willing to enter into conversation about different solutions that the home chooses and how to adapt them to meet the standards. Praise for things well done is laid on much more heavily by agency inspectors than by English or American inspectors. We observed a team of three Australian inspectors in 2005 give the assembled staff of the nursing home a round of applause at the end of an exit conference where perfect compliance was the result. Special commendation was institutionalized by the introduction of 'commendable' ratings for unusually outstanding homes that went well beyond compliance. This was simplified in 2003 because of the challenges of consistency of criteria by Better Practice in Aged Care awards to around 30 facilities who are granted Accreditation with Merit or Commendable Awards. These are publicized through the agency website, a booklet and training seminars on the learnings from the better practices. In addition there are Minister's Awards for Excellence in Aged Care for individual staff. Nominations are actively promoted; winners receive $10 000 to pursue training opportunities. All this adds up to a philosophy of improvement that is as much strengths based as it is problem based. This even extends to being willing to chat with homes about their business strategies because of the view that if the business is strong, funding of quality improvement is more likely. This part of the philosophy is shared with many old-style English inspectors, but not American inspectors. Accreditation is seen by top management as a 'customer service program', so if the customers would appreciate a chat about consequences of what they are doing to make their business stronger, the agency will indulge them, so long as agency personnel are not positioned as consultants who are seen as recommending any particular course of action.

An important part of building a strengths-based approach is to signal how this can displace blaming people for single incidents as staff learn to develop their strengths in crafting systemic solutions to problems. A Sydney nursing home in 2004 had an epidemic of falls and was failing to develop evidence-based approaches to solving it. Care staff would just pick residents off the floor, care for their needs and not document the fall. Staff from former Communist countries were afraid that recording falls of residents in their care could result in them being blamed. A smart quality assurance committee was able to identify from the limited data on falls that was available one simple root cause of their fall epidemic. It was the shoe/slipper/sock-wearing habits that had become common in the nursing home. All residents and relatives were sent information on what a safe shoe requires. Relatives were encouraged to give gifts of such safe footwear for the forthcoming Fathers' Day. Such a sweet no-blame intervention built confidence in the recording of falls to help the nursing home get on top of the other root causes of its problem.

One part of the case for a strengths-based approach by inspectors is that inspectors serve as role models of how managers can best secure improvement. There is, we observe, a degree of strengths-based contagion in Australian nursing homes today. The 'Recognition Board' for residents as well as staff, for fun things like the 'bowling winner', as well as for serious things, are certainly more visible in today's Australian nursing homes. The agency's strengths-based philosophy applies to inspectors themselves. Their CEO says to them, 'Don't be afraid to make a mistake. Use your judgement.' This is something US inspection managers would never say. While there are procedures, the agency does not have a procedures manual mentality (Braithwaite 2005b: 167–76), but rather one of encouraging inspectors to find their own ways of realizing the principles or sensibilities the agency seeks to animate through its training, the key ones being:

- continuous improvement
- resident focus
- being helpful
- evidence focus
- results focus
- systems and processes
- openness and transparency.

All but two of these – continuous improvement and systems and processes – express considerable continuity with the value shift of the old standards monitoring program. But these two are at the heart of their strengths-based approach.

CONTINUOUS IMPROVEMENT

The most common criticism we hear of the old standards monitoring process from the industry today is that homes would be found non-compliant on a standard for a single thing that happened to have been done wrong on the day of the inspection. This was interpreted by providers looking back as evidence that standards monitors were 'hiding behind the bushes waiting to jump on you'. The same criticism was often made by the industry in England and the US. This is what led to the US scope and severity grid, in which 'widespread' scope is interpreted to mean affecting virtually every resident in a facility. Australian accreditation has taken a different path on this issue. It is outcome oriented, and concerned to assure a focus on poor outcomes for residents that are serious rather than one-offs that are unlikely to be repeated. This necessitates a search for patterns. But more than that, the focus is on asking the question whether a poor system that is likely to fail again is a root cause of what may be just a single accident. The first major change from standards monitoring was the more determined focus upon evaluating systems and processes. The objective is to check that outcomes are good, improving, and improving because:

1.   good systems and processes are in place,
2.   are used,
3.   and are working.

If the home passes the systems and processes tests against outcomes, residents will be protected against roller-coaster compliance. Note this is still an outcome-oriented philosophy. Australian accreditation does not tick boxes that a long list of mandated systems and processes are in place. It requires evidence of improving outcomes and evidence that the nursing home has chosen systems and processes to guarantee those outcomes, and that these are used and working. The philosophy here is to make the industry more evidence based, more innovative and responsive in crafting processes. This means a learning culture of systems and processes rather than mandating them.

Over time the emphasis on evidence of continuous improvement has increased. Systems and processes that guaranteed minimum outcome standards would no longer be enough. A new burden of proof was shifted to nursing homes in the 2000s to demonstrate with evidence that they were improving.[12] There are two shifts here. One is from a minimum standards mentality to continuous improvement. The second is from it being the obligation of the inspectors to collect the evidence that the standard is being met to this being the responsibility of the provider. The job of the inspector is to ask the right questions to elicit the evidence providers have collected to prove continuous improvement. On a privacy standard this means shifting from an emphasis on inspectors interviewing residents about whether their privacy is respected, observing whether staff do things like pull curtains during treatments and knock on doors before entering. It means a shift to inspectors poring over resident and relative/carer survey results on the percentage of residents and relatives who say privacy is respected and whether this is going up or down over time (on the adequate reliability of such survey measurement in nursing homes, see Low et al. [2003] and Castle [2004]). Resident and relative interviews and observation continue to be important, but their importance is more in terms of raising red flags about the quality of systems and the quality of evidence those systems generate.

The job of inspectors has been redefined toward helping management learn how to demonstrate that they are achieving continuous improvement. So when a resident satisfaction survey is produced that shows satisfaction in the high 90 per cents on all manner of outcomes, the job of inspectors is to explain why that is not demonstrating any trend, any improvement over time. A common question is 'Are you graphing them?' This can be done directly or by advising managers of the various consultants who are specialists in doing more objective surveys to deal with the cognitive deficits in elderly populations. Or consultants can simply provide protocols for homes to follow on a regular routine and then they feed back to the home whether they are improving across time and against norms for the industry.

Many inspectors are cynical about how well the shift to a continuous improvement orientation is going. One referred to the 'huge paper shuffle that is continuous improvement'. Another said: 'Any old survey that shows residents are happy is the way they think.' This inspector went on to lament how nurses do not understand that they want quality data that demonstrates trends towards quality improvement and that a slap-dash survey that purports to show 100 per cent of residents satisfied with the nursing home is not useful for this purpose. Skills in root cause analysis were seen by inspectors as at a low level in the nursing home sector compared to the hospital sector: 'most of our nurses don't even understand what root cause analysis is, never mind having a clue how to run one'. Another inspector said getting homes to tell them what they had done to continuously improve standards was 'like pulling teeth'.

We agree there is a strong basis for this perception. The most common type of non-compliance in recent years has been failure to demonstrate continuous improvement on one or more of four general standards. Nursing homes do almost universally pull out a tabular list of continuous improvements (a 'continuous improvement log' that lists in columns priority problems that need improving, a planned action, who will be responsible for it, a planned completion date, and how the outcome will be measured). Inspectors ask to see this log; they expect to see a lot of improvement listed in it; they ask questions if it records no measurement of improvement. But many of the improvements listed are just fixing specific problems like repairing handrails that have come loose. This is an output not an outcome. Reporting routine maintenance is a poor excuse for evidence-based, system-driven, continuous improvement.[13] Fixing a handrail is not fixing a system that allows one maintenance problem after another to recur.

On the other hand, we observed that the biggest difference between what Australian nursing homes were doing in the 1980s and 1990s and what they are doing today is that they are more oriented to continuous improvement than they were, however limited and partial the shift. Rome was not built in a day, and on the longer view of regulatory history, we see a large change in progress. Consider 'Expected Outcome 2.8 All residents are as free as possible from pain.' The standards monitoring process worked to the identical outcome standard. Braithwaite et al. (1992: ch. 5) found this to be a problem standard and recommended a workshop focused specifically on how to improve evidence-gathering on it. We believed we saw residents suffering needless pain in the 1980s (as seems still the case today [Llewellyn-Jones et al. 2003; McClean and Higginbotham 2002]) and that inspectors were not picking this up. Ninety-four per cent of homes were rated as meeting the pain management standard, the second highest level of compliance on any standard. This was not because 94 per cent of homes were securing good outcomes but because, compared to what we observed American inspectors to do, Australian inspectors paid less attention to pain management in terms of:

1. Asking residents if they were suffering pain;
2. Observing whether staff were noting symptoms of pain and were trained in how to do this;
3. Checking documentation for evidence of attention to pain management; and
4. Observation of treatments (for example of pressure sores) for evidence of sound pain management.

The path we recommended was Australia lifting its game to that of the clearly superior American inspection of pain management in the 1980s and 1990s. Accreditation may be taking the improvement of pain management on a better path. Finding non-compliance is even more infrequent under accreditation than it was under standards monitoring. However, evidence-based improvement of pain management is being more effectively confronted in Australian nursing homes today than it was in the 1990s. We never saw a standards monitoring team do anything as effective to triangulate on a pain management problem and confront it as the single accreditation assessor on a support visit reported in Box 6.1. More importantly, accreditation has begun to force nursing homes to bring in consultants who know how to measure pain, its reduction and its management. There are standardized, well-validated instruments, such as the Abbey Pain Scale for the

BOX 6.1 AUSTRALIAN WOUND CARE, 2005

This was a planned half-day follow-up inspection (support visit) by a single inspector that became a full day because of a wound-care problem. A dressing was noticed on a wound that the resident reported during interview was causing her some discomfort. The dressing appeared old, curling up at the edges. When asked whether the wound had been checked by a nurse since the dressing was put on, the resident, who was alert, was emphatic it had not.

The inspector, not mentioning this incident, asked the nurse in charge (who happened to be acting director of nursing [DON]) how she finds out about wounds to check that they are being properly treated by staff. She says a new wound will be monitored in the incident report and she monitors them from that report. The inspector does not find the wound we observed recorded in the incident report. The acting DON is asked if she is aware of the resident's wound. She is not and she is not monitoring its progress.

The inspector then asks for files of other residents with wounds. There is only one other among the 40 residents. Her wound is properly recorded in the incident report and a wound chart was filled out. But the wound did not find its way into the care plan and was not followed through progress notes. The inspector decides an n of 2 is not enough to establish a pattern of poor care. She asks if there are recently deceased residents with wound problems. One is found. Like the others, it is not followed through in the care plan and progress notes.

At this point the inspector decides she is likely to write non-compliance on the wound-care issue and that management of the facility is going to resist this finding. She begins to record details carefully on when different things happen to which resident and whether or not they are recorded and in which charts.

This detective work suddenly raises the temperature in an explosive way. As the inspector pores over charts, the acting DON pleads that the quality of wound care is high; there are merely some documentation lapses. As she turns to enter a lift, she is upset and tells the inspector to 'eat it'. A doctor happens to be in the lift. She holds the door open: 'Dr Jones tell them how good my wound care is.' He looks stunned, seems relieved as the closing lift door absolves him of a need to say something.

After finishing follow-through on the records, the inspector looks for the acting DON. She has gone out 'for a smoke'; no one can find her for an hour. When she is found, the inspector sits down and asks: 'What is your wound-care policy?' She replies: 'What the standards say.' This is not a good answer as the standards do not tell homes what kind of management systems to put in place to guarantee wound care. The inspector explains that the standards do not say whether wound-care needs should be followed daily in progress notes. She shows progress notes to the acting DON: 'I can't see evidence of checking the dressing there. Can you see it?' 'No.' The inspector has by now responded to the rise in the emotional temperature (and to signals that management will resist a finding of non-compliance) by escalating her demeanour to a determinedly firm and fair evidence-gathering mode. She wants the acting DON to own the finding that wound care is not documented and to give her a last chance to correct any erroneous reading of the records.

The inspector then interviews staff to nail down discrepancies between what the home's policy says on recording wound care, what staff understand the policy to be and what staff record. After starting the first interview, the head of corporate quality for the nursing home group enters the room. The inspector says to him: 'Can I interview him alone please?' The quality manager says: 'I'll stay.' Then when the acting DON comes into the room as well, the inspector says: 'Not two. It's intimidating for your own staff.' She leaves.

At the exit, the inspector finds non-compliance for wounds not being recorded as required by the nursing home's policy and the responsible RN not knowing and therefore not monitoring the situation. She diagnoses the nursing home as not having a system that is used and working to guarantee monitoring of wounds. Management at the exit characterizes the failures as merely documentation oversights. It insists wound care is good. No continuous improvement study on wound care is submitted to support this assertion. It is asserted the home has had only one infected wound in the last six months. This does not seem very compelling as the home has such low care residents with so few wounds. The acting DON apologizes for telling the inspector to 'eat it'. The inspector says it did not worry her.

When the inspector hands over the evaluation feedback survey for the nursing home to fill out for the inspection, she is obviously afraid she will get poor ratings because, unusually, she makes a point of saying that even though she will be leaving as an inspector soon to take a job in the industry, she will be asking to see her ratings. The inspector tells John Braithwaite she was glad he was there as she would have felt intimidated, alone against all of them. She believes the home will contest the non-compliance with her superiors and might win. The quality manager tells John afterwards that he would not normally insist on sitting in on an interview, even though he has a right to do so. But his DON was terribly upset and he wanted to be there to support her.

This is not the kind of case that produces any sanction in Australia. Yet it is clear that the confrontation and allegation of non-compliance with a standard that goes to the professional competence of nurses causes tumultuous upset. The fact that it matters to everyone is palpable. It creates very real pressure to improve systems and processes, to continuously improve and collect the evidence that you have.

A second impressive thing was the way the inspector triangulated evidence from observation of a resident, interview with the resident, checking policies, checking correspondence of documentation with policies and with observed facts on the body of the resident, interviews with management, interviews with nursing assistants and requests for evidence of continuous improvement on the relevant standards. This was between-method triangulation; there was also within-method triangulation from three cases. When the n of 2 was the whole population of relevant cases, the boundary of the population was expanded to generate an n of 3 by including the recently deceased. The n of 3 was a persuasive pattern because in each case the same failings of the system to connect to the outcome were evident.

The third impressive thing was that even though the inspector was effectively alone and embattled by all around her, even though she worried her agency would side in the end with the nursing home, when nursing home management escalated the emotional pressure on her, she did not return abuse; she responded calmly by becoming firmer and more determined to record the facts carefully in the cause of better wound care for residents.

---

measurement of pain (Abbey et al. 2004). The evidence generated by monitoring pain with such instruments has delivered an evidence base for how better to train staff in recognizing and managing pain. Rather simple observational cues and monitoring of whether pain levels are increasing or decreasing, with simple survey questions to residents and their relatives and carers, can now be used. The demand for evidence of continuous improvement from accreditation is creating pressure to use them.

Survey methodology is quite useful for getting at some problems that have always been difficult if not impossible to assess in an inspection. Consider, for example, the important issue of whether residents have access to the spiritual comfort they need, to worship in the way they wish, and to clergy. How can inspectors evaluate if this is improving? When inspectors ask if homes can demonstrate this, a simple survey question to relatives like 'Are your loved one's spiritual needs attended to?' can produce a disappointing result. This can be discussed at meetings with residents and staff who come up with ideas for improving access to a wider diversity of opportunities for worship. If after implementing these ideas there is a big jump in the percentage of relatives who believe their loved one's spiritual needs are attended to, continuous improvement is convincingly demonstrated.

Consultants such as Moving ON Audits are playing an important role in creating a learning culture of continuous improvement in the Australian nursing home industry. They run workshops on how to interpret data on continuous improvement to target new interventions to solve emerging problems and measure whether the interventions work. This may be followed up with monthly emails advising the home what has to be audited this month; the completed data forms are emailed back, cleaned, analysed and graphed by the consultants. They enable benchmarking of a nursing home in comparison to many others of the same type, as these consulting organizations can have hundreds of clients. We were impressed with the quantity of useful benchmarking information such consultants generate for a home. At the same time we noted the existence in the quality consulting industry of some players whom we might characterize as charlatans. Larger chains also benchmark against the performance of all others in their own chain. Some medium-sized groups swap benchmarking data to evaluate how they are performing. The challenge seems more about assuring the quality of the data and using it well to test out root causes. One entry on outcome monitoring documents that impressed us was 'Reasons this data is collected.' For example, for a trending chart for new wound infections, it is explained that analysis of the results may reveal a need for new infection control processes or education, such as easier access to and education about hand-washing.

Other consultants specialize in assisting small facilities with their care planning. Care-planning software sends the plan automatically to the consultants who send back both more automated prompts on why this and that has not been followed through, and more qualitative diagnostic assessments, especially at the time of hands-on visits to the facility by the care-planning consultants. Other consultants work with medication advisory committees to track pharmacy quality by benchmarking whether, for example, psychotropic prescriptions or the risk of complex interactions through multiple drug use are higher than industry norms at the home. Some directors of nursing reported that these consultants were an expert resource for confronting doctors in ways they found hard to do, and worrying to do themselves, lest it endanger doctor's willingness to visit the home: 'The Meditracks pharmacist influences doctors by going and talking to them.' Consultancy and benchmarking from outside the health sector is also increasingly used, for example, benchmarking with a five-star restaurant the improvement of restaurant services in a facility.

One of the things these consultants benchmark is the percentage of staff in nursing homes who believe that their facility is in fact continuously improving and the percentage who believe that they are actively involved in continuous improvement processes. These data, collected independently of the accreditation agency for another purpose, are encouraging in showing across hundreds of facilities around 90 per cent of staff agreeing or partially agreeing on both these benchmarks. The accreditation agency claims from its compliance data that the single expected outcome that is most predictive of compliance with all the other standards is the overall continuous improvement outcome. This would be a persuasive datum on the power of continuous improvement innovation in ratcheting up everything else if we were able to verify it. Unfortunately the agency was not willing to share these actual numbers with us. Future published research is needed to test this claim.

As with all modalities of regulation, continuous improvement (CI) expectations engender their own kinds of ritualism and game-playing. Most depressingly of all, we were told of 'letting something slip so you can improve it later'. This shows why continuous improvement and a strengths-based pyramid can never stand alone as a regulatory strategy. An old-fashioned problem-based regulatory pyramid that can escalate intervention when homes allow things to get worse is needed for this scenario. We have no idea how common this is. One nursing home administrator who was in full flight listing continuous improvements from her CI log, pulled herself up during a support visit when she realized she had a full site audit in another six months: 'I'll have nothing left for next time if I'm not careful about all these CIs.' At the conclusion of another visit:

> *JB:* Maureen [the director of nursing] has a list of continuous improvements in the front of her black book and another list in the back that she is saving up for the next visit.
> *Maureen:* Gee you saw that.

Inspectors can be part of the problem of continuous improvement ritualism. In 2005 we saw one inspector as time was running out to complete an inspection: 'I need three continuous improvements on standard 4, standard

3.' Her attitude was 'give me 3, any old 3, so I can write you into compliance on continuous improvement'. Another inspector led a director of nursing: 'Can I put your new gardener down for a CI there?' We did not see accreditation reports reporting bad survey results to discern declining outcomes for residents. We only saw them used to demonstrate the upside of continuous improvement.

Some inspectors question ritualism. One home's quality assurance protocol asked the home to answer the question, 'Does the facility offer residents a varied, healthy and well balanced diet?' The home has ticked 'Yes' on its protocol. 'Who is going to tick no to that?', the inspector said. 'How do you check?' Even though the home replied that being asked the question made them look at the menus and think about how varied they were, this was not a protocol that invited management to drill down to the detail of improvement; it was just a 'gimme' tick on the way to generating some sort of high and improving score. Again the focus was on the ritual of achieving outputs to demonstrate continuous improvement but not on the underlying system that produces better outcomes for quality and care of residents.

On the other hand, we saw some anti-ritualistic performance indicators that were interesting. We know that one of the standard rituals of appearing to do something is to write a new page in a policy and procedures manual that makes it a more complicated and less useful document. So there is interest in monitoring whether agreement with the following staff survey item goes up or down over time: 'I find the policy and procedures manual easy to read.'

It may be that continuous improvement ritualism is being induced by the pursuit of continuous improvement across many standards. That is clearly mission impossible. Street-level bureaucrats use their discretion to moderate expectations of continuous improvement across the standards when major and challenging continuous improvements on a few are being executed well. Indeed, they are encouraged to use such discretion by top management. Policy learning is needed on the trade-offs between high quality continuous improvement on a narrow front versus medium quality on a wider front. Obviously, though, there is no virtue in vacuous, ritualistic continuous improvement on a wide front. Australian accreditation is at risk of this.

While we are seeing Australian continuous improvement as a major accomplishment of the present decade, like all the accomplishments discussed in this book, our data show it to be vulnerable to ritualism. Still, the best Australian providers are showing how to pull the industry up through new ceilings. They do things like include resident representatives on quality assurance committees that set ambitious evidence-oriented goals for the new ceiling they aspire to break through. They place family representatives on a board that is demanding that the home excel at continuous improvement. Indeed, they engage all staff, residents and families with prioritizing continuous improvement challenges through staff meetings and resident and family committees.[14]

One utterly non-ritualistic structural continuous improvement to which the government has committed is to increase the proportion of rooms that are single occupancy. This is carefully monitored and reported publicly, with average occupancy now down to 1.4 residents per room across the industry (falling to the level of the UK and Germany and way below the 2.8 in Japan [OECD 2005: 77]). This is accomplished by a certification process separate from accreditation that is administered by the Commonwealth Department of Health and Ageing. It has involved graduated supplementary funding for building work and graduated ten-year forward planning targets. This improvement is the antithesis of market-driven improvement, more like socialist five- and ten-year plans. The government has successfully adopted a similar approach to fire safety improvement in nursing homes. Australia has generally seen greater improvement in the quality of nursing home buildings over the course of this study than has the US or England.

SHAME AND PRIDE

In Chapter 5 we saw that English inspectors adapted to their enforcement weakness by becoming master street-level bureaucrats who enrolled webs of control in rather imaginative ways. Because Australian accreditation is less oriented to control of weaknesses, more oriented to development of strengths, the English path of consultation backed by indirect but potent deterrence had little appeal. The Australian resourcefulness that grew from its enforcement weakness was more about shame and pride management. Both shame and pride were important in how things were accomplished on the ground in nursing homes with both standards monitoring and accreditation, with shame more important in standards monitoring, pride in accreditation. Pride and shame were repeatedly referred to in our interviews as key motivators: 'When we are doing good things it's generally because we are taking pride in the home and in our job' (Perth nurse). 'In our home the whole staff attends the exit conference. It has an effect. I'm a cleaner. It's your dirty floor being talked about in front of everyone' (Washington cleaner). 'Everywhere I've worked in 25 years of geriatric nursing I've tried to improve the standard. To be told that I have not taken care of my residents would be a personal blow. I'd also feel disappointed for the girls because they would also feel upset. I wouldn't worry about the proprietor in this way' (Adelaide director of nursing).

Continuous improvement measurement can and does widely tap into the encouragement of pride by recognition for strengths with staff survey items such as:

- I receive informal recognition by the organization that I am doing a good job.
- I believe that my contribution to the organization is valued by the organization.

Australian nursing home accreditation is quite unlike any other inspection regime we have seen in the centrality it gives to encouraging regulated organizations to show pride in what they have accomplished. 'Please blow your trumpet', an inspector explains during an entrance meeting with the senior staff, 'Bring forward the good things you have done.' At another 2005 inspection, it was said: 'We want to listen to all the good things you have done. Don't be embarrassed to show off. Enjoy yourselves telling the story of what you have accomplished.' Ann Jenkins (1997) did a wonderful PhD on our Australian quantitative data showing that when directors of nursing scored high on a measure of their self-efficacy as managers, controlling for other variables, their compliance with standards was higher. Obversely, when CEOs disengage from the quality of care regulatory community, quality of care declines (Braithwaite et al. 1994). So there is a strong evidence base for nurturing pride in what one has accomplished so as to strengthen managerial self-efficacy to take on ever-bigger challenges. Hence, even when there is serious non-compliance, there is a case for the strategy of one American inspector who said at an exit: 'You've got some problems here but you've proved in the past that you can get on top of problems like this.' Moreover, as discussed in Chapter 4, there is direct evidence from our Australian quantitative research that informal praise is an inspection strategy that improves compliance (Makkai and Braithwaite 1993a).

Braithwaite (1989) and his co-authors (Ahmed et al. 2001) have argued that social control is ineffective if law enforcers simply natter at non-compliant actors. They need to confront it as the issue of deep community concern that non-compliance with nursing home standards is. This is what the inspector did on the wound-care issue described in Box 6.1. As we discussed in Chapters 3 and 4 in the context of American inspectors confronting physical restraint and following through on demands for change, this worked where simply nattering about restraint did not. Confronting managers with the reasons for why non-compliance warrants disapproval does not mean lecturing. It certainly does not mean calling people names.

Braithwaite's theory of reintegrative shaming argues that when we treat someone as if they are a bad or irresponsible person that is stigmatizing. It makes things worse. If you stigmatize a nurse as unprofessional or uncaring, he or she is likely to adopt the motivational postures of resistant defiance, game-playing or disengagement (see Chapter 9).

Our observation of nursing home inspections suggests that shame tends to bear heavily on nurses in particular when serious non-compliance is detected. But the effects of this shame are double-edged. Some deal with it by disengaging from their professional challenges; the number of nursing homes in our data where quality of care collapsed because the director of nursing or administrator slid into serious alcohol abuse was disturbingly high. Others deal with shame over poor quality care by displacing their shame (Ahmed et al. 2001) into anger toward the inspectors for treating them unfairly, toward their proprietor or the government for not giving them enough money. Sometimes they even blamed the victim – a complaining resident – as a troublemaker or ungrateful, or a complaining relative as riddled with guilt for putting their mother in a home.

One thing inspectors must do to avert this displacement of shame into accusing the accusers is to ensure that they are procedurally fair in everything they do. Makkai and Braithwaite (1996) found some, albeit partial, evidence from 341 Australian nursing home inspections that procedural justice on the part of inspectors is associated with improved compliance, injustice with declining compliance. The strong message from these data is that inspectors must avoid stigmatizing nurses. They must confront noncompliance firmly, while treating managers respectfully. This is what reintegrative shaming means in this context: treating the nurse as a respected professional in a caring organization that on this particular occasion has failed to meet standards that are important. Makkai and Braithwaite (1994b) found that 331 homes inspected by standards monitors with a reintegrative shaming philosophy experienced 39 per cent improved compliance with the law in a follow-up inspection two years later. Nursing homes inspected by stigmatizing inspectors suffered an equivalent drop in compliance two years later, while homes checked by tolerant and understanding inspectors suffered an intermediate fall in compliance (see Figure 6.2). Obviously the data suggest that this is a major issue with inspection effectiveness – the difference between making things 39 per cent better and 39 per cent worse. When this result was first published, one referee wondered whether inspectors 'can really have such an impact in one inspection'. Our qualitative fieldwork suggests they can. As we documented in Chapter 3, for example, reductions of physical restraint of much more than 39 per cent were achieved in one year after nattering about restraint was replaced with confrontations that made it crystal clear that this was unacceptable. With

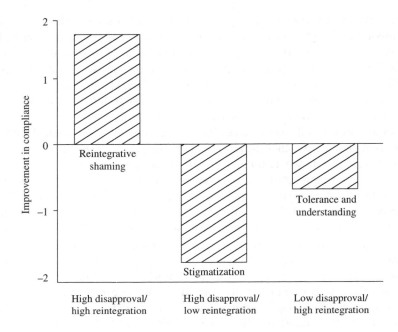

Source: Makkai and Braithwaite (1994b).

Figure 6.2   *Mean improvement in compliance for nursing homes where*
              inspectors used high disapproval and high reintegration styles,
              high disapproval and low reintegration styles and low
              disapproval and high reintegration styles

regulating organizations, the best inspections can be catalysts of a major process of corporate deliberation. It is not just the single encounter; it is the subsequent staff meetings, the soul-searching at subsequent quality assurance committee meetings that are triggered when inspection works well.

Our qualitative fieldwork suggested that inspectors were often perceived as stigmatizing – 'conducting a Spanish Inquisition', 'little Hitlers' or 'a Gestapo'. They were also often perceived as tolerant of non-compliance: 'They don't care, it's just a job for them'; 'They know I am doing the best I can with the limited resources I have even though we are not meeting the standards.' Inspector training that averts giving either of these impressions is a critical issue, according to our data, for inspection effectiveness. There is a lot of nuance in this, as one Massachusetts inspector explained when reflecting on how to communicate concern about how serious something is: 'Body language is important, eye contact. Tone of voice must be in keeping with the seriousness of the offence. Don't smile while you're telling them their home is in real trouble, otherwise they'll tell you later they didn't think it was that serious.'

Stigmatizing speech is most likely when anger explodes. Hence the advice of one Melbourne inspector: 'If shouting starts, you get out. Then make a new start the next day. Or if you can't, get your boss to take it over the next day.' Here is an example of a reintegrative encounter following a revelation of non-compliance that was felt as shameful by a nurse from a Sydney home:

> *Inspector:* We agree with your priorities.
> *Nurse:* Thank you.
> *Inspector:* We can see there's been an effort to improve and we're hoping for improvement.
> *Nurse:* Thank you again. There will be improvement.
> *(Later . . .)*
> *Inspector:* We hope that's history now.
> *Nurse:* It will be.

Here is how a Chicago inspector sought to be reintegrative in opening an exit conference with a home on the edge of the precipice:

> This is a follow-up and we have found many of the problems that we had two months ago still not corrected. And we have found further important deficiencies that we did not have last time. These things must be corrected. We will be back for a second follow-up and if they are not you will be definitely close to a provisional licence. [He pauses, looks up and around at all of them in a caring and concerned way.] You all seem like real nice people and I'd hate to see that happen to you.

The Makkai and Braithwaite (1994b) data also showed that respectful confrontation of the seriousness of non-compliance works best when inspectors know the director of nursing. It follows that it is a counterproductive inspection policy to be relentlessly rotating inspectors so they are always regulating nursing home managers they have never met before. Longer term relationships help inspectors do the critical emotion management parts of their job more effectively. In any case, with team inspections it is possible to get the advantages of 'a fresh pair of eyes' by rotating in one new inspector with one enjoying ongoing professional relationships at the facility.

CONCLUSION: PRIDE IN CARING, SHAME IN NEGLECT

Our data from the end of the 1980s suggest that while there was a formidable revolving door of Australian nursing home regulation, the theory of regulatory capture had minimal explanatory power. Later in the 1990s we saw, in contrast, formidable interest group politics that captured the nursing home policy process. While this permanently changed institutions of Australian regulation, while it seriously compromised its effectiveness for a short space of years in the mid and late 1990s, this capture no more neutered the effectiveness of Australian nursing home regulation in the 2000s than it did in the 1980s and early 1990s. Why was this? Two reasons.

First, the capture was so blatant that the Ministers in charge at the time were fatally wounded by the reaction of advocates, unions, the media and their deep throats in the bureaucracy. As a result, some of the most severe cutbacks for the aged – dismantled enforcement, abandoned unannounced inspections, reduced resources for regulation – were for the most part reversed.

Second, the agency and the government were put under pressure to deliver on the affirmative case on which accreditation was sold politically – continuous improvement instead of what had become minimum standards under the old regime. Our conclusion is that it is beginning to deliver, even though it has a long way to go and ritualism characterizes much, but not all, of the delivery of continuous improvement. As in all regulatory strategies, the riddle of how to resolve ritualism is still with us. In Part II of the book we try to show how we might solve it.

While Australian enforcement today has returned to much the same levels as a decade and a half ago, this is a much lower level than current levels of enforcement in the US.[15] We have also argued that while there seems to be a little more formal enforcement going on in Australia than in England, English street-level bureaucrats are effectively networking much greater levels of informal deterrence. Consequently, Australian inspection has the effect of shutting down fewer homes and pushing out fewer incompetent CEOs of nursing homes, for example, than either the American or the English regime. We will argue in Part II that this is a weakness of Australian regulation that needs to be remedied.

Continuous improvement, the positive story, is however in no sense driven by law enforcement. It would be problematic to attempt to enforce it in the courts, to punish the failure of a nursing home to demonstrate that it had not improved. Our conclusion is that professional pride is delivering that continuous improvement in the overwhelming majority of cases, and professional shame in a minority of cases where homes experience the shock of failing to meet a standard because they cannot demonstrate to the inspectors that they are improving. Praise (Makkai and Braithwaite 1993a) and reintegrative shaming (Makkai and Braithwaite 1994b) both seem to work in the context of Australian nursing home regulation. Moreover, our observations suggest that these are the weapons working to secure the tentative progress of continuous improvement.

NOTES

1. For more details on the methodology see Braithwaite et al. (1992: app. A).
2. This compares to 11 closures of social service providers by the UK Commission for Social Care Inspection from April 2004 to December 2005; it is not possible from the aggregated data to determine how many were aged care facilities but given that 91 per cent of complaints to the Commission were for adult care homes it seems reasonable to conclude that some were aged care facilities (Commission for Social Care Inspection 2005b: 247).
3. This was not just about standards monitoring. In the lead-up to accreditation commencing in the 1990s, there were perhaps 200 homes that decided not to apply for accreditation and closed.
4. Of course the reverse might be the explanation. Homes that announce they are planning to leave in a year might be more likely to get one-year accreditation.
5. For announced inspections and unannounced American inspections about which there had been tip-offs, we observed extra staff, extra pot-plants, flowers, pets, extra entertainment being brought in and updating of incomplete documentation. When we accidentally arrived 30 minutes early for a Sydney inspection in 2005, staff were completing a fragrant aerosol treatment of the entire home to dull the smell of urine.
6. At different times during this history, the Department was called the Department of Health, Housing and Community Services, the Department of Community Services and Health, the Department of Aged and Community Care, and the Department of Health and Ageing. It is referred to here as the Department or the Department of Health and Ageing for simplicity.
7. Following a meeting with the leadership of the standards monitoring program, on 28 October 1995, John Braithwaite wrote to his co-authors a long memo arguing that the theme and title of this book would perhaps best be 'Reform and Decay':

   > Had a depressing meeting yesterday with [the leadership group]. Have a profound sense of things going backwards. No serious enforcement seems to be happening as per our recommendations, though more 'conditions' are being imposed formally. Some homes are now not seeing a team for more than 3 years [because their risk profile was assessed as low]. No progress whatsoever on getting reports more user friendly and practically available to consumers. Worst of all, and this is why there is talk of accreditation, they see the regulatory regime as just about some basic minimum standards, rather than about continuous improvement. Begins to look like a classic captured regime. I feel so disappointed about this, as I am sure you do.

   Today, we think many of the losses from that decay have been recovered, especially on continuous improvement, thanks to a resurgent private industry overplaying its hand and advocates returning to the fray in the late 1990s.
8. There was, however, a reduction in the amount of notice of inspections to 24 hours in normal circumstances, with no notice for high-risk homes.
9. Experiments with peer involvement as standards monitors followed the same fate. Peer inspectors were often found to be opinionated compared to government inspectors – wanting things to be done the same way they were in their own facility. An attraction of government inspectors who spend their entire lives visiting nursing homes is that they become a resource for managers in their ability to explain the wide variety of ways different players in the industry tackle a particular problem.
10. Actually 'spot checks' because the 1997 legislative reforms required notice. With spot checks the notice became mostly a call from the home's car park as soon as the inspectors arrived.
11. Early on, the agency seemed even to lionize undemanding accreditation. Its October 1999 newsletter quoted a director of nursing approvingly: 'They gave a lot of positive feedback to the staff and they did not make excessive demands!'

12. An interesting issue is what attitude the courts would take to enforcement against homes that cannot prove they have continuously improved. The issue does not arise, however, because homes are never sanctioned formally for failing to continuously improve. When sanctions such as withholding Commonwealth funding for new admissions are applied, this only ever occurs with homes that are failing to meet minimum standards as well as failing to improve. We wonder what would happen in the courts if sanctions were appealed against a home that had very high absolute standards, but were failing to take themselves even higher. It is a shocking thought that withdrawing funding from a home could have the effect of forcing residents to seek beds in facilities with lower absolute standards than their outstanding closed home that refused to improve any further. Perhaps courts would stall at this as a disproportionate enforcement response and insist on more benign enforcement. What is hard to imagine is a judge flouting the clear purpose and language of the law – to require providers to demonstrate that they continue to improve – buying some argument that the deeper purpose of continuous improvement is to push everyone toward excellence, but not beyond excellence. Judges might fear 'slippery slope' effects of such a ruling. If they rule that an excellent provider does not have to prove that they are improving to get their funding, then perhaps next a slightly less excellent provider will opt out of continuous improvement, until ultimately providers who are barely above average try it on. Thanks to Peter Drahos for his thoughts on this note.

13. The 'Results and Processes' guideline accreditors follow for 'Expected outcome 1.1 Continuous improvement' (Aged Care Standards and Accreditation Agency 2005: 14) suggests considering the following question: 'Do improvements include genuine process improvement activity as opposed to routine maintenance activity?'

14. The 'Results and Processes' guideline accreditors follow for 'Expected outcome 1.1 Continuous improvement' (Aged Care Standards and Accreditation Agency 2005: 14) suggests considering the following processes, among others:

    - Provision of support mechanisms to ensure key stakeholders have active involvement in maximising outcomes, such as information to residents/representatives and specific training for staff.
    - Is there a link between resident needs, preferences and feedback, and representative feedback, with the home's continuous improvement activities?
    - Do staff have input into the home's continuous improvement activities?

15. That is, even after a period when Australian sanctions have gone up and US sanctions down, the US still has much tougher enforcement.

PART II

Rethinking Regulation and Governance

7. Dimensions of ritualism

The audit society is a society that endangers itself because it invests too heavily in shallow rituals of verification at the expense of other forms of organizational intelligence. In providing a lens for regulatory thought and action audit threatens to become a form of learned ignorance.

(Power 1997: 123)

REGULATORY CAPITALISM AND RITUALISM

The history of nursing home regulation we have described in three nations since 1970 fits in quite a strong way with David Levi-Faur's (2005, 2006) model of regulatory capitalism, which he developed with Jacint Jordana. What we have seen since 1970 is not only what Vogel (1996) found empirically to be *Freer Markets, More Rules*, but also 'more capitalism, more regulation'. In different ways, for-profit provision has expanded – at the expense of public provision in the UK and charitable provision in the US and Australia. In all three nations, the density of rules and resources to enforce them has increased and this capability has become more centralized in national regulatory agencies. At the same time strategy has shifted to meta-regulation (Parker 2002) with the effect that not only is there more public regulation today, there is also more regulation by corporations of their own facilities and more self-regulatory services offered by compliance consultants.[1]

In Chapter 1 we saw that the central planning era came to an end in the 1970s in the US. There have been many moments of reversal on the path toward regulatory capitalism. Starting with President Nixon's funding of state ombudsmen and more rigorous inspections, many conservative political leaders who came to power with a 'get government off the backs of business' ideology ended by increasing regulation. While the Thatcher and Major governments in the UK privatized a lot, they also increased regulation. The conservative Howard government in Australia in the 1990s began to both increase private sector participation in the nursing home industry and to deregulate. There was a backlash against the latter; re-regulation began from 2000.

The politics of this grudging regulatory growth conduces to regulatory ritualism. Those political leaders who would prefer to deregulate but are forced by the electorate to actually increase regulation are often attracted to ritualistic regulation that gives the appearance of being tough without compelling major substantive change. Then when politicians come to power who really want regulation that forces improvement, they are para-doxically at risk of attack from conservative ritualists when they dismantle rituals that give the appearance of toughness in favour of reforms that deliver more substance. This is the political dynamic of Michael Power's (1997) 'rituals of comfort' of the audit society. Even if street-level bureau-crats with a lot of discretion are actually getting a lot done, it is hard for politicians to prove to the people in a simple way that this is so. And when the street-level bureaucrat abuses discretion in a way that leads to a public scandal, the politicians want to be able to invoke an accountability mecha-nism, a ritual of comfort that will create the appearance that checks are now in place to ensure this cannot happen again. Since major public scan-dals are rare events in regulation, chances are the politician will be lucky and all the big problems will remain submerged from public view for a few years. The Minister's career will end in this portfolio with the successful appearance that his or her accountability mechanism has worked.

The forms of ritualism (see Table 7.1) we will consider in this chapter are rule ritualism (write a rule instead of solving the problem), objectivity rit-ualism, documentation ritualism and protocol ritualism, random sampling associated with overarching disciplinary traditions of legal ritualism and scientific ritualism. Finally, we consider technological ritualism and partic-ipatory ritualism. Many of the examples of ritualism we will discuss are at the same time examples of two or three of these recurrent kinds of ritual-ism. Thus the chapter is not organized in sections devoted to each kind of ritualism. First, we need to consider the wider array of actors, beyond the political actors discussed above, who are agents in the dynamics of ritual-ism. Then we consider how ritualism arises from misguided attempts to increase the reliability with which compliance is measured.

OTHER ACTORS IMPLICATED IN RITUALISM

Politicians are just one of the types of actors who deliver ritualism as a recurrent result of regulatory capitalism. Politicians, especially in the US, distrust regulatory bureaucrats, so they surround bureaucrats with rituals of discipline. As we saw in Chapter 3, regulators pass this discipline on to the management of nursing homes. Again, especially in the American polit-ical context, but to a lesser degree in England and Australia as well, the head of the regulatory agency disciplines inspectors to give a report that supplies comfort that can be passed on to his or her political masters that

Table 7.1   Types of ritualism

Rule ritualism	Write a rule instead of solving the problem
Objectivity ritualism	Follow an objective way of measuring something when a subjective way will better promote quality of care
Documentation ritualism	Get the documents right and the care wrong
Protocol ritualism	Follow the protocol when this makes outcomes worse
Random sampling ritualism	Select random sample, ignoring problem detection and legitimacy for statistical inference, thereby misrepresenting problems
Scientific ritualism	Do bad inspection by pretending to do good science
Legal ritualism	Follow the letter and not the spirit of the law
Technological ritualism	Fixate on a technological fix that misses the problem
Participatory ritualism	Follow procedures that pretend to enhance participation, but instead alienate (or put to sleep) supposed participants
Market ritualism (Chapter 8)	Persevere with free markets as good in themselves even when they reduce welfare

the home has been held to account. The inspector disciplines the administrator of the home to provide a trail of documentation that proves standards are met. The administrator then disciplines his or her nurses who in turn discipline their care assistants to create pieces of paper that accomplish the chain of comfort. Meyer's (2006) case study shows that the new administrative law that arrived in Australia in the 1970s became just another set of links in this chain of comfort. The whole chain is a hierarchy of distrust concerned with appearances more than substance.

The lines of distrust are more multidimensional than from the people to their politicians, to the layers of regulators, to the layers of service provision. There are the NGOs. Consumer groups in regulatory capitalism are an important check and balance on the industry capture of regulators that we discussed in Chapter 6. Unfortunately, they have often exercised NGO influence in a way that also conduces to ritualism. Their survival mechanism shares much in common with democratic politicians. Non-governmental organizations attract a membership, funding from donors and political support from the community by exposing regulatory failure. After the exposé, they want to prove their value to those constituencies by quick, concrete results. Most often that is a new law or regulation, typically one that imposes a new ritual of comfort. Hence an exposé of medication errors might lead to a new or expanded med-pass audit, or more commonly, simply a new requirement for extra documentation for medication. A new rule is often the cheapest thing for the politician to give marauding medical consumer groups. Both the politician and the consumer group get from the new rule that very concrete immediate reform that proves to their constituencies that they are making a difference.

The media are co-conspirators with NGOs in this process. Scandals sell newspapers; complex, nuanced stories do not. Ritualism is more likely when the media wants a scandal that is simple to understand, where there is a failure of the regulator to put in place a form of accountability that the consumer group stridently demands, or a politician is put on the spot and then responds to the demand. The journalist then shares the warm inner glow of the advocacy group that they have played their part in changing the world for the good. A new rule can involve almost zero cost to the state. Typically no extra time is provided for inspectors to check compliance with the new rule; they just spend proportionately a little less time checking all the other rules when the new one is added to their list of things to check. It is a doubtful victory for the advocacy group and the journalist when the cost of enforcing this year's new rule is that the rules that they won last year and the year before are checked less carefully. Since more rules are the dominant path of regulatory growth, in the next section we describe how it induces some paradoxes of ritualism.

RULE RITUALISM

Historically what happened in the US was that key political players became critical of broad, vaguely defined standards. At the macro level, one would think the industry were losers from an accumulation of rules. Surely they resist this? But rules do not accumulate at the macro level; they expand in a rather micro way. In these micro dynamics, it is sometimes the industry that drives the accumulation of rules. When home X is found non-compliant on a broad standard on which home Y in similar circumstances is found compliant, home X screams about inconsistency. It complains to its industry association about the vagueness of the standard leading to 'subjective' and 'unfair' judgments by inspectors. The industry association representing these members' grievances pleads for the standard to be 'tightened up'.

Paradoxically, when the regulator then consults with consumer groups on this grievance, for different reasons, they will agree that the standards should be made more specific. They are concerned that vague standards are unenforceable. Legislators can then see opportunities to please both by rule-making that portrays the same rule change in slightly different ways to the two constituencies. They tell the industry association they are responding to their grievance about the rules being vague and unfair; they tell the consumer group that they too are frustrated with the failure of inspectors to clean up the industry by enforcing these rules. Legislators think of the standards as so vague that they give inspectors too much discretion to subvert their legislative mandate.

On this, lawmakers and consumer groups often genuinely agree. Sometimes federal regulators also agree. They are frustrated that the states fail to deliver federal hopes. Lawyers – in roles that include judging, legal drafting and representing the conflicting interest groups – are professionally socialized to distrust vagueness in legal standards. So they reinforce the above streams of sentiment and help them converge into a river that runs in the direction of more rules that have greater specificity. Lawyers agree with the advocacy groups that vague standards are hard to enforce; they agree with the industry that vague standards result in abuse of discretion. The social and medical scientists have a similar view on vagueness to the lawyers. Scientists believe in tight protocols to ensure that inspectors assess the same things in exactly the same way using precisely defined criteria. In the US, the gerontological establishment has been a major contributor to the culture of distrust toward street-level bureaucrats. The scientists' solution to the discretion problem has been to seek to hem inspectors in with detailed protocols that they are audited to follow by federal US inspectors who check that state inspectors do their job.

The upshot has been convergence among all the key players of the nursing home regulatory game in the United States that broad standards that are not tightly specified must be narrowed. The consequence has been a long-run historical process of all these constituencies succeeding in having one broad standard broken down into two narrower standards; then later each of those two standards may be subdivided again into two or more. By 1986 this process had reached the point in the US where there were over 500 federal standards, complemented in most states by at least that number of state standards, sometimes by many times that number (the Illinois code for nursing homes included over 5000 quality of care regulations in the 1980s [Tellis-Nyack 1988: 10]). In the late 1980s there were some valiant efforts at rationalizing and reducing the numbers of standards and protocols. Even so, in most states inspectors continued to check compliance with around a thousand federal and state rules. And as the years rolled by, the micro-process of creating new regulations and protocols resumed.

How do inspectors cope with checking compliance with around a thousand standards? The answer is that they do not. Some of the standards are completely forgotten, not suppressed by any malevolent or captured polit-ical motive, just plain forgotten. Such standards are never cited in the states where they are forgotten. Then there are those that become familiar by some accident of enforcement history that gave prominence to a particu-lar standard in a particular state. Referring to state regulations, one Midwestern inspector said: 'We use 10 per cent of them repeatedly. You get into the habit of citing the same ones. Even though you could use others [for the same breach]. Most are never used.' Braithwaite and Braithwaite (1995) have analysed a variety of ways in which the accumulated existence of a large number of standards in the US drives huge interstate inconsis-tency and intrastate inconsistency in how the standards are enforced.[2]

For example, the professional background of inspection team members can frame which of the thousand odd standards will be attended to. Administrator: 'If you've got a nurse, it will be nursing deficiencies in the survey report; if a pharmacist, you'll get pharmacy deficiencies; a sanitar-ian, sanitary deficiencies; a lawyer, patient rights, etc.' We observed one Chicago inspection team to rate all dietary standards in a home 'met' for the reason that the dietary problems looked so serious! How can that make sense? The team felt that the dietary problems were so bad that they could not check them all out properly and get all the other standards checked in the time frame required by HCFA to complete the survey. So they 'deferred' the dietary problem for two weeks until a dietician could be booked for a specialist survey. When we accompanied the dietician on this inspection two weeks later, sure enough, a great number of the dietary standards rated met in the earlier inspection report that had already been submitted to the federal government were now rated 'not met'.

The point of these examples is that when inspectors have an impossible number of standards to check, arbitrary factors will cause particular stan-dards to be checked in some homes, neglected in others, causing endemic unreliability. Braithwaite and Braithwaite (1995) explored in this way the paradox of extremely low inter-inspector reliabilities of compliance for comparatively specific US standards[3] with extremely high reliabilities (inter-rater kappa coefficients for total compliance scores ranging from 0.93 to 0.96) for the 31 broad and vague Australian standards in force at that time. At its best, they concluded that the American process works in the following way:

> The inspectors meet together at the conclusion to their information-gathering, as they do at certain intermediate points during the inspection, to share the prob-lems they have found. When a number of negative findings are judged to con-stitute a pattern of non-compliance of a particular type, a search begins for a 'tag number' which can be written up as not met. Once all the problems have been agreed and tag numbers found to write not mets for them, the team leader

ticks met for all the remaining standards. As she does so, she does not read them or think about them and she certainly does not check with her colleagues that someone has collected the information necessary to reach that met rating. Usually she will not discuss with her colleagues the possibility that the same pattern of conduct that caused one standard to be rated not met should also cause several other standards to be out of compliance (for example, an inappropriate use of restraint may cause standards concerned with restraint, following physician's orders, resident choice, mobility and freedom of movement to all be out of compliance). In other words she makes one valid not met rating and several invalid met ratings as a result of this strategy.

(Braithwaite and Braithwaite 1995: 321)

This, Braithwaite and Braithwaite (1995) concluded, was the American process at its best. At its worst, inspectors partitioned responsibility for the standards, each writing up their own standards with little input from the other team members. What did we find was the relevant contrast with the highly reliable Australian process of that time? It was not easy for Australian inspection teams to keep 31 standards in their heads even though none of them had mandated protocols. Yet they could make a fist of it. More critically, at the end of an inspection the team could, and usually did, manage to sit down to discuss, standard by standard, the evidence collected by all team members relevant to each standard. This dialogue was formalized by the team agreeing on a list of positives and negatives to be written beside each standard. Sometimes they found that they had not collected the data necessary to reach a reliable rating on the standard. They then had to take steps to collect the extra information. There was no escape from this because the team was required to sit down with the management of the nursing home, to summarize the positives and negatives on each standard and give reasons for the final ratings. This differed from American exit conferences; they reported only exceptions. In the US nothing was and is said in exits about standards that are ticked 'met'. It would be difficult to do so since the inspectors have neither debated compliance with them nor assured themselves that they have collected the data relevant to them.

It was not the fault of American inspectors that they did not do this – the number of standards and protocols with which they coped made this quite impossible. The end result of demands for more specific standards with more defined protocols that cover all the things judged important for nursing homes is an inspection process that is structurally unreliable. The pursuit of the reliability of parts causes the unreliability of the whole.

If US inspectors give up on keeping all these standards in their heads, what is their cognitive coping strategy? It seems to us that they have a gestalt of the provisions codified in the regulation – for example, that good infection control is required, that privacy must be protected. It is likely that professional training informs these gestalts more than the law does. They then decide whether a deficiency ought to be written by deciding whether it offends against one of these gestalts. Then they search for an appropriate regulation under which to cite it: 'What will we call it? How about 1220 A? What about 1220 B? Why don't we use both of them?'

After explaining to a number of surveyors this interpretation, based on our observation of how they coped, they agreed that this was basically how they did it. When we pointed out that the most troubling implication of this process from the point of view of reliability was that depending on how hard they searched through the standards, they might find one or two or three deficiencies to write out, one of them said, tellingly: 'Or they might find none at all and have to mush it in.' Decisions about how hard to search for multiple citations for essentially the same problem were driven by a 'professional judgement' of 'how serious overall their problems have been' or 'how hard they've been trying'.

> You can write it out under [X] and create a repeat violation because they got a deficiency on [X] last time. Or you can write it out under [Y] so it's just an element, which has no real consequences. Or you can put it out under both [X] and [Y], putting out a whole standard.
>
> (Chicago inspector, 1989)

Hence, hand-in-hand with a paradox of reliability is a paradox of discretion. More and more specific standards are written by lawmakers in the misplaced belief that this narrows the discretion of inspectors. The opposite is the truth: the larger the smorgasbord of standards, the greater the discretion of regulators to pick and choose an enforcement cocktail tailored to meet their own objective. A proliferation of more specific laws is a resource to expand discretion, not a limitation upon it (Baldwin and Hawkins 1984).

The beauty of a small number of broad standards is therefore that one can design a regulatory process to ensure that the ticking of a met rating means that a proper process of information-gathering and team deliberation has occurred on that standard. One accountability check in Australia was that whenever enforcement action was appealed, the team's worksheets listing all of the positives and negatives they found under each of the 31 standards had to be tabled before the Standards Review Panel. Until 1990, teams were required to write a report for the nursing home with a statement in support of the rating for each of the 31 standards. This proved an impossible burden with reports often running over 50 typed pages. As a result, from 1990, the report gave a statement in support of the compliance ratings of standards grouped under seven objectives. This made for ten-page reports that were more consumer-friendly.

In summary, the smaller the number of standards, the better the prospects of ensuring that (a) the most vital information for assessing the total quality of life and quality of care of residents is pursued; (b) lying behind each rating is a collective deliberative process on what that particular rating should be; (c) there is effective public accountability to audit that (a) and (b) actually occurred; and (d) inspectors have the capacity to stand back to document the wider patterns in the problems they have identified.

PARADOXICAL EFFECTS OF PROTOCOLS ON RELIABILITY

The same argument against the proliferation of standards can be extended to the proliferation of protocols for rating standards. The misplaced faith of the legislator for narrowing broad discretion results in the enactment of more specific laws. The misplaced faith of the consultants of the scientific establishment of gerontology results in protocols to narrow discretion. When there are the number of protocols that are supposedly followed in the American process, all the inspector can do is fill out the forms mandated for certain protocols and essentially fudge the other protocols that cannot be checked. Realizing that this is the way the game is played, advocates of protocols for certain standards that they regard as especially important lobby the federal government to mandate auditable protocol forms that the state inspectors must fill out. While this improves the attention given to the lobbyists' cherished regulation, it further worsens the structural malaise of the process.

The commendable shift to resident interviews in the OBRA reforms to the survey process introduced in October 1990 quickly fell prey to the disease of the proliferation of protocols. Our observations during the early months of the new process illustrated the unintended consequences. Interviewers started at the beginning of the schedule for the resident interviews only to find either they ran out of time or the resident became exhausted before they got far into the schedule. Thus, items placed early in the schedule were done according to protocol, later items were fudged or ignored. For this and other reasons we will come to soon, we agree with the exasperated inspector who said to us: 'Our own questions are better than the nonsense on the OBRA forms.' When we raised this and other examples of OBRA protocols being selectively and partially followed, one state survey manager replied: 'We'll streamline it. In time we'll do it our way rather than follow the HCFA protocol.' The trouble is, of course, that every state has no choice but to streamline, and each state

streamlines in its own way. Streamlining error is the inevitable consequence of overly ambitious pursuit of reliability through the proliferation
of protocols.

Protocols can work well in the context of a social science evaluation, but
fail in practice because in the evaluation study the protocol does not have
to compete for limited time with 30 other protocols. There are other reasons
why a protocol that succeeds in the evaluation study fails in inspection practice. An evaluation might show that a protocol of putting a tick in a box for
the name of every resident that participates in each activity can be done
reliably. Moreover, scores from following the protocol are validated against
more sophisticated detailed assessments of the effectiveness of activities
programmes. Unfortunately, however, what was valid at the evaluation
stage quickly becomes invalid at the implementation stage.

Administrators are quick learners in the business of getting good inspection results. If ticks in activities boxes are what count, droves of sleeping
residents will be wheeled into activities programs to get the numbers up.
Never mind that the quality of the activities program will be compromised
by the clutter of sleeping bodies; it is beating the protocol that counts. This
is why nursing home administrators love protocols: 'Give us the rules and
we'll play the game.' Imprecision, undefined evidence-gathering procedures, make it harder for the efficient (read ritualistic) administrator to beat
the system. In Australia, because there were no defined protocols for
inspectors at the time of our reliability study, management had no choice
but to focus on the outcomes for which the inspectors were searching. This
made their life more painful and uncertain. When protocols were defined,
administrators showed us how they created a documentation system, a
paper trail that matched the protocols the inspectors followed: 'You can
achieve paper compliance without real compliance. You can fool most
inspectors on most standards with paper compliance.'

The source of unreliability then becomes the rare inspector who looks
behind the paper trail to the quality of care that is actually being given.
Validity then becomes the major source of unreliability! American evaluators have been systematically blind to these possibilities. When they fail to
find reliability after innovations to 'tighten up' the standards and protocols,
they call for more of the same. They conclude that the tightening and
refinement did not go far enough. Consider, for example, the evaluation of
the state of New York's methodologically sophisticated and pace-setting
Sentinel Health Events (Office of Health Systems Management 1985). The
Sentinel Health Events were not legal standards but outcome measures
designed to be at the heart of the innovative New York regulatory system
of the 1980s. When this study obtained poor reliabilities for nursing home
ratings using the sentinel events, the evaluators concluded:

It is important to note that although the Stage I and Stage I1 reliabilities were disappointing, it is expected that the old system in New York State of PaCS (the system to be implemented nationally in April 1986) would have even less reliability. This is because the new system in New York has far more structure than either the old system or PaCS.

(Office of Health Systems Management 1985: 105)

The assumption that more structure is better was particularly obstinate in light of the reasons for unreliability that were diagnosed in the New York study. The first and 'extremely prevalent' reason found was that 'some surveyors (incorrectly) extended protocol requirements by noting a quality issue when no such quality issue is defined in the Protocol' (Office of Health Systems Management 1985: 39). An illustration of an 'incorrect' deviation from protocol arose when one inspector who was supposed to assess improvement of a pressure sore on the basis of 'chart review' found inadequate care and deterioration by observing care being given: 'The protocol states that only a chart review is necessary for this protocol, so the first cause for difference of opinion was a result of one surveyor doing more than he/she was instructed to do' (Office of Health Systems Management 1985: 36). This clearly illustrates the pathology of punishing inspectors for looking to the wood beyond the trees specified in their protocols. The orthodoxy of science is to disapprove of the nurse who used initiative to follow their suspicion by digging deeper and to approve nurses who reached the wrong conclusion because they followed the protocol. The orthodoxy of science is naive here. It is naive to believe that nurses, who are socialized to care about the patients they encounter, who are trained to use their initiative as professionals to get to the bottom of problems, can be turned into uncaring, mindless automatons who simply stick to the protocols.

Given that many nurses will be caring enough and have the initiative to follow the evidentiary trail toward conclusions of poor quality care, we think it best to design inspection systems which both assume and encourage this, rather than systems that attempt to control it. When a resident is being seriously neglected, two different nurses, with free rein to follow whatever evidentiary trail they pick up, are both more likely to detect the neglect than are two nurses who we ask to be automatons by following a standard protocol. This is particularly so with the many idiosyncratic types of neglect that the designers of the protocol never foresaw. As one Australian inspector pointed out: 'There are a hundred different reasons for residents to be incontinent.' The advantage of wide procedural discretion over tight definition of protocols in generating valid ratings seem to us especially profound when we are considering team inspections. This is because when one team member fails to latch on to an evidentiary trail that will lead to a deficiency, the other team member may succeed in latching on to it. Or one may discover the missing link in an evidentiary chain pieced together by the other. Inspectors boxed in by a proliferation of protocols cope in another way that makes it difficult for them to see the wood for the trees: task specialization. One inspector takes responsibility for filling out the forms required from resident interviews and another completes the reviews of records. We observed very little reading by one inspector of the protocols filled out by another. In the busy work of getting the huge number of inspection forms completed, the process of following up problems identified in a resident interview by tracking down residents' records (and vice versa) is profoundly compromised. This is not to say such follow-through does not occur in the US; it is just to say that it occurs more freely in the more free-wheeling Australian and English processes. Protocols kill initiative under a pile of paper. With nursing home staff and inspectors alike, excessive demands for a task orientation distract attention from the outcomes that matter. The result is the creation of health bureaucracies and regulatory bureaucracies that miss the big picture.

This pathology of protocols is just a specific illustration of the more general problem of formalized regulation forgetting that 'policy problems can be solved only by taking account of numerous interdependent and highly variable factors which oblige decision-makers to manage a kind of cybernetic process involving tentative probe, feedback, adjustment, and reconciliation' (Schuck 1979: 29). The pursuit of precision, either by protocols or by the proliferation of ever-narrower rules, causes an unreliability that is a symptom of a deeper and many-sided malaise of regulatory failure. This is especially depressing since the pursuit of precision usually fails in its own terms – it fails to deliver precision. There might have been 30 or 40 US regulations for every one in Australia at the time of our reliability research, but the American standards still seemed vague. In the language game of regulation, the problem of one vague concept is solved by splitting into three vague concepts or by defining protocols with other vague concepts. An alternative we suggest to the perpetual struggle to get the words right is to concentrate more on getting the processes of dialogue right. Certainly there is merit in keeping the words simple. This is a necessary precondition to accomplish processes of dialogue that will deliver reliable judgements on those simple words.

THE EFFECT OF SUBJECTIVITY OF STANDARDS ON RELIABILITY

When we spoke to senior regulatory bureaucrats in the US and to social scientists who had been involved in the development and evaluation of nursing home inspections, a common type of comment was: 'There are some things that the process cannot do reliably. So you don't do them. Examples are: "Are the staff pleasant? Is the room tastefully decorated?" ' The thought occurred to us that if the Hyatt Hotel group adopted the view that decor and staff pleasantness were matters for which it could not set reliable standards (and therefore should not bother with), it would soon be bankrupt. In business, a head office effectively enforces all manner of 'soft' standards on franchisees by adopting a qualitative approach to evaluation of performance. In these cases, dialogue informs an evaluation that is made against the yardstick of 'What is it, subjectively, that consumers want?' Admittedly, some of these subjective assessments are easy and some are hard. You do not have to talk to many consumers to realize that they do not like vermin running around their hotel room or their nursing home. But to judge reactions as to how warm and non-institutional is the decor, or what they think of their continental breakfast, you really need to work hard at talking to consumers. Surely one reason that American nursing homes are so cold, institutional and unattentive to decor, notwithstanding a lot of improvement observed over the past 20 years, compared for example to the more pleasant decor of English homes, is precisely the attitude that such things are so subjective as to be beyond control.

The reliability of the subjective Australian 'homelike environment' standard (kappa inter-rater coefficients from 0.77 to 0.89) suggests that this American posture is in error. A properly subjective approach on a standard such as this involves talking to residents about whether they feel free to put up personal mementos in an area they define as their private space, whether there are spaces in the facility that they feel are inviting and homelike for chatting with friends, whether they feel there are inviting garden areas they can use. This subjectivity often came under attack in Australia. For example, managers of chains would complain to us that they had provided exactly the same food to two homes; the team in one home gave them a 'met' rating for the food and in the other home they got an 'action required' rating. There is no inconsistency here if the residents at the two homes had different subjective views about the food. Two teams will never agree on what is nice food, but we have found that they can agree, with high reliability, on whether the residents in a nursing home generally like the food they are getting. Reliability is accomplished by rejecting objectivity in favour of subjectivity.

The impetus to reform subjectivity in standards through objective criteria and protocols is dangerous because quality of life, which is what aged care should be about, is ultimately an irreducibly subjective matter. Inputs (the temperature of the food as it leaves the serving line; size of the room) are generally more 'objective' than outcomes (satisfaction of residents with the food and the comfort of the room). Objectivity disempowers residents and empowers managements who know how to get objective inputs in a row for inspection day – reams of documentation of the temperatures on food lines. Subjectivity, in contrast, means that residents are empowered because it is no longer the documents under the control of management that matter; it is what they as residents think and want that counts. Even the vision of outcomes which enjoys most support within the American gerontological establishment is an 'objective' conception – counting the number of residents with pressure sores or the number of restrained residents in the Minimum Data Set (MDS).

Collecting such objective outcome information can be useful. However, it must be pointed out that it is a process that does little to shift power over the definition of regulatory problems out of the hands of management into the hands of consumers. Administrators can handle a regulatory process that counts pressure sores or restraints. They can keep control of their own evaluation because they know what the score is objectively before the inspector walks through the door. Consequently, they are ready with a defensive documentary record to prove that the residents with the pressure sores were all turned two-hourly, that there are physicians' orders and assessments to justify the restraints they want to keep (Wiener and Kayser-Jones 1990). Hence, while the outcome of the number of restrained residents can be measured reliably and while this is an extremely valuable thing to do, it does not solve the problem of reliably assessing a law that requires proper use of restraints. Reliable assessment of a legal standard requires investigative common sense, determination and the imagination to uncover leads and follow them. The protocol-following automatons lauded by the objective outcomes movement will be incapable of doing this job reliably. Their protocols would not allow them reliably to find that over 90 per cent of the American nursing homes we observed between 1987 and 1991 failed to meet the then Australian restraint standard: 'Physical and other forms of restraint are used correctly and appropriately' (Australian Kappa reliability coefficients, 0.83 to 0.87). Instead, they mostly concluded that American homes where half the residents were tied up or chemically restrained met the US standards, and where they found restraint non-compliance, they found it unreliably.

THE EFFECT OF BEING RESIDENT-CENTRED ON RELIABILITY

Being resident-centred means two things: first, it means relying on residents as a source of information for rating standards; second, it means participation in a regulatory dialogue where quality of life outcomes for residents are the ultimate criteria of evaluation. Critics regard this as an orientation that is a prescription for unreliability because most residents are so sick or confused that what is a subjectively good outcome for them is unknowable in most particular cases. Moreover, for the same reason, they are incapable of being meaningfully interviewed. Our research has dealt with both these objections elsewhere at greater length (Braithwaite and Makkai 1993).

We should at least say here that most resident outcomes that are the focus of debate within any sensible regulatory system will not be controversial. We know that getting burnt in a fire, getting pills prescribed for someone else, or getting a pressure sore are outcomes that residents are keen to avoid without having to ask them. Second, we use our fieldwork data to argue elsewhere that skilled inspectors know how to find those residents in a nursing home who will be outstanding informants on those issues that do require subjective feedback from residents and they also know how to get some useful information even from residents who spend most of their life extremely confused (Braithwaite and Makkai 1993). The critics argued that it was harder, or even impossible, for a nursing home with many extremely high disability or demented residents to comply with standards under Australia's process of 1987–97, which was more resident-centred than any we know. Our data do not show this to be the case (Braithwaite and Makkai 1993).

We have seen that this resident-centred process seems to have high reliability. It is true, as the critics point out, that Australian inspectors were often misled by confused residents. However, we also found it true that these errors were almost invariably corrected long before they affected final ratings. In our reliability study, inspectors being misled by confused residents did not even register as a reason for disagreements, though one side picking up useful information from residents that the other side missed was one of the more important reasons for disagreements (Braithwaite et al. 1990). Moreover, with our study of reasons for 889 disagreements between inspectors and directors of nursing on ratings, in only 3 per cent of disagreements was one of the reasons that the director of nursing felt that the team had relied on misinformation from residents (Braithwaite et al. 1990: 73).

These data show that interpretive errors in a subjective, resident-centred process can be and are corrected through a process of dialogue. First, dialogue with residents and their carers is important. Second, with nursing home staff and within the inspection team, there is dialogue about whether the seven quality of life principles of the Australian standards were being secured: health care, social independence, freedom of choice, homelike environment, privacy and dignity, variety of experience, and safety. Consistency did not easily fall out of such processes of dialogue; it came painfully and with a lot of backtracking and moving in circles as new inconsistencies were discovered along the way. Ultimately, however, consistency will be greater to the extent that the debate is 'ultimately' only about resident outcomes. When the debate is theoretically only about whether an input required in a rule is delivered, in practice the outcomes that motivated the rule makers' specification of the input will unreliably intrude into ritualistic regulatory judgements. This is inevitable because sensible people do not like to enforce the law when its enforcement will defeat the very purposes for which the law was enacted. Because business regulatory laws (such as those that regulate health care) deal with complex, changing and individually variable problems, mismatch between legally mandated input and desired outcome is common.

Let us illustrate with a comparatively simple example. We observed a Chicago sanitarian point out during an exit conference that it is against the rules to have a male and female in adjoining rooms sharing the same toilet. The sanitarian concedes that in this particular case neither resident is capable of using the toilet and that moving either would be upsetting to them. He says he is going to turn a blind eye to the rule for the sake of the residents, but warns management that someone else from the department could come along and cite them for this. In other words, he is pointing out that because there is such a mismatch between rule and outcome, he is giving an unreliable ruling. With Australian standards monitors confronting such a predicament, there was no such unreliability. Since what was the best outcome for the residents was clear and since inspectors were instructed only to be concerned about outcomes, dialogue quickly led to a reliable result.

Our claim is that dialogue about resident-centred outcomes conduces to more reliability than recourse to authoritative interpretations of the meaning of words in rules. A word like 'privacy' is certainly a slippery word, as is 'health' or 'pain' for that matter. In a resident-centred process when the question arises 'But is this really an invasion of privacy?', the answer is discovered through a process of dialogue about what are the senses of privacy that are important to this particular resident. Dissension is more likely when the question is to be resolved by pitting one inspector's conception of what privacy means against another's; consensus is more likely when the professional responsibility of both is to focus on the practical sense of privacy that is subjectively important to that resident in that situation. There will always be inconsistency in trans-situational 'objective' judgements of whether privacy has been invaded. Resident-centred contextual dialogue about privacy outcomes, in contrast, can often reach reliable conclusions. It follows that progress with increasing reliability is less likely to come from handing down more sharply defined authoritative interpretations of what privacy is, and more likely to come from improving processes of dialogue.

Dialogue occurs at many levels, all of which allow scope for improvement. Inspectors can improve their dialogue with residents by learning how to deal with resident intimidation, how to capture the moments of clarity of thought that normally confused residents experience, how to communicate non-verbally with residents when verbal communication is poor, how to use third parties (roommates, relatives) to draw out uncommunicative residents, how to mobilize translation support with non-English-speaking residents. Moreover, group discussions with residents (for example, with residents' councils) can draw out some people who will not be engaged one on one. Other residents speak up on behalf of an intimidated resident who has been abused. While she has too much fear of reprisal to speak up herself, she nods agreement at the residents' council meeting when others speak up.

Inspectors can improve their dialogue with each other by scheduling interim discussions during the course of an inspection, learning how to be active listeners, learning how to break deadlocks by framing the sticking points on which more subjective information from residents is needed. They can also learn when it is wise to draw on the wider experience of a supervisor or to get the perspective of nursing home staff on an issue. They can learn how to select crucial conflicts over consistency to be put on the agenda for regular meetings of all inspectors. Training courses are improved by making them more genuinely dialogic – showing videotapes of real regulatory encounters and asking trainees to debate the appropriate compliance rating, for example. American inspector training has improved greatly in this regard.

Focusing reform energy on processes of dialogue rather than on rules recognizes something that the community of scholars who work on regulation and policing have begun to realize. This is that it is simply not true that police officers make decisions mostly by reference to rules (Shearing and Ericson 1991). They do not, should not and could not do so. Police culture, Shearing and Ericson (1991) point out, is not a rule book, but a storybook. Police learn how to handle difficult situations by hearing stories about how competent officers handled similar situations or by themselves experiencing and retelling such stories: 'Stories constitute a consciousness, a sensibility, a way of being out of which action will flow without recourse to specific instructions. Unlike rules, stories do not address action directly but rather constitute a sensibility out of which action flows' (Shearing, personal communication, 1993). Stories instruct the participants in a regulatory culture how to 'read', via a 'poetic apprehension', the layers of meaning in a situation. Shearing and Ericson (1991) show how this poetic apprehension is communicated through analogous reasoning – like advising young officers to avoid provocation in difficult situations by 'acting as if you were on holidays'. Nursing home inspectors communicate a resident-centered sensibility, for example, with the analogous reasoning: 'Is this a home that you could be happy for your mother to live in?' Reliable ratings will be maximally possible with a regulatory culture that accomplishes a common set of sensibilities through dialogue. Hence, a hotel chain can get staff and decor to a state that appeals to consumers, but it will not accomplish this with a set of decor rules. Rather, it seeks to cultivate the right sort of sensibilities in its management and quality assurance staff with stories, concrete examples and analogies. Staff civility and pleasant decor then follow from these sensibilities.

The importance of legal standards is more in setting the framework and focus for storytelling, less as words that utter explicit guidance. To be good at framework-setting and focusing dialogue, standards must be simple and few in number. Like good poetry, they must engage us by being replete with silences, leaving us to make of them what we can: 'For in leaving to us the talk of making sense of what is before us, this silence forces our continuous and attentive engagement with the poem itself' (White 1984: 27).

THE EFFECT OF RANDOM-SAMPLING RITUALISM ON RELIABILITY

Yet another way in which the paradox of reliability came about in the past was on the question of the random sampling of residents. The behavioural and medical scientists who were influential in shaping the American process as it emerged in the 1980s believed that randomness was important to valid and reliable ratings. The old-fashioned inspection practice of allowing inspectors to concentrate evidence-gathering on residents of their choice was viewed as unscientific. Many key players in industry associations were also vigorous advocates of random sampling, but for more sophisticated reasons. Some regulators alleged that these industry players supported random sampling because it would inhibit inspectors from following their noses to the residents who were getting the worst deal out of the home. The lawyers had a hand in this shift as well. Up until October 1990, when the US abandoned random sampling of residents for nursing home inspections, standard training practice would confront the American inspector with the scenario of a company lawyer challenging their findings by questioning their competence in the statistical theory which would warrant the judgement that a 'pattern' of non-compliance existed.

Our observations of the random-sampling process revealed endemic cheating by inspectors. They would cheat for both principled and unprincipled reasons. When on the initial tour of the home the inspector met a resident who complained of mistreatment or who manifested signs of neglectful care, the inspector would sometimes cheat by putting that resident into the sample even though she was not randomly selected. On one occasion, an inspector from another part of the state asked the team to put a friend of hers who was suffering from a pressure sore in the sample. On another occasion, a complainant was fudged into the sample to protect her – so that the problem would appear to have been discovered by the team. In another multistorey nursing home, where care seemed to vary by floor, the team decided to 'improve' on the standard sampling protocol by stratifying the sample by floor. These were all examples of principled cheating.

Examples of unprincipled cheating included the following. The team member met a resident on the tour who was an old friend she enjoyed talking to. After a 20-minute chat with her over lunch, she realized that she had already collected half the information she needed from this resident. So she slipped her into the random sample. In another type of fudging repeatedly observed, the inspector would find a resident with multiple problems – restraint, catheter, pressure sores and others. Because the sampling protocol demanded a number of residents with each of these types of special problems, this resident became 'a good one to do'. Slipping such a resident into the sample reduced the total number of residents investigated. We say these latter examples are of unprincipled cheating, but the teams did not view it this way. We have already made the point that systematic data collection to rate hundreds of regulations is impossible; the cheating, they contended, made an impossible job a little more possible. Even when the cheating was clearly principled rather than designed to cut corners, inspectors were under no illusion that it was cheating that required concealment:

Inspector: There are ways of bending these things [the sample]. That doesn't cause us any problem.
JB: How do you mean?
Surveyor: Well you can just number the list of patients where you are selecting every fifth one: 1, 2, 3, 4, 6, 5.

It is a sad commentary on the unreflexive empiricism of the behavioural sciences that so many books are written on the statistics of sampling, while empirical studies of random sampling in practice are virtually non-existent. Our own observations are of a wide gulf between science in the books and science in action, even with inspectors with considerably more education and training in sampling protocols than the average opinion survey interviewer, for example.

The reasons for the gulf in this domain are multiple, but include: (a) laziness; (b) job survival; (c) the view that inspectors have more serious professional obligations than to the numbers games of scientists; and (d) the view that inspectors have a more sophisticated or rounded practitioner's view of randomness than the theoreticians. The last of these is the most interesting: inspectors who stratified by floor or who put into the sample someone they bumped into on the tour had a social construction of randomness which they would defend as superior to the protocol. This then is just a special case of the naiveté of assuming that because protocols exist, they will be followed; because something works in a pilot, it will work in day-to-day practice. Behavioural scientists are empirically neglectful of behaviour in science. One lesson of observing nursing home inspections is that trained professionals expect and exact working conditions where they exercise professional judgement: they simply refuse to succumb to demands to follow instructions like machines. Inspection procedures should never be based on the hope that this will not happen; they should be designed on the expectation that it will.

Hence, random sampling in nursing home inspection in the US up to 1990 tended to fail in one of two ways. In some cases the team cheated by slipping bad cases into the sample, thereby defeating randomness. In other cases, they refrained from cheating when they saw bad cases; they settled for the randomly selected case and let the bad case slip by that might have been their best chance of getting to the deepest problems in the facility. As argued earlier, our view is that inspectors are most likely to find problems of non-compliance reliably when their initiative in following evidentiary leads is cultivated instead of controlled.

The final reason why random sampling reduces reliability in regulatory inspections is that it is extraordinarily time-consuming. It distracts a great deal of time from the more important work of gathering evidence on the standards. We would observe one inspector on the first day of a pre-1990 US inspection do little more than participate in the initial tour and gather all the information on residents and their categories of care in order to select the sample, selecting it with the correct number in each category (variably according to the number of qualified residents in the home), and recording the selected sample to prove that the sampling protocol had been followed. On one occasion, we observed four nurses debate for 37 minutes whether, for sampling purposes, group therapy counted in the 'physical therapy' category. A call to the supervisor was eventually needed to resolve the dispute. All this effort for the dubious statistical virtue of randomly selecting 16 residents from a population of 80! The US made a sound scientific decision when it abandoned random sampling in October 1990.

The first point we should make toward a conclusion of this journey through reliability ritualism versus actual reliability is that our finding of a decade and a half ago that the US inspection process was much less reliable than the Australian process may simply not have been true. None of the quantitative studies had large samples, and all had design flaws. They do, nevertheless, amount to superior information on the reliability of nursing home inspection than we have on any other area of business regulatory inspection we know. We would be surprised if our hypothesis were wrong, however, not only because of the dramatically different results of the quantitative reliability studies but because of the convergent conclusion from our extensive qualitative fieldwork.

It could be argued that even if our empirical claim about the comparative reliability of nursing home inspection were right, this is simply a statistical artefact. When American inspectors found a problem that should be cited, there were 499 different ways they could cite it under the wrong standard (when there were 500 standards). When Australians decided to give a 'not met' rating, there were only 30 ways they could get it wrong (with 31 standards). Of course this is an overstatement because clearly there is little risk of fire-safety citations being written under a quality of food standard. Nevertheless, the basic point remains that more standards mean more ways classification errors can occur.

To point this out, however, is not to erect a defence of the American standards. It is no comfort to proprietors who feel they have been treated inconsistently to tell them that they unfortunately have been victims of a statistical artefact. If inspectors give the wrong ratings because of the many standards under which they might write non-compliance, then this is a bad feature of the design of a system with too many standards. It is the design features of this system that cause the unreliability.

We have seen that a fundamental problem in thinking about reliability in nursing home inspection is that it has been captured by the rituals of quantitative science. These are rituals of objective observation and recording that do not sit naturally with professionals socialized in more diagnostic, problem-solving traditions. Our qualitative diagnosis is that scientific ritualism has greatly compromised the efficacy of nursing home inspection in the US. Like the police officer, for a nursing home inspector it is more important to follow leads than to follow protocols, though protocols have a place. A police department that relied exclusively on the most sophisticated regimen of random patrol would never solve a single murder.

We have suggested the following three conditions for rendering nursing home standards more reliable: (1) opt for standards that are simple broad principles and few in number (in preference to many specific rules and many protocols); (2) structure the regulatory process to be normally resident-centred and outcome-oriented; and (3) trust dialogue (not just top-down 'training') among people who have been persuaded to care about those

outcomes. It is the challenge of persuading to care that makes the movement to commitment from a variety of more ritualistic motivational postures a critical issue in Chapter 9.

RESOLVING RULE RITUALISM

In this section, we treat the ritualism that comes of writing more rules, more
protocols or a new kind of audit as variants of the same problem. We have
argued that by creating as productive a culture of storytelling among regulatory inspectors more or less consistent sensibilities can issue. Broad, vague
principles can deliver consistency when they are informed by shared sensibilities (see further Braithwaite 2002b, 2005b: ch. 10). Detailed protocols
can be part of such a regime. But a detailed protocol for inspectors to follow
to assess a standard should not be the preferred approach, even when a randomized controlled trial shows using the protocol delivers measurement of
superior reliability and validity than not using it. This is because improved
measurement integrity is likely to be achieved at the expense of reduced
measurement integrity for other standards that are neglected because of the
rigours of implementing the protocol. Extra protocols should only be introduced when funding is added for extra inspection hours to implement them.
Even with infinite inspector funding, the number of days of the year that
staff will be distracted from the provision of care by the implementation of
protocols to measure the quality of care is a constraint. Detailed protocols
are best saved for unusually intractable measurement problems or for use
only in homes that fail a more qualitative initial test; only when there is
probable cause of serious non-compliance as American lawyers say.

In an era of meta-regulation, one temptation is to require the home to
implement a protocol that good science shows to measure quality of care
well. If the home cannot produce documentary evidence of meeting the standard based on implementation of or exceeding that protocol, they fail the
standard. This can be a sound policy so long as there is space for providers
to innovate with new and better ways of doing the protocol, with good evaluation of the innovation. It has its own limits, however. We have observed a
great deal of evidence that when providers are required to document compliance even with very simple protocols, such as a two-hourly turning schedule, fabricated evidence of protocol-compliance is often recorded.

A study by Schnelle et al. (2003a) of 779 residents in 30 US nursing
homes found that MDS recording of incontinence was associated with documentation of two care processes: evaluation of the resident's incontinence
history and toileting assistance rendered by staff. The disturbing thing
was that, among residents capable of accurately reporting their care, no

difference was found in the reported frequency of toileting assistance between those recorded as receiving scheduled toileting and those not. There was also no difference between the two groups in the discrepancy between received and preferred toileting. There was no difference in residents' reports of received toileting between residents scored differently on the MDS incontinence quality indicators. It appears that while being incontinent mobilized the ritual of documenting a toileting assistance plan, it did not result in the reality of more toileting assistance. This is the ugly face of ritualism – documentation of incontinence history and documented evidence of responding to it as a ritual of comfort. The regulatory state gets comfort while the incontinent suffer extreme discomfort.

More disturbing still, residents who received three to four assists with their toileting per day were more than twice as likely to be able to stand without human assistance as those who received zero assists per day. In other words, it appears that more mobile residents who objectively need less assistance with toileting get more, presumably because they are the easiest ones for staff to assist. Schnelle et al. (2003a: 920) interpret their results somewhat more charitably than this: 'the finding that residents listed as being on scheduled toileting were less cognitively and physically impaired than residents who were not on scheduled toileting suggests that NH [nursing home] staff used invalid assessment criteria to determine a resident's appropriateness for scheduled toileting'.

Simmons et al. (2002) and Pokrywka et al. (1997) found discrepancies between chart documentation of food intake and direct observations of eating. This evidences the rituals of comfort that cause the widespread malnutrition in nursing homes:

> *Chicago dietary inspector:* They think they can solve their problems by designing a fancy sheet [that records percentage of food eaten for each meal]. Paper compliance we call it. They like to show the state that they're doing something. Give them a new documentation and that will get them off our back, they think. But then even the food service supervisor tells us she can't understand why all this food comes back on the trays when the sheets say that they are eating well. But she can't say work out who it is who is not eating their food because the sheets say they are all eating in cases where we've found that they did not eat today.

Bates-Jensen et al. (2003) found that repositioning on a two-hour schedule was documented for 95 per cent of residents at risk of pressure sores – impressive charting for the state of this ritual of comfort. The observed reality of resident comfort in the study was that 78 per cent of the residents were not moved on a schedule of three hours or less. Cotton (1993: 2338) discussed a study by Joseph Oslander that tested the reality of documentation of two-hourly release of physical restraints and repositioning of residents.

Research staff put an invisible fluorescent mark in the centre of knots. A light can then detect whether the restraint has been untied for repositioning. In the majority of cases the documentation was falsified; the restraint was not released when it was recorded as having been. We observed inspectors mark the knot of restraints with felt pen in the 1980s. Mostly they too would find a discrepancy between the documentation of release and the unobtrusive measure of it. We will never forget the emotion of seeing one old woman cover the mark with her hand when she realized the inspector had put it there to help her win back some of her freedom. It follows from this kind of evidence that we should heed the wisdom of the crusty old inspectors who say: 'Don't take too seriously the ticks in the boxes they show you. Kick the tyres.' The US system makes this hard to do, however, as an Oklahoma dietary inspector complained: 'I can't see the whole picture like I used to. I'm so busy checking off these forms and following through on my sample cases that I can't follow a special problem I see.' Ironically, as she was saying this, another inspector was failing to notice that a group of residents were asleep in the dining room with trays of uneaten food in front of them as he was preoccupied with working out who was in his sample of selected residents.

The most endemic form of ritualism documented in the earlier chapters was the tendency for nursing homes in the US more than 90 per cent of the time to accept a deficiency without disagreement, even if they did not agree it was correct, so long as it was not going to result in a sanction. Then a ritualistic plan of correction would be submitted – often to create a new policy, hold an in-service, fire a staff member they were going to fire anyhow. The root cause of the non-compliance would not be addressed and roller-coaster compliance would be observed at subsequent visits, when this and other problems would recur. There was even ritualism in the frontline documents essential to delivering quality care, and openness about it:

Chicago inspector 1: These care plans are not accessible to the care staff.
Inspector 2: So what's the point in having them if they can't see them?
Nurse: To show the state surveyors, that's what.

Later the inspectors explained that many homes like this one keep the documentation away from aides lest they write something in them 'that gets them in trouble with us'. The documentation is rendered ineffective as a working tool to improve care in order for it to be more effective as a ritual of comfort for the state.

Texas inspector: They must have policies to deal with theft.
Resident: Yes their policy is to make a police report, nothing happens and they blame the police for that.

In God we trust . . . All others document.
[Sign in Washington nursing home]

Sometimes a ritualistic response is used in an attempt to pre-empt a citation. An Indiana inspector pointed out that a kitchen hand had left food uncovered.

> *Owner to the staff member:* You're fired. Out.
> *Inspector:* You know I won't be intimidated by that from telling it how it is. If you want to fire people that's your business.

An example of ritualism to prevent enforcement action occurred in 1988 when both federal and state inspectors in New South Wales were conducting separate inspections, but the state inspectors were signalling the new expectations of the federal government. Between a visit by state inspectors on a Friday and an expected federal inspection on the Monday, care plans for 105 residents were written!

In Chapter 9, we argue that meta-regulation only holds out the prospect of improving on what can be accomplished by command-and-control regulation if providers can be moved from the motivational postures that conduce in different ways to ritualism – game-playing, disengagement, resistant defiance and capitulation – to commitment to the principles of the regulatory order.

But even if that is accomplished, even for nursing homes utterly committed to doing protocols right because they are committed to what high-integrity pursuit of the protocols can accomplish, there is another constraint to confront, another reason why an excess accumulation of protocols can compromise quality of care. This was a discovery of Chapter 3. There is a deal of evidence that small homes find it easier to create a home-like non-institutional environment, a less custodial and disciplinary environment. Historically, Chapter 3 argued, in the US as regulatory demands became more exacting, smaller homes could not survive. Today a US home needs to be large enough to have an MDS nurse, or several such nurses, specialized and dedicated to ensuring that all the MDS protocols are correctly followed. Whether the demands are delivered through direct command and control or regulated self-regulation, homes need to grow to a certain size to have the economies of scale and division of labour to implement a large burden of regulatory protocols.

While we should very much want our regulation to be evidence-based, evidence-based ritualism counts as a danger alongside other ritualisms. Even when the evidence is methodologically strong and powerful that following a certain protocol will improve the measurement of quality of care, we must pause to ask the following questions:

1. Will requiring inspectors or providers to follow this protocol take time away from other quality assurance activities that will do even more good?

2. Will the improvements that are likely from applying the protocol be greater than the benefits that will be lost from moving provider time from hands-on care to protocol implementation, especially when the latter requires the time of the most qualified care staff?
3. What is the evidence on fraudulent completion of such protocols?
4. What are the enforcement costs of detecting and punishing the fraud in 3?
5. To what extent will the protocol add to the costs of regulation?
6. Will these costs be compensated for by economies of scale, leaving residents to live out their lives in colder, more institutional nursing homes?

If we do not come up with compelling answers to these questions, we can fall prey to rituals of being evidence based that, in a given implementation context, will make outcomes worse.

TECHNOLOGICAL RITUALISM?

According to some scenarios, new technologies will solve many of the pathologies of documentation that have so concerned us. Professionals will no longer have to keep such a myriad of protocols in their heads (that end up forgotten) because all the protocols can be designed to come to them as an electronic prompt. Since the exponential take-off of clinical practice guidelines in the 1990s, when more than 1600 were written in the US (Heimer et al. 2005), all health providers have found it quite impossible to manage the cross-cutting, multiple clinical practice guidelines they are expected to take seriously. Guidelines and care plans can be coded into a palm pilot hanging from a care assistant's belt. If Mrs Jones is to be turned every two hours and this is the responsibility of that care assistant, his palm pilot will beep, reminding him to do the turn. Elsewhere in this book we argue that very often staff have a will to comply; they fail to because they are overwhelmed, often just needing a tap on the shoulder about their most crucial priorities. On this account, the new technology can be seen as an automated tap on the shoulder, albeit not as human a tap as that of the caring reminder of a supervisor or inspector. But it is delivered every time and with utter precision.

If the care assistant ignores this electronic tap, at the end of his shift his supervisor gets a beep on her palm pilot to tell her to give the staff who did not complete their tasks on time that human tap on the shoulder. If the supervisor fails to close that loop by speaking to the staff and ensuring at least that the resident is turned at the end of the shift, the supervisor's supervisor will get a printout that says so, and so on up the line to state inspectors who can get an automated electronic report of compliance with care plans for the whole population of residents. Not only can the inspectors check this for the whole population of residents instead of the sample they currently check in inspections, they can do it at any time without notice, not just at inspection time, and they can do it without leaving their office.

So why would nursing homes invest in such new technology when it creates the potential of enhanced external control over them? The proprietors we spoke to who are moving in this direction are more interested in the new technology for the way it can increase their efficiency in claiming reimbursement. They believe that nurses have more love for providing care than for recording it. Their analysis is that their staff are doing a lot for residents that is not recorded in their documentation. The new technology will allow them to capture this better and make a case for increased reimbursement. For example, they believe it is often months after the condition of a resident deteriorates to the point where there is a case for higher case mix reimbursement that management start getting documentary evidence to support that claim. While it might increase their exposure to being fined for non-compliance with standards, they think the reimbursement benefit will far outweigh this.

Besides, by being an early mover into new technologies that increase multiparty accountability for their performance, they get a reputational benefit with the regulators for their openness. Rickwood and Braithwaite (1994) have shown empirically that 'Openness with Inspectors Pays.' Pro-technology proprietors think it will allow their internal quality assurance systems to more effectively pick up problems before an inspector notices them, so when the inspectors do check they will actually get credit for documented good care. It will be the late movers who regulation forces into the new technology who will be at risk of the most serious regulatory threats. There is an evidence base for seeing computerized decision support in health care more broadly as one of the more promising innovations for improving quality, that is, mostly effective across a number of credible studies (Grimshaw et al. 2001: II-34–II-37; Grol 2001: 2579).

While the capital investment in the new technology is large, the early-mover proprietors also believe it will deliver large recurrent savings in staff time. Consider the turning scenario. At the moment it sometimes takes more time to record the turning of Mrs Jones than it takes to do the actual turning. The days when the progress notes were always hanging at the end of the bed are long gone for reasons of privacy and multidisciplinary engagement with care plans. So when the care assistant looks for the record on which she must record the care she has just provided, the activities' director might have it in her office, or the physical therapist in his therapy room. In the high-tech scenario, the care assistant just clicks 'done' on the palm pilot or the computer kiosk in the corridor outside this little cluster of rooms (or says 'turn done' to the voice recognition software). This single click pulses through all the relevant documents where it could conceivably be relevant for this to be recorded for purposes of monitoring delivery of a care plan, measuring impacts in a quality assurance study, coding clinical outcomes for the MDS, clinical processes for compliance with a multitude of clinical practice guidelines, coding for reimbursement, and so on.

Not only might this information become available to everyone in the care team, to all levels of the supervisory hierarchy, external quality assurance consultants and state inspectors, it might also go to relatives of the resident. Progress with a care plan that the resident's son participated in crafting can be delivered in a suitable form (also with an access code to honour privacy and patient consent standards) to the son's computer 1000 miles away. Technological innovation therefore holds out the possibility of nudging greater ongoing participation of that son in his mother's struggle, pushing the son to make that phone call to empathize with mother's latest setback. It could also deliver a very practical form of tripartite supervision of compliance with regulatory standards. A challenge for the software is to 'translate' (Black 2000, 2001), in a way the son can understand, complex medical and pharmacological concepts in the standards and in the specific care plan to guarantee their delivery. If the son is a Portuguese speaker, there is also the challenge for translation software to send the summary report in Portuguese. Those electronically generated Portuguese reports may help even more the son's participation in the quarterly care planning meetings with the professionals on the care team that he attends with his English-speaking sister to assist in the translation of the translation.

Of course the external monitoring by relatives and inspectors enabled by the new technology is less important than the horizontal monitoring of peers. This is the connection to the civic republican ideal of non-hierarchical accountability to circles of widening circles of accountability (Braithwaite 2006). Elsewhere in this book we have discussed the importance of informal social control from peers at handover meetings between shifts. When a carer hands over a resident to the new shift without mandated care processes completed, for example dumping the changing of the soiled sheets onto the carer on the next shift, the horizontal social disapproval can be potent. An aspiration for the new technology is greater transparency and improved coordination between multiple shifts and multiple disciplines. This is especially important when non-routine 'alert' events occur that are beyond the experience of these nurses, but that prompt additional tasks or activities that also trigger prompts at the desks of consultant physicians or pharmacists. In addition, the frontline caregiver can probe for a prompt. He or she can key in that he or she is proposing to give the resident paracetamol before giving it. The paracetamol administration guideline is checked against that resident's care plan and progress notes, and a prompt comes back: 'No. Check with your consulting pharmacist or physician before doing that.'

More than that, the electronic loop can increase the rigour of that consulting. In a recent incident in Maryland, a nurse called a doctor to query a written instruction to administer 300 units of insulin. The doctor commended the nurse for picking up what was surely a transcription error. She was told it would have to be 30 rather than 300. The nurse duly administered the 30 units and the resident collapsed almost immediately and died. On investigation, the intended dose proved to be 3. An objective of a system where the nurse probed electronically the 300 instruction first would be electronic feedback that both 300 and 30 were beyond the guidelines in such a case.

We spoke with Walt Wheeler, recently retired head of health systems in the Michigan Department of Community Health, now a visionary consultant for the most ambitious experiment in rolling out this technology in the US industry. It involves a dozen homes across Michigan in 2006. Wheeler agrees with the analysis of Chapter 3 that regulation has been the driver of growth in the size and institutionalism of American nursing homes that has not been in the interests of residents. He sees documentation as the most fundamental driver of this. Documentation is the biggest cost of regulation in the nursing home industry. Because the current regime regulates space through paper, the paper needs to be housed under one roof. It is not possible for one paper system to satisfactorily regulate a cluster of buildings in a bushland setting, for example. Nurses cannot run from building to building in search of care plans. They, their immediate supervisors and the paper that operationalizes all the day-to-day supervision must be under one roof. As the webs of paper and the webs of supervision get wider, the roof gets bigger.

Wheeler thinks the wireless capability that has emerged since 2000 can change this: space can be regulated at a distance by computers talking to one another. Tiny clusters of homelike, non-institutional, housing for small groups of residents, their full-time carers and a full-time supervisor of those carers can be widely dispersed. Part-time specialized carers and their supervisors can move between these clusters with the assurance that all the records they need, updated in real time, move with them wherever they go. Such a system might also translate to a dispersed cluster of a dozen suburban houses converted into an electronically integrated nursing care monitoring system, so more of the infirm elderly might be housed within walking distance of the homes of their children, grandchildren or friends. Indeed, it could enable hybrid home-institutional care clusters integrated into suburbia.

But there is a pessimistic scenario about this new technology as well. The technology might make more difficult the common practice of recording at the end of a shift or the end of a month that all the turns and toiletings mandated by care plans have been done when they were not done. This would become more risky because there would be an electronic trace of when the entry was recorded. But when the palm pilot beeps to tell the carer he must turn Mrs Jones, it is only a little fraud for him to instantly press done, telling himself he will get to that in a minute or two. It is easy to see how little habits of cheating to avoid grief with one's supervisor could aggregate into wider patterns of cheating that generate convincing but utterly false rituals of cyber-comfort. We must remember that the archipelago of discipline which is the American nursing home industry (see Chapter 3) has at its base the poorest workers of the US labour market. They are oppressed by the most formidable webs of discipline imaginable. How are they going to react to this new technology? Will they embrace its noble vision? We fear they will systematically subvert it, just as our qualitative data and the quantitative data of Schnelle et al. (2003a) suggest they systematically subvert paper documentation. Indeed, they are likely to read it as a stepping up of the technology of domination that rules their working lives.

In Chapter 10 we argue that unless these carers can be moved from motivational postures like game-playing and disengagement that conduce to ritualism, they will subvert the noble vision of the likes of Walt Wheeler. Moreover, we argue that they will not move to a motivational posture of commitment to the regulatory order and to continuous improvement in quality of care until the facts of their working lives cease being facts of domination. This means that inevitable webs of regulation are complemented by webs of support that increase freedom in their lives, that give them more meaning, that help them build on their strengths to develop a career trajectory from more decent base incomes to even higher incomes as their skills grow. Without this, it seems almost inevitable that handheld health technologies will become locks on invisible new wireless chains that aides will have even more reason to pick apart than the paper that currently oppresses them. As one quality manager put it, palm pilot technology will encourage 'task focused care that emphasizes resident dependency needs'. That is not to say that we cannot identify the conditions for flipping these new technologies from being webs of domination to nets of liberation for both residents and staff. Those conditions we argue involve simultaneously changing the status of the resident as a person in a rite of passage between adulthood and death (Shield 1988) and of the care assistant trapped in a rite of passage from welfare dependency to the working poor. Both must cease being 'other' – neither adult nor dead for the resident, neither welfare dependent nor full citizen of the health and social care workforce for the care assistant. Only then can the new technology avoid imposition of new rituals of compliance. Only then can it enable inclusion of both residents and staff in rituals of regeneration, rituals that interdependently regenerate the lives of those who care and those cared for.

THE CASE FOR THE MINIMUM DATA SET

The biggest single set of protocols in US nursing home regulation since 1991 have been those associated with the Minimum Data Set. In a standard way for every home in the nation, the MDS records 'objective' indicators of various health outcomes. There is little evidence of consumers using these objective comparators to choose a home. It could hardly be desirable for them to try, as without risk adjustment,[4] and even with it, the MDS would be a misleading guide to the quality of care residents could expect, for reasons explained below. Inspectors use the MDS in a useful way to target issues of concern and select residents for review. Before arriving, inspectors print out the MDS outcomes for the home that are worse than the seventy-fifth percentile for the state. A sample is then selected using MDS codes to target residents who have those problems.

Because inspectors use it this way, so do quality assurance staff within nursing homes. They can see where they are above the seventy-fifth percentile and they know this will attract regulatory scrutiny. Being above the seventy-fifth percentile may not be a worry if they know the inspectors know that they take residents who are unusually sick compared to other homes, especially if they have a reputation for referrals of high-risk or demented residents because of their excellence.

On the other hand, a home that does not have a good reputation, and has low-risk residents, will feel vulnerable when they exceed the seventy-fifth percentile on a health outcome. In this situation, insiders told us that down-coding of MDS outcomes is common. We also concluded earlier that down-coding of outcomes (or up-coding of risk categories to the same effect) is almost universal to avert MDS coding of the sentinel events of fecal impaction, dehydration and pressure sores on low-risk residents. While the evidence is encouraging that different appropriately trained nurses can come into a nursing home to run MDS codings with high inter-rater reliability (Mor et al. 2003b), appropriately trained nurses consistently code fecal impaction and dehydration as something else. Even more sadly, as Schnelle et al. (2003a) and other data discussed above suggest, MDS nurses have to deal with a great deal of fraudulently recorded information in resident records. Different MDS nurses often reliably code on the basis of information recorded by care staff that is systematically false.

Even if MDS nurses were reliably coding valid data, which they are not, their codes would still be misleading. This is because of the sample size US nursing homes offer. In a small facility, one or two residents admitted with a pressure sore can move it from below average to above the seventy-fifth percentile. Obversely, if two residents with pressure sores have died in the months since the last MDS results were published, at the facility level MDS results quickly become an outdated trigger of concern. Health outcomes have large standard errors or bands around the true level. For example, Mor et al. report:

> [I]f the true 3-month incidence of pressure ulcers is 5%, the 95% confidence interval around the estimate for any given facility would range from 1% to 11% in a facility with 100 residents in the denominator. Not until the number of observations exceeds 200 do the confidence intervals around the observed rate drop to less than twice the size of the point estimate.
>
> (Mor et al. 2003a: 39)

This would be an even bigger problem for homes in Australia and the UK, which on average have around 40 residents. An MDS that can be a good policy idea for large institutions such as hospitals can be a statistical non-sense for care homes. The idea, of course, also makes more sense in hospitals because they are primarily health-care institutions, while nursing homes are primarily social care institutions. If all the rigour and all the regulatory risk for nursing homes attaches to the health outcomes in the MDS, then social outcomes can be neglected, and indeed are neglected more than they should be (Vladeck 2003). The more MDS-measurable can drive out the more important.

Minimum Data Set trends are also monitored at the national level and inform the setting of national objectives and priorities. On the other hand, there seems to be a kind of data-ritualism in this. As one senior CMS officer put it: 'We're collecting huge amounts of data, but we're drowning in it.' At all the levels it is (mis)used, MDS data underwrite pseudo-science – up-coding and down-coding to reduce regulatory risk and optimize reimbursement, facility-level quality assurance targeting based on dated information with unacceptable standard error, inspection targeting based on fraudulent data input, consumer choice based on non-risk-adjusted outcomes. Sadly the scientific ritualism of the MDS is another of those costly regulatory burdens on the aged care industry that pushes up the diseconomies of small scale in nursing homes.

PARTICIPATORY RITUALISM

Just as being evidence based is a central virtue that can be corrupted by ritualism, so is empowerment a central virtue in our analysis, and likewise it is susceptible to ritualism. We saw in Chapter 6 that residents' committees were pushed by standards monitoring at the end of the 1980s to become a feature of almost all Australian nursing homes in a short period of change, a change that occurred some years earlier in the US and that has yet to occur in England. The 1980s also saw in the US the promulgation of many state regulations requiring both residents and their carers to be invited in writing to quarterly care planning meetings. The 1990s saw state ombudsmen successfully push for family councils in nursing homes. While we do not know of studies on the effect of resident participation on the quality of decision-making,[5] there is evidence that relatives being engaged with the nursing home and visiting it regularly improves quality of care (Barney 1974; Chou 2002; Institute of Medicine 1986: 184; Tellis-Nyack 1988: ch. 8; Zischka and Jones 1984) and that richer participation of staff in decision-making improves care (Anderson et al. 2003; Rantz et al. 2003).

We were able to observe a great number of instances of these forms of participation, especially in the US. Whichever modality it was, whether pitched at residents or relatives, our observation was mostly of rituals of participation as opposed to participation that changed the substance of care for good or ill (see Gibson 1998; Tilse 1998). Many care planning conferences were conducted in a technical language of medical care that clearly left a resident who sat in the room throughout the meeting mystified and irrelevant to the professional conversation. Most residents said nothing at most meetings. Often presidents of residents' councils had been coached by facility staff to keep the agenda on discussion of what sort of outings or activities the residents would like to see over the next month. When complaints with real edge about care or food were raised, the standard response would often be 'That's something you should take up with Mrs Gatekeeper.'

On the other hand it is important to evaluate residents' committee meetings not just in terms of more democratic decision-making, but also more mundanely as some residents expressed it – 'something to do' – 'something different' to break the monotony of nursing home life. In that frame, discussing outings can be a good priority because it can interest and animate more than nursing care. Val Braithwaite became our expert at attending residents' meetings because residents so much wanted to talk to her about her recent shopping expeditions. She learnt this at a 1988 residents' council meeting at a home tucked away in the mountains of Tennessee. One of the elderly ladies said she was bored with the meeting and wanted the visitor to tell us what Australia was like. Val, taken by surprise, said: 'Well Australia has free universities [it did at that time].' The inspector replied in her ear: 'They don't want to know about that. They're mountain people, not interested in universities.' Here are Val's notes from a residents' committee in an Australian country town soon after she had learnt to be a skilful shopping raconteur:

> *President:* 'You're late Mrs Moriarty. The meeting's already started. You should have been here.' Mrs Moriarty shuts the door. It's still almost impossible to hear with a floor cleaner going outside. Two items were brought up. One was the positioning of a picture. Then there was some business from the last meeting I did not grasp. Then: President: 'Anything you want to raise?' Silence. 'Well that's it then. This happens all the time. They won't say anything in the meeting but they say it afterwards. But I can't write that down, can I? I talked to Sister about it. She said if they don't say it in the meeting I can't write it down. [To Val, unobtrusive observer] Am I doing the right thing? I thought you were here to see if I was doing the right thing. I know we have to have these meetings. Someone from the government says we have to have them. But this happens all the time. No one says anything in the meetings.'
>
> *Val:* 'You run these meetings as you want. It's not for me to say how you do it. There is not a right or wrong way. You talk about whatever you want. The government has been very concerned that people in nursing homes have more say and a chance to make things better. That's why they have suggested resident committees. They want you to regard this as your home. It's your home. [Discussion follows about how some of them still go home for the weekend. One wouldn't be here at all if her daughter didn't work during the day.] In your home you have a say about how things are done and you should have a say here.'
>
> *President:* 'But no one will say anything. What should we do? Am I doing it right?'
>
> *Val:* 'Well it's not for me to tell you but perhaps you could talk about social functions. Do you have social activities? Perhaps you could plan those? I've seen that work in other places. Once people start talking about things they like to do, they sometimes move on to talk about things they would like to be done differently . . .'
>
> *President:* 'Can I write that down in the book? What will I write? Mrs Braithwaite said that we should talk about social events.'
>
> We then talked about Christmas, about their plans for a shopping expedition to Grace Brothers, their families, their Christmas shopping. I described the skirt I was making for myself and Sari [my daughter]. We had a nice chat with much interest after prolonged silences and vacant stares. The secret of success in the end was that we talked about the things that gave them pleasure.

The entire meeting reminded us of the question members of the Older Persons' Action Group put to us in Victoria: 'Have residents' committee meetings been tried and failed or do residents need to know where to begin?' Since Val's residents' committee encounter of 1988, there has been some learning on how to make committee meetings a locus of activity. Many Australian nursing homes today periodically ask attendees on surveys if they 'highly enjoy, enjoy, are indifferent, dislike or highly dislike' the meetings. While many choose 'indifferent', typically five to ten times as many residents are on the enjoy than on the dislike side of this mid-point.

Julia Black has put her finger on one critical obstacle to participatory empowerment:

> it is not sufficient simply to call for deliberation for there is a real likelihood that even if all deliberants can be brought together true communication will be blocked by difference; difference in the modes of discourse, the techniques of argument, language and validity claims. Discourse may therefore have to be mediated through the adoption of strategies of translation, mapping and dispute resolution.
>
> (Black 2001: 33)

We have already said that these days the strategies of dispute resolution are mostly in place through resident, family, staff, care planning and quality improvement committees, exit conferences and the like, hard as it is to get them animated as Val's notes testify. Because many health and social care professions contribute to nursing home care (as do engineers, architects, sanitarians, lawyers and accountants), there are many technical discourses to be mapped (see Shield 1988). There are two reasons for this: first, no field of endeavour has more diversification of disciplinary specializations than health care (though nursing homes do not approach the 50-plus disciplines in a metropolitan hospital); second, nursing home care covers not just health but every aspect of life – from banking to bedding, even to booking appointments at a brothel – such that the mundane is professionalized (cooking is the realm of a qualified dietician, activities of a 'diversional therapist'). While the jargon is maximally pluralized and highly educated and technical at the top end of medicine, its subjects are the least educated and least alert cohort of the community. So the nursing home supplies us a least likely case (Eckstein 1975) for the problems of translation to be solved in order to make deliberative regulation work.

This is more so because some standard kinds of difference assume exaggerated form in nursing homes, not least gender, class and race. Hands-on care staff, especially in the US, are at the very bottom of the class structure and commonly members of racial minorities. Some residents of white middle-class and 'respectable working class' backgrounds looked down on them. In Chicago, where Jewish proprietors were common, some residents openly resented having 'our lives run by a Jew'. Men often viewed themselves as a 'valiant minority' (Shield 1988: 57) surrounded and dominated by gossipy, acid-tongued women, while the women thought the men were stupid and swore too much. Our observations suggest that women often did indeed dominate deliberative fora, for example by deciding on activities that were not of interest to men. And of course nursing homes are feminized institutions on the care staff side and in terms of who the influential visitors are (including inspectors). This has led to the peculiar Australian nursing home institution of one of the activities listed beside bingo, sewing circle, and so on, becoming 'Men's activity', where this will vary between visits to the pub/club, gambling, football, whatever. This form of difference is in other words settled by the men deciding an agenda on their own and then doing something that they see as getting them out from under the women in the way men of this generation were wont when younger.

What breaks down difference in able-bodied contexts is reciprocity. Wax (1962: 130) observed that even where there are great similarities of status, history and culture in a nursing home community, barriers between them can be very slow to break down because communication through those barriers is 'built upon reciprocity, and those who lack possessions, strength and health have relatively little to exchange with each other'. And as Shield (1988) points out, the absence of reciprocity, receiving care but not giving it, is a reason why the rite of passage from adulthood to death is so demoralizing. Residents often come to terms with the impending fact of death better than with the fact that nothing is expected of nursing home residents during this rite of passage. In the rest of life's rites of passage, there are things we must accomplish to gain admission to the next phase or status.

In Chapter 9, we discuss how a philosophy of regenerative care is changing this in the most inspiring nursing homes where residents care for pets, mentor children who visit them and educate them about what life was like in the past. Jewish residents teach Yiddish to children in local Hebrew schools and teach it to care staff who want to interact better with uncommunicative residents (Berman et al. 1986). One Victoria home wrote to the Alliance Française to say they had French speakers who would like to help students of French. Participatory fora also create political spaces where some of the very reciprocity that facilitates translation across difference can be constituted. I can trade my support for the bus trip to the beach in return for his support for the shopping expedition.

What did we observe to be the conditions of the rare event of the substance of participation across difference? One was relatives, community visitors and ombudsmen acting as bridges between the staff and residents. This was a theme of one of our first interviews in 1987 with the Chair of the Australian Affiliation of Voluntary Care Associations. He said that the resident committee model and the advocacy model were both weak participatory checks and balances, but that by linking the two models there could be strength in the convergence of weaknesses (see also Tilse 1998: 22). Twenty years of further observation affirm his analysis.

Relatives at care planning conferences were almost always more assertive than residents. When the health professionals were talking a language they did not understand, relatives would be more demanding of translation. Some said to us that they were more emboldened in this because they were speaking up for their mother – if it were their own care, they would not have asked. So we observed in a 2004 California inspection: 'Moma, can you understand what they are saying?' We even observed an uneducated nurses' aide being recruited to this kind of translation project: 'You're the one who has to do this Delores [the aide], do you follow what the nurse and the doctor are talking about, or is it just me?' Ombudsmen who attended residents' council meetings or exits at the end of an inspection would often draw residents into more genuinely participatory engagement with real quality of care issues in these fora. These would not necessarily be about these residents' own personal issues.

> *Ombudsman to president of residents' council at exit:* A number of residents have complained to me about being pushed into the shower very early in the morning. Have they being saying that at your meetings George?
> *President:* Yes. I think Mrs Jones should come and talk about the plan of correction she has in mind at our next meeting to see if we can stop that.

In other words translation is a collective project of sensitized medically educated professionals, residents and less educated staff emboldened by support in deliberative fora such as staff and resident meetings by advocates – be they ombudsmen, official community visitors, union representatives, or more educated children of some residents translating not only for their own residents but for others as well. Occasionally we saw inspectors doing translation at residents' council meetings, though never at care planning meetings. The tension between the regulator and translator roles that caused Julia Black (2001: 53) so much concern was in practice not such a major issue. Why? Because when translation did happen it was mostly at the hands of assertive non-professionals who, while not professionals, were repeat players who as a result had acquired enough translation skill to know when they should demand translation by the professional and when they could proffer their own translation for the resident and give the professional a chance to correct its errors. In this collective project of translation, some of the younger, more articulate residents would also translate for other residents. We have also illustrated how roommates can translate even the silence, the grunts, screams or grimaces of residents who cannot speak at all into communications a nurse or an inspector can encode. We observed inspectors to sometimes have an important role in reinforcing inspiring translation initiatives:

> *Resident at a residents' council meeting in Alabama 1993:* We have so many deaf folks I would like us to organize sign language classes.
> *Inspector:* You're wonderful.

Finally, we should remember that collective encounters such as exit and care planning conferences are multidisciplinary meetings. While nurses have more technical jargon than social workers, nurses sometimes get a buzz from explaining with a wry smile to everyone else: 'That's social-work-speak for . . .'

In those wonderful and all too rare homes with a regenerative culture, all the disciplines, all the stakeholders, take responsibility for helping one another with the task of translation. At the Julia Farr home in South Australia, residents decide who cares for them; they sit on selection panels for those positions that have a resident focus, such as all senior nursing positions. That mandates, even in the process of applicants preparing for their job interview, engagement with the challenges of translation from professional discourses. All such participatory processes are, of course, so much more challenging in homes where many of the residents do not speak English. In Australia over the past two decades there has been great progress in establishing nursing homes that specialize in residents who speak a particular language(s), in searching for care staff who speak the language of particular residents and even in staff learning the rudiments of new languages.

Our conclusion is by no means that it is inevitable that resident participation is ritualistic. A US administrator who ignores any sensible recommendation that is recorded in the minutes of the residents' council is a poor regulatory risk manager. To get the strength from a converging of weaknesses to enable more deliberative planning of care, there is perhaps a need to combine the level of public funding and networking of advocacy that we see with the ombudsman's programs in many US states, the mandating of resident and relative invitations to quarterly care planning meetings and exit conferences, inspection protocols that require not only interviews with residents individually but collectively as well (as in the US), the culture of smallness and local connectedness to communities that we see in English nursing homes that are more populated by assertive visitors, and some of the funding support for community visitors that we see in Australia that ranges from provision of free beverages and cookies for visitors to state funding of community visitor programs. As Tilse (1998: 20) points out, there is also a need to address some of the structural impediments to assertiveness by relatives, most notably a fear of residents having nowhere else to go in a system that has full bed capacity and waiting lists. We turn to this in Chapter 8. But most fundamentally, we see Black's (2001) challenge of translation as one of the culture shift to regenerative care that is now underway (Chapter 9).

So we have concluded that translation in the regulation and self-regulation of quality of care is difficult and routinely does not happen. When it does occur it is a collective accomplishment. The most important work of translation is done by third-party advocates of various kinds who build bridges between residents and those in more powerful positions that make deliberative fora like care planning conferences, meetings of inspectors with residents' committees and exit conferences more effectively participatory. Yet when translation is a collective accomplishment of a regenerative culture of care, the translating contribution can come from any member of the collective. In this extended account of a care planning conference from Renee Rose Shield's fieldwork notes, the senior physician is actually the key translator of a mother's wishes to her son:

The next resident to be presented is Evelyn Tischler. The social worker says she is 89 years old and she and her son have had a very difficult relationship. She was admitted three years ago for several months. While she was here she was adamant about returning to the community, and she did. Now she is back because her eyesight had become so bad that she is unable to remain in her apartment alone. The social worker explains that the doctor has discussed the possibility of surgery to remove the cataract. The son is determined that his mother not have surgery. He is certain she is against it also, and he wishes to spare her. He is furthermore concerned that his mother wants to make this stay a temporary one again, like the last time, but he knows that this is her last stop. He does not dare discuss this with her. He tells all of us that she is not a woman who can be crossed. Before Mrs. Tischler comes in, the staff and the son discuss whether the surgery is feasible or not. It seems that she had made a fairly good adjustment in the nursing home, and she is able to get around quite well. The surgery is more straight forward than the son was originally led to believe, and it is likely to have dramatically beneficial results. Nonetheless, the son insists that he knows his mother, and he will never consent to her surgery. Dr. Corning repeats that surgery may not be necessary, considering her adaptation, but because it is simpler than expected, it may be something his mother desires. 'Remember', Dr. Corning cautions, 'your mother is entirely competent to make her own decision in the matter. This will be her decision, not yours', he finishes, carefully.

The mother is asked to come in. Dr. Corning introduces himself and Mrs. Tischler remembers him immediately. 'I'll never forget the time', she says laughing, 'when I was in your office, and you yelled at me, "Don't waste my valuable time!" because I didn't want to do what you wanted me to do!' She seems to cherish the memory, and Dr. Corning and the rest of us are laughing, too. She holds his arm roughly and strongly. He asks defensively, 'Have you forgiven me yet, Evelyn?' and she says immediately 'No!' 'But Evelyn, that was years ago. I'm not so set in my ways anymore; I've gotten better – haven't I, Mrs. Rubin?' he asks the social worker, who backs him up by saying, 'Yes. He has, Mrs. Tischler; he has gotten better with age.' Mrs. Tischler laughs appreciatively and says again how she'll never forget that day.

Now Dr. Corning leans very close to her and signals a serious tone. 'Mrs. Tischler', he says solemnly, 'I have to ask you something today. When you were admitted this time, who made the decision to come here?' She answers quickly that it was her decision. 'Do you think it was a good decision?' he asks her carefully. She answers immediately that it was the right decision because she couldn't manage by herself anymore. Now, he asks, 'Do you think you are going to leave here or are you staying?' 'Oh, there's no question about that', she responds without hesitation. 'I have to stay here. I've already given notice that my apartment should be closed up. My son will take care of that.' As she speaks, the son's face is transformed; he looks astonished and relieved. The social worker whispers to Dr. Corning that he should ask about the surgery. He waves her question away, saying he does not want to ask that, but then he asks it. He says that her physician is pleased to see that she has adjusted very well to the new setting and that she has managed to get around the nursing home quite well. Gingerly he continues: there is some question that cataract surgery could be performed quite easily and might help her become more independent than she already is. If that were her physician's recommendation, and she and he reviewed all the risks and benefits to the surgery, what might she say? 'Well', Mrs. Tischler answers slowly, 'I might want to go along with it and do it then if that was the case.' Again, the son's jaw drops. Dr. Corning continues, 'It's my job to give you all the facts and to make recommendations because you can't make decisions without all the facts, right, Mrs. Tischler?' She says yes and again grabs his arm, pinches his cheek vigorously, and repeats the story about his long-ago anger in his office. Dr. Corning and Mrs. Tischler look like they thoroughly enjoy one another. After she leaves with her nursing assistant, the social workers compliment him on a job well done. The son looks happy and relieved. With modesty and pleasure, Dr. Corning says that when this meeting works it's because the family members and the resident are genuinely part of the group decision-making process. He looks as if he could crow.

(Shield 1988: 212–13)

CONCLUSION

In the era of regulatory capitalism, it is impossible for health and social care providers to ignore regulation. We did not embark on this research with the hypothesis that ritualism is the dominant response of our age to regulation. Across many domains we have attempted to show that this is the hypothesis that has emerged from our many years of data collection. The ritual of pretending to solve a problem by writing a new rule aggregates at the micro level in a way that at the macro level makes the system of rules unreliable and unserviceable for regulatory purposes.

Most stakeholders deplore this at the macro level. Yet at the micro level, business, advocacy groups, professions, the legislature, the executive, the media and the legal establishment all act to seek to fix a part of the system by making the whole system of rules more unworkable. The scientific establishment makes the macro picture worse still by pushing at the micro level for their favoured protocols to measure their priority feature of care. The way random sampling made both the care and the science worse in the 1980s is just one of the extended analyses of this problem provided in this chapter. When there are an unrealistic number of protocols to honour, the result is rule ritualism compounded by protocol ritualism. More reliable parts frequently make for less reliable wholes.

Law and science have allowed themselves to become ritualized by the inattention of their practitioners to the empirics of the behaviour of law and the behaviour of science. Contrary to the ideals of their foundation, law and science have become rituals of learned ignorance in the terms of Michael Power's opening to this chapter. They have taught many of the street-level bureaucrats of the US state to stop thinking, to stop doing detective work to protect the vulnerable elderly. They have not done this to nearly the same degree in England and Australia. Wireless information technology holds out the potential to loosen the chains in which care staff and residents have been enslaved, excessively institutionalized, by the overreach of law and science. On the other hand, the new technologies have the potential to become new wireless chains of Foucaultian discipline. Likewise empowerment strategies can continue to go the way of participatory ritualism or link productively to new possibilities like the changes to scale enabled by wireless technology and the new movements for regenerative care. The era of regulatory capitalism is also one when the custodians of the old welfare state cannot ignore markets. In the next chapter, we will conclude that not only is regulatory ritualism a dominant response to regulatory capitalism, so is market ritualism.

NOTES

1. In nursing home regulation today we find public mandating of the preparation of all manner of compliance plans, often combined with a requirement for committee meetings associated with them, with obligations to provide minutes of such meetings to inspectors and the risk of citations from inspectors if these processes are not working. Examples are nursing home plans for quality assurance, individual care plans for all residents, in-service training plans, staff planning, building design, infection control, pharmacy, social services, even grooming plans. In some jurisdictions, with some of these there are public requirements that outsiders be required to participate on committees that revise plans and monitor continuous improvement, as in US state rules that require family members of residents to be invited in writing to quarterly care planning meetings for their loved one. All of the features of Braithwaite's (1982) enforced self-regulation model can be identified in these practices.
2. While the literature on US inspectors' writing of deficiencies shows extremely low inter-rater reliability, the literature on nurses' MDS assessments from the same nursing home records shows high inter-rater reliabilities (Mor et al. 2003a).
3. Interstate differences in how compliance is rated are also much greater in the US. Even two seemingly similar states can be very different in deficiencies per facility – for example 1.8 in New Mexico and 14.3 in Nevada (Winzelberg 2003: 2554).
4. Risk adjustment is necessary lest homes that skim low-risk residents are rewarded. Risk adjustment statistically controls for the effect of levels of risk on health outcomes. Unfortunately, risk adjustment is technically difficult (Mukamel and Brower 1998) and it is possible to overadjust (Zimmerman et al. 1995).
5. No significant effects were found in our Australian research, which was afflicted with limited variation (for example, over 90 per cent of homes with residents' committees).

8. Market ritualism

In the US three ages of health governance might be discerned: the nineteenth and early twentieth centuries age of the liberal nightwatchman state when doctors were trusted to run the health system, a provider capitalism era from World War II to 1970 when it was believed central planners should take control of health systems from doctors, then the current era of regulatory capitalism (see Chapter 1, Table 1.3). Profound disillusionment with comprehensive central planning to solve the problems of the health system set in after the Johnson administration in the US.

Under President Nixon, regulatory capitalism was born with a huge growth in nursing home regulation alongside the creation of many other new regulatory bureaucracies such as the Environmental Protection Agency and the Occupational Health and Safety Administration. Regulatory capitalism saw trust in the professions and trust in central planning wane and trust in markets and in regulation of market externalities rise. But there was also growing trust in local communities to do their own regulation. Nixon also funded a nursing home ombudsman program in each state to organize citizens in local communities to increase oversight of their nursing homes. In the last chapter we considered the participatory ritualism that has been the upshot three decades on. And we foreshadowed the hopeful signs in new ideologies of regenerative care that are retrieving some of the promise of local community control. This chapter considers market ritualism and also seeks to salvage some of the potential of health and social care markets that has not been realized in practice. While the details are different, in Australia and England, like the US, we have seen the same basic transitions of the fall in trust in the professions and comprehensive planning and unresolved tension over how much markets and regulation that empowers local communities should be trusted.

WHY NURSING HOME MARKETS DO NOT WORK

Markets for nursing home care were never allowed to work during the central planning era of Keynesian welfare state economics. If the state were going to pay for nursing homes, their licensing would ensure that they were full. A half-empty publicly funded facility was a scandal of wasteful planning. The road to deregulation of capacity of nursing homes was slow in all three countries. There is not empirical evidence on whether a licensing regime that ensures publicly funded homes are full delivers worse value for public money than a deregulated market where poorly run facilities are half-empty and the best providers are expanding their bed capacity. But given what we know about deregulated markets in other contexts, it might be reasonable to assume it does. While we are inclined to make this assumption about the efficacy of more deregulated markets for bed capacity, because of the analysis that follows about the limits of markets in the aged care sector, we do not assume deregulation will make a major difference. Therefore, we part company with those who say that with deregulation and consumer choice, the worst providers will be driven out of the market, and so quality of care inspection can also be deregulated. An example of the kind of analysis we question is that of a Bush administration response in the *New York Times* to a study of inadequate staffing levels in nursing homes: 'instead of imposing new [staffing] rules . . . [we should] publish data on the number of workers at each nursing home in the hope that staffing levels may simply increase due to the market demand created by an informed public' (Pear 2002: 151). The idea is that when consumers see on the Internet that staffing levels in a home are comparatively low, they will not go there.

One limit on the power of markets to control poor quality is what Mancur Olsen has called the indivisibility problem:

> The consumer reveals his marginal valuation of the goods the economist traditionally has studied by taking a little more or less until the marginal evaluation equals the price; the goods that do not readily come under the measuring rod of money are those which, because of one type of indivisibility or another, the individual cannot take a little more or less, at least within some pertinent range.
>
> (Olsen 1988: 14)

The nursing home resident is in a situation where almost all the goods and services she depends upon in her life are bundled into one package supplied by the nursing home. Even goods and services that are not chosen through markets in normal life, in the nursing home are bundled into the package you buy. You no longer choose the church you go to, the pastor whose sermons you like; you go to the chapel in the nursing home with the clergy the home invites. Outside, if you dislike a brand of tea you stop buying it and purchase a more expensive brand. The nursing home does not have this individual consumer sovereignty over the quality of the tea. If the resident does not like the tea, she will generally lump it because the quality of the tea is not an important enough issue to move to another nursing home. The story of the consumer who loses her sovereignty over the market for tea and the choice of sermons is repeated with countless other little markets that have been important in her life. No purchase is quite like the purchase of a nursing home place in the way it bundles almost everything we need for the rest of our life into one indivisible package.

Many nursing home goods and services are also non-excludable. Non-excludable goods are those from which non-purchasers cannot be excluded. National defence is the classic example; you get defended by the army whether you pay taxes or not. Most of the critical goods and services in a nursing home are non-excludable – the fire alarm and sprinkler system, the medical care equipment, the social work staff, the cook and dining room, the lawns and garden – as also are most of the non-critical things that aggravate us – the screeching parrot inside the front door. Dividing these things up into units that are provided to some consumers and not others, that can then be given in greater quality or numbers to consumers who pay more, is mostly not feasible. Faced with this non-excludability, markets are hamstrung as a source of control over quality.

Geography is another major constraint on markets, especially for Australians and Americans living in remote country towns with one nursing home. Our interviews revealed geography loomed large even in the biggest cities where we conducted our research:

> *Relative of a Sydney resident:* I wish I could put her in Pleasant View Home or Gentle Rest, but they are just too far away for us to visit. We have no choice but to leave her here.

Unfortunately, markets in aged care do not work as well as markets in haircuts for reasons beyond our ready access to many barbers who can exclude others from our haircut, and who can offer us all manner of divisible extras. We know a bad haircut when we see it. But we may never know that if only we had put our mother into a different nursing home she would have lived a longer and happier life. The mistakes that nurses, doctors, dieticians, social workers and physical therapists make in the care of our mother will mostly never become known to us in retrospect; in prospect it is even more difficult to judge where care will be best. Even if we are a nurse ourself, and we interview all the nurses before putting our mother in there, because of the high turnover of staff in nursing homes in the US at least, a year later most of them will have moved on.

One response is to say if consumers make the wrong choice, they can vote with their feet and move to another facility. But there is contested evidence that a move of facility is very bad for the health and well-being of the frail elderly and is a cause of mortality (Borup 1983; Bourestom and Pastalan 1981). It causes much more stress than a move of house does for healthy young people. Familiarity with an environment is a good in itself in preventing falls and supplying established relationships one can lean on. So it can be better for the well-being of the aged to stick with a poor quality facility than move to an outstandingly good one. The risk of moving can also be compounded by the fact that the inspiring administrator who makes the new facility so excellent is also statistically likely to move up or away. In any case, it is often not a financially feasible option in the growing proportion of cases where the elderly have years earlier locked their capital into a unit in a retirement community that bundles nursing home care. So we just cannot be starry-eyed about capacity deregulation encouraging consumers to vote with their feet. In the face of all the above challenging information problems, unfortunately what consumers mostly do is judge nursing homes in the same way as they judge haircuts – by the way they look. One company we visited prioritized on the 'customer checklist' of its quality program a rating of 'curb appeal', meaning what the home looked like from the curb. At first we thought it was a joke because inspectors often refer to perfunctory inspections as 'drive-by surveys'.

Capacity deregulation is only one path to markets working better. And we do not totally discount it; in Australia while there is full capacity and no genuine market for high-care residents, there is spare capacity, a degree of competition and a degree of willingness of residents to move when service is poor among the low-care aged. In the US, Hirth et al. (2003) found that facilities with twice the number of deficiencies of their state average had a 2.9 per cent higher incidence of residents transferring out of the home to another home. While this is a small effect upon a small total amount of movement,[1] it is a statistically significant effect. In turn we will now consider league tables or report cards to improve the quality of technical information available to consumers in a digestible way, quality incentive reimbursement and shifting the object of competition.

QUALITY REPORT CARDS

In the US, England and Australia, inspection reports have been published for some years on the Internet, as well as being required to be displayed or easily accessible to residents and families at the home. The discursive qualities of reports are often more useful than compliance scores that might be converted to a league table. For example, a resident who has special physical therapy needs might learn most from an inspection report that explains a long list of problems with the physical therapy program, staff and equipment. In all three countries the text of inspection reports is more consumer-friendly than it used to be, but is still not as useful as it could be and not very widely used by consumers.

Our research in Australia suggested that, where there is a modest number of standards each of some breadth, inter-correlations among compliance scores on different standards are sufficiently high to make it statistically sensible to add compliance scores across 31 standards to form a total compliance score (Braithwaite et al. 1990, 1991). Then it is a small step to tell consumers on a website that the home is in the top 10 per cent, the top 20 per cent, and so on, in its overall compliance score. The inter-inspector reliability of total compliance scores in Australia was 0.93 to 0.96. Unfortunately, inspector ratings of compliance in the US have extremely low inter-rater reliabilities (Braithwaite and Braithwaite 1995). So it would be problematic to use them to constitute an American league table of compliance with nursing home standards for consumers. At least our Australian data show it is technically feasible to do so.

In practice, however, the integrity of the published Australian compliance data by nursing home has also been compromised by compliance ritualism itself. The smartest nursing homes at playing the regulatory game in Australia, even more so in the US, do not resist findings of non-compliance by inspectors. They get to work immediately at finding a low-cost way of coming into compliance. In previous chapters we have discussed the many ways they can do this – fire an allegedly responsible staff member on the spot who management was planning to shed anyway, conduct in-service training to retrain staff in this sort of compliance, fix Mrs Smith's call-bell that does not work. If the problem is fixed before the inspectors leave the home there is a good chance they will not write it in their report. If it is fixed soon after the report arrives but before it is published on the Internet, there is a good chance the final report on the Internet will say the home is in compliance on this standard. Moreover, some proprietors are more adept than others at twisting the arm of regulators to change posted compliance ratings once something has been fixed. A problem is, if Mrs Brown's call-bell does not work because there is no maintenance system for call-bells and no routine repair loop when they break down, by the time the compliance is posted on the Internet Mrs Black's and Mrs White's call-bells will not be working. We have seen that ritualistic plans of correction make for yo-yo compliance. This makes for profound problems of unreliability in using compliance scores to create league tables. League tables require a principled method of recording whether the yo-yo is up or down. The best way is to record non-compliance that existed on the day of the inspection regardless of when it is fixed. That does create tension with inspectorial practices of forbearance when something not too serious is fixed on the spot, a forbearance that we argued in Chapter 4 can build voluntary commitment to comply in future.

Such tensions can be resolved, however, as can the non-user-friendly access to nursing home inspection reports in all the countries studied, as can the unreliability of US compliance ratings. The fact that consumers in these three countries do not consult inspection reports greatly at the moment does not rule this out as a possibility in future. It is early days in the history of consumer–regulator interface on the Internet. Most of the best learning on how to do it well is yet to come.

Health outcomes measured by the MDS do deliver US report cards of nursing homes. They appear as quality indicators on the CMS Nursing Home Compare website and on 25 state sites, some of which are more user-friendly than the federal site, for example California Nursing Home Search. Harrington et al. (2003) argue for the value of these websites for comparing homes in terms of their staffing levels, given that there is considerable evidence that investment in staffing predicts quality of care. The quality indicators can tell a consumer if the incidence of pressure sores, weight problems, physical restraint and the like are in the bottom quartile or the top quartile of nursing homes, or average. These are not consulted by most consumers because they are not easy to comprehend and access. In any case, it would not be good if consumers did use the MDS as a league table because the standard errors of the estimates from the MDS are statistically unacceptable and because the percentile rankings are not risk adjusted: 'The difference between the best and the worst facilities (two standard deviations above and below the average) is eight new residents with improvement in UI [urinary incontinence] outcomes out of 25 annual admissions' (Mukamel et al. 2003: 467). If the MDS provides a league table of limited use for consumers, it does not follow that the idea is in principle bad. In principle it is a good idea because it responds to the key problem identified in the last section – that consumers need simplified comparative information on a quality of care that they are technically obscured from assessing directly.

Still, we must confront the fact that the experience of league tables in the health sector more broadly is mixed. In 1989 the HCFA started publishing death rates for what became 6000 US hospitals. These rates had more acceptable standard errors, related to an event that is hard to down-code or up-code (a corpse is a corpse is a corpse), and were risk adjusted for the severity of illness. Even so, the empirical experience was that neither consumers nor hospitals made much use of them (Brennan and Berwick 1996). They also caused a great deal of anger and resistance from hospitals and doctors. The HCFA ceased publishing the mortality league tables because if the benefits were not clear, the costs were ($16 per patient discharge [Marshall et al. 2000: 1873]). Costs are naturally greater in nursing homes because standardization challenges are greater with smaller providers.

A considerable amount of evaluation research of hospital report cards has been done since then, some of it of high quality, though only two randomized controlled trials. Marshall et al. (2000) reviewed 21 peer-reviewed studies. The subsequent research confirms the basic pattern of results summarized here. Individual consumers rarely use statistical information on the performance of health providers; they are much, much more influenced by stories of poor quality care than by published numbers, be they stories in the mass media or from friends (Mennemeyer et al. 1997; Robinson and Brodie 1997). Doctors do read report cards relevant to their referring practices, but they discredit them and mostly do not discuss them with patients during the process of referral (for example, less than 10 per cent of cardiologists discussing cardiac surgery report cards with more than 10 per cent of their patients [Schneider and Epstein 1996]). Corporate purchasers of health care (mostly employers in the US and primary care trusts in the UK) also rarely let league tables influence their purchasing decisions. In sum, league tables in health seem to fail to have significant impacts on health through market mechanisms – through consumers, referring health professionals, corporate purchasers making decisions to buy from those at the top of the table. Consumers are not interested in the data (Goldfield et al. 1999), do not trust it (Robinson and Brodie 1997), do not understand it (Hibbard et al. 1998; Jewett and Hibbard 1996), confront problems with timely access (Schneider and Epstein 1998) and in any case feel there is in practical terms no choice of provider available to them (Schoen and Davis 1998).

In spite of this, and in spite of the fact that all the key health stakeholders widely resist, even angrily resist them, quality report cards often seem to work in a major way in improving health quality. The first startling suggestion that this might be the case was the Hannan et al. (1997) study of the Cardiac Surgery Reporting System in New York. Actual mortality rates decreased by 21 per cent between 1989 and 1992. The risk adjusted decrease was actually greater – 41 per cent – because the illness severity of New York hospital heart surgery patients increased during this period. This big result triggered a lively literature on whether there really was a causal relationship between the quality report card and such a large improvement (for example, Epstein 1998; Marshall et al. 2000: 1872; Schneider and Epstein 1996). Peterson et al. (1998) found that it was not the case that the existence of the report card drove sicker heart surgery referrals to other states. They confirmed a reduction in 30-day mortality for New York of 33 per cent compared to a national average of 19 per cent. Rosenthal et al. (1997) at the same time reported improved outcomes associated with mortality league tables for 101 060 Ohio hospital discharges for six common medical conditions and two surgical operations. There were again significant and sustained reductions in risk-adjusted mortality following publication for most conditions. Longo et al.'s (1997) quasi-experimental design evaluated the impact of an obstetrics consumer report for Missouri hospitals. A number of clinical outcome indicators improved after publication, including patient satisfaction and caesarean delivery rates. Fifty per cent of hospitals implemented process improvements as a result of publication, such as infant car-seat programs, breastfeeding nurse educators and the like. Clearly these seemed effects of more discursive consumer reports as opposed to risk-adjusted statistical analysis. A Wisconsin experiment assigned hospitals to a highly public consumer-friendly form of comparative quality reporting, a private report on the performance of their own hospital only and no report (Hibbard et al. 2003). For obstetric care and cardiac care, the public-report hospitals had by far the highest number of quality improvement activities implemented in the year after reporting, followed by private-report hospitals, with no-report hospitals implementing fewest improvement activities.

So why did it seem these quality report cards changed hospital performance if referrers, consumers and corporate purchasers do not vote with their feet as a result of reading them? Among hospital CEOs, quality improvement directors and medical directors in the Wisconsin study, there were no differences among the control and experimental groups on whether public reporting would damage the market share of hospitals. Where there were big differences was on how public reporting would enhance or detract from a hospital's public image (Hibbard et al. 2003). A number of researchers suggest the anecdotal evidence is of hospitals being sensitive to the public-image effects of reports of poor performance (Marshall et al. 2000, 2004). This is consistent with evidence that commercial corporations are like non-commercial organizations such as universities and individual human beings in valuing reputations for their own sake, as opposed to valuing them only because of market returns from reputational assets (Fisse and Braithwaite 1983). Even though cardiac surgeons (and the hospitals they work for) may know that cardiologists do not refer to them on the basis of where they stand on the league table, they know that the cardiologists know where they stand, and they care about this for purely reputational reasons. While the medical players feel critical and angry about league tables, this is not dismissive defiance; it is what we will call in Chapter 9 resistant defiance. Resistant defiance is certainly resistant and defiant, but it is much easier to flip to cooperation with a need to improve than is the disengaged posture of dismissive defiance.

A second explanation sometimes mentioned in the literature for the impact of quality reports on providers that is not mediated by market pressures is that providers may fear that regulatory agencies or accreditation agencies may target them because of a poor report card, or tort litigation might target them (Marshall et al. 2004: 158). In turn, for this reason we saw in Chapter 5 that it is good British banking practice before lending to a nursing home to check their latest inspection report on the Internet. These possibilities suggest that the power of league tables to improve quality might be enhanced by thinking of them less as a tool for strengthening markets and more as a tool for bolstering regulation via reputational threats.

Compelling nursing home as opposed to hospital data on this policy question is scarce. The most apposite study by Castle (2003) gave improved comparative outcome data on quality of care to 120 nursing homes and compared their outcomes a year later with 1171 nursing homes that did not receive the comparative report card. The data simply went to the home without being publicized. There were significant positive effects, though not large ones. The report card homes had a 5.7 per cent reduction in risk-adjusted use of restraints and a 5 per cent decrease in psychotropic drug use. Four other outcomes were not significantly different.

As encouraging as the above studies are that quality report cards improve health care through feared reputation or regulation effects, worries remain about their side effects. A common objection to the New York cardiac surgery report cards was that it frightened surgeons away from high-risk patients. A New York survey of cardiologists' attitudes confirmed that it was widely believed that this was happening in New York (Hannan et al. 1997). Of course, cardiologists perceiving this to be a problem does not necessarily mean that it actually was. In fact, the evidence suggests that underlying the drop in mortality were some highly desirable ways in which cardiac surgeons were discouraged from operating. There was an exodus of low-volume and high-mortality surgeons after publication of the report cards, probably driven by hospitals restricting surgery privileges to higher-volume, lower-mortality surgeons (Marshall et al. 2000: 1872).

Another survey of cardiologists concerning a similar report card program in Pennsylvania, however, had more worrying results. Nearly two-thirds of cardiologists there reported they found it harder to find surgeons to operate on high-risk patients; two-thirds of cardiac surgeons in turn reported that they were less willing to operate on high-risk patients (Schneider and Epstein 1996).

The second major concern about league tables is the same one we have discussed with the MDS, that the more measurable becomes a bigger concern than the more important. To move up the league table, providers may neglect other quality concerns that are not captured by the league table. Because league tables have the problem of being highly selective in what they target, they are vulnerable to gaming effort into measured areas. This has been a major concern with league tables in education – that schools neglect other education values in a scramble to improve results on test scores. We end up with schools populated by children who are good at filling out tests, but uneducated.

A connected concern with education league tables is that middle- and upper-class schools will top the list and schools in poor neighbourhoods will be stigmatized when they fall at the bottom. This will drive brighter students and students from upwardly mobile families away from poor schools in their neighbourhood, worsening class and race inequality in the education system. While this is hardly a major concern with hospitals, it is with nursing homes. In the US, Mor et al. (2004) have shown that nursing home care has become two-tiered. There is a bottom tier of nursing homes that almost completely serve welfare residents, with no private pay residents, and predominantly African-American clients. Mor et al. (2004) worry that one of the bad effects of the quality indicators movement for nursing homes may be to further drive the system into racially segregated socio-economic tiers, chasing out the 9 per cent of white residents who are still in lower tier facilities.

If the main good effects of league tables are about reputational and regulatory effects of the publication, and if the main worries are skimming low-risk patients, neglect of unquantified issues and widening the care gap between rich and poor, then there is a case for discretionary regulatory use of quality indicators that is vigilant on these worries. Marshall et al. (2004: 161) argue that if we are serious about using quality report cards in an evidence-based way, we will take note of the evidence that what stakeholders attend to is not tables of numbers but stories that connect to numbers. They expect that television news or current affairs programs are the best option for this in that 'human interest' of patients suffering terrible injuries or inspiring recoveries are visual, and therefore perfect for the high-impact medium. Using the power of television, however, would obviously require selectivity. The demands for selectivity mean that regulators can target the story of the hospital or nursing home chains that are at the bottom of the quality league table in a way that is sensitive to the bad side-effects of league tables. The wise regulator might not target a chain that did poorly on the quantitative indicators in the report card because they were doing a great job of concentrating their resources on turning around a bigger quality problem that was not quantifiable. They certainly would not target a provider that had poor outcomes because they were specializing in the highest risk cases. Indeed, they might even target them for positive publicity for performing as well as they did on the league table against the odds of some of the daunting and inspiring cases they were taking on. And wise regulators might hesitate about stigmatizing a facility which had poor outcomes because it had very poor clients who had no family support and where management, good though they were, found it difficult to attract quality staff because of the stigma of the community in which the facility was located.

In sum, the pattern of the evidence suggests that a good policy might be open publication on the Internet of quality report cards without a large investment in publicizing them. No point in ritualistically flogging a dead (market) horse. Just publishing them would be sufficient to make them available to bankers, professional reputational networks, inspectors and internal quality assurance staff who might make some strategic use of them, and would honour good governance values of transparency. Then regulators might use evidence of shocking and outstanding report card performance with engaging stories of how peoples' lives were affected in the electronic media. This would make providers care acutely about the reputational risk of poor report card performance, while feeling assurance that if there were a good reason why their shocking performance would be an unfair target for publicity, they would be welcomed in making a submission to the regulator, and given a fair hearing in advance of any rush to publicity. Indeed a policy of sending a draft press release to the targeted poor quality provider in advance, sometimes responding by shredding it in response to a cogent rebuttal from them, and then moving on to another provider who would be the more deserving target, would have two good effects. It would communicate perceptions that the regulator is procedurally fair, when we know this improves compliance (Makkai and Braithwaite 1996; Tyler 1990). Second, it puts more providers on notice through a close call that these dimensions of performance matter, while they are certainly not the only things that matter.

MONETARY INCENTIVES FOR QUALITY

Another attempt to mimic the effect of markets has been initiatives by a number of large US states (perhaps as many as 15 [HCFA 1998: 322]), including Michigan, Massachusetts and Florida, to graduate Medicaid benefits so homes with higher quality received higher benefits. The most famous of these was the QUIP (Quality Incentives Program) in Illinois from 1985 to 1992. Harvard's Kennedy School of Government and the Ford Foundation gave QUIP their top innovations in government award in 1986. Yet QUIP and all other state programs like it were abandoned as failures in the 1990s. Why? One reason was a concern that scarce resources were diverted to the best nursing homes instead of those with the greatest problems. But the deeper concerns were actually about the administrative detail of how these programs worked. When rewards were put in place for the number of residents participating in activity programs, we observed sleeping residents in wheelchairs being pushed into the room where an activity such as craft or a game was going on so that they could be recorded on the head count as participating.

One standard that was incentivized by QUIP related to the existence of a homelike interior environment. One aspect of this is the capacity of residents to domesticate their little piece of institutional space by putting up pictures of their choosing on the wall. This kind of empowerment could take many forms – rearranging the bed and other furniture, carpets, bringing a beloved pet in to deinstitutionalize the space. But counting the pictures on the wall was the easiest quantitative way of operationalizing this standard. And, of course, quantitative measures that can be calibrated unambiguously are what inspectorates like when quantitative incentives which could be contested in a court of law hang on their ratings. Sure enough, nursing home staff told us that the large numbers of pictures of movie stars we would notice, often torn from the same magazine, had been slapped up around the nursing home on the instructions of management in anticipation of the arrival of the inspectors. Of course, they were not supposed to know when the inspectors would be arriving; but we found that game-players had a way of knowing these things. Our fieldwork even revealed cases of large numbers of pot-plants on short-term hire that were returned as soon as the inspection was completed. The bigger the incentive, the more complex the phenomenon regulated, the worse creative compliance gets.

One scientific study is sometimes discussed as demonstrating the efficacy of incentive regulation of nursing (HCFA, 1998: 326–37; Norton 1992). Thirty-six San Diego nursing homes were matched into 18 pairs, with one of each pair randomly assigned to an incentive payment scheme. The homes in the incentive scheme had lower mortality and lower rates of discharge to hospital than controls. A problem is whether the result is about incentive payments or just more payment. Homes in the control group got fewer dollars on average than homes in the experimental group. So the result may simply reflect the fact that homes in the incentive group had more staff resources to provide certain critical kinds of care. Beyond nursing homes, a considerable number of studies of financial incentives to physicians and health providers to achieve specific targets (such as for immunization of children or cancer screening compliance) suggest that the incentives mostly work at least partially (Petersen et al. 2006). However, consistent with our ritualism theme, this literature also shows that financial incentives for hitting health targets also result in avoidance of sicker patients (Shen 2003). In addition, financial incentives in three studies produced statistically significant improvement in documentation of a preventive service but not in actual use of that service (Fairbrother et al. 1999, 2001; Roski et al. 2003).

THE TROUBLE WITH REWARDS

As a general matter, rewards are less useful in regulation than they are in markets. Firms respond to market incentives because most markets are contestable. In the next section, we argue that in markets that are not oligopolies, it makes more sense to adopt a competitor mentality than a fixer mentality. Regulatory power in contrast is mostly not contestable. Firms are therefore more likely to adopt a fixer or game-playing posture. We will argue below that reactance to regulatory control through rewards is likely to be greater than reactance to market discipline. If a responsive regulatory pyramid is a good strategy for optimizing compliance, then punishment is more useful in regulation than reward. Reward at the middle of a regulatory pyramid brings about a moral hazard problem. Finally, we will say something about the limited conditions where quality incentives can be useful at the base of a regulatory pyramid.

Jeremy Bentham believed that while rewards were powerful in markets and while they had some uses in law, rewards were a less valuable tool for the legislator than punishments (Bentham 1825: 6, 51–2; Bentham 1977: 75–7, 79). On markets he was in agreement with Adam Smith, but he did not share Smith's enthusiasm for rewards in regulation (Bentham 1825: 52). 'Punishment is an instrument for the extirpation of noxious weeds: reward is a hot bed for raising fruit, which would not otherwise be produced' (Bentham 1825: 51). We will advance in turn a contestability argument, a reactance argument and a responsiveness argument for why rewards do not enjoy the superiority over punishment in regulation that they do enjoy in markets.

CONTESTABILITY

The rewards provided by markets generally work in motivating productive efficiency. But not always. Most firms respond to the challenge of a market for the product they sell by competing with a customer service mentality. An alternative path is to seek to fix the market, to rig bids with competitors, to form cartels that fix prices or allocate markets geographically. Most business opts for the competitive mentality rather than the fixer mentality because cartels are hard to hold together. Fixers also find ways to cheat on other members of the cartel to attract business to themselves, for example, by under-the-table rebates to customers. When monopoly prices are being charged, markets are always contestable by new entrants that are not members of the cartel. This is especially so in contemporary conditions of global markets where foreign competition can always enter the market to contest for the business of local cartels.

Regulation of commerce, however, is different from commerce itself in that it is not always the case that the competitor mentality dominates the fixer mentality. When a regulator puts in place a system of rewards for achieving an outcome like pollution reduction, firms that already have leading pollution control capabilities will compete aggressively for those rewards. The majority of firms that have poorer capabilities, however, tend to do what they can to put in the fix to prevent the compliance leaders from getting this competitive jump on them (Keohane et al. 1998: 351–3). Their pursuit of the fixer mentality takes many forms. They lobby through industry associations to subvert or delay the reforms industry-wide, they make special pleadings for exemptions for themselves, they fudge their compliance data, bribe inspectors, or complain to their political masters about regulatory unreasonableness. Most commonly of all, they indulge in what Doreen McBarnet and Christopher Whelan (1999) have called 'creative compliance'. Business regulatory outcomes tend to be complex, not black and white. Hence the dominant fixer mentality is to play for the grey.

One might say that in markets there are fixers who dupe consumers by fudging compliance with product quality or safety standards. The difference is that when duped consumers discover they have been duped they punish the supplier in the market. Inspectors generally do not do this when firms are clever enough to creatively comply with the standards they have written. Regulators figure that if they punish firms in these circumstances the agency will come under political attack for failing to write the rules of reward in a competent fashion and that courts will overturn their decisions to withhold the reward. This was the feeling among Illinois regulators in the late 1980s and early 1990s who understood very clearly that QUIP was being gamed. Instead, inspectors in a way admire the ingenuity of the firm; the inspector does not suffer personally for it, the intended beneficiaries of the regulation do. Beneficiaries such as nursing home residents are not empowered to use rewards that are issued by the state to assert their claims to quality and safety.

But the more fundamental fact of this situation is that while a consumer in a market who is duped simply goes to another supplier, an inspector who is duped cannot simply walk away from the transaction. The nursing home will get some level of Medicaid payment; it would be irresponsible to cut off payments that are made to care for the residents unless the situation is life-threatening. Fraud and creative compliance in market relationships are effectively contested by other suppliers. In the regulatory relationship they are not. This is reciprocally true. In general, the firm faces only one regulator with responsibility for a particular issue. The threat the regulator poses to the profits of the regulated firm is not a threat that is contested by other regulators. This is quite different from the situation with a cartel. The threat to cartel profits is posed by a number of potential entrants to the market.

It is harder to put in the fix with all of them than it is with one regulator. There is just one regulator to corrupt, capture or outwit.

Hence the competitor mentality dominates the fixer mentality in markets because there are too many market players to fix; the fixer dominates the competitor mentality with regulatory rewards because this contestability is absent: fix one regulator and you may fix the whole game.[2] The absence of contestability is therefore a fundamental structural reason why reward has less power in regulation than in markets.

REACTANCE

Experimental research on children and college students demonstrates the counterproductive effect salient rewards and punishments can have: long-term internalization of values like altruism and resistance to temptation are inhibited when people view their action as caused by a reward or punishment (Dix and Grusec 1983; Hoffman 1983; Lepper 1973; Lepper and Greene 1978). Over 100 studies examining the effect of extrinsic incentives on later intrinsic motivation indicate that inducements that are often perceived as controlling (for example, tangible rewards, surveillance, deadlines), depending on the manner in which they are administered, reduce feelings of self-determination and undermine subsequent motivation in a wide variety of achievement-related activities after the reward is removed (Deci et al. 1999).

These findings seem to be of fairly general import, being supported in domains including moral behaviour, altruism, personal interaction, aggressive behaviour, and resistance to temptation (Boggiano et al. 1987; Dienstbier et al. 1975; Dix and Grusec 1983; Lepper 1973). Just as strong external incentives retard internalization, using reasoning in preference to power assertion tends to promote it (Baumrind 1973; Cheyne and Walters 1969; Hoffman 1970; Parke 1969; Zahn-Waxler et al. 1979). This is an important part of the case for conversational regulation.

Brehm and Brehm (1981) constructed a theory of psychological reactance on the basis of the kinds of studies we have been discussing. Figure 8.1 shows that the net effect of threats of control is the sum of a control effect and a reactance effect. According to this theory, intentions to control are reacted to as attempts to limit our freedom, which lead us to reassert that freedom by acting contrary to the direction of control. Reactance applies to attempts to control through rewards just as it applies to threats to control through punishment, though reactance effects are not as great with rewards as they are with punishments (Brehm and Brehm 1981: 229). Figure 8.1 also shows that reactance is least when freedom is restricted to do something that is not very important to us, and greatest when the

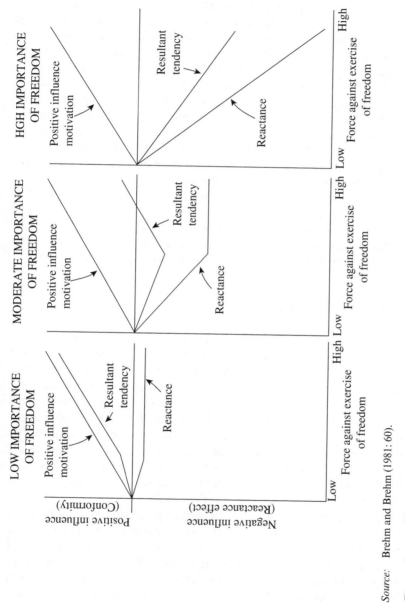

Source: Brehm and Brehm (1981: 60).

Figure 8.1   The interactive effects of force and importance of freedom

freedom subjected to control is something the regulated actor deeply cares about. Tom Tyler might suggest that naked attempts to control us give us some negative information about our identity – that we have a subordinated identity, that we are a slave to the will of another – and this is an identity we do not want (Tyler 1990; Tyler and Blader 2000; Tyler and Dawes 1993; Tyler and Huo 2001). We do not get this negative information if it is the rewards of the market that control us; we do if it is a regulator who seeks to control us through rewards. Hence we can expect the invisible hand of the market to generate less reactance than the visible hand of a controlling regulator. The rewards we get in a market come from the prices consumers are willing to pay to get something they want; the rewards a regulator gives for good performance in contrast are motivated by an 'intention to control' by the regulator. According to reactance theory, it is when we see an intention to control us that we defy or react to this control. The more important the freedom being regulated, the greater this reactance effect will be according to the evidence generated by this theory.

While the theory explains why reactance to regulatory rewards should be greater than reactance to rewards in markets, and therefore why rewards should be less effective than we might expect in making regulation work, reactance theory does not explain why regulatory incentives should be less useful than punishment. For that result we turn to responsive regulatory theory.

RESPONSIVENESS

A more fundamental policy debate about regulatory strategy than that between reward and punishment has been the contest between punishment and persuasion. Responsive regulation hypothesizes that it is best to have a presumption in favour of trying persuasion first, generally reserving punishment for when persuasion fails (Ayres and Braithwaite 1992; Gunningham and Grabosky 1998). Persuasion is cheaper and a more respectful way of treating the regulated actor. However, it is argued that persuasion will normally only be more effective than punishment in securing compliance when the persuasion is backed up by punishment. And punishment will seem fairer, and therefore be more effective, when persuasion has been tried first and has failed.

The most distinctive feature of responsive regulation is the regulatory pyramid. It is an attempt to solve the puzzle of when to punish and when to persuade. At the base of the pyramid is the most restorative, dialogue-based approach we can craft for securing compliance with a just law. As we move up the pyramid, more and more demanding and punitive interventions in people's lives are involved. The idea of the pyramid is that our presumption

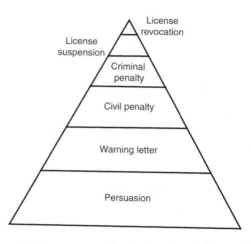

Note: The proportion of space at each layer represents the proportion of enforcement activity at that level.

Source: Ayres and Braithwaite (1992: 35).

Figure 8.2 An example of a regulatory pyramid

should always be to start at the base of the pyramid. Then escalate to somewhat punitive approaches only reluctantly and only when dialogue fails. Then escalate to even more punitive approaches only when the more modest forms of punishment fail. Figure 8.2 is an example of a responsive business regulatory pyramid from Ayres and Braithwaite (1992: 35). The regulator here escalates with the recalcitrant company from persuasion to a warning, to civil penalties, to criminal penalties and ultimately to corporate capital punishment – permanently revoking the company's licence to operate.

If it is right, as responsive regulation claims, that cooperative approaches such as education, persuasion and restorative justice are normally better, though not invariably so, as a first strategy, then regulators are best to be presumptively cooperative and only override this presumption when strong reasons to do so appear.[3] When the cooperative approach fails, the regulator escalates up the pyramid. According to the theory, this escalation involves an abandonment of the motivational assumption that the regulated actor is a responsible citizen who is capable of complying (see Figure 8.3). The next port of call assumes the regulatee to be a rational actor who must be deterred. But, of course, if the regulatee is a rational firm, it can be motivated by reward just as well as, or better than, by punishment. The problem with a responsive regulatory strategy that would have the regulator escalate from trust and cooperation to reward is moral hazard.[4] The

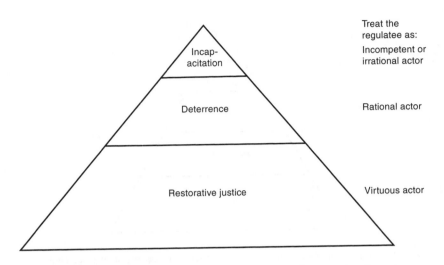

Figure 8.3   Towards an integration of restorative, deterrent and incapacitative justice

regulatee who really is a rational actor will exploit the opportunity that a regulator's first preference for trust provides by failing to invest in compliance. Then such a firm will reap the rewards for compliance provided at the next rung up the pyramid. Unpunished free-riding is followed by rewarded free-riding. Escalation to punishment is what is needed to provide incentives for the rational actor to invest in cooperation and risk management.

So why not make reward the first port of call at the base of the pyramid? One reason is that paying rewards is more expensive than asking for voluntary compliance. Second, rewards commonly cause reactance, as we saw in the last section. Third, as we saw in the section before that, rewards foster a culture of game-playing. Gaming is productive in the context of a market; in the context of regulation, games of 'cat and mouse' tend to be expensive, inefficient and result in a win for the corporate cat, defeating the purposes of the regulation (Bardach and Kagan 1982; Kagan and Axelrad 2000). From the theoretical perspective of responsive regulation, putting rewards at the base of the pyramid creates the wrong kind of regulatory culture, the wrong kind of regulatory community (Meidinger 1987). It would give businesses the message that they are not expected to be responsible corporate citizens. The policy framework would give the message that government only expects businesses to meet their obligations when it pays. The moral content of the law is eroded as nobler motives are eclipsed by baser ones (Goodin 1980: 139–40).

Finally, attempts to replace punishment with reward in a regulatory pyramid tend to be illusory. You cannot reward providers for excellence in aged care without requiring them to report that excellence in some way. This creates incentives to cheat in those reports in order to collect the reward. Those who cheat must then be punished. So the policy of replacing punishment with reward in one quick step takes us back to a policy of punishment. The effect of the reward strategy is to replace quality of care inspectors with fraud auditors. This is a bad outcome because financial auditors are technically incompetent to do the diagnostic troubleshooting of quality problems, which is among the most effective things inspectors do (see Chapters 4 and 10; also Bardach and Kagan 1982; Gunningham and Grabosky 1998; Hawkins 1984; Hutter 1999).

All of that said, there are some conditions where rewards at the base of an enforcement pyramid work well and deliver the economic efficiency advantages of a market for regulatory outcomes contrived by the regulator. One of those conditions is that non-compliance is so transparent that financial auditors are not needed (Coglianese and Lazar 2003). For example, the policy many governments introduced in the late 1970s and 1980s of reducing taxes on unleaded fuel was part of a package that successfully reduced lead in the environment (Gunningham and Grabosky 1998: 435). While there was some cheating by petroleum suppliers, it was limited by the fact that putting the wrong kind of fuel in certain kinds of engines would cause problems for consumers. In other words, there was sufficient transparency for the regime to be self-enforcing in the market. A second condition this case meets is of a large imbalance of power between regulator and regulatee in favour of the regulator. Here the regulatee is primarily the vehicle user: they pay the tax, not the vehicle manufacturer. If it were the vehicle manufacturer that was provided with an opportunity to reduce tax on a large scale, we might have seen regulatory 'cat and mouse' in the engineering of vehicles in pursuit of that tax benefit. But most of us did not have the economic or technological capability to re-engineer our car in pursuit of tax advantages. We were simply too weak (economically and technically) in comparison with the state's power, so we just went along with the regime and took the rewards in the way intended by the policy makers. In contrast we know when the tax system is used to reward powerful corporations, say to invest in research and development (R&D), they often manage to use tax incentives to avoid tax altogether without securing the policy intent of the tax break (claiming cleaning as R&D on detergents!) (Braithwaite 2005b).

Neither of these conditions for the efficacy of rewards at the base of the pyramid applies to aged care regulation. It is literally not transparent how many residents have pressure sores. To see them, you need to remove clothing. Technically, it is not transparent how many residents are being over-medicated or wrongly medicated. Also, as we saw in Chapters 2 and 6, nursing homes are politically powerful actors, especially in the context of Australia and of most US state governments, where they have proved to be among the top contributors to political campaigns.

Where these conditions are not met, there is a risk that reward at the base of the pyramid not only can fail, it can make the problem worse. For example, if you pay farmers bounties to plant trees in pursuit of a biodiversity objective (Grabosky 1996: 7–8), you had better be sure your monitoring of the number of trees on large properties is credible (something more possible with satellite technology). If not, you create incentives to cut down and sell trees in order to gain the bounty from subsequently replanting the area. In a variety of more complex ways we observed this phenomenon with the now defunct state Medicaid incentive schemes of the 1980s and 1990s. Under one of the QUIP criteria for payment, it was necessary to achieve a certain number of care-planning goals every three months. This led to some of the most shocking gaming we have observed in regulatory fieldwork, particularly staff being pulled into line when they were setting care-planning goals that were too ambitious and therefore at risk of not being achieved within the three months. This made Illinois care planning ridiculously ritualistic. Here are some examples of goals that received their QUIP tick as accomplished:

> Goal: Will not use profanity at least one time a week.
> Approach: Will explain it's not nice to use profanity.

Another QUIP fiddle was to set a goal the resident had already accomplished:

> *Nurse:* Will go to bible study one day a week.
> *Resident:* I usually go anyway.

As with the MDS today, we saw a lot of evidence of desired QUIP financial outcomes being achieved by false documentation as opposed to good quality care. We were also told of rumours of bribes being paid to secure the highest QUIP rating as a six-star facility. But the worst ritualism of all was when new goals were proposed for residents and the boss would say 'No we have already achieved our goals for the current three-month period, we will move onto delivering that for the resident in a month or two.'

QUALITY AS ITS OWN REWARD

Of course there are many specific contexts where regulation is required to force providers to invest in quality in ways their economic interests tell them not to. Yet in general it may be that improving quality reduces costs rather than increases them. If this is true, it is irrational public policy to pay extra rewards in a way that distorts the distribution of welfare away from homes with the deepest resource needs and the worst quality problems. This is an argument for leaving the actual market be; forget playing with the phoney market ritualism of competition for welfare system incentives, as in QUIP.

Weech-Maldonado et al. (2003) have presented the most compelling empirical evidence on this question. Their data was outcomes for 705 homes from five US states in HCFA's 1996 'Multi-state case-mix and quality demonstration.' One of the biggest effects in their structural equation model was from quality of care to lower costs, and thence to higher profits. Homes that were able to achieve higher quality care seemed to be able to reduce costs. Weech-Maldonado et al. (2003) argue that other studies show that higher nursing home quality is not associated with higher costs (Linn et al. 1977; Mukamel and Spector 2000; Nyman 1988). In health care more broadly, higher quality results in fewer defects and lower amounts of waste (Binns 1991), increased productivity from quicker patient recovery and more efficient processes (Harkey and Vraciu 1992), and more appropriate absolute and experience-based economies of scale (Phillips et al. 1983). On more specific issues, in this book we have already discovered, for example, that contrary to industry prejudices, the evidence is that upfront investment in dealing with the problems that caused physical restraint produced long-run reductions in demands on staff time after restraint reduction (Chapter 3).

The most fascinating aspect of the Weech-Muldonado et al. (2003) analysis is that quality increased profits by lowering costs; it did not increase profits by increasing consumer demand. In their model there was no significant effect from higher quality to higher revenues, nor from higher quality to attracting more residents willing to pay a higher price (private-pay market share). Essentially, high quality in health and aged care increases economic efficiency, but not through market mechanisms. Again we return to the conclusion that markets in aged care simply do not work well enough to deliver these effects. On the other hand, these results imply that regulation that delivers improved quality can reduce costs. Regulation in the 1990s that reduced physical restraint is a good illustration of this economic efficiency dividend.

The second big implication of these results is that for reasons similar to the thinking of Michael Porter (1990, 1995a, 1995b, 1995c) on competitive advantage, it can make commercial sense for aged care corporations to train their staff to be quality-conscious and conscious of professional standards rather than bottom-line conscious. On this view the mentality that allows the contemplation of unprofessional practice to cut corners on costs is a mentality that in the long run delivers lower profits. Here is one inter-view with a regional director of a medium-sized chain which at the time of the interview was the most profitable nursing home corporation in the US:

> *Executive:* I've worked for three long-term care companies. This one is different because quality is number 1; quality comes before profit. Sure we're concerned about profit too.
> *JB:* At the end of the day you have to make some profit.
> *Executive:* Yeah but we believe if we aim for quality the profit will take care of itself. We'll get a reputation in the community, among physicians, surveyors and quality staff we attract as a place that gets quality.
> *JB:* But in particular choices you must have to choose between a decision that will improve quality for one patient that no one will ever know about and cutting great cost.
> *Executive:* Yes, sure we have to think about both the quality and the profit in par-ticular situations. But when we do, compared with other companies I've worked for, we are willing to give less weight to profit. If we think it's right, we'll do it even if it's bad for profit.

The philosophers would say that this corporation lexically orders quality before profit; the presumption that quality considerations trump profit con-siderations is difficult to override in the culture of the corporation. Paradoxically, by having a mentality that is less profit-oriented, the corpo-ration might become more profitable. This might also be one reason for the many cross-national findings that not-for-profit aged care providers achieve higher quality of care (Aaronson et al. 1994; Harrington 2001; Jenkins and Braithwaite 1993; O'Neill et al. 2003; Weech-Maldonado et al. 2003: 56), that residents in for-profit institutions are more afraid of staff retaliation if they complain (Monk et al. 1984), and that a corporate culture with a stronger emphasis on profit-seeking is associated with even lower standards (Jenkins and Braithwaite 1993). Makkai and Braithwaite (1993c) found compliance was higher when the director of nursing had professional autonomy vis-à-vis control of purse strings and control of staff by the pro-prietor. We found US companies that did a variety of interesting things to lexically order a professional orientation ahead of a profit orientation. Some kept secret from staff who were Medicaid (welfare) residents and who were private residents, the latter paying a premium that increased profits. We encountered Australian homes with elderly illegal immigrants in them, who were not entitled to welfare benefits, being cared for free. The opposite mentality of lexically ordering money before care is manifest by an Australian director of nursing: 'It all comes down to money here. It will only happen if it's free.' Another director of nursing who worked for a pro-prietor like that, herself having the reverse lexical ordering, often paid for services for residents out of her own pocket.

SALVAGING REWARD

Rewards in markets that do work are effective in shaping behaviour. This implies that indirect regulatory strategies which have the effect of enhancing market rewards for desired behaviour can be effective. Hence green labelling, mandated disclosure of the fuel efficiency of motor vehicles and other mandatory disclosure rules can achieve regulatory objectives by enabling consumers to supply rewards in the market for desired behaviour. Of course, the outcomes specified on green labels still have to be easily measured, which they can be with fuel efficiency but not with most health and environmental impacts. And unfortunately, as we found earlier in this chapter, labelling nursing homes as high or low quality on a league table is not easily done.

A form of reward that seems to have unequivocally positive effects on compliance is informal praise – inspectors giving a word of encouragement when they see an improvement. Makkai and Braithwaite (1993a) found that when nursing homes were monitored by inspection teams that used a lot of praise, subsequent compliance with quality-of-care standards improved, after controlling for other factors. We therefore went on to commend other slightly more formal forms of praise such as letters from local members of Congress congratulating homes that achieved excellence in quality of care (which we often observed to be framed in nursing home lobbies) and the state of New York Department of Health's practice of putting out a press release on a regular basis announcing the names of nursing homes found to be totally free of deficiencies.

Praise is a gift. It is not required. Like a smile, it is supererogatory. While a smile of approval can motivate us enormously, because it has the character of a gift more than that of a reward, we do not normally interpret it as an attempt to manipulate us. So there is mostly not a reactance problem, not a problem of extrinsic incentive driving out intrinsic satisfaction in doing the right thing. Informal praise is compatible with cooperative problem-solving at the base of a regulatory pyramid. The more voluntary compliance is elicited at the base of the pyramid the more fulsome the praise dispensed. When there has been non-compliance that moved regulation up the pyramid, the return to compliance and movement back down the pyramid can be associated with praise for putting things right. Hence, while punishment is associated with movement up the pyramid, praise is associated with movement down. In practice there does not seem to be much of a problem of regulatees being non-compliant so they can get the benefit of informal praise in a sequence following formal punishment. This is because the power of praise does not reside so much in it being a reward that can be balanced against the cost of punishment. Its power resides in the affirmation of identities – law-abiding identities in the case of regulation – communicated by praise.

Now let us try to pull together our conclusions on regulatory rewards for quality. Punishment is not the most important lever of compliance in a responsive regulatory framework. However, we have argued here it is in most contexts a more useful regulatory tool than reward. The form of direct regulatory reward that avoids persistent dangers of counterproductivity in nursing home regulation is informal praise. And it works because it is not seen as a conscious reward by regulated actors, at least not when it is communicated with finesse. Extrinsic rewards undermine intrinsic motivation, foster gaming and defiance in response to attempts at control. Punishment as an escalation up a regulatory pyramid combats free-riding, reward exacerbates it. Reward not only increases the danger of risks being uncontrolled, there is reason to increase risk if subsequent reward is calibrated in proportion to the degree to which risks are brought under control. Reward therefore must only be used at the base of a regulatory pyramid and in association with movements down the pyramid.

In Chapter 10 we will argue that so long as we have a regulatory pyramid that enables sanctions to effectively control risks, we can also erect a strengths-based pyramid that uses reward to build strengths. Even in that kind of pyramid, informal praise of the person oriented to affirming their identity as a responsible citizen may be more useful than monetary rewards. Praise projects encounters into the rhetoric of obligation, monetary rewards into calculative game-playing that strips norms of their moral content.

SHIFTING THE OBJECT OF COMPETITION

Porter and Teisberg (2004) have written a thoughtful paper pondering why it is that when the United States has the most competitive markets in health services in the world, when it spends so much more on health than other developed economies, it has among the worst health outcomes in the developed world. Their answer is that vibrant as this American health sector competition is, it is not improving outcomes because it occurs at the wrong level, over the wrong things. The dominant form of competition is in cost-shifting. Costs are shifted from payer to patient, health plan to hospital, hospital to nursing home or physician, insured to uninsured, and so on. Payment of a set amount per admission for a given ailment creates an incentive for cheaper treatments, but not more effective, innovative ones.

In the US nursing home industry, one pathological form of competition of the type that concerns Porter and Teisberg is competition in optimizing

MDS up-coding and down-coding to maximize reimbursement and mini-mize regulatory burdens. Firms with the cleverest nurses at gaming the MDS will be most skilful at skimming the lowest-risk residents within any partic-ular case-mix category. Another is competition to attract younger Medicare patients who are unprofitable for hospitals when they are shifted out of them, but highly profitable under the lower cost structure of nursing homes. These younger acute care patients might distract nursing homes from their core business of long-term social care for aged residents and, as Vladeck (2003) fears, thereby take nursing homes back to medical model dominance.

The right level of competition according to Porter and Teisberg is com-petition to heal individual patients, as opposed to competitive excellence in the cost-shifting game. That is the level at which value is created in the health industry. It is also created by providers competing at being the best at addressing a particular set of problems. So we want nursing homes that compete at being best at long-term care for the elderly, eschewing excellence at cost-shuffling with hospitals on their acute care cases. Porter and Teisberg use the example of the Texas Heart Institute becoming a special-ist institution for heart surgery – priding itself on having surgical costs a third to a half lower than other medical centres as it takes the most difficult cases. 'Doing the right thing first time' improves outcomes as it cuts costs. It follows that Porter and Teisberg should applaud the effect of the New York heart surgery report cards in driving low-volume, high-mortality sur-geons out of the market.

While it does follow from the Porter and Teisberg critique that quality report cards are one of the ways to focus competition at the level of curing patient by patient, disease by disease, the foregoing data suggest it is more a market in esteem for professionals (Brennan and Pettit 2004) than a financial market. Deregulation of bed-capacity licensing is another impli-cation of the Porter and Teisberg diagnosis. This is because under deregu-lation of bed capacity, homes that fail to improve things patient by patient may lose patients.

Because good nursing home management simultaneously reduces costs and increases quality, competition in the market for management would seem critical. This form of competition actually works quite well in nursing homes. The industry, particularly in Australia (driven by the push for con-tinuous improvement), has seen a lot of growth in the nursing home con-sulting market, especially for quality assurance. Administrators and directors of nursing must compete for control of certain functions with these outsourced managers. In the US market, large premiums are paid to administrators for good performance on quality, sometimes bigger than 10 per cent salary bonuses. Lower-level managers such as dietary directors get lesser bonuses, but they can still be much more than $1000 in one year. Just one inspection with serious deficiencies can cost an administrator his or her job; several of them are almost sure to. The latter is mostly also true in England and Australia, but US proprietors are considerably more ruthless in punishing poor regulatory outcomes. The best most directors of nursing and administrators can expect for an outstanding result for an inspection in England and Australia is, one of them said, 'a box of flowers'.

Still proprietors pay for excellence in quality leadership in all three countries. These pay rates are contestable by the healthy incomes quality leaders can make as outsourced quality consultants. In Chapter 2 we argued that the health sector is like the university sector in this regard. Price competition on fees in countries where most universities are public (such as Australia and the UK) is limited and students do not move from one university to another very much. But there is massive reputational competition among universities, lots of league tables that have precious little market implication but that universities are nevertheless status-conscious about. Competition among universities for the most outstanding scholars is intense and is very much about the price they are offered for their labour.

While markets for management labour seem to work well in the nursing home industry, regulation could help them work better. It is easy for other universities to assess how good a scholar is at another institution 1000 miles away. They just read their work, the reviews they get, how cited they are, and so on. In contrast, it is difficult for a prospective employer to know how good a job the administrator of a nursing home is doing 1000 miles away for the same reasons that the quality of care at a nursing home is opaque to consumers. Inspectors are uniquely well qualified to judge how good a job an administrator is doing at managing quality. This is why we observed astute proprietors to consult inspectors discreetly on how their administrator is performing. These proprietors know the inspectors are more independent than their own staff under that administrator; and inspectors have the advantage of seeing large numbers of outstanding and ordinary administrators *in situ* and under pressure.

Hence it would make sense and have minimal cost to ask all inspectors who visit a nursing home to code a confidential rating of how well the CEO of the home is doing at improving quality of care. It would be best that these ratings not be disclosed to the CEO, lest it jeopardize working relationships. We hypothesize that in the course of three years, administrators in the US would collect on average about 20 such inspector ratings, mostly by different inspectors. Such a large average number of rating points would be desirable because, while we know that peer ratings of health-care professionals can be highly reliable, with a small number of raters they are vulnerable to outliers. Peer ratings of physicians are reliable, but only with at least 11 raters (Ramsey et al. 1993). These three-year average ratings could be posted on the Internet by the regulator. This would increase the efficiency of the market for nursing home management enormously, given the evidence we have on the importance of the CEO to driving quality outcomes. Such a quality manager report card could also be usefully consulted by consumers. The same could be done for other key roles such as the dietary director, the director of nursing, the social work director, and so on. To maintain an equitable balance of power, nursing home managers can also be asked to rate the inspector's performance on a number of dimensions, as already happens in Australia and England.

CONCLUSION

We have concluded that, as in universities, in nursing homes the most critical and vibrant markets are labour markets for the most senior people. These are the markets that drive quality. They could be helped to drive it even more by linking peer review of managers to nursing home inspection. We have concluded that bed-capacity deregulation might to a limited degree drive out some of the very worst providers by leaving them with half their beds empty and allow some of the very best to expand.

Markets are likely to be only slightly strengthened by consumers having access to reliable quality-of-care league tables. Yet health providers are extremely sensitive to the reputational effects of poor league table results and market outstanding results to enhance their reputation. Regulators can and should use the electronic media to communicate poor quality reports of providers who have been irredeemably and consistently poor performers. Banks can also motivate regulatory responsiveness by using published inspection reports to withhold loans to homes that are a regulatory risk. Public inspection reports also make it more difficult for homes to fudge or fail to implement a plan of correction. This is because public reports put residents, relatives and advocates in a position to know that there is a plan of correction in place that should be implemented.

We have therefore identified multiple dimensions of market power to increase quality. Most of them are weak. Yet we will see in Chapter 10 that they can count among the weak strands in a web of regulatory controls that work. Perhaps it seems strange to talk of multiple strands of market influence and stranger still to talk about weaving them into a web of regulatory controls. But we have seen that some of these market strands enable regulation (for example, league tables enable regulators to use adverse publicity to regulate), and some strands of regulation enable markets (for example, inspector peer review of administrators enabling a more vibrant market in management).

At the same time, we have seen that if we tie some ritualistic modes of mimicking a market into webs of regulation, it can cause them to unravel. This was our conclusion about quality incentives programs such as QUIP, and indeed about all 15 of the quality incentive programs of the 1980s and 1990s in the US. While we conclude that rewards can create profound moral hazard in a regulatory pyramid, and therefore are much less useful than punishments in this context, in Chapter 10 we argue that rewards have the central place in a new pyramid that we call a strengths-based pyramid.

Complex and demanding coding of quality indicators such as the MDS can also cause both regulation and markets to unravel into ritualism. For units of small N, the standard errors of such quality indicators are unacceptable. There is no escaping a need for nursing homes with more at-risk residents to get more money. Better for street-level bureaucrats to use discretion, somewhat in the style of Australian Aged Care Assessment Teams, to make more aggregated assessments of how sick is the resident profile for a given home over a given period. The main accomplishment of the MDS has been to shift resources in a major way so the most talented nurses moved from providing care to gaming quality indicators. This shifts the system from one of competition in caring to competition in gaming. Such a shift is an instance of what Porter and Teisberg (2004) identify as the pathology of health competition: failing to compete at healing patient by patient, disease by disease. Instead it competes code by code, document by document.

NOTES

1. Mor et al. (1997) found only a total of 3 per cent of nursing home residents transferring over a six-month period.
2. We can attenuate this to a degree by making the regulatory game a tripartite one in which the power to pay rewards is contested by the monitoring of non-governmental organizations (Ayres and Braithwaite 1992: ch. 3). But here the NGO is only a proxy regulator of sorts; there is still just one state agency that can pay the rewards. Non-governmental organizations cannot pay them.
3. Responsive regulation, moreover, argues that this approach is best even with hardened law-breakers. The most irresponsible of us has a socially responsible self. Responsive regulation is a strategy for persuading the worst of us to put our best self forward.
4. Wikipedia defines moral hazard as 'increased risk of problematical (immoral) behavior, and thus a negative outcome (hazard), because the person who caused the problem doesn't suffer the full (or any) consequences, or may actually benefit'. Fire insurance increasing the incentive to commit arson is the classic moral hazard. With reward in the middle of an enforcement pyramid, the moral hazard is that the person will cheat on compliance at the base of the pyramid and subsequently receive a benefit for cheating when the reward for moving to compliance is paid higher up the pyramid.

9. Transcending ritualism

> We would not have great symphony orchestras if conductors focused only on keeping musicians from playing out of tune.
>
> (Carol Heimer 1997)

Eugene Bardach and Robert Kagan became the first to theorize commitment and regulation when they said:

> The risk of having the state push accountability requirements into the farthest reaches and deeper recesses of social life is that, in the long run, everyone will be accountable for everything, but no one will take responsibility for anything. Thus the social responsibility of regulators, in the end, must be not simply to impose controls, but to activate and draw upon the conscience and the talents of those they seek to regulate.
>
> (Bardach and Kagan 1982: 321)

Carol Heimer (1997) has construed care planning meetings, physician rounds and protocol development committees as examples of activities in the health sector that are more oriented to encouraging actors to take active responsibility rather than just to be held accountable. These are indeed the kind of deliberative fora that throughout this book have been found to be sites where commitment to quality of care, and to taking active responsibility for doing specific things to realize it, is constructed.

The last two chapters can be read as showing how quality improvement has been poorly served by following the rituals of three disciplines – economics (Chapter 8), law and medicine (Chapter 7). Disciplines play a useful role in universities in disciplining young minds to apply themselves to learning various methodological competencies. Delivering these methods to the world of solving policy problems is also useful so long as it does not induce method myopia in the policy thinker. Nursing home residents, we have argued, have suffered deeply at the hands of policy makers who have been more oriented to fidelity to the rituals of their disciplinary background than fidelity to the problem, in this case the care needs of the aged. The protocol ritualism of the gerontological establishment is a good example in Chapter 7. Another is the market ritualism of the health economists in Chapter 8, who naturally think that if the problem is not being solved, this must be because the market settings are not right.

Our first prescription for transcending ritualism is to apply the evidence-based methods of each discipline in turn to the presuppositions of the ritualistic solution of each other discipline. Then indeed we might identify, as we did in the last chapter, some ways that sharpened competition might improve quality of care. We might identify, as we have in previous chapters, that ritualism can be transcended by principle-based law, discerning use of quality protocols, resident-centred methods displacing some document-centred methods, thoughtful use of new technologies, an orientation to improving systems more than blaming people, dialogue that builds commitment to improve quality of care by linking conversational inspection to conversational advocacy (for example, by ombudsmen) to conversation in residents' councils, staff meetings and care planning meetings.

Commitment to quality, really caring about quality improvement, as a result of all of these different kinds of dialogue, is the most recurrent ingredient of improvement that flows from our text and from the mouths of our informants. Belief in the standards predicts compliance with them (Makkai and Braithwaite 1991). Commitment means more than just belief. Commitment transcends obstacles, even sees obstacles as an opportunity to develop our strengths. But commitment is just one of five motivational postures of actors toward authority in research Val Braithwaite initially led on our nursing home data (Braithwaite et al. 1994) and has since developed further in the domain of tax compliance (Braithwaite 2003, forthcoming). It was work that built on and started by testing Kagan and Scholz's (1984) classic typology: amoral calculators who are best responded to by deterrence, political citizens with principled disagreements with regulation who require responses that enable negotiation, education and persuasion, and organizational incompetents who require consultancy to help them manage compliance. Elegant as this typology is, the thinking of Australian nursing home regulators did not conform to it.

MOTIVATIONAL POSTURES AND TRANSCENDING RITUALISM: DEFINITIONS

Braithwaite (forthcoming) defines motivational postures as sets of beliefs and attitudes that sum up how actors feel about and wish to position themselves in relation to another actor. Actors send signals to a regulator about how it is regarded and how much social distance is being placed between them and the regulator. Beliefs and attitudes comprising each posture are based on an appraisal of what the regulator stands for, what it is demanding, and how it engages with the needs and aspirations of those it regulates.

From her factor analytic studies of beliefs and attitudes of directors of nursing and ordinary and sophisticated taxpayers toward nursing home and tax authorities, she has found five[1] motivational postures:

1. *Commitment* means willingly embracing the mission of the regulator.
2. *Capitulation* means surrender to the will of an authority, to the letter of a rule without fully embracing its spirit.
3. *Resistance* means strident opposition to the power the regulator has and how it uses it.
4. *Disengagement* means psychological dissociation that renders an actor immune to attempts by a regulator to steer their actions.
5. *Game-playing* is a more imaginative and bold practice for escaping regulatory constraint by redefining rules, moving goalposts or repositioning one's self. It implies keen engagement with regulatory codes, analysing regulatory systems with disarming acuity and clarity of purpose. Regulators are not thought of as resented or resenting; they are playing the game too, just on a different team.

We could apply the postures to the nursing home regulator who wants the nursing home to jump in a certain direction over a bar at a certain height:

1. *Commitment:* 'We jump as high as we can in that direction.'
2. *Capitulation:* 'We jump to just clear the bar.'
3. *Resistance:* 'That's ridiculous. You have no right to ask it. This is where you should set the bar to benefit residents.'
4. *Disengagement:* 'What will they come up with next? Pass me a drink.'
5. *Game-playing:* 'You might think your rule says the bar is at 2 metres; my legal advice is 1.5, and I am not obliged to jump at all before 2008. In 2008 I may change my licence from being a nursing home to assisted living, so this rule will not apply.'

DISENGAGERS

The role in nursing homes where it is hardest to be a disengager is as administrator of an American home. Disengaging, as by not getting your plan of correction prepared and submitted in time, is almost certain to cost you your job. In the mom-and-pop English and Australian nursing home industry of the 1980s, we encountered many matrons who were disengagers, some of them alcoholics or suffering depression. They were disengaged from industry-wide conversations about quality as well:

In New South Wales the backward nursing homes are isolated. They are not in the industry associations. They don't come along to professional meetings because they are embarrassed. They don't want to reveal to their peers that they're not keeping up. They're not doing the things that the others in the group are doing.

(1989 director of nursing interview)

Yet even in those less disciplined places and times, such disengaged matrons tended eventually to be pushed out by a combination of regulatory pressure, angst from their proprietor and staff sick of covering for them. Because the Valerie Braithwaite et al. (1994) data show disengaged directors of nursing are so dangerous, it is a priority for regulators either to flip them to commitment or to evict them from the industry. In the conditions of the fairly intense corner of regulatory capitalism that is aged care, there are survival niches for the three other motivational postures.

RESISTERS COMPARED TO DISENGAGERS

Resisters are political citizens in Kagan and Scholz's (1984) terms. They are often politically active in industry associations. They lodge complaints about inspectors to their superiors; they argue with inspectors to their face, for example at exit conferences. The Braithwaite et al. (1994) data show resisters often lose the argument and succumb to become a compliant citizen of the regulatory order over time. One reason they do this is that they also often win arguments with inspectors. When resisters conclude that inspectors listen to their objections and sometimes concede they were wrong, resisters become more willing over time to calm down and yield to the perspective of the inspectors on other issues. Dialogue, our fieldwork together with our quantitative data suggest, works in flipping resistance to commitment. Quantitatively, resistant Australian nursing home CEOs are less likely to flip to commitment and compliance when they perceive regulators as coercive rather than cooperative (Braithwaite forthcoming). Similarly, when resistant people are treated by regulators in a way they perceive as procedurally fair, their future compliance improves compared to those who perceived themselves as treated unfairly (Braithwaite forthcoming).

This procedural justice effect was not found among disengagers (the dismissively defiant as they are labelled in Braithwaite's (forthcoming) most recent work). Similarly, for resisters, Braithwaite (forthcoming) found that feeling trusted by the regulator improved subsequent compliance; but trust did not work for the dismissive defiant.[2] Braithwaite (forthcoming) therefore sees 'institutional integrity' that involves fairness, trust and lived commitment to the principles in its mission (as opposed to regulatory ritualism) as something that works in turning around resistance. Institutional integrity does not accomplish this so effectively, if at all, with dismissiveness. That is why with disengagers, and sometimes game players, there is little option but to incapacitate them. Winning them over means winning their commitment to the purpose of the institution, which is not always going to be possible.

On the positive side, while Braithwaite's (forthcoming) data suggest that dismissive defiers are not rational calculators about deterrent threats, they do respond to a regulator's 'aura of power'. Mind you the dismissively defiant are less likely than other actors to believe that regulators have an aura of power. An aura of power requires seriousness of intent as well as credible and effective means for delivering this intent. Yet when the dismissively defiant recognize there is an aura of power, regulators have the capacity to bring them to heel by signalling their willingness to escalate right to the top of the pyramid and shut them down (say as a business or a licensed professional). This is consistent with the shape of the reactance curve in Figure 8.1 (Chapter 8). For defiant actors for whom the reactance curve is steeper than the deterrence curve (so that increasing threat just increases defiance in a way that reduces compliance), there is a point where extremely large threats ultimately cause actors to give up on defiance.

All this is an important part of the evidence base for believing that a regulatory pyramid needs a high peak that includes very tough options such as imprisonment or licence revocation. On Braithwaite's (forthcoming) account, being a tough incapacitator in these circumstances where incapacitation is required to defend an important regulatory mission such as protecting the aged, then signalling and using an 'aura of power' is part of what regulatory integrity means.

It is because dialogue more often fails with disengagers that it is frequently necessary to cull rather than converse. To make life even more difficult, disengagers are the group with whom deterrence is least effective, again commending escalation to incapacitation for disengagers. Resistance and disengagement are both the least compliant postures, and in these different ways the least stable: resisters change, disengagers are culled. Resisters change very quickly if they are managers of US chains. Large corporate providers do not like 'loose cannons' who argue with regulators. They tape exit conferences so they can counsel managers against resistance in almost every situation where they hear it on the tape. This is not to say that top management wants commitment, though in the best corporations they do. It is to say that they prefer ritualism – that can be manifest in either capitulation or game-playing – to resistance or disengagement.

THE RITUALISTIC POSTURES – GAME-PLAYING AND CAPITULATION

Game-playing is another posture associated with poor compliance that can be quite persistent. Gaming is not the central challenge for nursing home regulators in the way it is for tax or corporations' law regulators. Disengagers and capitulators are where most of the energy of aged care regulators is directed. Yet MDS up-coding and down-coding is classic game-playing. Game-playing that was too flagrant in this area would quickly become fraud quite visible to the energetic inspector. Minimum Data Set gaming has to be clever and below the surface. Then it can survive and flourish. In a sense we could think of the MDS nurse in the US system having the role of being the specialist in game-playing. Of course we have seen that there is a lot of outright cheating as well, but the MDS nurse normally is above this. Fabrication of records to indicate that care has been given when it has not is more likely to be the work of disengaged aides, licensed practical nurses or charge nurses.

In nursing homes there can be a fine line between game-playing and capitulation. Capitulation rather than game-playing is the dominant motivational posture of managers, particularly in the US. There it is a very dominant attitude of 'the regulator says jump and I say how high?' – so long as other homes are asked to jump the same bar and so long as the reimbursement system covers that cost. If not, capitulation will be mixed with resistance to the unfair circumstances of being asked to jump that high. The trouble with capitulation is once the manager has cleared the bar, he or she will not necessarily keep jumping. The manager will jump again when next the inspector comes around and tells the manager he or she is not jumping high enough. This is the idea of roller-coaster or yo-yo compliance. That is how the capitulator is different from the committed manager who keeps jumping because he or she believes in it. Committed managers keep jumping higher to lead the industry up through new ceilings and they keep their staff jumping for as long as they can to keep them all above the mandated floor. Commitment then is the antithesis of ritualism; capitulation is the heartland of ritualism in nursing home regulation and game-playing its cutting edge.

DRAWING OUT THE BEST IN US

The same managers have their moments when they are committed, when they care about soaring way above the bar, moments when they are struggling and delighted to barely clear it, moments when they resist because, for example, the bar is not set as high for other providers, moments when they game the system, and moments when they just drop their bundle and disengage. They have multiple selves. The responsive regulatory ideal is to draw their best self to the fore, their committed self. Even when sophisticated inspectors know that a particular act of compliance manifests capitulation or game-playing, they will impute commitment to management when they discuss it with them, because commitment is the posture they want to reinforce as normal and expected. Collectively the organization also has multiple postures, as in the MDS nurse specializing in game-playing. Again the responsive regulatory strategy is to find the committed members of the organization and strengthen their hand in the power structure of quality assurance policy. We encourage management to put their best self forward and their best people. This is how the strengths-based pyramid of the next chapter connects to the theory of motivational postures.

An important finding about motivational postures is that during an enforcement crisis (concerning tax schemes), all of the motivational postures become stronger (Braithwaite et al. 2007). This makes intuitive sense. Consider, for example, the nurse subject to an abuse investigation by the police. During the investigation, the issue of her (let us assume 'her' in this instance) commitment to non-violent care becomes more salient. She defends herself by telling everyone, telling herself, that no professional is more gentle in her care than she. At the same time she becomes resistant about aspects of the regulatory state that are deployed against her for the first time in her life, such as an intrusive, gruelling and demeaning police interrogation of her and her colleagues. She considers all manner of game-playing, from constructing a record of evidence of what an unreliable witness the complainant is to reinterpreting records of care that already exist. At times she disengages with the whole idea of continuing to work in the industry. As one nurse said in a case like this: 'Who would want to work in an industry that treats its employees the way it has treated me? Que sera sera. I'll drop out of life until this nighmare blows over.' And if the police offer her a deal, she is likely to capitulate quickly to its terms.

It follows from the Braithwaite et al.'s (2007) data that we need to see the regulatory challenge as one of increasing commitment more than gaming and disengagement are increased. We actually do not want to crush capitulation because we want defendants to respond to just settlements. Nor should we want to crush resistance because we seek robust defence of allegations, and critique of conduct during an investigation that is unfair. We wish the drama of the investigation and the trial to heighten everyone's commitment to the value of non-violence, to stay engaged with fair process, to vigorous debate and contestation of facts, and to a capitulation that might be a foundation for restorative justice and regeneration for abuser and abused.

Till now, we have been considering how nursing home managers adopt the different motivational postures. In most respects it would be tedious to work through the motivational postures again in application to lower-level staff of nursing homes because we would say rather similar things. The really major exception is that we would say something radically different about disengagement. While it is almost impossible for disengagement to be a survival strategy for US nursing home administrators or directors of nursing, disengagement is one of the dominant survival strategies of US nurse aides. Chapter 10 argues that because disengagement is not the minority strategy it is with managers, but perhaps the dominant strategy with US aides, the root causes of their disaffection must be tackled. Incapacitation of an entire aide workforce is hardly an option. So, just as institutional integrity requires incapacitation of bosses who abuse the privilege of power by being dismissive, institutional integrity requires empowerment of powerless care assistants who are dismissively defiant. Regulatory strategies cannot conquer dismissiveness except at the peak of the pyramid. But we will argue in Chapter 10 that capacity-building strategies can.

The root causes of care assistant disengagement are seen to revolve around exclusion, poverty and racism. They feel reluctance to commit to the mission of an authority because they have never been given a stake or a voice in any authority structure. Disengaged care assistants are in the aged care system, but not of it. Empirically, low trust is a correlate of disengagement. Large gestures are needed to extend trust and in time to expect trust from a structurally disadvantaged segment of the society. Chapter 10 lays out a vision of the aged care sector as a micro site of the macro struggle to build a more inclusive democracy for the excluded. Participating in serving and empowering one excluded, voiceless minority (the very old and sick) can be conceived as a strategy for care assistants to find their own voice and to find a career trajectory. The idea of the new pyramid in this context is to regenerate hope and strengths that care workers already have in their families, their communities and their workplaces.

STRATEGIC EXAMPLES OF COMMITMENT-BUILDING

It is one thing to see an imperative to build the ratio of commitment to the other four motivational postures. It is another to imagine how one would accomplish that. In Chapter 4 and elsewhere we have had a lot to say about how inspectors can and do manage regulatory encounters to persuade managers to put their committed self forward. Christine Parker (2006) warns that responsive regulation can lead regulators out of a 'deterrence trap' into a 'compliance trap',[3] when webs of deterrence are leveraged in the absence of business commitment and political commitment to a law. Leveraging webs of deterrence in the absence of commitment is likely to be viewed as unfair by business leaders who then mobilize sympathetic political leaders against regulators. Our nursing home data suggest there was a time when business leaders frequently mobilized political leaders against regulators perceived as too vigorous in their enforcement. However, politicians learnt that they could suffer politically when frail elderly were perceived as hurt by enforcement failure in which the politician was implicated. So this is no longer a domain where the conditions for Parker's compliance trap strongly apply. Even so, our data are instructive about the conditions for building both business and political commitment to the law. In a more general sense, Braithwaite's (forthcoming; also Braithwaite et al. 1994) data suggest that resistant defiance, the motivational posture that concerns Parker, is not the compliance difficulty that dismissiveness is. Resistant defiance poses a democratically healthy challenge to regulatory authority that a sophisticated enforcement policy can flip to commitment much more readily than disengagement.

In the next section we will use the US data to conclude that even in the most ritualistic regime of them all, there have been major national political forces for commitment. In the UK case, in the section after that, we will find the most strategic and instructive interventions to build commitment at the street level. Finally, in the Australian data we will find the most interesting interventions at the national regulator level in shifts to a continuous improvement philosophy.

TRANSCENDING RITUALISM AT THE NATIONAL LEVEL – THE OBRA CAMPAIGN

In Chapters 3 and 4 we concluded that the campaign led in the 1980s and early 1990s by the National Citizens' Coalition for Nursing Home Reform (NCCNHR) for change in nursing home law and regulation built a lot of industry and political commitment to improved quality of care. The OBRA reform package was enacted into law in 1987, but full implementation was not complete until 1995. The empirical record is fairly clear that OBRA was associated with improved quality of care on various dimensions, though some were not affected (HCFA 1998: vol. 3, 53–4; Mor et al. 2004). At the end of this process there were actually fewer standards on the books than there had been in the mid-1980s when Illinois had 5000 nursing home standards. Contrary to common perceptions, levels of enforcement fell sharply and almost continuously for eight years from their peak in 1989. So we concluded in Chapter 3 that the OBRA impact was not a product of more laws more firmly enforced. It happened in circumstances of fewer laws being more leniently enforced than in the 1980s. What changed things, according to our account in Chapter 3, was the OBRA campaign itself.

So what were the features of this campaign that had an effect? One was a mobilization of some 200 NGOs around quality-of-care scandals and how to respond to them with constructive law reform, and telephone trees of their rank and file members calling political leaders. These NGOs showed media shrewdness in getting their stories into the popular press (Ulsperger 2002: 397). They engaged political leaders not only by getting their attention through the media, but directly as well, as in the Untie the Elderly Campaign meetings on Capitol Hill. The NCCNHR made heroes of restraint-free nursing homes, gave them a platform on places like Capitol Hill and standing ovations at their conferences. They had a political sense of which were the providers who could grab the imagination of the industry as role models that a better way was possible.

The NCCNHR then engaged the industry on a wide front with the remarkable consensus-building effort that was the Campaign for Quality Care. In an interview with Elma Holder and her colleagues in 1990, she told us that in 1986 the American Health Care Association (AHCA), representing nursing homes, had said: 'We want to be the ones wearing the white hats.' Holder's philosophy was: 'We want everyone to get credit for what they do.' Her philosophy was to take the high road of cooperation with her industry adversaries, openness and consensus-building. The AHCA was less open and would frequently go behind Holder's back to the Hill with proposals. 'But someone always told us. And we got copies of their proposal, distribute them to everyone else. We said at the [Campaign for Quality Care] meeting "AHCA has a different point of view on that" and force them to tell everyone what they were doing.' When Holder would say to the industry 'Would you like to share that with us?', they would look and feel embarrassed because they knew the NCCNHR was being so open.

Holder and her deputy, Barbara Frank, were gifted at consensus-building, knowing how to focus on the little that had been agreed as a strength from which the campaign could build outwards. 'Barbara will have a room full of people yelling at each other for half an hour. She would then get up and say: "Now we have consensus on these issues"' (state ombudsman, 1989). The Omnibus Budget Reconciliation Act was in an important sense a new law drafted collaboratively between NGOs, health professions and the industry. It was outside-in regulatory design, where organizations representing residents, workers and owners sent the pulses of reform from outside-in to the regulatory system. As Braithwaite (2005b: 156–66) has argued, outside-in regulatory design is superior for building commitment than the more conventional process of inside-out design where the state crafts regulation, then sells it to users.

We saw in Chapter 3 that scientific researchers played an important role in the epistemic community that built commitment to untie the elderly. They produced the research showing that lowering restraint actually reduced staff costs and reduced tort risks (Phillips et al. 1993; Tinetti et al. 1990). Obviously this helped build commitment. The Untie the Elderly Campaign built commitment among the best state regulatory leaders; those lead states in collaboration with their industry associations started to compete to be the state with the lowest levels of restraint. This in turn changed the commitments of inspectors for whom it ceased being an acceptable answer in a high-restraint home that appropriate doctors' orders existed to vindicate the restraints. In Chapter 3 we characterized inspectors as moving from ineffectually nattering about restraint to confronting it. When inspectors started demanding evidence of programs to try alternatives to restraints, staff found intrinsic commitment to further change when, to their surprise, they saw residents released successfully, and appreciating their freedom. This was why the progress was so cumulative, restraint dropping further and further year after year from the late 1980s through to 2006. Commitment to the reform became internalized into the mentalities of the industry. Restraint-reduction was not the accomplishment of a rule book; it was the accomplishment of a storybook, as Shearing and Ericson (1991) put it, stories of what could be tried to free the most difficult of restrained residents.

In Chapter 3 we sought to tie things together by seeing the NCCNHR as a node in a network of governance that increased pride in caring and strengthened commitment to a range of more resident-centred standards. The biggest blow this nodal governance struck for nursing home residents was to shift the mentalities of various kinds of actors from institutionalized rituals for regulating things like restraint to commitment to reducing levels of restraint and improving quality of care generally. They moved from wanting to fill out their restraint authorization correctly to caring about untying the elderly.

STREET-LEVEL TRANSCENDENCE OF RITUALISM IN ENGLAND

Our account of English inspection in Chapter 5 was also of networked governance that, at its best, cut through ritualism. But it was a networking of regional as opposed to national club governance. There was no national advocacy networker that was anything like the national node of outside-in governance of the NCCNHR in the US. One of the critiques of responsive regulation is that it requires a great deal of resources to work. Yet we saw in Chapter 5 that English regulation is much less adequately resourced than American regulation, yet more responsive and less ritualistic. English inspectors compensate for their puny enforcement powers in comparison with their US counterparts by networked escalation, where the street-level inspector does the networking. For example, failure to achieve regulatory goals may result in escalation first to a repeat inspection, then a stern letter from a senior official, then networking in of more senior officials who the proprietor is called in to meet at increasingly formal encounters, then scathing reports might be written that network in the concern of banks that lend to the home, industry associations, professional registration authorities, hospitals that refer new residents, and the like. It is extremely difficult to motivate interest from such network partners to support enforcement that is merely ritualistic. The inspector must be seen as responding to a failure to improve poor quality outcomes. The provider must not be seen as merely playing at ritualistic compliance; motivation for networked effort comes from seeing genuine improvement in the lives of old folks. Ritualism and networked responsive escalation are simply not very compatible.

CONTINUOUS IMPROVEMENT AND AUSTRALIAN REGULATORY INSTITUTIONS

When the Australian standards monitoring program was introduced in 1987, the ambition was to 'raise the bar' over time. This did not happen in the conditions of industry capture of regulatory initiative that prevailed during most of the 1990s. We saw in Chapter 6 that one of the ironies of the move from state inspection to accreditation in the late 1990s was that it was justified in terms of a move to a continuous improvement philosophy. Over time, partly in response to internal dynamics in the Accreditation Agency and partly in response to external pressures such as from scandals and advocacy, the Australian continuous improvement philosophy has gradually acquired more substance.

In practice, we have seen that this means that inspectors at the street level are responsive to initiatives of the industry to continuously improve, or lack thereof. Inspectors do not operate by setting the bar at a particular spot, but rather by encouraging the industry to innovate in strategies that generate evidence of the substance of continuous improvement. The Australian nursing home industry of the 1990s had pockets of innovation, but was in general an industry characterized by extremely low levels of innovation and a dearth of sophisticated management. Today there is more investment in management and a more competitive management labour market (see Chapter 8), as well as an extremely innovative market in quality assurance consultancy to smaller providers.

While there remain many respects in which the American and English industries set higher quality-of-care standards than Australia, Australia is laying a foundation for the future of becoming more innovative in designing quality improvement initiatives and evaluating the improvements that flow from them. Some of the best professionals in the Australian industry are learning from the significant cultural transformation that seems to be dawning on the Australian hospital sector for greater openness with data that reveals its mistakes and collaborative root cause analysis to correct those mistakes. By collaborative root cause analysis, we mean a micro version of outside-in design, where instead of having a root cause analysis expert on staff who specializes in doing these analyses, residents and their relatives directly affected by the quality or safety failure are invited to participate in the root cause analysis with all staff involved (and perhaps with an outside consultant to facilitate the process).[4] This, however, is no more than a stirring of outside-in quality improvement. Most nursing home managers have no idea of what root cause analysis is. They are stuck at event-driven analyses of problems that do not attend to systemic causes that prevent the same events from bobbing up again and again.

Embryonic though it is, what is encouraging about current Australian developments is that they begin to transcend Michael Power's concern about 'the audit society' as 'a society that endangers itself because it invests too heavily in shallow rituals of verification at the expense of other forms of organizational intelligence. In providing a lens for regulatory thought and action audit threatens to become a form of learned ignorance' (Power 1997: 123). The Australian push for continuous improvement is allowing a thousand flowers to bloom that include both new blooms of organizational intelligence and some highly ritualistic approaches to demonstrating continuous improvement (as we saw in Chapter 6). To escape the latter trap, regulators need to continuously improve their demands for and responsiveness to continuous improvement. This is not to say when continuous improvement fails, we need more of the same. It is to suggest a reflexive commitment to continuous improvement, continuously improving our strategies for continuously improving. Moreover, as Chapter 6 concluded, our evidence does suggest that continuous improvement transcends ritualism when there is pride in caring and shame at neglect.

CONCLUSION

We have concluded that ritualism on the part of regulators is interpreted by regulatees and incorporated into their motivational postures. The costs of ritualism are seen in the postures of managers and their staff – resistance to unfairness and meaninglessness that is not addressed, game-playing that mirrors enforcement ritualism, disengagement that shows lack of respect for regulatory goals and means. Regulatory ritualism induces gaming, defiance and disengagement that in turn produce compliance ritualism. We end up with both regulators and providers of care who do the regulatory dance ritualistically, without commitment to what can be done to help old folks to more comfortable and fulfilled lives. Responsive regulation is an approach that requires non-ritualistic regulators to read motivational postures, understand the sensibilities that shape them and tailor regulatory interventions accordingly.

There is an association in quantitative survey research between shame acknowledgement (but not stigmatizing shame) and humble pride (but not narcissistic pride)[5] in doing right and making a commitment to a normative order (Ahmed and Braithwaite 2007; Braithwaite forthcoming). There is also quantitative evidence, both from our nursing home data (Braithwaite and Makkai 1994; Makkai and Braithwaite 1996) and beyond (Tyler et al. forthcoming), that communicating trust and procedural justice are also connected to normative commitment and thence compliance in a similar way to reintegrative shaming (Makkai and Braithwaite 1994b) and praising (Makkai and Braithwaite 1993a). Our qualitative fieldwork suggests that even programs that are abysmal failures because they collapse into market ritualism, such as QUIP in Illinois, can have redeeming qualities because staff of facilities that were in fact six-star facilities on dozens of occasions reported pride to us in being a QUIP six-star facility. Our qualitative fieldwork suggests that strong inspectors do mobilize shame, but in a reintegrative way, when professional standards of care are not met.

When they announce in an exit conference that dietary standards are not met, we observe them make a point of looking the head of dietary in the eye as they say this. They then leave a silence at the end of announcing the failure to meet the dietary standards, a silence that seems to last forever with so many eyes on the responsible kitchen manager. The manager then fills that silence by accepting responsibility and foreshadowing his or her commitment to a rigorous plan of correction. That in turn elicits kindly and respectful nodding from the inspectors who seem to say with their body language that they knew the kitchen manager was the kind of dietary professional who would take responsibility in just such a determined way. These reintegrative gestures of the inspectors then create an atmosphere where the dietary manager's boss says he or she has confidence that in putting things right the management and staff of the kitchen will set a new quality benchmark. Squaring the circle of reintegration and hope, the inspectors again nod their concurrence with this expectation that there will be pride in putting things right.

Weak inspectors do not do this. We observed an exit conference in a Southern US state after the director of nursing was found to have fabricated minutes of an infection control committee meeting that had not occurred (as required by the rules).[6] There had been tears from the attractive nurse that had caused the male head of the inspection team to crumble before the exit with assurances that this would not be treated harshly in their report, that she had 'been very cooperative and helpful' during the inspection and everything would be OK. At exit, an inspector who used to be a nurse says in a firm, understated way, with much eye contact with the director of nursing: 'I have not seen records that satisfy me that the infection control committee does meet quarterly.' The director of nursing nods, mutters unconvincing puzzlement at which of her staff could have fabricated these minutes, and says: 'I wish I had an answer for it. All I can do is stop myself from crying.' The nurse inspector replies, poker faced, 'You can do that', then opens a long silence with eyes of both nurse inspectors on the director of nursing, waiting for her to do better at accepting professional responsibility. Then their weak-kneed team leader lets her off this hook as well, ending the excruciating silence with: 'You need to keep on top of the temperature with the bath. You need to fix that son of a gun.'

Our conclusion is that the micro-politics of pride and shame at street level, that can be a gender politics and a nursing professional politics, as in this example, are fundamental to building commitment to quality and integrity in particular organizations. As English inspection of decades past so vividly illustrates, high integrity street-level bureaucrats can mobilize pride, shame and networked escalation when commitment is lacking, to great effect. They repeatedly accomplished this in the most structurally difficult contexts of being poorly resourced, ill equipped with enforcement tools and devoid of political backing from either national or local political elites. Skilful micro-politics at the street level routinely kept these encounters out of Parker's (2006) compliance trap.[7] However, our data also suggest that no amount of skill is likely to flip disengagers, as opposed to resisters, to commitment and compliance. Nor is any amount of deterrence. For them, a credible capability to escalate to incapacitation is needed.

What follows from Chapters 7 and 8 is that there are many dimensions of the problem of ritualism, any of which might thwart a strategy intended to transcend it. The present chapter shows that there are many levels at which ritualism can be transcended – through nodes of national and state NGO politics cleverly networked with industry and professional associations, through continuous improvement and strengths-based national regulatory strategies for building commitment, responsive enforcement escalation to incapacitation, and street-level tactics to build pride in caring. That establishes the empirical foundation for wanting to grapple with an epistemology of webs of explanation and webs of governance. This we seek to do in Chapter 10.

NOTES

1. These postures have been refined over time. In the original Braithwaite et al. (1994) publication on motivational postures there were four: resistance was called resistance then and now, as was disengagement; managerial accommodation then is now called commitment, capture (meaning capture *by* the regulator) then is now called capitulation. The game-playing posture was discovered in the subsequent work. In terms of Merton's (1968: 194) typology, commitment is similar to conformity (yet allows innovation to better achieve desired goals as a form of commitment), resistance is similar to rebellion, game-playing is a form of ritualism, and disengagement is similar to retreatism.
2. In this more recent work, commitment and capitulation are seen as the motivational postures that disable compliance, resistance of course as the posture that enables resistant defiance, and disengagement and game-playing the postures that enable dismissive compliance (Braithwaite forthcoming).
3. The deterrence trap is the inability of corporations, especially highly leveraged ones, to pay fines of the amount needed to reflect the gravity of offences with low risk of detection and conviction (Coffee 1981). It is the trap of making it rational for corporations to comply when the rewards of offending are high and the probability of detection low by setting the penalty so high as to create unjust overspills (for example, when lawbreaking worth $1 million has odds of detection of 1 in 100 and a rationally deterrent fine of over $100 million will bankrupt a company, putting innocent workers out of work). 'The compliance trap suggests that where a regulator does not have political and community support for the morality of its interpretation of compliance with the law it enforces, it will be trapped between choosing to go soft on enforcement in order to avoid criticism (but doing nothing to ensure compliance), or it can take formal enforcement action in more matters (but fall into the deterrence trap) or it can utilise deterrence leveraged with creative moral and political enforcement statements (but this will create resistance and political backlash from regulatees) (Christine Parker, personal communication).
4. One the problems with root cause analysis is people who feel they might be held responsible just sitting around and justifying themselves. Outsiders are needed in this context to look at what happened through a different lens and a critical one, and to ask simple questions. It would be a good idea to enhance the quality of non-professional engagement by providing root cause analysis training on the Internet oriented to non-professionals. Second, professionals with wide experience of moving beyond event-based and 'who is responsible' analyses to forensic search for systemic causes are desirable.
5. Narcissistic pride is vaunting pride that puts ourself above others; humble pride is pride in doing something well in a way that gives credit to others for their contribution to the accomplishment.
6. It was detected because the minutes purported to discuss the condition of a resident who had died months earlier.
7. Admittedly, these were contexts of regularly repeated inspections rather than the episodic enforcement encounters that were the context of Parker's (2006) data, and Parker points to repeat versus episodic encounters as a critical variable.

10. The new pyramid

One of the important moments in the history of regulatory science was the finding of Scholz and Gray (1990) that occupational health and safety inspections seemed to reduce accidents even when expected punishment costs of breaching health and safety laws were trivial. Detection probabilities were low and the average Occupational Safety and Health Administration penalties more than two decades ago were $37 (Kelman 1984), meaning that the direct cost of fixing a problem was virtually always a lot more than the expected punishment cost. In this study we have also found that expected punishment costs overall do not explain compliance (Braithwaite and Makkai 1991; Makkai and Braithwaite 1994a), but that there are a considerable number of other conditions that specify when inspection does improve compliance quantitatively, such as inspector praise (Makkai and Braithwaite 1993a), reintegrative shaming (Makkai and Braithwaite 1994b), fostering managerial self-efficacy (Jenkins 1994), having an all-female inspection team (Makkai and Braithwaite 1991) and trust (Braithwaite and Makkai 1994).

Qualitatively, our observations of 157 inspections supply some insights into the variety of contextual ways that inspectors frequently succeed in improving compliance, only a few of them about deterrence (see Table 10.1). Whether it is nursing home inspectors, or inspectors checking for weapons of mass destruction in Iraq, it is myopic to see inspection as something that works mainly through deterrence. The chapter will now move on to show why it is fortunate that nursing home inspection empirically does deploy such a web of different types of controls. Webs of disparate controls are necessary in a world where phenomena have complex webs of explanation. Then we move on to consider how complementing a regulatory pyramid with a strengths-based pyramid can enhance the redundancy of regulatory strategy in a strategic way. Finally, we connect the idea of strengths-based governance to a politics of structural, even global, transformation that works out from regenerative micro contexts.

RESPONSIVENESS TO LEVELS OF COMPLEXITY

Jeffrey Sachs (2005) in *The End of Poverty* argues that development economics should be more like medicine. On the one hand, development

*Table 10.1   Strategies that improved compliance in certain contexts
observed in this study*

Strategy	Process
Reminds	Tapping a staff member on the shoulder reminds of an obligation believed in but lost sight of
Commits	Persuading someone who was not persuaded that compliance would benefit residents
Shows	Shows how to do something necessary to compliance that the person does not know how to do
Fixes	Inspector fixes something themselves (for example, releases a restrained resident)
Incapacitates individual	Reports a professional to a licensing body that withdraws/suspends their licence
Incapacitates home	Withdraws/suspends licence for home
Protects future residents	Bans new admissions until problem fixed
Management change	Orchestrates sale or management takeover of the home by signalling escalation up a regulatory pyramid
Shames	Disapproves non-compliance
Exposes	Reports non-compliance to the public on a website or the nursing home notice board, inducing either reputational discipline or market discipline, or both
Praises	Congratulates improvement
Deters	Imposes a penalty
Signals escalation capability	Displays a capability to network escalation up a pyramid, a capability threatening in the background more than threatened
Wears down	Keeps coming back until the home wants closure to rid themselves of the inspector
Changes resource allocation	Sanctions withheld only if there is a change in resource allocation
Voluntary acceptance of responsibility on the spot	By asking a question, causes a professional to jump in and accept responsibility to put something right immediately
Voluntary acceptance of responsibility in a plan of correction	Asking the right questions brings about a long-term plan that accepts responsibility
Root cause analysis	Asking the right questions induces an insightful root cause analysis
Triggers continuous improvement	Asking the right questions reveals the benefits of commitment to continuous improvement
Triggers consultancy	Asking the right questions persuades the home to hire a consultant

Table 10.1   (continued)

Strategy	Process
Stimulates the home's deliberative problem-solving	Asking the right questions is a catalyst of problem-solving conversation at a staff meeting or other forum
Triple-loop learning	Inspector spreads generative learning from mistakes to one part of a facility from another and to one facility from another
Educates	Provides in-service training on the spot
Builds self-efficacy	Helps management and staff to see their own strengths
Awards and grants	Supports. Nominates the home or staff for an award or grant
Empowers	Empowers friends of compliance within the organization through some combination of the above strategies that puts pro-compliance factions of the organization in the driver's seat
Triggers pre-emption	The home fixes problems before the inspector arrives to pre-empt the deployment of any of the above strategies
Triggers third-party engagement with any/all of the above	A word to an advocacy organization, a key shareholder, a lending bank, the media, a provider association, a tort lawyer, the ombudsman, the residents' council, relatives

economics certainly needs more randomized controlled trials with their stronger warrant for inferences on the root causes of phenomena and less emphasis on non-experimental econometrics, which has become rather good at allowing economists to find whatever answers they want by putting extra variables into the model. On the other hand, Sachs suggests development economists need training and experience as clinical economists. This means learning how to diagnose a single case when that case is fraught with complexity. Randomized controlled trials allow us to be more credibly evidence based. Their problem is that they allow us to look at just one or a few causes at a time and do not help us understand the dynamics of how these causal factors push system effects across thresholds. Their findings offer limited guidance when we are dealing with complexes of many interacting causes.

How does this work in medicine? Consider regulation of infection. A doctor visits a patient in a hospital who gets one infection after another. Research on infection-management provides in effect a checklist of things the evidence-based doctor looks at. One infection for this doctor's patient starts by moving from one eye to another. It has been empirically demonstrated that this can be caused by the poor nursing practice of wiping one eye with a swab after applying drops and then using the same swab to dab the other eye. The existence of one symptom leads the doctor to do detective work checking other symptoms associated with a certain syndrome. They look for side effects. In the body/environment system, they watch for and seek to understand feedback loops that can render the cure worse than the disease or that can take the patient up to a new level of well-being. We have all experienced how good clinicians do this kind of detective work to diagnose the often complexly interacting root causes of our health weaknesses and strengths.

Then there is an intermediate level of science between randomized controlled trials on thousands of cases and clinical diagnoses of the complexly interacting problems of one patient. An example is the infection control study in a nursing home that plots on a computer map of the facility a blue dot for each eye infection, a red dot for each wound infection, and so on. Then the quality improvement committee looks at the patterns of dots over time. Aha, these dots cluster around where we leave soiled sheets awaiting pick-up by the laundry man! In hospitals this kind of intermediate science of root cause analysis in a particular context often happens at the ward level, generating lessons for triple-loop learning – rolling out the learnings from the infection study on the management of laundry to all the wards in the hospital, then to all hospitals in the system.

At both clinical and ward study levels on small Ns without a control group, we have a theory of what caused the infection. We keep trying one theory after another until the infection goes away. We never have a scientific warrant for knowing that it went away because of our intervention. The fact that the infection went immediately after the intervention is a kind of evidence that our theory was right, but poor quality evidence.

What we do know is that by being well-trained detectives, by being a doctor who is a good clinician rather than a clairvoyant, and being detectives who work through checklists that are based on evidence from randomized controlled trials, we cure more infections on average. Theory provides reflective practitioners with generative metaphors. Conversations among clinicians through clinical rounds and other means provide new lenses, new ways of seeing or framing the problem (Morgan 1986). Root cause analyses that engage both insiders and outsiders also do that, as we saw in the last chapter. Plural lenses push us to ask questions about the similarities and differences between the clinical problem and the metaphorical scenario of the theory. The good clinician is a detective who asks a lot of journalists' questions – what, who, how, when, where, why – to get the time line of the story clear. The good clinician 'thinks in a stream of time' (Neustadt and May 1986) to develop a contextual, integrated, joined-up, multiple-mechanism strategy to fix the problem (Braithwaite 1993). But because this beneficent new equilibrium in the system will eventually break down, regular checkups watch for this, especially with a worn system. The outstanding clinician is also regenerative, seeking to use each bout of illness not merely to restore the status quo, but as an opportunity to move the patient to a higher level of well-being.

Now from medicine to surfing. Doctors do not know enough to predict when and which of their patients will contract a particular disease; but they can identify common diseases when they do arise and can suggest treatments that improve the odds of recovery. Surfers are in a similar situation. Good surfers know what would be useless waves to attempt and they have a broad sense of how they are going to approach riding a wave of a particular type that is likely to break in a particular place. Yet good surfers are hardly logical positivists. They do not have a fixed theory of waves that they execute by strictly following the sequence of a wave-riding protocol. They adapt to the wave – a lot. When they are heading up toward a section of the wave that is breaking, they turn their board away from the foam. They shift their weight as the shape of the wave changes, even feel the wave as they interact with it, putting their hand into it. Their approach is partly ready–aim–fire, partly fire–aim–ready. This means a view that all waves are different, and it is hard to predict exactly how they will unfold. So you need to change your aim when the wave is not working for you. You keep adapting to the complexity of the wave until you find something that works and you never fully understand why it worked. Much of life is like riding waves. There is some good theory of what sort of waves are good riding. It would be possible to be a better surfer with the benefit of randomized controlled trials that show competitors score higher in championships when they use this design of board for surf condition X and that design for condition Y. Yet any number of randomized controlled trials will not change the fact that to be a great surfer we need to probe the wave, feel how it reacts to our body, and be responsive to that reaction. You need experience that only comes from 'doing', from learning to recognize and use patterns, and that requires investing in people over a long period of time. Good surfers are neither determinedly deductive theorists of wave-riding nor determinedly inductive. They are skilled at shuttling backwards and forwards between deduction and induction (Scheff 1990).

We are not competent to say anything of value on the technical subject of how to use a small amount of well-networked leverage to cause large change in complex systems, nor on how stable patterns emerge from chaos. Complexity science has taught us that many systems adapt over time, without a global equilibrium, generating perpetual novelty. Or as Karl Popper (1972: 210) put it, we misapprehend the world, if we assume that 'All clouds are clocks – even the most cloudy of clouds.' The Australian military uses the Cynefin model (Kurtz and Snowden 2003) to sensitize

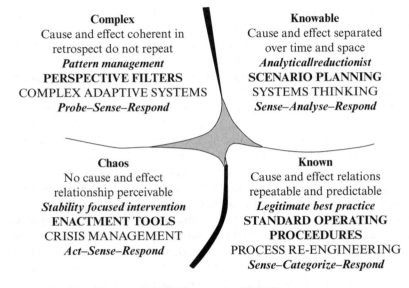

Complex
Cause and effect coherent in
retrospect do not repeat
Pattern management
PERSPECTIVE FILTERS
COMPLEX ADAPTIVE SYSTEMS
Probe–Sense–Respond

Knowable
Cause and effect separated
over time and space
Analytical/reductionist
SCENARIO PLANNING
SYSTEMS THINKING
Sense–Analyse–Respond

Chaos
No cause and effect
relationship perceivable
Stability focused intervention
ENACTMENT TOOLS
CRISIS MANAGEMENT
Act–Sense–Respond

Known
Cause and effect relations
repeatable and predictable
Legitimate best practice
**STANDARD OPERATING
PROCEEDURES**
PROCESS RE-ENGINEERING
Sense–Categorize–Respond

Sources: Kurtz and Snowden (2003); Warne et al. (2005: 47).

Figure 10.1 Domains of the Cynefin framework

soldiers to the options (Figure 10.1). We find this useful for thinking about how to intervene to improve quality of aged care. In less complex, less networked times, more was known about what makes for success in warfare. Two centuries ago, good soldiering was much more about standard operating procedures such as drilling soldiers to hold a straight line under fire (the 'known' quadrant of Figure 10.1). This is no longer true in a world where your adversary can network in a varied web of options against you.

In warfare today, inaction from analysis paralysis can be fatal, either when there is too much that is known, or because you are in the dark and unwilling to risk imposing some order on the chaos. The winner can be the soldier who thinks he or she knows the cause and effect relations and deploys some forces to act on that theory, yet at the same time thinks his or her theory may be wrong because the environment is more complex than the theory allows, and hence deploys some other forces to 'probe–sense–respond'. Yet others may be deployed to 'act–sense–respond', to test whether imposing order rather than reacting to it will work or backfire. It is quite possible that it is correct that some aspects of the situation are known or knowable and prove tractable to our theory. Other aspects may be embedded in complex systems where we do better by probing and sensing for patterns. And it is possible that by succumbing to analysis paralysis, leaving our troops huddled in the dark, an enemy who more aggressively probes the patterns of a complex environment or imposes order upon chaos will come out and kill them, group by group.

Whether we are a soldier, a board rider or a clinician, we may do better to be sensitized to all these possibilities. This means being reflexively evidence based – being evidence based about when it is stupid to be paralysed by the want of a randomized controlled trial to tell you what to do. It also means being evidence based about when we should completely stop a certain kind of intervention until large randomized controlled trials are published (for example, when clinicians observe some patients to die after the intervention).

To conclude this section, responsiveness to the environment and to actors in it means being reflexively evidence based. It means understanding that only some things are known and knowable. It means clinical wisdom. We must not suffer an analysis paralysis that sees us do nothing as we ponder the unknowable, just allowing the patient to die. Regulators, like doctors, need wisdom in when to 'probe–sense–respond', when to 'act–sense–respond'. They must be social scientists of what works in regulation, diagnosticians of the N of 1, root cause analysts of intermediate quantification with small N, no control group, in a specific context, and consummate monitors of system change. We have found in our fieldwork that master practitioners of nursing home inspection do indeed combine the skills of the detective, the skills of the reflective practitioner of problem-oriented policing (Goldstein 1979) and the skills of gerontological science.

MULTIPLE CAUSATION

Even simple things human beings do have multiple causes. Consider why we chose to order pork in a restaurant tonight and beef last night. Realities of networked governance of social life multiply the causes that exist at different points in the network. Wars have become less winnable by following known standard operating procedures; this is not an idiosyncratic example. As Manuel Castells (1996) has shown with great synoptic sweep, over time we have come to live in societies that are governed more through networks. Hierarchical machine bureaucracies, such as in the Soviet Union, that was quite good at building efficient subways and armies (Castells 1996), no longer rule the world. Today's world belongs more to Bill Gates than to Joseph Stalin.

For this reason, it should not surprise us that policy science increasingly shows that multidimensional interventions often work better than unidimensional interventions. In peace-building operations, for example, Doyle and Sambanis (2000) show in a study of 124 civil wars that multidimensional peace operations that attack a range of perceived root causes of a war are more successful in preventing future war than peacekeeping that just patrols a border or polices a ceasefire. Grimshaw et al. (2001) show from a review of 41 reviews (one of them [Gurwitz et al. 1990] of 16 nursing home studies, another [Shortell et al. 1998] of 55 continuous improvement evaluations) that unidimensional approaches to changing the behaviour of clinicians (for example, just posting them clinical practice guidelines) do not change their behaviour. It takes a multifaceted approach (of which posting guidelines might be a part). Passive universal interventions do not work as well as active multidimensional interventions that engage with the complexity of a local context (Grimshaw et al. 2001: II-11). In the same year Grol (2001) published a review of 36 reviews of health quality improvement strategies that also found 'combined and multifaceted interventions' to be 'mostly (very) effective'. ' "Give attention to many different factors and use multiple strategies" is the conclusion of this study' (Grol 2001: 2584). Integrated strategies are needed that combine 'evidence-based guidelines, clinical pathways, indicators for continuous assessment, and quality improvement projects embedded within a wider quality system of a hospital or practice'.

In rehabilitation of criminals, Farrington and Welsh (2002), among others, find an evidence base for multisystemic therapy having more promise than single-system therapies. Whole-school anti-bullying programs seem to work much better in reducing bullying than more narrowly targeted interventions (Smith et al. 2004: 310–22). Whole-school approaches are not only distinguished by their engagement of peers, parents, teachers, janitors, as opposed to just bullies; they engage many different dimensions of the culture and policies of a school. Based on a micro–macro ethnography of world systems, Braithwaite and Drahos (2000) concluded that something as difficult as globalizing a business regulatory regime or a nuclear non-proliferation regime does not happen without the engagement of a whole web of actors at different levels mobilizing a web of mechanisms of globalization.

It is simple-minded to look at these large literatures and just say well of course simple solutions do not work for complex problems. Regulators who wish to learn how to become more effectively responsive need to unpack what we mean when we say that complex webs of explanation imply webs of intervention. Gunningham and Grabosky's (1998) classic, *Smart Regulation*, is the most powerful analysis in the regulatory literature of the dangers of 'smorgasbordism' – try a little bit of everything. After unpacking the arguments for multidimensionality, we will return to the dangers of a 'kitchen sink' approach to regulatory strategy.

Briefly let us consider seven reasons why multiple regulatory interventions are likely to be needed.

Different Causes Require Different Weapons

It will be likely that the same control strategy will not work with different root causes of a problem. Different barriers to change will need different weapons to attack them. We should want to turn around as many of the root causes and side effects of a problem as possible. This requires us to be open to the likelihood that different causes require different solutions.

The Redundancy Principle

Because it is best to assume that instrument failure or implementation failure occurs, and that such failure will be contextually unpredictable, it is best to have multiple strings to our bow. A complaints hotline is one way of detecting resident abuse. But it will mostly fail because the most severely abused residents fear retaliation if they complain. Hence we need mandatory reporting laws for other staff in the nursing home who have good reason to suspect abuse. Military commanders need offensive capacity and defensive capacity that will mean different kinds of tools. Nursing home reformers need tools to attack barriers to change and different tools to erect barriers to counterchange. They need to attack homes that tie up residents; they must defend against ritualistic compliance followed by reversion to physical restraint once the inspectors have left.

Swiss Cheese Defence

Redundant defence will not work if it has just any old strings to its bow. Very different kinds of strings are needed to cover the weak spots of one intervention with the strengths of another. James Reason (1990) has developed the Swiss cheese model (Figure 10.2) in application to domains such as aircraft accident prevention. A multitude of different types of controls are needed to cover weak spots of one barrier with other barriers that have their weak spots in other places. Covering a pilot with a co-pilot, or a computer with a backup computer, may be less effective than covering a pilot with a computer and a computer with a co-pilot. Two pilots flying over snow may both suffer the same whiteout; two computers may be simultaneously attacked by the same virus. The Swiss cheese model is about multiple defensive protections against an unwanted confluence of factors, as opposed to multiple offensive capabilities. Yet in the last section we saw that we need offence as well as defence.

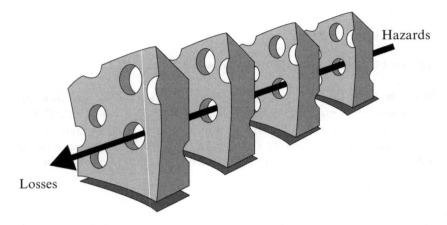

Source: Reason (1990).

Figure 10.2   Swiss cheese model of risk prevention

Strengthen the Fabric Principle

It is possible to tie together thin reeds that snap on their own to form a strong basket. But tying an extra strand into a web of controls can strengthen the fabric when we tug on it, or when tugged can cause the web to unravel. Therefore, we need to do the instrument analytics of complementary and incompatible instruments in Gunningham and Grabosky's (1998) *Smart Regulation*. Empirically, in regulatory science, this can mean testing interaction terms in regression models that predict regulatory effectiveness. It can mean randomized controlled trials that send one group of nurses just a clinical guideline in the mail, and another, the mailing plus a follow-up conversation on the importance of the guidelines by a respected peer. It can mean the kind of conceptual analysis of complementary and incompatible strategy combinations that we find in Gunningham and Grabosky (1998). Most of all, it means thinking in time about how a system of interacting variables might be leveraged in a particular context.

The Check and Balance Principle

A fuse box that checks excessive current is an example of a check and balance. The value of many regulatory mechanisms is that they show up errors in other mechanisms so learning can occur. Conversation[1] is the most important of these; hence the preference for conversational regulation (Black 1997) such as we have discussed with exit conferences, quality improvement committees, residents' councils and care planning conferences. Conversation regulates while checking excesses of regulation. It checks responses by helping us see them through multiple lenses. In Donald Schon's (1983) *The Reflective Practitioner*, he suggests that the art of practice is about the reflective practitioner shaping the situation in accordance with an initial view of it. The situation 'talks back' and the practitioner responds to the situation's back talk. Inspectors reflect in action through conversations with the situation (see Chapter 4). As John Dewey put it, they learn the art of practice by doing. Of course, conversations with others can suggest a new lens to reframe the situation, a different evaluation methodology to assess our epistemology of practice. Strategic conversations are the key to reflection-in-action. Keynes is reputed to have said in 1936: 'It is astonishing what foolish things one can temporarily believe if one thinks too long alone.'

The Pyramid Principle

By having multiple strategies we can layer them into a pyramid. The regulatory pyramid does more than cover the weaknesses of one strategy with the strengths of another (as the Swiss cheese model does); it orders strategies from more minimalist, more conversational interventions to progressively more coercive ones. It normatively privileges persuasion ahead of punishment. Its explanatory model is that punishment is likely to be more effective when persuasion is tried first. It is also that persuasion is likely to be more effective when it is viewed as inevitable that when dialogue fails there will be escalation to coercion. Conversation works better when we have an aura of power in the eyes of the other.

The Networked Pyramid Principle

Networked escalation – nodes that tie together networks at each layer of the pyramid (Drahos 2004) – combine the pyramid idea with the strengthening of the fabric idea (see Figure 10.3). Weak regulators, such as English inspectors, US ombudsmen, Australian advocates or community visitors, can and do use a networked pyramid. They escalate their regulatory capabilities less by ratcheting up their own enforcement response, more by widening their networks to the regulatory capabilities of other actors, progressively enrolled at escalating layers of their pyramid.

The Dual Pyramid Principle

In addition to a pyramid that gives us networked escalation of regulation, we can have a pyramid of progressively more expanded networking of

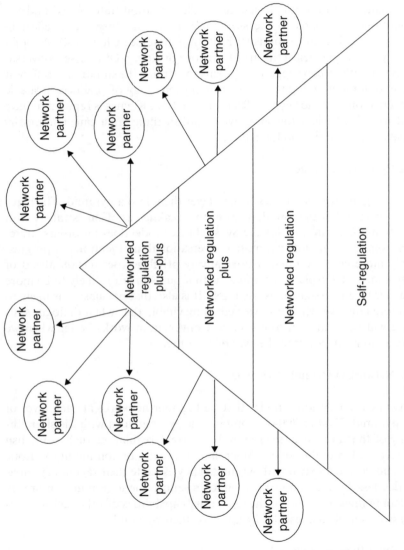

Figure 10.3 An example of a pyramid of networked escalation

capacity-building. This is the new pyramid – the strengths-based pyramid – that will be the focus of the remainder of this chapter.

THE STRENGTHS-BASED PYRAMID

In Chapters 6 and 9 we found that the paradigmatic change of Australian nursing home regulation in the current decade is toward continuous improvement of strengths. But even in the most risk-based of our three country case studies – the US – we saw in Chapter 4 that strengths-based inspection is well and truly alive at the street level as part of the multifaceted approach inspectors use in practice. Strengths-based quality improvement is also evident at the self-regulatory level in all our cases, though care planning still mostly enumerates deficits rather than capabilities.

One of the dilemmas of responsive regulation has always been that in a regulatory pyramid, as argued in Chapter 8, punishments are more useful than rewards. Moral hazard is the most important of a number of reasons for this. If we try to control a risk with dialogue first and then with a reward at the next rung of the pyramid, rational actors will shun the dialogue until they have collected their reward. Gunningham and Grabosky (1998: 438, but see the qualification at p. 435) reached a similar conclusion: command and control and broad-based economic instruments (like tax breaks) that target the same problem are an inherently counterproductive combination of tools.

In Chapter 4, we saw that the theory of strengths-based intervention is that the best way to improve is to build out from strengths; ultimately these strengths will grow to conquer more weaknesses, or to compensate for them. In an organization, if we build out from everyone's strengths, the chances that the weaknesses of one individual in a work group will be covered by the strengths of another will be much improved. Finally, we have concluded in this book that inspectors often achieve more by working with the friends of continuous improvement than by working against its enemies (see also Parker 2002). A good example from our data of how a strength can compensate for a weakness is Ann Jenkins's (1997) finding that nursing home CEOs with high managerial self-efficacy were not discouraged from commitment to compliance by procedural injustice on the part of inspectors. Jenkins found that when CEOs believed the regulator was moving the goalposts, they just kicked the ball further (Jenkins 1997). Obversely, weakness engendered collapse into further weakness. So Jenkins (1997) revealed an interesting deterrence–self-efficacy interaction. When managers with low self-efficacy are concerned about legal sanctions, this seems to cause them to drop their bundle. This was a similar result to that of Makkai and Braithwaite (1994) that for directors of nursing high in emotionality, perceived threats of deterrence reduced compliance. Deterrence only increased compliance for low emotionality directors of nursing who were cool and calculating. High self-efficacy managers in Jenkins's (1997) analyses responded to the challenge of perceived legal threats with resilience and high compliance. On a number of dimensions, Jenkins showed high self-efficacy to compensate for the adversities and obstacles that caused poor quality of care in homes run by managers with low self-efficacy.

The impossibility of satisfactorily integrating rewards into a sanctions pyramid has always been one of the unappealing features of responsive regulation, for we know rewards often work better than sanctions. The dual pyramid solution is to build more redundancy, to complement defensive capability with offensive capability, to build strengths to check and balance, to cover the weaknesses of one strategy with the strengths of another. It is to enhance our capability to temporally order supportive strategies before punitive ones, by complementing the regulatory pyramid with a quite separate strengths-based pyramid.

In Chapter 1, we found virtue in Malcolm Sparrow's prescription to 'Pick problems and fix them.' This is what escalation up an enforcement pyramid is designed to accomplish. The strengths-based pyramid, in contrast, is designed to 'Pick strengths and expand them.' Table 10.2 shows that while the regulatory pyramid responds to a 'fear' about a 'risk', the strengths-based pyramid responds to a 'hope' that 'opportunities' can be built upon. This means the strengths-based pyramid is not preoccupied with guaranteeing a minimum standard; rather it seeks to maximize quality by pulling standards up through a ceiling.

Dual pyramid regulation would be about continuous improvement, building on the recent Australian experience in Chapter 6. The regulatory framework would require continuous improvements based both on identifying the biggest remaining problems and fixing them, and on identifying the biggest remaining opportunities and building out from them by expanding opportunities.

Table 10.2   Distinguishing the design principles of a regulatory enforcement pyramid and a strengths-based pyramid

Regulatory pyramid	Strengths-based pyramid
Risk assessment	Opportunities assessment
Fear	Hope
Prompt response before problem escalates	Wait patiently to support strengths that bubble up from below
Pushing standards above a floor	Pulling standards through a ceiling

Under such a framework, inspectors would fail their performance review if they had not ensured both that the organization had a risk management system that was working in identifying its biggest problems and fixing them, and a strengths diagnosis system that was identifying the largest opportunities to expand out from strengths. Inspectors would be accountable for both strengths-based and problem-based evidence of continuous improvement diagnosis. If the regulated organization could not identify both the strengths and the weaknesses it was targeting and how it was evaluating improved performance, then it would fail its inspection. A considerable departure from existing regulatory practice in all three countries is involved in the suggestion of this paragraph.

Figure 10.4 allows us to compare and contrast examples of a regulatory pyramid and a strengths-based pyramid. The two pyramids are linked at the bottom because education and persuasion about problems and about strengths might well have the same delivery vehicle. However, they should not be joined up as separate sides of a multisided pyramid (Gunningham and Grabosky 1998) because at the same level the different activities on adjoining sides of the pyramid would have to be complementary. This is not the case with this model. Shame versus pride, sanctions versus prizes, are alternative rather than complementary strategies.

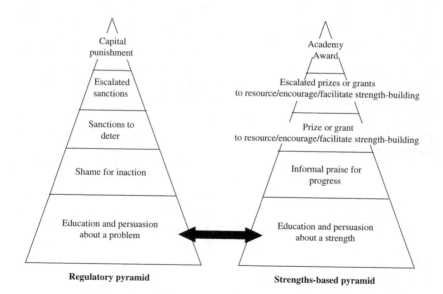

Figure 10.4   Comparison of a regulatory pyramid and a strengths-based pyramid

The opposite of disapproval and shame for failing to manage a risk in the regulatory pyramid is praise and pride for realizing an opportunity in the strengths-based pyramid. As the regulatory pyramid escalates between deterrent and incapacitative sanctions, the strengths pyramid can alternate between prizes and grants. Prizes are awarded to encourage those who are developing new benchmarks that might take the industry up through a ceiling. Prizes build strength in those who are most excellent. Of course, there is great virtue in giving a prize to an actor who is terrible in most other things, but unusually good in this thing. That virtue is finding a strength in the weakest of us that can be a base to build out new strengths that conquer our weaknesses. This is the ideal of redemptive education that finds something excellent in the capacities of every student. There is no moral hazard in awarding prizes because they go to those who have laboured unusually hard to build their strength.

Grants can be attached to prizes when doing so would provide resources for R&D on improved paths to quality. But in general it makes sense to devote most scarce grant dollars to help actors who are on the move in building a strength from a starting point of great weakness. This means grants are concentrated where needs are greatest, while prizes are concentrated where excellence is greatest. To get a strength-building grant, however, an actor must be already on the move with building the strength. Yet they must need more resources to move it upwards. This makes the grant simultaneously a reward for effort and a way of directing resources where needs are great. The combined effect of the two pyramids is to eliminate moral hazard in rewards. An actor who lets a weakness get weaker will not get a grant or a prize. Indeed, when this weakness causes problems, there will be punitive escalation up the regulatory pyramid until the problems are fixed and the poor systems that allowed them to occur reformed. Once a non-compliant actor is driven down to the base of the regulatory pyramid, the emphasis of inspector engagement with them can shift to strength-building.

A worry that remains about escalated prizes and grants in the strengths pyramid is that that the biggest wins might be captured by those who are the best fixers rather than the best performers on that strength. Remedies to this are to insist on independent evidence that a strength is growing, such as resident satisfaction surveys conducted by an outside consultant and having an external academic assessor of that evidence, such as happens with the Australian Better Practice in Aged Care Awards. While it is harder to fix the inspector, the external consultant, the data and the independent academic than it is to just fix the inspector, even more multiparty engagement is still desirable. One path is for inspectors to make a proposal to the exit conference on which strength-building might be targeted and for how much special state resources. Resident, staff and family representatives then have a chance to comment on that joint management–inspector proposal, as would ombudsmen or other advocates if they were present.

One of the interesting ways practice is ahead of theory in laying a foundation for strengths-based and risk-based pyramids that are linked at their bases is the way Australian homes lay a foundation for quality improvement by aggregating in the same folder 'accolades, concerns and suggestions'. Books that collate these are usually found prominently placed in the staff room so they will be read as a foundation for motivation and action. Other homes capture 'compliments' and 'complaints' quantitatively in corporate quality improvement plots. When compliments spike up in one of their homes, head office reads the qualitative content and, where justified, sends out certificates of commendation to individual staff and the home.

Following the theory in this chapter, inspectors would assess interventions as presumptively weak if they were unidimensional. Interventions that mobilized multidimensional webs of self-regulation and webs of capacity would be regarded as presumptively more promising. But in the theory we are struggling to develop, there is a major difference between webs of regulation and webs of capacity. At the base of the regulatory pyramid, dialogic webs of regulation need to be soft and weak. If the constraint is unjust or unreasonable, the regulated organization must be able to crash through the web of controls and contest the regulatory order at higher levels of the pyramid – for example, in a criminal trial in which the accused is found not guilty, or litigation in which a court strikes down the regulation as unreasonable. Resistant defiance, as opposed to dismissive defiance, should be seen as something that works, as democratically healthy (see Chapter 9).

Criminologists may feel discomfort at this idea because they remember the saying of Daniel Drew, a robber baron of Wall Street in the 1880s: 'Law is like a cobweb: it's made for flies and the small kind of insects, so to speak, but lets the big bumblebee break through. When technicalities of the law stood in my way, I have always been able to brush them aside easy as anything' (Sutherland 1983: 57).

Part of the idea of the Ayres and Braithwaite (1992) enforcement pyramid is to make a web of regulation so soft at the base of the pyramid that both the bumblebees and the flies can break out of it to escalate the contest. But ultimately at the peak of the pyramid there is a web of controls so strong even the biggest bumblebee, even presidents of great corporations and great nations must submit to it.

Webs of capacity, in contrast, must be safety nets. At the base of the pyramid they must be strong enough so no one falls through them. No one misses the opportunity for a basic education to build their strengths, for example. But not everyone may be singled out for praise when they use that education to build a special strength. Not everyone will have further strength rewarded with further resources and further education. Not everyone will win an academy award.

Strengths-based pyramids are also different from regulatory pyramids in that they weave a tapestry through time. We get this idea from the motto of the Live Oak Regenerative Community of nursing home care: 'Live in the present, draw from the past and prepare for the future' (Barkan 2003: 213).[2] Healthy ageing means regenerative care by building on the webs of the past, using webs of support in the present and constructing new webs of capacity into the future (as in a 90-year-old learning to use the Internet for the first time). Peter Reddy (2006) has also picked up this regenerative theme in his work on peace-building. Peace-building might be similarly conceived as regenerative – weaving a tapestry through time. Peace-building that regenerates relationships severed by war builds out from the webs presently surviving in islands of civility and constructs new webs of a future civil society.[3] It follows that webs of capacity aspire to a more holistic quality than webs of regulation. Webs of regulation are meant to just switch on until a problem is fixed and then switch off. Webs of capacity are meant to grow organically, weaving that tapestry of support through time. Through the weaving together of the tapestry, the whole becomes greater than the sum of the parts, growing like a flourishing organization.

In the long run we hypothesize that the most important thing regulators do is catalyse continuous improvement. The hypothesis of responsive regulatory theory is that a regulatory pyramid that creates a flexible space for innovation at the base of the pyramid will do better by continuous improvement than prescriptive command and control. Our new hypothesis is that a combination of a regulatory pyramid and a strengths-based pyramid (both for self-regulators and for public regulators) will do better still by continuous improvement.

The second contribution of this work is in seeing the pyramid as just a special case of the need for a multidimensional response based on a conversation with a complex situation to solve a problem or expand a strength. Both pyramids require nodal governance to enrol webs of actors and webs of mechanisms (Shearing and Wood 2003). Complex situations mostly will not yield to unidimensional responses such as applying a rule or a standard operating procedure. Enforcing a rule has a place in at least one of our two pyramids. Even there, it is a place that is presumptively subsequent (higher in the pyramid) to collegial circles of conversation.

One worry that people have about the idea of a web of controls organized into a progressively more interventionist pyramid is that it will tangle and constrain our liberty in its web. Yet we saw in Chapter 3 that it is a contingent matter whether webs of discipline work to constrain freedom or to enable it. Webs can control those who crush freedom. We need a normative theory, such as the republican theory of freedom as non-domination, to guide the design of the strands of regulatory webs (Braithwaite and Pettit 1990; Pettit 1997). But the idea of linking a strengths-based pyramid to a networked enforcement pyramid is also a check on tyranny by the enforcement pyramid. By building strength, we build capability to resist domination.

We have discerned five critical steps in the governance of matters such as health or social care:

- *Step 1*. Understand the historical dynamics of webs of explanation as best we can.
- *Step 2*. Understand what is too complex for us to understand well, yet too important to leave ungoverned.
- *Step 3*. Be prepared with responsive pyramids specifically designed for problems known to emerge unpredictably but commonly (for example, riots).
- *Step 4*. Understand how to clinically construct multidimensionality in our response to multiple root causes by networking up through multiple layers of regulatory capacity. When 'sense–categorize–respond' fails because the category is wrong, have options in the pyramid that 'probe–sense–respond' and/or 'act–sense–respond'.
- *Step 5*. Understand how to network to expand strengths.

REGENERATIVE CARE, REGENERATIVE POLITICS

A normative problem with responsive regulation theory has been that while it informs a progressive politics of checking abuse of power, it has been an impoverished theory of how to build power among those who lack it. Linking it to restorative justice in *Restorative Justice and Responsive Regulation* (Braithwaite 2002a) was certainly a step in this direction. Regulation for regeneration seems a bigger step to tapping a life-cycle politics of structural transformation.

The reader might remember that an initial motivation in our choice of topic was that nursing home residents, as the most challenging subjects to empower through either exit or voice, seemed a least likely case of empowerment. When we started the research, however, we did not realize that aged care and social care staff are the most disadvantaged fraction of the workforce and that they are among the most massive workforces of the service economy (2 million workers in US nursing homes alone – excluding assisted living and community care workers). They are a workforce oppressed by the lowest pay in the legal economy, extraordinary conditions of discipline (as documented in Chapter 3) that make Foucault's discipline of factory work seem benign, high-risk work especially as a result of lifting and slipping, all compounded by sex and racial discrimination in a workforce where white males are a small minority, especially at the bottom of the heap (Diamond 1992). Many of these deficits are compounded by unusual unpleasantness – slips that are in human faeces, racial discrimination communicated as explicit abuse and ugly degradation by depressed aged who inflict their own suffering upon the only easy targets close at hand.

The first point toward a regenerative politics of the nursing home workforce is understanding that the disciplinary society that so oppresses both residents and staff is not what is best for residents. Hence the conditions for liberation of nursing home residents are also conditions for liberation of staff. Even key facets of discipline that were thought to make life easier for staff, like tying up residents who were proving difficult or doping depressed residents with barbiturates rather than treating their depression, have now been shown empirically to make life harsher for staff. When underlying depression or other root causes of behaviour management problems are addressed instead of disciplined, staff have to deal with less cantankerous people; demands on their time go down. This kind of liberating de-disciplining of aged care is not a pipe dream. In some major ways, including reduced use of physical restraint and more energetic treatment of depression, there has already been substantial de-disciplining during the lifetime of this research project.

A structurally more profound way in which this has been happening in all three countries has been a large shift of the society's aged care resources from nursing homes to community care and integrated retirement community clusters. In retirement communities most living is fairly independent yet nursing home beds are incorporated into the design. This radical restructuring of aged care is actually happening because the state correctly sees it in the short term as reducing public spending by shifting burdens of care from the state back to families.[4] It is these developments that allow us to see a bowls competition between aged care homes in our town today, something we did not have at the beginning of this project.

One might say community care is hardly in the interests of workers; it means fewer aged care jobs. History suggests in the long run this may be otherwise.[5] Remember that the nursing home itself was invented as a cheaper and less institutional form of care than geriatric wards of hospitals. While it still is, scandals, advocacy and the regulatory state have combined over the decades to demand higher standards of nursing homes. Moreover, demand to alleviate burdens of care in the community by creating more nursing home beds exploded in the second half of the twentieth century. The final legacy of the welfare state and the regulatory state was a nursing home sector of aged care that employed many more people than geriatric wards ever did. This is also likely to be the long-run upshot of the explosion of community care and social care residential homes. Moreover, at the very bottom of the aged care job market, opportunities are already greatly expanded by the restructuring. Consider domestic cleaning. It takes a lot more state-subsidized cleaning jobs to assist a hundred wheelchair aged to live at home than it does to clean one institution where they all live together.

Just as the aged control their own lives much more in their own home, likewise the care staff of community care are more their own bosses than in institutional work. There is not much choice but to evaluate their work in a rather customer-centred way, as by satisfaction surveys, and by completed care plans that are initialled by the consumer who is the only one in a position to observe the care being delivered, as opposed to initialled by a charge nurse. In turn this should mean that the frail aged have to be helped to understand their care plan. Palm pilot monitoring of care delivery also has the potential for large-print consumer-friendly printouts of care delivered to be initialled, combined with the potential of simultaneous dispatch of electronic reports to the computers of relatives to get them more engaged with the content and delivery of the care plan.

The evidence is now strong that more staff,[6] with higher skill levels[7] and lower turnover,[8] improves quality in aged care. There can be no doubt that it is long-term economically rational for us to pay more taxes or more aged care insurance premiums to pay for more staff to care for us when we are old. It is even intergenerationally rational, because while we suffer more taxes to buy staff support for our parents, our children will pay us back even more through their taxes because each generation will live longer than their parents. Sadly though, people are not long-run economically rational; they have a shorter time horizon. We prefer to spend our money on a comfortable single-occupancy hotel room today and look forward when we are 90 to a run-down multiple-occupancy room sharing every hour of the day with someone we do not know. Even so, we can expect the public sphere to continue to get progressively a little more economically rational over time; in future decades, as in past decades, gradually increasing the amounts we as a society are willing to invest in aged care staff. So aged care jobs as a proportion of the workforce will continue to expand.

We know not only that more skilled staff are needed to improve quality of care, but that there is a massive skills shortage, especially with nurses, in all three of our countries, indeed in most developed economies. This is why we see such large numbers of aged care nurses arriving on our shores from places like the Philippines. Beyond plucking desperately needed nurses away from poor countries, our purported solution to this problem is to have our universities train more graduate nurses. The trouble today is that not enough of our young people want to train as nurses. The Y generation are not the Florence Nightingales that their mothers and grandmothers were. Believe it or not, when they visit their grandmother in the nursing home, they decide gerontological nursing is the last thing they would like to do with their life!

The solution has to be a radical restructure of the health, aged care and social care workforces. Some Northern European societies such as Sweden have found a kind of solution in high-quality, comparatively well-paid cadres of middle-aged women returning to part-time paid caring work after years of unpaid care in families. This may not be a robust solution for a future in which there are fewer Florence Nightingales to start with, and fewer women of any kind who suspend full-time work for a long period while they raise children.

For a nation like the United States, the solution must surely lie in a redemptive politics for the feminized working poor of the lower reaches of its massive aged and social care workforce. Crudely, this means loosening our commitment to solving the problem through middle-class white college graduates following the Florence Nightingale trajectory into care for the aged. It means creating totally new career trajectories for underclass Americans, male and female, to move from unemployment, from casual low pay in jobs such as fast food or supermarkets, from disappearing factory jobs, to unskilled aged care jobs that provide a variety of career development trajectories. The most important of these would be to higher levels of nursing skill, but also trajectories to activities professionalism, social work, dietary and hospitality professionalism, physical therapy, occupational therapy, and so on.

This would require a more modularized model for the development of professional skill. Poor black mothers in their thirties with children to feed cannot drop out of those responsibilities to study nursing at college for a few years. They could move from base-level skill development from episodic workplace in-service training to publicly supported short courses that run for blocks of weeks rather than years. Each one of these short-course completions can bestow a new module of professional credentialing to do a new set of more highly skilled tasks in aged care – from managing the diet calculations for diabetic meals, up to managing the administration of medication (something that has already been devolved in the US from registered nurses to Licensed Practical Nurses with one or two years of training), and beyond to higher skill tasks. Again, this is not a fanciful idea; already in all three of our countries there exist labour market programs that are being used to create more modularized skill-based trajectories. In

Australia they seem to be working to a degree in reducing turnover in the aged care workforce. What we advocate is a more concerted marriage of public policy to govern aged care skill sets and public investment in labour market programs to tackle unemployment and the skill deficits of the least skilled in the economy.

It is not inevitable that lifetime professionalism, gradually renewed into new skills through fresh modular training challenges throughout the life course, would be an inferior professionalism. Indeed, for the poor it might mean training that is more highly motivated because it is purposively selected to move into a specific form of more skilled work. The poor may target this as of immediate interest to them in delivering a higher pay cheque upon graduation from the module. It is far from true that vocational training integrated with work experience in the field is inferior. Skills are not inferior when updated with knowledge of the evidence base that applies to their effective delivery near the time when this evidence will be put to use. Grol's (2001: 2580–81) review on the effectiveness of health professional development suggests that interactive, self-directed, problem-based, port-folio learning may be more effective than classic education delivery.

Redemptive aged care might make the frail aged agents of the skill upgrading needed for their own regeneration. A central part of a labour market reform package for aged and social care could be to educate the elderly (and their families) to encourage their carers in their daily interac-tions to develop their skill levels (for the sake of the elders, and for the sake of the families of the care workers). This means restoring the dignity of elders as life-course mentors, as respected experts in workforce and family trajectories in which they have the wisdom of experience.

As discussed earlier, regenerative care means institutionalizing this in many ways: having students who are learning German at school practise conversation with German-speaking elders, making it part of the education of all children to provide some voluntary care for an aged person who in turn is given the obligation of mentoring and educating the child through an oral history of what life was like in their town, their school, 70 years ago, or what life was like in a faraway concentration camp 70 years ago. An increasingly popular outing for Australian nursing homes is bus trips to schools for oral history encounters. In high school media courses as well, because adolescents gravitate toward filmmaking about the lives of young people, an assignment can ask them to capture on film the world through the eyes of an elder. To get a feel for the extent to which this is hap-pening around the world, you can go to the Generations United website (www.gu.org).

Giving, receiving and repaying are a crucial mark of personhood (Shield 1988: 215). By creating expectations that part of the resident role is to mentor and encourage the staff, we begin to solve two problems together – the problem that carers for the aged get less thanks than other kinds of workers, and the problem that nursing home residents are treated as less than full persons because they are not expected to do emotional work. There are many ways of fostering this, such as access to simple compliment cards and a standing agenda item to invite compliments for inclusion in residents' council minutes.

Psychologists have provided us with a strong evidence base that one of the best ways of transcending one's own adversity is to help others transcend their's (Seligman 2002). Parents experience this regularly with children: helping their children overcome fear in a situation is one of the best ways of dealing with their own fear; helping them deal with a disappointment or grief helps them to come to terms with their own disappointment or grief. More recently, some of the best criminology has supplied the same lesson. Maruna (2001) found that serious criminals who 'make good' find redemptive scripts to 'restory' their lives. Empirically, Maruna found that one of the best ways of discovering their own redemptive scripts is by helping younger criminals avoid the pitfalls they walked into by failing to take earlier trajectories out of their criminal careers.

Other advantages flow from residents and care assistants feeling obligations to empower each other. Residents can ask for help to learn how to do things for themselves so they can become less of a burden. Staff can shift their mission from 'doing for' (care) and 'doing to' (discipline), to 'doing with' (facilitating self-empowerment). Ageing that is interactive and facilitative will be active, and therefore regenerative. Obversely, there is evidence that care staff engender atrophy by rewarding dependency of elders (Baltes and Lascomb 1975; Barton et al. 1980; Birren and Renner 1980). There is also evidence that empowering the lowest level of care staff alongside more senior staff in care planning with residents reduces turnover of care assistants (Banaszak-Holl and Hines 1996; Waxman et al. 1984).

This is the great strength-building opportunity of the aged care work of regulatory capitalism that was not present in the factory work at the bottom of the class structure of industrial capitalism. It is that possibility of mutuality in regeneration. On the assembly line, careful work was directed at an inanimate object. In the nursing home, caring work is shared with a suffering, needy subject. It is possible for the one to see themselves as helping the other to find new joys and fulfilments on the rite of passage from old age to death (such as learning how to email distant loved ones). It is possible for the elder to see themselves as helping the carer on a rite of passage from poverty to a decent, secure existence for them and their family.

Redistributional politics certainly needs to be macro-structural. Indeed, what we are considering here is a macro restructuring of a huge sector of the labour market that is emerging from industrial capitalism as larger than the factory sector. Yet what we have discovered through the long empirical journey of this project is that we must not neglect the micro, for transformation can be micro–macro, starting with micro interactions between an elder once viewed as on the scrapheap of industrial capitalism and a young black woman once viewed as welfare dependent. We can find the best sites of micro-regenerative politics by finding spaces where highly disempowered and discarded fractions of capitalist societies have historically come together to afflict misery one on the other, then restructuring the politics of these spaces in a regenerative way.[9] Labour market regulation as well as health and other forms of regulation that are strengths based as well as risk based supply the levers of that transformation.

Nursing homes and places like them such as institutions for the disabled are not the only such sites. Prisons bring together over 2 million poor Americans with about that number of correctional officers and almost that number of other criminal justice officials whose job it is to keep them there, not to mention larger numbers of private security people. Redemptive, regenerative imprisonment, such as we see in the LIFERS (2004) project at the Graterford Penitentiary near Philadelphia, where lifers and justice workers are developing together promising strategies to transform the culture of street crime, to move from the current rehabilitation sequence of:

conviction → rehabilitation → replacement on the street,

to

conviction → personal transformation → transformation of the culture of street crime.

The idea is that long-term prisoners with street credibility are released on parole to work with young people on their old block to broker peace agreements between gangs and deploy other strategies to transform the culture of street crime.

There are a multitude of such contexts that are idiosyncratic and more micro: the citizens of native American reservations and the low-level civil servants who get postings as welfare officials in what to them are unattractive locations such as the Arizona desert, or as career casino regulators posted to a reservation casino. Globally, the most important context of such regenerative labour market transformation could be among the large numbers of mostly poor Americans who seek employment as privates and non-commissioned officers in the military. In the era of the 'networked warrior', the 'strategic corporal' (Liddy 2004: 139) can be a powerful street-level bureaucrat. Instead of these disadvantaged Americans being agents of the domination of weaker peoples, as we saw in Somalia, Iraq and many other parts of the globe, a regenerative vision is of the military as partners in multidimensional peace operations that create opportunities for experienced peacekeepers (military or police) to pursue career trajectories not only in military and police peace-building, but in development assistance as well. In Australia's region we are seeing more of this: military and police 'leaving a piece of their heart behind'[10] with a war-torn people and returning later in their lives to help them with development.

CONCLUSION

This has been a story about regulatory flux and change from the 1980s to the present. Throughout this period there has been a relentless drive toward more, not less, regulation of nursing homes in all three countries. The response to this has been that small and less capable homes have disappeared, inspectors have sought innovative and creative ways of trying to ensure that nursing homes are better places than they used to be, and regulators have grappled with the nightmare of bad publicity, strong lobbying by the industry and advocacy groups and political edicts. Today the government is a regulator, the firm is a regulator, the profession is a regulator and we are embattled by regulatory oversight; the most widespread response is regulatory ritualism. Sometimes by design, and sometimes unwittingly, inspectors, nursing home management and care staff engage in the game of regulatory ritual in order to 'get by' in the regulatory society. The outcome is less than desirable care for the frail elderly.

We have argued that there are ways forward; ways based on our findings from a multi-country study spanning the 1980s, 1990s and 2000s that is both qualitative and quantitative. One is to craft a new regulatory environment that has two complementary models – a regulatory model backed by enforcement and a strengths-based model backed by rewards. The former is designed to ensure that the standard of care in nursing home reaches the minimum standard set by the regulator; the latter is designed to build out from micro and macro strengths within nursing homes and the industry to lift the standard of care beyond the minimum to continuously higher levels.

Our work has identified many strategies that are used to encourage, educate, goad and threaten managers to improve (see Table 10.1). Four ingredients seem essential to transforming the quality of care. The first is that the regulator has to be prepared to develop a framework that is not so prescriptive and detailed that it slides into ritualistic inspection.

Second, inspectors must be sophisticated strengths-based professionals who identify real problems and promote investigation of them through to their root causes. When inspectors find serious problems they must be prepared to make tough but fair assessments (and the regulatory leadership must support them); equally they must reward and encourage those managers who pursue continuous improvement in the standard of care. Third, nursing home managers must be persuaded to be dissatisfied with anything less than continuous improvement. When they are not so persuaded, inspectors need to either flip them into caring or incapacitate them. The industry should want to embrace root cause analyses, triple root learning from them and building an evidence base that shapes the practice of care staff. Fourth, inspectors, managers and advocates all do better in a regulatory environment that recognizes their professionalism and specialist expertise and builds on those strengths to secure improving standards.

Pseudo-scientific method that legitimates poor outcomes, careerist political opportunism and cheap publicity stunts by advocates are all less rewarding when the regulatory culture is about listening for ideas that improve as opposed to ritualism. In such a culture, careers, scientific accolades and other good things flow to those who make the most useful contributions to the conversation. Quality of care in this study is demonstrably a street-level accomplishment of nursing home communities and inspectors. Yet street-level accomplishment is endemically at risk of being soured to ritualism by moves at the level of national politics. Even so, poisonous national politics can be nodally governed by a National Citizens' Coalition for Nursing Home Reform.

The two groups who are the weakest in the industry need to be empowered – care staff and residents. Care staff provide the day-to-day environment in which the frail elderly move from life to death. It is they who make the difference in the care provided on the ground. If they are to be active participants in continuous improvement, home owners and managers need to provide the kind of work environment that builds a committed workforce. Their staff require access to the opportunities and skills that would genuinely enable them to be emancipated participants in the nursing home's vision of high quality social care as well as being advocates for the frail elderly. Finally, of course, residents need to be treated with respect and dignity, to be given the opportunity to impart their wisdom and their experience, and to be able to participate in the decisions that the industry tends to make for them rather than with them.

Our method for this project was to select a site of maximum disempowerment to test theories of regulatory empowerment on a least likely case. Through a micro method of regenerative politics we have shown that it is possible, but extremely difficult, to empower the least empowered. The test is whether policy makers can embrace the challenge of a new wave of regulatory reform that marries regulatory institutions to developmental institutions, that finds a path to build strength in the midst of seemingly inexorable enfeeblement.

NOTES

1. Or as Majone (1986) puts it, 'colleagium' to manage complexity by mutual adjustment as opposed to hierarchy. Day and Klein (1987c: 249) have provided one of the most eloquent statements of the conversational perspective: 'The emphasis of public policy has been to respond to complexity by setting up new institutions of accountability . . . this may, in turn, bring about excessive complexity in the machinery of accountability and at the same time create dead ends. So, why not concentrate less on formal links or institutions and engage more in a civic dialogue to recreate at least something of the high visibility and directness of the face to face accountability.'
2. Eaton's (2000) study concluded that while the overwhelming majority of US nursing homes she studied fitted a 'traditional law service quality' model, one-fifth fitted a 'regenerative community' model. This pretty much fits the picture we saw of US nursing homes. In traditional facilities residents spent at least 91 of 112 waking hours a week doing nothing whatsoever.
3. Reddy argues that a sense in which regeneration is a more attractive ideal than restoration is that restoration to a state of domination and disempowerment that existed before a war can be an impoverished ideal. Even for children it might be argued that regeneration is also a more attractive ideal than development. Child development is about preventing children from slipping back at times because of a setback in their emotional intelligence due to a major failure in their young life, a feeling of rejection or an endogenous change such as puberty. Child development on this analysis is mostly about the child regenerating by recovering from the setback and returning to build on their pre-puberty, pre-setback strengths.
4. There are estimated to be 5 million unpaid carers in England (Commission for Social Care Inspection 2005b: 2).
5. A combination of demographic and health factors makes this unlikely – an ageing population in most Western countries, a low birth rate with increasing numbers of women choosing not to have any children, and longevity resulting in more elderly people requiring social care for dementia and Alzheimer's disease.
6. Higher staffing levels have been associated with outcomes such as improvements in mortality rates, physical functioning, antibiotic use, pressure sores, catheterization rates, hospitalization rates, weight loss and dehydration (see Abt Associates, Inc. 2001; Cotton 1993; Eaton 2000; Harrington 2004; Harrington et al. 2000b; Institute of Medicine 1996, 2001; Schnelle et al. 2003b; Wells 2004).
7. Higher skill levels that in most studies predict better quality of care include higher formal professional qualifications among the care staff, greater exposure to inservice training and greater management skill on the part of the CEO of the home (see Gibbs and Sinclair 1991; Pearson et al. 1991; Proctor et al. 1999; Zhang and Grabowski 2004).
8. Burnfeind and O'Connor (1992), Makkai and Braithwaite (1993a: 85), Harrington (1996: 466), Christensen and Beaver (1996), Singh et al. (1996), Castle (2001), Anderson et al. (2003) and Rantz et al. (2003) found an association between high turnover and poorer resident care outcomes or deficiencies.
9. Some of the continuous quality improvement work in nursing homes now targets work-life quality through a variety of measures – turnover, injuries, surveys of staff

satisfaction with various dimensions of the job, and the rather interesting indirect measure of plotting decline in numbers of days of sick leave.

10. Interview with Sergeant Bob Sobey, an Australian peacekeeper who returned after a stint of peacekeeping in Guadalcanal with dozens of Australian scouts to rebuild a school there. John Braithwaite's next research project is on regenerative peacekeeping with Hilary Charlesworth and Leah Dunn.

References

Aaronson, W.E., J.S. Zinn and M.D. Rosko (1994), 'Do for-profit and not-for-profit nursing homes behave differently?', *The Gerontologist*, **34** (6), 775–86.

Abbey, J., N. Piller, A. De Bellis, A. Esterman, D. Parker, L. Giles and B. Lowcay (2004), 'The Abbey Pain Scale: a 1-minute numerical indicator for people with end-stage dementia', *International Journal of Palliative Nursing*, **10** (1), 6–13.

Abt Associates, Inc. (2001), *Appropriateness of Minimum Staffing Ratios in Nursing Homes. Phase II Final Report to the Centers for Medicare and Medicaid Services*, Cambridge, MA: Abt Associates, Inc.

Aged Care Standards and Accreditation Agency (2004–05), *Annual Report 2004–05*, Parramatta: Aged Care Standards and Accreditation Agency.

Aged Care Standards and Accreditation Agency (2005), *Results and Processes in Relation to the Expected Outcomes of the Accreditation Standards*, Parramatta: Aged Care Standards and Accreditation Agency.

Ahmed, E. and J. Braithwaite (2007), 'Shame, pride and workplace bullying', in Susanne Karstedt, Ian Loader and Heather Strang (eds), *Emotions, Crime and Justice*, Oxford: Hart Publishing.

Ahmed, Eliza, Nathan Harris, John Braithwaite and Valerie Braithwaite (2001), *Shame Management through Reintegration*, Cambridge: Cambridge University Press.

American Association of Homes for the Aging (1991), *ANHA Questionnaire on OBRA Surveys*, Washington, DC: American Association of Homes for the Aging.

Anderson, G.F., P.S. Hussey, B.K. Frogner and H.R. Waters (2005), 'Health spending in the United States and the rest of the industrialized world', *Health Affairs*, **24** (4), 903–14.

Anderson, R.A., L.M. Issel and R.R. McDaniel (2003), 'Nursing homes as complex adaptive systems: relationship between management practice and resident outcomes', *Nursing Research*, **52** (1), 12–21.

Arai, Yumiko (1992), 'Implementation of the 1984 Registered Homes Act: quality assurance for care of the elderly in private nursing homes', dissertation for Master of Arts in Health Service Studies, Leeds University.

Auditor-General (1981), *Efficiency Audit: Commonwealth Administration of Nursing Home Programs*, Canberra: Auditor-General.

Australian National Audit Office (2003), *Managing Residential Aged Care Accreditation: The Aged Care Standards and Accreditation Agency Ltd, Audit Report No. 42, 2002–2003*, Canberra: Australian National Audit Office.

Axelrod, Robert M. (1984), *The Evolution of Cooperation*, New York: Basic Books.

Ayres, Ian and John Braithwaite (1992), *Responsive Regulation: Transcending the Deregulation Debate*, New York: Oxford University Press.

Bagshaw, M. and M. Adams (1986), 'Nursing home nurses' attitudes, empathy, and ideologic orientation', *International Journal on Aging and Human Development*, **22** (3), 235–46.

Baldwin, R. and K. Hawkins (1984), 'Discretionary justice: Davis reconsidered', *Public Law*, **1984**, 570–99.

Baltes, M.M. and S.L. Lascomb (1975), 'Creating a healthy institutional environment: the nurse as change agent', *International Journal of Nursing Studies*, **12**, 5–12.

Banaszak-Holl, J. and M.A. Hines (1996), 'Factors associated with nursing home staff turnover', *The Gerontologist*, **36**, 512–17.

Bardach, Eugene and Robert A. Kagan (1982), *Going by the Book: The Problem of Regulatory Unreasonableness*, Philadelphia, PA: Temple University Press.

Barkan, B. (2003), 'The Live Oak Regenerative Community: championing a culture of hope and meaning', *Journal of Social Work in Long-Term Care*, **2** (1/2), 197–221.

Barney, J.L. (1974), 'Community presence as a key to quality of life in nursing homes', *American Journal of Public Health*, **64** (3), 265–8.

Barton, E.M., M.M. Baltes and M.J. Orzech (1980), 'Etiology of dependence in older nursing home residents during morning care: the role of staff behavior', *Journal of Personality and Social Psychology*, **38** (3), 423–30.

Bates-Jensen, B.M., M. Cadogan, D. Osterweil, L. Levy-Storms, J. Jorge, N. Al-Samarrai, V. Grbic and J.F. Schnelle (2003), 'The Minimum Data Set Pressure Ulcer Indicator: does it reflect differences in care processes related to pressure ulcer prevention and treatment in nursing homes?', *Journal of the American Geriatrics Society*, **51** (9), 1203–12.

Bauman, Zygmunt (1982), *Memories of Class: The Pre-history and Afterlife of Class*, London: Routledge & Kegan Paul.

Baumrind, D. (1973), 'The development of instrumental competence through socialization', in A.D. Pick (ed.), *Minnesota Symposium of Motivation*, vol. 7, Minneapolis, MN: University of Minnesota Press.

Bennett, J. (1986), *Private Nursing Homes: An Exploratory Study into the Contribution They Make to Long Stay Care of the Elderly in the Brighton Health District*, Brighton: Brighton Health Authority.

Bennett, J. (1987), 'Who inspects the inspectors?', *Nursing Times*, **16** (83), 32–6.

Bentham, Jeremy (1825), *The Rationale of Reward*, London: John & H.L. Hunt.

Bentham, Jeremy (1977), *Collected Works of Jeremy Bentham: Principles of Legislation: A Comment on the Commentaries and a Fragment on Government*, eds J.H. Burns and H.L.A. Hart, London: Athlone Press, University of London.

Berman, R.U., A.S. Weiner and G.S. Fishman (1986), 'Yiddish: it's more than a language: in-service training for staff of a Jewish home for the aged', *Journal of Jewish Communal Service*, **62** (4), 328–34.

Bernstein, Marver H. (1955), *Regulating Business by Independent Commission*, Princeton, NJ: Princeton University Press.

Binns, G.S. (1991), 'The relationship among quality, cost and market share in hospitals', *Topics in Health Care Financing*, **18** (2), 21–32.

Birren, J.E. and J. Renner (1980), 'Concepts and issues of mental health and ageing', in J.E. Birren and R.B. Sloan (eds), *Handbook of Mental Health and Ageing*, Englewood Cliffs, NJ: Prentice-Hall.

Black, Julia (1997), *Rules and Regulators*, Oxford: Clarendon Press.

Black, J. (2000), 'Proceduralizing regulation: part I', *Oxford Journal of Legal Studies*, **20** (4), 597–614.

Black, J. (2001), 'Proceduralizing regulation: part II', *Oxford Journal of Legal Studies*, **21** (1), 33–58.

Blum, S.R. and E. Wadleigh (1983), *The Bureaucracy of Care: Continuing Policy Issues for Nursing Home Services and Regulation*, Sacramento, CA: Commission on California State Government Organization and Economy.

Boggiano, A.K., M. Barrett, A.W. Weiher, G.H. McLelland and C.M. Lusk (1987), 'Use of the maximal-operant principle to motivate children's intrinsic interest', *Journal of Personality and Social Psychology*, **53**, 866–79.

Bond, J., S. Bond, C. Donaldson, B. Gregson and A. Atkinson (1989), *Evaluation of Continuing-Care Accommodation for Elderly People, Health Care Research Unit Report 38*, vol. 7, Newcastle: University of Newcastle upon Tyne.

Borup, J.H. (1983), 'Relocation mortality research: assessment, reply and the need to refocus on the issues', *The Gerontologist*, **23**, 235–42.

Bourestom, N. and L. Pastalan (1981), 'The effects of relocation on the elderly: a reply to Borup, J.H., Gallego, D.T. & Heffernan, P.G.', *The Gerontologist*, **21**, 4–7.

Bowman, C.E. (1997), 'Institutional care in the community: from chaos to integration of health and social care', *Reviews in Clinical Gerontology*, **7**, 189–91.

Brady, J.G. (2001), 'Long-term care under fire: a case for rational enforcement', *Journal of Contemporary Health Law and Policy*, **18**, 1–52.

Braithwaite, J. (1982), 'Enforced self-regulation: a new strategy for corporate crime control', *Michigan Law Review*, **80**, 1466–507.

Braithwaite, John (1984), *Corporate Crime in the Pharmaceutical Industry*, London: Routledge & Kegan Paul.

Braithwaite, John (1985), *To Punish or Persuade: Enforcement of Coal Mine Safety*, Albany, NY: State University of New York Press.

Braithwaite, John (1989), *Crime, Shame and Reintegration*, Cambridge: Cambridge University Press.

Braithwaite, J. (1993), 'Beyond positivism: learning from contextual integrated strategies', *Journal of Research in Crime and Delinquency*, **30**, 383–99.

Braithwaite, John (1994), 'The nursing home industry', in M. Tonry and A.J. Reiss (eds), 'Beyond the law: crime in complex organizations', *Crime and Justice: A Review of Research*, **18**, 11–54.

Braithwaite, John (2002a), *Restorative Justice and Responsive Regulation*, New York: Oxford University Press.

Braithwaite, J. (2002b), 'Rules and principles: a theory of legal certainty', *Australian Journal of Legal Philsophy*, **27**, 47–82.

Braithwaite, J. (2002c), 'Rewards and regulation', *Journal of Law and Society*, **29** (1), 12–26.

Braithwaite, J. (2005a), 'Neoliberalism or regulatory capitalism?', Regulatory Institutions Network Working Paper, Australian National University.

Braithwaite, John (2005b), *Markets in Vice, Markets in Virtue*, Oxford, New York and Sydney: Federation Press.

Braithwaite, J. (2006), 'Accountability and responsibility through restorative justice', in M. Dowdle (ed.), *Public Accountability: Designs, Dilemmas and Experiences*, Cambridge, Cambridge University Press.

Braithwaite, J. and V. Braithwaite (1995), 'The politics of legalism: rules versus standards in nursing-home regulation', *Social and Legal Studies*, **4**, 307–41.

Braithwaite, John and Peter Drahos (2000), *Global Business Regulation*, Cambridge: Cambridge University Press.

Braithwaite, J. and T. Makkai (1991), 'Testing an expected utility model of corporate deterrence', *Law and Society Review*, **28**, 7–40.

Braithwaite, J. and T. Makkai (1993), 'Can resident-centred inspection of nursing homes work with very sick residents?', *Health Policy*, **24**, 19–33.

Braithwaite, J. and T. Makkai (1994), 'Trust and compliance', *Policing and Society*, **4**, 1–12.

Braithwaite, John and Philip Pettit (1990), *Not Just Deserts: A Republican Theory of Criminal Justice*, Oxford: Oxford University Press.

Braithwaite, J., V. Braithwaite, D. Gibson, M. Landau and T. Makkai (1991), *The Reliability and Validity of Nursing Home Standards*, Canberra: Department of Health, Housing and Community Services.

Braithwaite, J., T. Makkai, V. Braithwaite, D. Gibson and D. Ermann (1990), *The Contribution of the Standard Monitoring Process to the Quality of Nursing Home Life: A Preliminary Report*, Canberra: Department of Community Services and Health.

Braithwaite, J., T. Makkai, V. Braithwaite and D. Gibson (1992), *Raising the Standard: Resident Centred Nursing Home Regulation in Australia*, Canberra: Department of Health, Housing, and Community Services.

Braithwaite, Valerie (1990), *Bound to Care*, Sydney: Allen & Unwin.

Braithwaite, V. (1995), 'Games of engagement: postures within the regulatory community', *Law and Policy*, **17**, 225–55.

Braithwaite, V. (2003), 'Dancing with tax authorities: motivational postures and non-compliant actions', in Valerie Braithwaite (ed.), *Taxing Democracy: Understanding Tax Avoidance and Evasion*, Aldershot: Ashgate, pp. 15–40.

Braithwaite, Valerie (forthcoming), *Defiance in Taxation and Governance*, Cheltenham, UK and Northampton, MA: Edward Elgar.

Braithwaite, V., J. Braithwaite, D. Gibson and T. Makkai (1994), 'Regulatory styles, motivational postures and nursing home compliance', *Law and Policy*, **16**, 363–94.

Braithwaite, V., K. Murphy and M. Rinehart (2007), 'Taxation threat, motivational postures and responsive regulation', *Law and Policy*, **29** (1), 137–58.

Brehm, Sharon S. and Jack W. Brehm (1981), *Psychological Reactance: A Theory of Freedom and Control*, New York: Academic Press.

Brennan, Geoffrey and Philip Pettit (2004), *The Economy of Esteem: An Essay on Civil and Political Society*, Oxford: Oxford University Press.

Brennan, Thomas A. and Donald M. Berwick (1996), *New Rules: Regulation, Markets and the Quality of American Health Care*, San Francisco, CA: Jossey-Bass.

Brennan, T.A., L.L. Leape, N.M. Laird, L. Hebert, A.R. Localio, A.G. Lawthers, J.P. Newhouse, P.C. Weiler and H.H. Hiatt (1991), 'Incidence of adverse events and negligence in hospitalized patients', *New England Journal of Medicine*, **324**, 370–76.

Brooke Ross, R. (1987), *The Registered Homes Act 1984 and the Registered Homes Tribunal*, London: Social Care Association.

Brown, R.N. (1975), 'An appraisal of the nursing home enforcement process', *Arizona Law Review*, **17**, 304–56.

Burnfeind, J.D. and S.J. O'Connor (1992), 'Employee turnover and retention rates as predictors of nursing home code violations', paper presented to Annual Meeting of American Academy of Management, Las Vegas.

Butler, P.A. (1979), 'Assuring the quality of care and life in nursing homes: the dilemma of enforcement', *North Carolina Law Review*, **57**, 1317–82.

Cape, R.D.T. (1983), 'Freedom from restraint', *The Gerontologist*, **23**, 185–217.

Castells, Manuel (1996), *The Information Age: Economy, Society and Culture, Volume 1: The Rise of The Network Society*, Oxford: Blackwell.

Castle, N.G. (2001), 'Administrator turnover and quality of care in nursing homes', *The Gerontologist*, **41** (6), 757–67.

Castle, N.G. (2003), 'Providing outcomes information to nursing homes: can it improve quality of care?', *The Gerontologist*, **43** (4), 483–92.

Castle, N.G. (2004), 'Family satisfaction with nursing facility care', *International Journal for Quality in Health Care*, **16** (6), 483–9.

Castle, N.G. and V. Mor (1997), 'Physical restraints in nursing homes: a review of the literature since the Nursing Home Reform Act', *Medical Care Research and Review*, **55** (2), 139–70.

Centers for Medicare and Medicaid Services (2001), *Nursing Home Data Compendium 2001*, Baltimore, MD: Centers for Medicare and Medicaid Services, Department of Health and Human Services.

Centers for Medicare and Medicaid Services (2005), *Nursing Home Data Compendium 2005*, Baltimore, MD: Centers for Medicare and Medicaid Services, Department of Health and Human Services.

Cherry, R.L. (1993), 'Community presence and nursing home quality of care: the ombudsman as a complementary role', *Journal of Health and Social Behavior*, **34**, 336–45.

Cheyne, J.A. and R.H. Walters (1969), 'Intensity of punishment, timing of punishment, and cognitive structure as determinants of response inhibition', *Journal of Experimental Child Psychology*, **7**, 231–44.

Chou, S.-Y. (2002), 'Asymmetric information, ownership and quality of care: an empirical analysis of nursing homes', *Journal of Health Economics*, **21**, 293–311.

Christensen, C. and S. Beaver (1996), 'Correlation between administrator turnover and survey results', *Journal of Long-Term Care Administration*, **24**, 4–7.

Christie, Nils (1993), *Crime Control as Industry: Towards Gulags, Western Style?*, London: Routledge.

Coffee, J.C. (1981), 'No soul to damn: no body to kick: an unscandalised inquiry into the problem of corporate punishment', *Michigan Law Review*, **79**, 386–459.

Coglianese, C. and D. Lazer (2003), 'Management-based regulation: pre-scribing private management to achieve public goals', *Law and Society Review*, **37**, 691–730.

Cohen, J. (1986), 'The dynamics of "the revolving door" on the FCC', *American Journal of Political Science*, **30** (4), 689–708.

Commission for Social Care Inspection (CSCI) (2005a), *Annual Report and Accounts 2004–05*, London: The Stationery Office.

Commission for Social Care Inspection (CSCI) (2005b), *The State of Social Care in England 2004–05*, London: Commission for Social Care Inspection.

Commission for Social Care Inspection (CSCI) (2005c), *Social Services Performance Assessment Framework Indicators 2004–05*, London: Commission for Social Care Inspection.

Commonwealth/State Working Party on Nursing Home Standards (1987), *Living in a Nursing Home: Outcome Standard for Australian Nursing Homes*, Canberra: Australian Government Publishing Service.

Connolly, M.T. (2002), 'Federal law enforcement in long-term care', *Journal of Health Care Law and Policy*, **4** (2), 230.

Cotton, J. and J. Tuttle (1986), 'Employee turnover: a meta-analysis and review with implications for research', *Academy of Management Review*, **11**, 55–70.

Cotton, P. (1993), 'Nursing home research focus on outcomes may mean playing catch-up with regulation', *Journal of the American Medical Association*, **269** (18), 2337–8.

Cotton, P. and P.M. Hart (2003), 'Occupational wellbeing and performance: a review of organisational health research', *Australian Psychologist*, **38** (2), 118–27.

Curry, T.J. and B.W. Ratliff (1973), 'The effects of nursing home size on resident isolation and life satisfaction', *The Gerontologist*, **13**, 295–8.

Dalley, G., L. Unsworth, D. Keightley, M. Waller, T. Davies and R. Morton (2004), *How Do We Care?*, Newcastle: National Care Standards Commission.

Darton, R.A. (1987), 'Survey of residential and nursing homes in Canterbury and Thanet', unpublished paper, University of Kent.

Davis, A. (1987), *Managing to Care in the Regulation of Private Nursing Homes*, Hayle, Cornwall: Patten Press.

Day, P. (1988), 'The public regulation of private welfare – the case of resi-dential and nursing homes for the elderly', *The Political Quarterly*, **59** (1), 44–55.

Day, P. and R. Klein (1987a), 'Maintaining standards in the independent sector of health care', *British Medical Journal*, **290**, 1020–22.

Day, P. and R. Klein (1987b), 'The regulation of nursing homes: a comparative perspective', *The Milbank Quarterly*, **65** (3), 303–47.

Day, Patricia and Rudolf Klein (1987c), *Accountabilities: Five Public Services*, London: Tavistock.

Day, P. and R. Klein (1990), *Inspecting the Inspectorates: Services for the Elderly*, York: Joseph Rowntree Memorial Trust.

Day, P., R. Klein and S. Redmayne (1996), *Regulating Residential Care for Elderly People: Social Care Research Findings 78*, York: Joseph Rowntree Foundation.

Day, P., R. Klein and G. Tipping (1988), 'Inspecting for quality: services for the elderly', Bath Social Policy Papers, no. 12, University of Bath.

Deci, E.L., R.M. Ryan and R. Koestner (1999), 'A meta-analytic review of experiments examining the effects of extrinsic rewards on intrinsic motivation', *Psychological Bulletin*, **125** (6), 627–68.

Department of Health (1990), *Making Sense of Inspection: A Training Course for Registration and Inspection Staff*, London: HMSO.

Department of Health and Human Services, Office of the Inspector General (1996), 'Summary of IOG study of 19 survey directors', *Nursing Home Regulations Manual*, July, New York: Thompson, p. 22, table 400.

Diamond, Timothy (1992), *Making Gray Gold: Narratives of Nursing Home Care*, Chicago, IL and London: University of Chicago Press.

Dienstbier, R.A., D. Hillman, J. Lenhoff and M.C. Valkenaar (1975), 'An emotion-attribution approach to moral behavior: interfacing cognitive and avoidance theories of moral development', *Psychological Review*, **82**, 229–315.

Dingwell, R, J. Eekelaar and T. Murray (1983), *The Protection of Children: State Intervention and Family Life*, Oxford: Basil Blackwell.

Dix, T. and J.E. Grusec (1983), 'Parental influence techniques: an attributional analysis', *Child Development*, **54**, 645–52.

Doyle, M.W. and N. Sambanis (2000), 'International peacebuilding: a theoretical and quantitative analysis', *The American Political Science Review*, **94**, 779–801.

Drahos, P. (2004), 'Intellectual property and pharmaceutical markets: a nodal governance approach', *Temple Law Review*, **77**, 401–24.

Drahos, Peter with John Braithwaite (2003), *Information Feudalism*, New York: New Press.

Duffy, M., S. Bailey, B. Beck and D.G. Barker (1986), 'Preferences in nursing home design: a comparison of residents, administrators, and designers', *Environment and Behavior*, **18**, 246–57.

Durkheim, E. (1961), *Mural Education: A Study in the Theory and Application of the Sociology of Education*, trans. E.K. Wilson and H. Schnurer, New York: Free Press.

Eaton, S.C. (2000), 'Beyond "unloving care": linking human resource management and patient care quality in nursing homes', *International Journal of Human Resource Management*, **11** (3), 591–616.

Eckstein, H. (1975), 'Case study and theory in political science', in F. Greenstein and N. Polsby (eds), *Handbook of Political Science, Vol. 7: Strategies of Inquiry*, Reading, MA: Addison-Wesley.

Edelman, T. (1998), 'What happened to enforcement?', *Nursing Home Law Letter*, **1–2**, 1–46.

Epstein, A. (1998), 'Rolling down the runway: the challenges ahead for quality report cards', *Journal of the American Medical Association*, **279**, 1691–6.

Ermann, M.D. (1976), 'The social control of organizations in the health care area', *Milbank Memorial Fund Quarterly/Health and Society*, **53**, 167–83.

Evans, Harry (1926), *The American Poor Farm and its Inmates*, Mooseheart, IL: Loyal Order of Moose.

Evans, L.K. and N. Strumpf (1989), 'Tying down the elderly: a review of the literature on physical restraints', *Journal of the American Geriatrics Society*, **37**, 65–74.

Evans, L.K. and N. Strumpf (1990), 'Myths about elderly restraint', *Image: Journal of Nursing Scholarship*, **22**, 124–8.

Fairbrother, G., K.L. Hanson, S. Friedman and G.C. Butts (1999), 'The impact of physician bonuses, enhanced fees, and feedback on childhood immunization coverage rates', *American Journal of Public Health*, **289**, 434–41.

Fairbrother, G., M.J. Siegel, S. Friedman, P.D. Kory and G.C. Butts (2001), 'Impact of financial incentives on documented immunization rates in the inner city: results of a randomized control trial', *Ambulatory Pediatrics*, **1**, 206–12.

Fairman, R. and C. Yapp (2005), 'Enforced self-regulation, prescription, and conceptions of compliance within small businesses: the impact of enforcement', *Law and Policy*, **27** (4), 491–519.

Farrington, D.P. and B.C. Welsh (2002), 'Family-based crime prevention', in Lawrence W. Sherman, D.P. Farrington, B.C. Welsh and D.L. MacKenzie (eds), *Evidence-Based Crime Prevention*, London: Routledge.

Faunce, T.A. and S.N. Bolsin (2004), 'Three Australian whistleblowing sagas: lessons for internal and external regulation', *Medical Journal of Australia*, **181**, 44–7.

Fawcett, G., D. Stonner and H. Zepelin (1980), 'Locus of control, perceived constraint and morale among institutionalized aged', *International Journal of Aging and Human Development*, **11**, 13–23.

Feeley, Malcolm (1979), *The Process is the Punishment*, New York: Russell Sage Foundation.

Feeley, M. (2002), 'Entrepreneurs of punishment: the legacy of privatization', *Punishment and Society*, **4**, 321–44.

Fine, M. (1999), *The Responsibility for Child and Aged Care: Shaping Policies for the Future*, Sydney: Social Policy Research Centre.

Fisse, Brent and John Braithwaite (1983), *The Impact of Publicity on Corporate Offenders*, Albany, NY: State University of New York Press.

Foucault, Michel (1977), *Discipline and Punish: The Birth of the Prison*, London: Peregrine Books.

Foucault, Michel (1984), *The History of Sexuality*, vol. 1, London: Peregrine Books.

Foucault, Michel (1991), 'Governmentality', in G. Burchell, C. Gordon and P. Miller (eds), *The Foucault Effect: Studies in Governmentality*, London: Harvester Wheatsheaf.

Gardiner, J. and K.L. Malec (1989), *Enforcement of Nursing Home Regulations: OBRA Plus Two, a Report to the US Senate Special Committee on Aging*, Chicago, IL: University of Illinois at Chicago, Office of Social Science Research.

Garland, David (1990), *Punishment and Modern Society: A Study in Social Theory*, Chicago, IL: University of Chicago Press.

Garrard, J., V. Chen and B. Dowd (1995), 'The impact of the 1987 federal regulations on the use of psychotropic drugs in Minnesota nursing homes', *American Journal of Public Health*, **85** (6), 771–6.

General Accounting Office (1987), *Medicare and Medicaid – Stronger Enforcement of Nursing Home Requirements Needed: Report to the Ranking Minority Member, Special Committee on Aging, US Senate*, Washington, DC: United States General Accounting Office.

Gibbs, I. and I. Sinclair (1991), *A Checklist Approach to the Inspection of Old People's Homes: Report to the Department of Health*, York: University of York.

Gibson, Diane (1998), *Aged Care: Old Policies, New Problems*, Melbourne: Cambridge University Press.

Giddens, Anthony (1976), *New Rules of Sociological Method*, London: Hutchinson.

Giles Report, Senate Select Committee on Private Hospitals and Nursing Homes (1985), *Private Nursing Homes in Australia: Their Conduct, Administration and Ownership*, Canberra: Australian Government Publishing Service.

Goldfield, N., C. Larsen and D. Roblin (1999), 'The content of report cards', *Joint Commission Journal of Quality Improvement*, **25**, 423–33.

Goldstein, H. (1979), 'Improving policing: a problem-oriented approach', *Crime and Delinquency*, **25**, 236–58.

Goodin, R. (1980), 'Making moral incentives pay', *Policy Sciences*, **12**, 131–45.

Gormley, W.T. (1979), 'A test of the revolving door hypothesis on the FCC', *American Journal of Political Science*, **27** (1), 86–105.

Grabosky, P. (1996), 'Regulation by reward: on the use of incentives as regulatory instruments', *Law and Policy*, **17** (3), 256–81.

Grabosky, Peter and John Braithwaite (1986), *Of Manners Gentle: Enforcement Strategies of Australian Business Regulatory Agencies*, Melbourne: Oxford University Press.

Greenwald, S.R. and M.W. Linn (1971), 'Intercorrelation of data on nursing homes', *The Gerontologist*, **11** (4), 337–40.

Grimshaw, J.M., L. Shirran, R. Thomas, G. Mowatt, C. Fraser, L. Bero, R. Grilli, E. Harvey, A. Oxman and M.A. O'Brien (2001), 'Changing provider behavior: an overview of systematic reviews of interventions', *Medical Care*, **39** (8), II-2–II-45.

Grol, R. (2001), 'Improving the quality of medical care: building bridges among professional pride, payer profit, and patient satisfaction', *Journal of the American Medical Association*, **286** (20), 2578–84.

Gunningham, Neil and Peter Grabosky (1998), *Smart Regulation: Designing Environmental Policy*, Oxford: Clarendon Press.

Gurwtiz, J.H., T.S. Field, J. Avorn, D. McCormick, S. Jain, M. Eckler, M. Benser, A.C. Edmondson and D.W. Bates (2000), 'Incidence and preventability of adverse drug events in nursing homes', *American Journal of Medicine*, **109**, 87–93.

Gurwitz, J.H., S.B. Soumerai and J. Avorn (1990), 'Improving medication prescribing and utilisation in the nursing home', *Journal of the American Geriatric Society*, **38**, 542–52.

Handler, Joel F. (1986), *The Conditions of Discretion: Autonomy, Community Bureaucracy*, New York: Russell Sage Foundation.

Hannan, E.L., C.C. Stone, T.L. Biddle and D.A. DeBuono (1997), 'Public release of cardiac surgery outcomes in New York', *American Heart Journal*, **134**, 55–61.

Harkey, J. and R. Vraciu (1992), 'Quality of health care and financial performance: is there a link?', *Health Care Management Review*, **17** (4), 55–63.

Harrington, Charlene (1996), 'Nursing facility quality, staffing, and economic issues' in G.S. Wunderlich, F. Sloan, and C. Davis (eds), *Nursing Staff in Hospitals and Nursing Homes: Is It Adequate?*, Washington, DC: National Academy Press, pp. 453–502.

Harrington, Charlene (2001), 'Regulating nursing homes: residential nursing facilities in the United States', *British Medical Journal*, **323**, 507–10.

Harrington, C. (2004), 'Saving lives through quality of care: a blueprint for elder abuse', *Alzheimer's Care Quarterly*, **5** (1), 24–38.

Harrington, C.H. and H. Carrillo (1999), 'The regulation and enforcement of federal nursing home standards', *Medical Care Research and Review*, **56** (4), 471–94.

Harrington, C.H., H. Carrillo, S.C. Thollaug, P.R. Summers and V. Wellin (2000a), 'Nursing facilities, staffing, residents, and facility deficiencies, 1993 through 1999', Department of Social and Behavioral Sciences, University of California, San Francisco.

Harrington, C., H. Carrillo and C. Mercade-Scott (2005), 'Nursing facilities, staffing, residents, and facility deficiencies, 1998 through 2004', US Health Care Financing Administration, and Department of Social and Behavioral Sciences, University of California, San Francisco.

Harrington, C., J.T. Mullan and H. Carrillo (2004), 'State nursing home enforcement systems', *Journal of Health Politics, Policy and Law*, **29** (1), 43–73.

Harrington, C., J. O'Meara, E. Collier and J.F. Schnelle (2003), 'Nursing indicators of quality in nursing homes', *Journal of Gerontological Nursing*, **29** (10), 5–11.

Harrington, C., D. Zimmerman, S.L. Karon, J. Robinson and P. Beutel (2000b), 'Nursing home staffing and its relationship to deficiencies', *Journal of Gerontology: Social Sciences*, **55B** (5), S278–S287.

Hawkins, Keith (1984), *Environment and Enforcement: Regulation and the Social Definition of Pollution*, Oxford: Clarendon Press.

Hawkins, Keith (2002), *Law as Last Resort: Prosecution Decision-Making in a Regulatory Agency*, Oxford: Oxford University Press.

Hayek, Frederick A. (1949), *Individualism and Economic Order*, London: Routledge.

Health Care Financing Administration (HCFA) (1988), *New Long Term Care Survey Process: Procedural Guidelines*, Baltimore, MD: Health Care Financing Administration.

Health Care Financing Administration (HCFA) (1998), *Report to Congress: Study of Private Accreditation (Deeming) of Nursing Homes, Regulatory Incentives and Non-Regulatory Initiatives, and Effectiveness of the Survey and Certification System*, Baltimore, MD: Health Care Financing Administration.

Healy, J. (2007), *Reluctant Regulators: Mapping the Governance of Patient Safety in Australia*, Canberra: Australian National University.

Heimer, C. (1997), 'Legislating responsibility', American Bar Foundation Working Paper #9711, Chicago, IL: American Bar Foundation.

Heimer, C., J.C. Petty and R.J. Culyba (2005), 'Risk and rules: the legalization of medicine', in Bridget Hutter and Michael Power (eds), *Organizational Encounters with Risk*, Cambridge: Cambridge University Press, pp. 92–131.

Hibbard, J.H., J.J. Jewett, S. Engelmann and M. Tusler (1998), 'Can Medicare beneficiaries make informed choices?', *Health Affairs*, **17**, 181–93.

Hibbard, J.H., J. Stockard and M. Tusler (2003), 'Does publicizing hospital performance stimulate quality improvement efforts?', *Health Affairs*, **22** (2), 84–94.

Hirth, R.A., J.C. Banaszak-Holl, B.E. Fries and M.C. Turenne (2003), 'Does quality influence consumer choice of nursing homes? Evidence from nursing home to nursing home transfers', *Inquiry*, **40**, 343–61.

Hoffman, M.L. (1970), 'Moral development', in P.M. Mussen (ed.), *Carmichael's Manual of Child Psychology*, New York: Wiley.

Hoffman, M.L. (1983), 'Affective and cognitive processes in moral internalization', in E.T. Higgens, D.N. Ruble and W. Hartup (eds), *Social Cognition and Social Development*, New York: Cambridge University Press.

Hughes, C., K. Lapane and V. Mor (2000), 'Influence of facility characteristics on use of antipsychotic medications in nursing homes', *Medical Care*, **38** (12), 1164–73.

Hutter, Bridget M. (1999), *A Reader in Environmental Law*, Oxford: Oxford University Press.

Institute of Medicine (1986), *Improving the Quality of Care in Nursing Homes*, Washington, DC: National Academy Press.

Institute of Medicine (1996), *Nursing Staff in Hospitals and Nursing Homes: Is It Adequate?*, Washington, DC: National Academy Press.

Institute of Medicine (2000), *To Err is Human: Building a Safer Health Care System*, Washington, DC: National Academy Press.

Institute of Medicine (2001), *Improving the Quality of Long-Term Care*, Washington, DC: National Academy Press.

Jenkins, A. (1994), 'The role of managerial self-efficacy in corporate compliance', *Law and Human Behaviour*, **18**, 71–88.

Jenkins, A. (1997), 'The role of managerial self-efficacy in corporate compliance with regulatory standards', PhD dissertation, Australian National University.

Jenkins, A. and J. Braithwaite (1993), 'Profits, pressure and corporate lawbreaking', *Crime, Law, and Social Change*, **20**, 221–32.

Jewett, J.J. and J.H. Hibbard (1996), 'Comprehension of quality of care indicators', *Health Care Finance Review*, **18**, 75–94.

Johnson, S. (1985), 'State regulation of long term care: a decade of experience with intermediate sanctions', *Medicine and Health Care*, **13**, 173–87.

Jost, T.S. (1983), 'The Joint Commission on Accreditation of Hospitals, private regulation of health care and the public interest', *Boston College Law Review*, **25**, 525–98.

Jost, T.S. (1985), 'Enforcement of quality nursing home care in the legal system', *Law, Medicine and Health Care*, **13** (4), 160–72.

Jost, T.S. (1988), 'The necessary and proper role of regulation to assure the quality of health care', *Houston Law Review*, **25**, 525–98.

Kagan, R.A. (1991), 'Adversarial legalism and American government', *Journal of Policy Analysis and Management*, **10** (3), 369–406.

Kagan, Robert A. and Lee Axelrad (eds) (2000), *Regulatory Encounters: Multinational Corporations and American Adversarial Legalism*, Berkeley, CA: University of California Press.

Kagan, R.A. and J. Scholz (1984), 'The "criminology of the corporation" and regulatory enforcement strategies', in K. Hawkins and J.M. Thomas (eds), *Enforcing Regulation*, Boston, MA: Kluwer-Nijhoff.

Kahn, Arnold S. (1984), *Social Psychology*, Dubuque, IA: Wm C. Brown.

Kane, Robert L. and Rosalie A. Kane (1985), *A Will and a Way: What the United States Can Learn from Canada about Caring for the Elderly*, New York: Columbia University Press.

Kapp, M.B. (2002), *Issues in Conducting Research with and About Older Persons, Ethics, Law, and Aging Review*, vol. 8, New York: Springer Publishing.

Kelman, Steven (1984), 'Enforcement of occupational safety and health regulations: a comparison of Swedish and American practices', in Keith Hawkins and John M. Thomas (eds), *Enforcing Regulation*, Boston, MA: Kluwer-Nijhoff.

Keohane, N.O., R.L. Revesz and R.N. Stavins (1998), 'The choice of regulatory instruments in environmental policy,' *Harvard Environmental Law Review*, **22**, 313–67.

Kerrison, S.H. and A.M. Pollock (2001), 'Absent voices compromise the effectiveness of nursing home regulation: a critique of regulatory reform in the UK nursing home industry', *Health and Social Care in the Community*, **9** (6), 490–94.

Kurtz, C.F. and D.J. Snowden (2003), 'The new dynamics of strategy: sense-making in a complex-complicated world', *IBM Systems Journal*, **42**, 462–506.

Leape, L.L. and D.M. Berwick (2005), 'Five years after "to err is human": what have we learned?', *Journal of the American Medical Association*, **293** (19), 2384–90.

Lepper, M.R. (1973), 'Dissonance, self-perception and honesty in children', *Journal of Personality and Social Psychology*, **25**, 65–74.

Lepper, M.R. and D. Greene (1978), *The Hidden Costs of Reward*, Hillsdale, NJ: Erlbaum.

Lessig, L. (1999), *Code and Other Laws of Cyberspace*, New York: Basic Books.

Levi-Faur, D. (2005), 'The global diffusion of regulatory capitalism', *Annals of the American Academy of Political and Social Science*, **598**, 12–32.

Levi-Faur, D. (2006), 'Varieties of regulatory capitalism: sectors and nations in the making of a new global order', *Governance*, **19**, 363–6.

Liddy, L. (2004), 'The strategic corporal: some requirements in education and training', *Australian Army Journal*, **2** (2), 139–48.

Lieberman, M.A. and S.S. Tobin (1983), *The Experience of Old Age: Stress, Coping and Survival*, New York: Basic Books.

LIFERS Public Safety Steering Committee of the State Correctional Institution at Graterford, Pennsylvania (2004), 'Ending the culture of street crime', *The Prison Journal*, **84** (4), 48–68.

Linn, M., L. Gurell, and B. Linn (1977), 'Patient outcomes as a measure of quality of nursing home care', *American Journal of Public Health*, **6**, 337–44.

Lipsky, Michael (1980), *Street-Level Bureaucracy: Dilemmas of the Individual in Public Services*, New York: Russell Sage Foundation.

Llewellyn-Jones R., K.A. Baikie, H.E. Smithers and P.D. Funnell (2003), 'Pain management programs in residential aged care', *Medical Journal of Australia*, **178** (1), 44–5.

Long, Steven (1987), *Death Without Dignity: The Story of the First Nursing Home Corporation Indicted for Murder*, Austin, TX: Texas Monthly Press.

Longo, D.R., G. Land, W. Schramm, J. Fraas, B. Hoskins and V. Howell (1997), 'Consumer reports in health care: do they make a difference in patient care?', *Journal of the American Medical Association*, **278** (19), 1579–84.

Lowe, T.J., J.A. Lucas, N.G. Castle, J.P. Robinson and S. Crystal (2003), 'Consumer satisfaction in long-term care: state initiatives in nursing homes and assisted living facilities', *The Gerontologist*, **43** (6), 883–96.

Majone, Giandomenico (1986), 'Mutual adjustment by debate and persuasion', in F. Kaufmann, G. Majone, V. Ostrom with W. Wirth (eds), *Guidance, Control, and Evaluation in the Public Sector*, Berlin: Walter de Gruyter.

Makkai, T. and J. Braithwaite (1991), 'Criminological theories and regulatory compliance', *Criminology*, **29**, 191–220.

Makkai T. and J. Braithwaite (1992), 'In and out of the revolving door: making sense of regulatory capture', *Journal of Public Policy*, **12**, 61–78.

Makkai, T. and J. Braithwaite (1993a), 'Praise, pride and corporate compliance', *International Journal of the Sociology of Law*, **21**, 73–91.

Makkai, T. and J. Braithwaite (1993b), 'The limits of the economic analysis of regulation', *Law and Policy*, **15**, 271–91.

Makkai, T. and V. Braithwaite (1993c), 'Professionalism, organizations, and compliance', *Law and Social Inquiry*, **18** (1), 33–59.

Makkai, T. and J. Braithwaite (1994a), 'The dialectics of corporate deterrence', *Journal of Research in Crime and Delinquency*, **31**, 347–73.

Makkai, T. and J. Braithwaite (1994b), 'Reintegrative shaming and regulatory compliance', *Criminology*, **32**, 361–85.

Makkai, T. and J. Braithwaite (1996), 'Procedural justice and regulatory compliance', *Law and Human Behavior*, **20** (1), 83–98.

Mann, Michael (1986), *The Sources of Social Power, Volume 1: A History of Power from the Beginning to AD 1760*, Cambridge: Cambridge University Press.

Marshall, M.N., P.S. Romano and H.T.O. Davies (2004), 'How do we maximise the impact of the public reporting of quality of care?', *International Journal for Quality in Health Care*, **16** (Supplement I), 157–63.

Marshall, M.N., P.G. Shekelle, S. Leatherman and R.H. Brook (2000), 'The public release of performance data: what do we expect to gain? A review of the evidence', *Journal of the American Medical Association*, **283** (14), 1866–74.

Maruna, Shadd (2001), *Making Good: How Ex-Convicts Reform and Rebuild their Lives*, Washington, DC: American Psychological Association.

McAdams, R.H. and J. Nadler (2005), 'Testing the focal point theory of legal compliance: the effect of third-party expression in an experimental hawk/dove game', *Journal of Empirical Legal Studies*, **2** (1), 87–123.

McBarnet, D. and C. Whelan (1999), *Creative Accounting and the Cross-Eyed Javelin Thrower*, London: John Wiley.

McClean, W.J. and N.H. Higginbotham (2002), 'Prevalence of pain among nursing home residents in rural New South Wales', *Medical Journal of Australia*, **177** (1), 17–20.

McLeay Report, House of Representatives Standing Committee on Expenditure (1982), *In a Home or At Home: Accomodation and Home Care for the Aged*, Canberra: Parliament of the Commonwealth of Australia.

Meidinger, E. (1987), 'Regulatory culture: a theoretical outline', *Law and Policy*, **9**, 355–86.

Meijer, A., C. van Campen and A. Kerkstra (2000), 'A comparative study of the financing, provision and quality of care in nursing homes. The approach of four European countries: Belgium, Denmark, Germany and the Netherlands', *Journal of Advanced Nursing*, **32** (3), 554–61.

Mendelson, M.A. (1974), *Tender Loving Greed*, New York: Alfred A. Knopf.

Mennemeyer, S.T., M.A. Morrisey and L.Z. Howard (1997), 'Death and reputation: how consumers acted upon HCFA mortality information', *Inquiry*, **34**, 117–28.

Merton, Robert K. (1968), *Social Theory and Social Structure*, New York: Free Press.

Metcalfe, L. (1994), 'The weakest links: building organisational networks for multi-level regulation', in Organisation for Economic Co-operation and Development, *Regulatory Co-operation for an Interdependent World*, Paris: OECD.

Meyer, L. (2006), 'The shame of aged care in Australia', www.agedcarecrisis.com.

Meyers, E.M. (2002), 'Physical restraints in nursing homes: an analysis of quality of care and legal liability', *Elder Law Journal*, **10**, 217–62.

Miles, S.H. and P. Irvine (1992), 'Deaths caused by physical restraints', *The Gerontologist*, **32**, 762–66.

Minichiello, Victor (1989), 'The regular visitors of nursing homes: who are they?', *Australian and New Zealand Journal of Sociology*, **25** (2), 260–77.

Monk, Abraham, Lenard W. Kaye and Howard Litwin (1984), *Resolving Grievances in the Nursing Home: A Study of the Ombudsman Program*, New York: Columbia University Press.

Moos, R.H. (1981), 'Environmental choice and control in community care settings for older people', *Journal of Applied Social Psychology*, **11**, 23–43.

Mor, V., J. Angelelli, R. Jones, J. Roy, T. Moore and J. Morris (2003a), 'Inter-rater reliability of nursing home quality indicators in the U.S.', *BMC Health Services Research*, **3** (1), 20.

Mor, V., K. Berg, J. Angelelli, D. Gifford, J. Morris and T. Moore (2003b), 'The quality of quality measurement in U.S. nursing homes', *The Gerontologist*, **43** (Special issue II), 27–46.

Mor, V.O., B.E. Intrator, B.E. Fries, C. Phillips, J. Teno, J. Hiris, C. Hawes and J. Morris (1997), 'Changes in hospitalization associated with introducing the resident assessment instrument', *Journal of the American Geriatrics Society*, **45**, 1002–10.

Mor, V., J. Zinn, J. Angelelli, J.M. Tenno and S.C. Miller (2004), 'Driven to tiers: socioeconomic and racial disparities in the quality of nursing home care', *The Milbank Quarterly*, **82** (2), 227–55.

Moran, M. (2003), *The British Regulatory State: High Modernism and Hyper-Innovation*, Oxford: Oxford University Press.

Morgan, Gareth (1986), *Images of Organization*, Beverly Hills, CA: Sage.

Mukamel, D.B. and C.A. Brower (1998), 'The influence of risk adjustment methods on conclusions about quality of care in nursing homes based on outcome measures', *The Gerontologist*, **38**, 695–703.

Mukamel, D. and W. Spector (2000), 'Nursing home costs and risk-adjusted outcome measures of quality', *Medical Care*, **38** (1), 78–89.

Mukamel, D.B., N.M. Watson, H. Meng and W.D. Spector (2003), 'Development of a risk adjusted urinary incontinence outcome measure of quality for nursing homes', *Medical Care*, **41** (4), 467–78.

National Center for State Long Term Care Ombudsman Resources (1989), *A Study of the Use of Volunteers by Long Term Care Ombudsman Programs: The Effectiveness of Recruitment, Supervision, and Retention*, Washington, DC: National Center for State Long Term Care Ombudsman Resources.

National Citizens' Coalition for Nursing Home Reform (1987), *Campaign for Quality Care in Nursing Homes*, Washington, DC: National Citizens' Coalition for Nursing Home Reform.

National Healthcare Quality Report (2004), 'Alabama State summary table', www.qualitytools.ahrq.gov/qualityreport, accessed 30 July 2005.

National Patient Safety Agency (2004), *Seven Steps to Patient Safety: An Overview Guide for NHS Staff*, London: National Patient Safety Agency.

Neustadt, Richard E. and Ernest R. May (1986), *Thinking in Time: The Uses of History for Decision Makers*, New York: Free Press.

Nicol, D. and J. Hope (2007), 'Cooperative strategies for facilitating use of patented inventions in biotechnology', *Law in Context*, **24**, 85–112.

Norton, E.C. (1992), 'Incentive regulation of nursing homes', *Journal of Health Economics*, **11**, 105–28.

Nyman, J.A. (1988), 'Improving the quality of nursing home outcomes: are adequacy or incentive oriented policies more effective?', *Medical Care*, **26** (4), 1158–71.

O'Connor, J.T. (1974), 'Comprehensive health planning: dreams and realities', *Milbank Memorial Fund Quarterly/Health and Society*, **51**, 223–51.

O'Malley, P. (1992), 'Risk, power and crime prevention', *Economy and Society*, **21** (3), 252–75.

O'Neill, C., C. Harrington, M. Kitchener and D. Saliba (2003), 'Quality of care in nursing homes: an analysis of relationships among profit, quality and ownership', *Medical Care*, **41** (12), 1318–30.

Office of Fair Trading (2005), *Care Homes for Older People in the UK: A Market Study*, London: Office of Fair Trading.

Office of Health Systems Management (1985), *Evaluation of the New York State Residential Health Care Facility Quality Assurance System*,

Albany, NY: Office of Health Systems Management, New York State Department of Health.

Office of the Deputy Prime Minister (2005), *Securing Better Outcomes: Developing a New Performance Framework*, London: HM Treasury.

Ohio Nursing Home Commission (1978), *A Program in Crisis*, Columbus, OH: Ohio Nursing Home Commission.

Olson, Mancur (1988), 'Can jurisprudence, economics and other social sciences be integrated?', unpublished manuscript, University of Maryland.

Organisation for Economic Co-operation and Development (OECD) (2005), *Long-Term Care for Older People*, Paris: OECD.

Osborne, D. and T. Gaebler (1992), *Reinventing Government: How the Entrepreneurial Spirit is Transforming the Public Sector*, Reading, MA: Addison-Wesley.

Parke, R.D. (1969), 'Effectiveness of punishment as an interaction of intensity, timing, agent nurturance and cognitive structuring', *Child Development*, **40**, 213–35.

Parker, Christine (2002), *The Open Corporation*, Cambridge: Cambridge University Press.

Parker, C. (2006), 'The "compliance" trap: the moral message in responsive regulatory enforcement', *Law and Society Review*, **40** (3), 591–622.

Parker, C. and J. Braithwaite (2003), 'Regulation', in P. Cane and M. Tushnet (eds), *Oxford Handbook of Legal Studies*, Oxford: Oxford University Press.

Parker, R.A. (1987), *The Elderly and Residential Care: Australian Lessons for Britain*, Aldershot: Gower.

Parliament of Australia, Senate (2005), *Quality and Equity in Aged Care*, Canberra: Commonwealth of Australia.

Patterson, G.R. (1982), *Coercive Family Process*, Eugene, OR: Castalia.

Pear, R. (2002), '9 in 10 nursing homes lack adequate staff, study finds', *The New York Times*, 18 February, A1.

Pearson, A., S. Hocking, S. Mott and A. Riggs (1991), *Optimal Skills Mix for Desired Resident Outcomes in Non-Government Nursing Homes*, Canberra: Department of Community Services and Health.

Petersen, L.A., L.D. Woodard, T. Urech, C. Daw and S. Sookanan (2006), 'Does pay-for-performance improve the quality of health care?', *Annals of Internal Medicine*, **145** (4), 265–72.

Peterson, E.D., E.R. Delong, J.G. Jollis, L.H. Muhlbaier and D.B. Mark (1998), 'The effects of New York's by-pass surgery provider profiling on access to care and patient outcomes for the elderly', *Journal of the American College of Cardiology*, **32**, 993–9.

Pettit, Philip (1997), *Republicanism: A Theory of Freedom and Government*, Oxford: Oxford University Press.

Phan, J.N. (2002), 'The graying of America: protecting nursing home residents by allowing regulatory and criminal statutes to establish standards of care in private negligence actions', *Houston Journal of Health Law and Policy*, **2**, 297–335.

Phillips, C.D., C. Hawes and B.E. Fries (1993), 'Reducing the use of physical restraints in nursing homes: will it increase costs?', *American Journal of Public Health*, **83**, 342–8.

Phillips, L.W., D.R. Chang and R.D. Buzzell (1983), 'Product quality, cost position, and business performance: a test of some key hypotheses', *Journal of Marketing*, **47**, 26–43.

Pillemer, K. and D. Moore (1989), 'Abuse of patients in nursing homes: findings from a survey of staff', *The Gerontologist*, **29**, 314–20.

Pokrywka, H.S., K.H. Koffler, R. Rensburg, J. Roth, M. Tayback and J.E. Wright (1997), 'Accuracy of patient care staff in estimating and documenting meal intake of nursing home residents', *Journal of the American Geriatric Society*, **45**, 1223–7.

Popper, Karl (1972), *Objective Knowledge: An Evolutionary Approach*, Oxford: Clarendon Press.

Porter, Michael (1990), *The Competitive Advantage of Nations*, New York: Free Press.

Porter, Michael and Claas van der Linde (1995a), 'Green and competitive: ending the stalemate', *Harvard Business Review*, September–October, 120–34.

Porter, Michael and Claas van der Linde (1995b), 'Reply to Portney's critique of Porter and van der Linde (1995) "Green and competitive: ending the stalemate"', *Harvard Business Review*, November–December, 206–8.

Porter, Michael and Claas van der Linde (1995c), 'Toward a new conception of the environment–competitiveness relationship', *Journal of Economic Perspectives*, **9** (4), 98–118.

Porter, M.E. and E.O. Teisberg (2004), 'Redefining competition in health care', *Harvard Business Review*, **82** (6), 64–77.

Power, Michael (1997), *The Audit Society: Rituals of Verification*, Oxford: Oxford University Press.

Pranis, K. (2000), 'Democratizing social control: restorative justice, social justice, and the empowerment of marginalized populations', in G. Bazemore and M. Schiff (eds), *Restorative Community Justice*, Cincinnati, OH: Anderson.

Pray, John (1986), 'State v. Serebin – causation and the criminal liability of nursing home administration', *Wisconsin Law Review*, **2**, 339–66.

Proctor, R., A. Burns, H.S. Powell, N. Tarrier, G. Faragher, G. Richardson, L. Davies and B. South (1999), 'Behavioural management in nursing and residential homes: a randomised controlled trial', *Lancet*, **354**, 26–9.

Quirk, Paul J. (1981), *Industry Influence in Federal Regulatory Agencies*, Princeton, NJ: Princeton University Press.

Ramsey, P.G., M.D. Wenrich, J.D. Carline, T.S. Inui, E.B. Larson and J.P. LoGerfo (1993), 'Use of peer ratings to evaluate physician performance', *Journal of the American Medical Association*, **269** (13), 1655–60.

Rantz, M.J., V. Grando, V. Conn, M. Zwygart-Staffacher, L. Hicks, M. Flesner, J. Scott, P. Manion, D. Minner, R. Porter and M. Maas (2003), 'Getting the basics right: care delivery in nursing homes', *Journal of Gerontological Nursing*, **29** (11), 15–25.

Ray, W.A., J.A. Taylor, K.G. Meador, M.J. Lichtenstein, M.R. Griffin, R. Fought, M.L. Adams and D.G. Blazer (1993), 'Reducing antipsychotic drug use in nursing homes: a controlled trial of provider education', *Archives of Internal Medicine*, **153**, 713–21.

Reason, James (1990), *Human Error*, New York: Cambridge University Press.

Reddy, Peter (2006), 'Restorative justice and peace operations', PhD dissertation, Australian National University.

Rees, Joseph V. (1994), *Hostages of Each Other: The Transformation of Nuclear Safety since Three Mile Island*, Chicago, IL: University of Chicago Press.

Reiss, Albert J. (1984), 'Selecting strategies of social control over organizational life', in K. Hawkins and J.M. Thomas (eds), *Enforcing Regulation*, Boston, MA: Kluwer-Nijhoff.

Rhodes, Rod (1997), *Understanding Governance*, Buckingham, UK and Philadelphia, PA: Open University Press.

Rickwood, D. and J. Braithwaite (1994), 'Why openness with health inspectors pays', *Australian Journal of Public Health*, **18**, 165–70.

Rigert, J. and M. Lerner (1990), 'Company and FDA have done little to prevent deaths', *Star Tribune*, 3 December, 1, 10A.

Robinson, S. and M. Brodie (1997), 'Understanding the quality challenge for health consumers: the Kaiser/AHCPR Survey', *Journal of Quality Improvement*, **23**, 239–44.

Ronalds, C., P. Godwin and J. Fiebig (1989), *Residents' Rights in Nursing Homes and Hostels: Final Report*, Canberra: Australian Government Publishing Service.

Rosenthal, G.E., L. Quinn and D.L. Harper (1997), 'Declines in hospital mortality associated with a regional initiative to measure hospital performance', *American Journal of Medical Quality*, **12**, 103–12.

Roski, J., R. Jeddeloh, L. An, H. Lando, D. Hannan and C. Hall (2003), 'The impact of financial incentives and a patient registry on preventative care quality: increasing provider adherence to evidence-based smoking cessation practice guidelines', *Preventive Medicine*, **36**, 291–9.

Rudder, C. with C.D. Phillips (1995), *The Nursing Home Enforcement System in New York State: Does It Work?* Albany, NY: Nursing Home Community Coalition of New York State.

Sachs, Jeffrey D. (2005), *The End of Poverty: How We Can Make it Happen in our Lifetime*, London: Penguin Books.

Scheff, Thomas J. (1990), *Microsociology: Discourse, Emotion, and Social Structure*, Chicago, IL: University of Chicago Press.

Schmidt, I., C. Claesson, and B. Westerholm (1998), 'Resident characteristics and organizational factors influencing the quality of drug use in Swedish nursing homes', *Social Science and Medicine*, **47**, 961–71.

Schneider, E.C. and A.M. Epstein (1996), 'Influence of cardiac-surgery performance reports on referral practices and access to care', *New England Journal of Medicine*, **335**, 251–6.

Schneider, E.C. and A.M. Epstein (1998), 'Use of public performance reports', *Journal of the American Medical Association*, **279**, 1638–42.

Schnelle, J.F., M.P. Cadogan, J. Yoshii, N.R. Al-Samarrai, D. Osterweil, B.M. Bates-Jensen and S.F. Simmons (2003a), 'The Minimum Data Set Urinary Incontinence Quality Indicators: do they reflect differences in care processes related to incontinence?', *Medical Care*, **41** (8), 909–22.

Schnelle, J.F., S.F. Simmons and M.G. Ory (1992), 'Risk factors that predict staff failure to release nursing home residents from restraints', *The Gerontologist*, **32** (6), 767–70.

Schnelle, J.F., S.F. Simmons, C. Harrington, M. Cadogan, E. Garcia and B. Bates-Jensen (2003b), 'Nursing home staffing information: does it reflect differences in quality of care?', working paper, UCLA, Department of Medicine, Los Angeles.

Schoen, C. and K. Davis (1998), *Erosion of Employer-Sponsored Health Insurance Coverage and Quality*, New York: Commonwealth Fund.

Scholz, J.T. and W.B. Gray (1990), 'OSHA enforcement and workplace injuries: a behavioral approach to risk assessment', *Journal of Risk and Uncertainty*, **3**, 283–305.

Schon, Donald A. (1983), *The Reflective Practitioner: How Professionals Think in Action*, New York: Basic Books.

Schuck, Peter H. (1979), 'Litigation, bargaining and regulation', *Regulation*, **3**, 26–34.

Schudson, C.B., A.P. Onellion and E. Hochstedler (1984), 'Nailing an omelet to the wall: prosecuting nursing home homicide', in E. Hochstedler (ed.), *Corporations as Criminals*, Beverly Hills, CA: Sage, pp. 131–46.

Seligman, Martin E.P. (2002), *Authentic Happiness*, New York: Free Press.

Shearing, C. and R.V. Ericson (1991), 'Towards a configurative conception of action', *British Journal of Sociology*, **42**, 481–506.

Shearing, C. and P. Stenning (1985), 'From the panopticon to Disney World: the development of discipline', in A.N. Doob and E.L. Greenspan (eds), *Perspectives in Criminal Law*, Toronto: Canada Law Book, pp. 335–49.

Shearing, C. and J. Wood (2003), 'Nodal governance, democracy and the new "denizens" ', *Journal of Law and Society*, **30** (3), 400–419.

Shen, Y. (2003), 'Selection incentives in a performance-based contracting system', *Health Services Research*, **38**, 535–52.

Sherman, D.S. (1988), 'Psychoactive drug misuse in long-term care: some contributing factors', *Journal of Pharmacy Practice*, **1** (3), 189–94.

Sherman, L.W. (1993), 'Defiance, deterrence and irrelevance: a theory of the criminal sanction', *Journal of Research in Crime and Delinquency*, **30**, 445–73.

Shield, Renée Rose (1988), *Uneasy Endings: Daily Life in an American Nursing Home*, Ithaca, NY: Cornell University Press.

Shimizu, Y., W. Hotori, K. Horikawa and D. Maeda (1985), 'Residential care for the elderly in Japan', in L. McDerment and S. Greengross (eds), *Social Care for the Elderly: An International Perspective*, Surbiton, Surrey: Social Care Association Publications.

Shortell, S.M., C.L. Bennett and G.R. Byck (1998), 'Assessing the impact of continuous quality improvement on clinical practice: what it will take to accelerate progress', *Milbank Quarterly*, **76** (4), 1–37.

Simmons, R.F., S. Babineau, E. Garcia and J.F. Schnelle (2002), 'Quality assessment in nursing homes by systematic direct observation: feeding assistance', *Journals of Gerontology Series A: Biological Sciences and Medical Sciences*, **57**, M665–M671.

Singh, D.A., R.A. Amidon, L. Shi and M.E. Samuels (1996), 'Predictors of quality of care in nursing facilities', *Journal of Long-Term Care Administration*, **24** (3), 22–6.

Smith, Peter K., Debra Pepler and Ken Rigby (eds) (2004), *Bullying in Schools: How Successful Can Interventions Be?*, Cambridge: Cambridge University Press.

Social Welfare Action Group (1982), *A Report on the Phone-in on Abuse of the Elderly*, Sydney: Australian Consumers' Association.

Sparrow, M. (2000), *The Regulatory Craft: Controlling Risks, Managing Problems and Managing Compliance*, Washington, DC: The Brookings Institution.

Special Committee on Aging, United States Senate (1990a), *Federal Implementation of OBRA 1987 Nursing Home Reform Provisions, 101st Congress, May 18, 1989*, Washington, DC: US Government Printing Office.

Special Committee on Aging, United States Senate (1990b), *Untie the Elderly: Quality Care without Restraints, 101st Congress, December 4, 1989*, Washington, DC: US Government Printing Office.

Spector, W.D. and M.L. Drugovich (1989), 'Reforming nursing home quality regulation: impact on cited deficiencies and nursing home outcomes', *Medical Care*, **27** (8), 789–801.

Spiegel, C. (1991), 'Restraints, drugging rife in nursing homes health: industry admits 68% of patients are involved while critics say 80%. State is not enforcing new U.S. law', *Los Angeles Times*, 25 March, A1, A20.

Starr, Paul (1982), *The Transformation of American Medicine*, New York: Basic Books.

Stenning, Philip C., C.D. Shearing, S.M. Addario and M.G. Condon (1990), 'Controlling interests: two conceptions of order in regulating a financial market', in W.L. Friedland (ed.), *Securing Compliance*, Toronto: University of Toronto Press.

Stevenson, D.G. and D.M. Studdert (2003), 'The rise of nursing home litigation: findings from a national survey of attorneys', *Health Affairs*, **22** (2), 219–29.

Sutherland, Edwin H. (1983), *White-Collar Crime: The Uncut Version*, New Haven, CT: Yale University Press.

Sykes, G. and D. Matza (1957), 'Techniques of neutralization: a theory of delinquency', *American Sociological Review*, **22**, 664–70.

Tellis-Nayak, V., with J.A. Day and D.J. Ward (1988), *Nursing Home Exemplars of Quality*, Springfield, IL: Charles C. Thomas.

Thomas, William C. (1969), *Nursing Homes and Public Policy*, Ithaca, NY: Cornell University Press.

Tilse, C. (1998), 'Family advocacy roles and highly dependent residents in nursing homes', *Australian Journal on Ageing*, **16** (1), 20–31.

Tinetti, M., W.L. Liu and S. Ginter (1990), 'Falls and injuries among high risk nursing home residents who are and are not physically restrained', *Clinical Research*, **38** (2), 517A.

Tinetti, M.E., W.L. Liu and S.F. Ginter (1992), 'Mechanical restraint use and fall-related injuries among residents of skilled nursing facilities', *Annals of Internal Medicine*, **116**, 369–74.

Tinetti, M.E., W. Liu, R.A. Marottolil and S.F. Ginter (1991), 'Mechanical restraint use among residents of skilled nursing facilities: prevalence, patterns and predictors', *Journal of the American Medical Association*, **265**, 468–71.

Tingle, L. (2001), 'Moran the big winner as aged care goes private', *Sydney Morning Herald*, 16 March, 2.

Townsend, P. (1962), *The Last Refuge*, London: Routledge & Kegan Paul.

Tyler, Tom (1990), *Why People Obey the Law*, New Haven, CT: Yale University Press.

Tyler, Tom and Steven Blader (2000), *Cooperation in Groups: Procedural Justice, Social Identity, and Behavioral Engagement*, Philadelphia, PA: Psychology Press.

Tyler, Tom and Robyn M. Dawes (1993), 'Fairness in groups: comparing the self-interest and social identity perspectives', in B.A. Mellers and J. Baron (eds), *Psychological Perspectives on Justice: Theory and Applications*, Cambridge: Cambridge University Press.

Tyler, Tom and Yuen J. Huo (2001), *Trust and the Rule of Law: A Law-Abidingness Model of Social Control*, New York: Russell Sage.

Tyler, T., L. Sherman, H. Strang, G.C. Barnes and D. Woods (forthcoming), 'Reintegrative shaming, procedural justice and recidivism: the engagement of offenders' psychological mechanisms in the Canberra RISE drinking-and-driving experiment', *Law and Society Review*.

Ulsperger, J.S. (2002), 'Geezers, greed, grief, and grammar: frame transformation in the nursing home reform movement', *Sociological Spectrum*, **22**, 385–406.

Vladeck, Bruce C. (1980), *Unloving Care: The Nursing Home Tragedy*, New York: Basic Books.

Vladeck, Bruce C. (2003), 'Unloving care revisited: the persistence of culture', *Journal of Social Work in Long-Term Care*, **2** (1/2), 1–9.

Vogel, Stephen K. (1996), *Freer Markets, More Rules: Regulatory Reform in Advanced Industrial Societies*, Ithaca, NY and London: Cornell University Press.

Waldman, D.E. (1978), *Antitrust Action and Market Structure*, Lexington, MA: Lexington Books.

Waldman, Saul (1983), 'A legislative history of nursing home care', in Ronald J. Vogel and Hans C. Palmer (eds), *Long-Term Care: Perspectives from Research and Demonstrations*, Baltimore, MD: Health Care Financing Administration.

Walshe, K. (2001), 'Regulating U.S. nursing homes: are we learning from experience?', *Health Affairs*, **20** (6), 128–44.

Walshe, K. (2003), *Regulating Healthcare: A Prescription for Improvement*, Maidenhead: Open University Press.

Walshe, K. and A. Boyd (2006), *Designing Regulation: A Review for the Healthcare Commission of the Systems for Regulation in Seven Sectors, and a Synthesis of the Lessons and Implications for Regulatory Design in Healthcare*, Manchester: Centre for Public Policy Management, University of Manchester.

Walshe, K. and S. Shortell (2004), 'Social regulation of healthcare organizations in the United States: developing a framework for evaluation', *Health Services Management Research*, **17**, 79–99.

Warne, Leoni, Irena Ali, Derek Bopping, Dennis Hart and Celina Pascoe (2005), *The Network Centric Warrior: The Human Dimension of Network Centric Warfare*, Canberra: Defence Science and Technology Organisation, DSTO-CR-0373.

Wax, M. (1962), 'The changing role of the home for the aged', *The Gerontologist*, **2**, 128–33.

Waxman, H.M., E.A. Carner and G. Berkenstock (1984), 'Job turnover and job satisfaction among nursing home aides', *The Gerontologist*, **24**, 503–9.

Weech-Maldonado, R., G. Neff and V. Mor (2003), 'The relationship between quality of care and financial performance in nursing homes', *Journal of Health Care Finance*, **29** (3), 48–60.

Weimann, G. (1982), 'Dealing with bureaucracy: the effectiveness of different persuasive appeals', *Social Psychology Quarterly*, **45** (3), 136–44.

Wells, J.C. (2004), 'The case for minimum nurse staffing standards in nursing homes', *Alzheimer's Care Quarterly*, **5** (1), 39–51.

Werner, P., J. Cohen-Mansfield, J. Brown, and M.S. Marx (1989), 'Physical restraints and agitation in nursing home residents', *Journal of the American Geriatrics Society*, **37**, 1122–6.

White, James Boyd (1984), *When Words Lose Their Meaning: Constitutions and Reconstitutions of Language, Character and Community*, Chicago, IL: University of Chicago Press.

Wiener, C.L. and J. Kayser-Jones (1990), 'The uneasy fate of nursing home residents: an organisational interaction perspective', *Sociology of Health and Illness*, **12** (1), 84–104.

Wilson, R.M., W.B. Runciman, R.W. Gibbert, B.T. Harrison, L. Newby and J.D. Hamilton (1995), 'The quality in Australian health care study', *Medical Journal of Australia*, **163** (9), 458–71.

Winzelberg, G.S. (2003), 'The quest for nursing home quality', *Archives of Internal Medicine*, **163**, 2552–6.

Wolfensberger, W. (1972), *The Principle of Normalization in Human Services*, Toronto: National Institute on Mental Retardation.

Wolfensberger, W. (1983), 'Social role valorization', *Mental Retardation*, **21**, 234–9.

Wolfensberger, W. (1985), 'Social role valorization: a new insight, and a new term, for normalization', *Australian Association for the Mentally Retarded Journal*, **9** (1), 4–11.

Wolk, S. and S. Telleen (1976), 'Psychological and social correlates of life satisfaction as a function of residential constraint', *Journal of Gerontology*, **31**, 89–98.

Yeh, S.-H., L.-W. Lin and S.K. Lo (2003), 'A longitudinal evaluation of nursing home care quality in Taiwan', *Journal of Nursing Care Quality*, **18** (3), 209–16.

Zahn-Waxler, C.Z., M.R. Radke-Yarrow and R.A. King (1979), 'Child rearing and children's prosocial initiations towards victims in distress', *Child Development*, **50**, 319–30.

Zartman, I. William and Maureen R. Berman (1982), *The Practical Negotiator*, New Haven, CT: Yale University Press.

Zhang, X. and D.C. Grabowski (2004), 'Nursing home staffing and quality under the Nursing Home Reform Act', *The Gerontologist*, **44** (1), 13–23.

Zimmerman, D.R., S.L. Karon, G. Arling, B.R. Clark, T. Collins, R. Ross and F. Sainfort (1995), 'Development and testing of nursing home quality indicators', *Health Care Finance Review*, **16**, 107–27.

Zischka, P.C. and I. Jones (1984), 'Volunteer community representatives as ombudsmen for the elderly in long-term care facilities', *The Gerontologist*, **24** (1), 9–15.

Index

problem ID
root Cause
innovation
opportunity exploitation
p320 ther is (prizes)
catalize continuous improv